Ed Schoonveld does an extraordinary job of making one of the most complex and vital topics in the industry intelligible to both new and experienced audiences. Best of all, he leverages case studies and straightforward frameworks to provide a pragmatic approach for mastering the theory of global pricing and access. I keep his book in easy reach for my own reference or to share with others.

Susanne Laningham, Executive Director
Global Value Access & Policy, Amgen

This book gives a great overview and offers several perspectives on drug pricing issues. It provides comprehensive new insights such as the need to take benefits assessments of pharmaceuticals into consideration during all steps of drug development and market access. The mix of theory, in the form of underlying arguments and analytical frameworks, along with practical and up-to-date real-world solutions, makes this book an outstanding reference.

Thomas Mueller, Head of Pharmaceutical Department
Gemeinsamer Bundesausschuss (Federal Joint Committee), Germany

The Price of Global Health *is the most informative and comprehensive book I have read on the topic of global pharmaceutical pricing and market access. Ed is able to distill complex topics into simplified and pragmatic frameworks, including insightful perspectives on market segmentation, communicating value, and pricing. The final section provides a useful reference, describing how key global healthcare systems are structured and their approach for assessing value. I have recommended this book for members of my team as part of their initial training.*

David Kaplan, Senior Advisor
Global Payer Market Research, Eli Lilly

Ed's book has been a huge addition to the global pharmaceutical pricing educational process. I have used the book to teach pharmaceutical pricing since the book first arrived on the market. It fills a huge unmet need. The students find that Ed's book transforms the complex global pricing environment and the factors that influence the pricing process into an understandable and manageable entity. The book takes a lot of data and transforms the information into key concepts. I can't imagine teaching global pharmaceutical pricing without Ed's book.

Richard Truex Ph.D., Adjunct Professor
St. Joseph's University, Philadelphia

The Price of Global Health *is a rare book in pharmaceutical market access strategy that develops an understandable strategic perspective. It is based on considerable real-world experience and has been updated as the dynamics of the global pharma market have evolved. We used it as an important part of our onboarding process for all junior market access staff. Highly recommended.*

Keith Hendricks, Vice President,
Decision Support Group, Corporate Strategic Planning, AbbVie

This book should be on the shelves of every pharmaceutical company executive—in whatever discipline—and will prove invaluable to anyone interested in providing and financing modern healthcare.

Joe Zammit-Lucia, President and CEO
Cambridge Pharma Consultancy

This book is fantastic! ... People will love it. It's very well suited for a broad audience from student to professionals to non experts and will hopefully be useful to demystify the subject a little. ... THE pharma pricing book!

Ulf Staginnus, Executive Director,
Head Market Access & Pricing Europe at Endocyte

The Price of Global Health *is a compelling and holistic introduction into the art and science of pricing.*

Andreas Altemark, Head of Global Pricing & MACS Reporting
Bayer HealthCare Pharmaceuticals

The Price of Global Health

To my wife, Hana:
my love and true partner in life

The Price of Global Health

Drug Pricing Strategies to Balance Patient Access and the Funding of Innovation

Second Edition

ED SCHOONVELD

GOWER

Published by
Gower Publishing Limited
Wey Court East
Union Road
Farnham
Surrey, GU9 7PT
England

Gower Publishing Company
110 Cherry Street
Suite 3-1
Burlington, VT 05401-3818
USA

www.gowerpublishing.com

British Library Cataloguing in Publication Data
A catalogue record for this book is available from the British Library

The Library of Congress has cataloged the printed edition as follows:
Schoonveld, Ed.
  The price of global health: drug pricing strategies to balance patient access and the funding of innovation / by Ed Schoonveld.
    pages cm.
  Includes bibliographical references and index.
  ISBN 978-1-4724-3880-5 (hardback: alk. paper)—ISBN 978-1-4724-3881-2 (ebook)—ISBN 978-1-4724-3882-9 (epub) 1. Drugs—Prices. 2. Pharmaceutical industry—Prices. 3. Medical care. 4. Globalization. I. Title.

  HD9665.5.S364 2014
  338.4'36151—dc23

2014018598

ISBN 9781472438805 (hbk)
ISBN 9781472438812 (ebk – ePDF)
ISBN 9781472438829 (ebk – ePUB)

Printed in the United Kingdom by Henry Ling Limited, at the Dorset Press, Dorchester, DT1 1HD

Contents

List of Figures

List of Tables

List of Abbreviations

€	Euro Currency
ACA	Patient Protection and Affordable Care Act
AD	Alzheimer's Disease
AEMPS	Agencia Española de Medicamentos y Productos Sanitarios (Spain)
AFP	Average Foreign Price (Japan)
AFSSAPS	Agence Française de Sécurité Sanitaire des Produits de Santé (France)
AHFS – DI	American Hospital Formulary Service – Drug Information (US)
AIDS	Acquired Immunodeficiency Syndrome
AIFA	Agencia Italiana del Farmaco (Italy)
AIOCD	All India Organization of Chemists and Druggists (India)
AMCP	Academy of Managed Care Pharmacy (US)
AMNOG	Arzneimittelmarktneuordnungsgesetz (Act on the Reform of the Market for Medicinal Products; Germany)
AMP	Average Manufacturer Price
ANS	Agência Nacional de Saúde Suplementar (Brazil)
ANSM	Agence Nationale de Sécurité du Médicament et des Produits de Santé (France)
ANVISA	Agência Nacional de Vigilância Sanitária (Brazil)
AOK	Allgemeine Ortskrankenkasse (Germany)
ASMR	Amélioration du Service Medical Rendu (France)
ASP	Average Selling Price (US)
ATC	Anatomical Therapeutic Classification
AWP	Average Wholesale Price (US)
AZT	Azidothymidine
BEST PRICE	Framework: Benefits, Evidence, STory, PRICE
BfArM	Bundesinstitut für Arzneimittel und Medizinprodukte (Germany)

BGTD   Biologics and Genetic Therapies Directorate (Canada)
BHIS   Basic Health Insurance Scheme (China)
BKK   Bundesverband Betriebskrankenkassen (Germany)
BMG   Bundesministerium für Gesundheit (Germany)
BMS   Bristol-Myers Squibb
BRIC   Brazil, Russia, India, China
CADTH   Canadian Agency for Drugs and Technologies in Health
            (Canada)
CAP   Competitive Acquisition Program (US)
CCDSM   Collaborating Centre for Drug Statistics Methodology (WHO)
CCG   Clinical Commissioning Group (UK)
CCOHTA   Canadian Coordinating Office for Health Technology
            Assessment (now CADTH; Canada)
CDF   Cancer Drug Fund (UK)
CDR   Common Drug Review (Canada)
CED   Coverage with Evidence Development
CEESP   Commission Evaluation Economique et de Santé Publique
CEPS   Comité Economique des Produits de Santé (France)
CGHS   Central Government Health Scheme (India)
CHIP   Children's Health Insurance Program (US)
CHMP   Committee for Medicinal Products for Human Use (EU)
CIPE   Comitato Interministeriale per la Programmazione Economica
            (Italy)
CIPM   Comisión Interministerial de Precios de los Medicamentos
            (Spain)
CMED   Câmara de Regulação do Mercado de Medicamentos (Brazil)
CML   Chronic Myelogenous (or Myeloid) Leukemia
CMS   Center for Medicare and Medicaid Services (US)
CODEM   Comité de Evaluacion de los Medicamentos de Uso Humano
            (Spain)
COMP   Committee for Orphan Medicinal Products (EU)
CONITEC   Comissao Nacional de Incorporaca de Technologias
COPD   Chronic Obstructive Pulmonary Disease
CPI   Consumer Price Index
CT   Commission de Transparence (France)
CTS   Commissione Tecnico Scientifica (Italy)
CUF   Commissione Unica del Farmaco (Italy)
DBCAC   Drug Benefit Coverage Assessment Committee (S. Korea)
DDD   Daily Defined Dose (WHO)
DH   Department of Health (UK)

DMARD	Disease Modifying Anti-Rheumatic Drug
DoD	Department of Defense
DP	Direct Price
DPCO	Drugs Price Control Order (India)
DRG	Diagnosis-Related Group
DTC	Direct To Consumer (Advertising)
ECJ	European Court of Justice
ECT	Electroconvulsive Therapy
EMA	European Medicines Agency
EMEA	see EMA
EORTC	European Organization for Research and Treatment of Cancer
ESIS	Employee State Insurance Scheme (India)
ESRD	End-Stage Renal Disease
EU	European Union
EU-5	France, Germany, Italy, Spain, UK
FDA	Food and Drug Administration (US)
FPA	Foreign Price Adjustment (Japan)
FSS	Federal Supply Schedule (US)
FUL	Federal Upper Limit (US)
G-BA	Gemeinsamer Bundesausschuss (Germany)
GDP	Gross Domestic Product
GI	Gastro-Intestinal
GSK	GlaxoSmithKline
GVS	Geneesmiddelen Vergoedings Systeem (Netherlands)
HAM-D	Hamilton Depression Rating Scale
HAS	Haute Authorité de Santé (France)
HbA1C	Haemoglobin A1C
HE	Health Economics
HEOR	Health Economics and Outcomes Research
HER-2	Human Epidermal growth factor Receptor 2
HHS	(Department of) Health and Human Services (US)
HIPC	Highest International Price Comparison (Canada)
HIRA	Health Insurance Review and Assessment Service (South Korea)
HIV	Human Immunodeficiency Virus
HMO	Health Maintenance Organization (US)
HO	Health Outcomes
HPFB	Health Products and Food Branch (Canada)
HQ	Headquarters
HTA	Health Technology Assessment

ICP	Internally Calculated Price (Japan)
IKK	Bundesverband der Innungskrankenkassen (Germany)
IPP	Indifference Price Point
IRDA	Insurance Regulatory Development Authority Bill (India)
IQWiG	Institut für Qualität und Wirtschaftlichkeit im Gesundheitswesen (Germany)
IV	Intravenous
GKV	Gesetzliche Krankenversicherung (Spitzenverband Bund der Krankenkassen; Germany)
KFDA	Korean Food and Drug Administration (S. Korea)
KOL	Key Opinion Leader
LDL	Low Density Lipoprotein
LEEM	Les Enterprises du Médicament (France)
MA	Market Access
MA	Medical Aid (S. Korea)
MA&P	Market Access and Pricing
MAC	Maximum Allowable Cost (US)
MAP	Minimally Acceptable Profile
MBS	Medicare Benefits Schedule (Australia)
MCO	Managed Care Organization (US)
MEA	Managed Entry Agreements
MHRA	Medicines and Healthcare product Regulatory Agency (UK)
MIPC	Median International Price Comparison (Canada)
MLSS	Ministry of Labor and Social Security (China)
MMA	Medicare Modernization Act (US)
MS	Multiple Sclerosis
NCCN	National Comprehensive Cancer Network (US)
NCE	New Chemical Entity
NDRC	National Development and Reform Commission (China)
NEDL	National Essential Drug List (China)
NGO	Non-Governmental Organization
NHI	National Health Insurance (S. Korea, Japan)
NHIC	National Health Insurance Corporation (S. Korea)
NHS	National Health Service (various countries)
NICE	National Institute for Health and Care Excellence (UK)
NIH	National Institute of Health (US)
NPPA	National Pharmaceutical Pricing Authority (India)
NRCMS	New Rural Cooperative Medical System (China)
OPP	Optimal Price Point
OPPI	Organization of Pharmaceutical Producers of India (India)

OS	Overall Survival
OTC	Over-the-Counter
P&L	Profit and Loss
P&MA	Pricing and Market Access (also MA&P)
P&R	Pricing and Reimbursement
PA	Prior Authorization (US)
PBAC	Pharmaceutical Benefits Advisory Committee (Australia)
PBM	Pharmaceutical Benefit Manager (US)
PBMI	Pharmacy Benefit Management Institute (US)
PBS	Pharmaceutical Benefits Scheme (Australia)
pCODR	pan-Canadian Oncology Drug Review (Canada)
PCP	Primary Care Physician
PCPA	pan-Canadian Pricing Alliance (Canada)
PCT	Primary Care Trust (UK)
PDL	Preferred Drug List
PEI	Paul Ehrlich Institute (Germany)
PFN	Prontuario Farmaceutico Nazionale (Italy)
PFS	Progression Free Survival
PLA	Provincial Listing Agreement (Canada)
PLFSS	Projet de loi de financement de la sécurité sociale (France)
PMC	Point of Marginal Cheapness
PMDA	Pharmaceutical and Medical Devices Agency (Japan)
PME	Point of Marginal Expensiveness
PMPRB	Patented Medicine Prices Review Board (Canada)
PODiUM	Framework: Treatment **P**ractice, Promise **O**ptions, **D**irect Competition, **U**nmet Needs, **M**oney Flow
PP	Public Policy
PPO	Preferred Provider Organization (US)
PPRS	Pharmaceutical Price Regulation Scheme (UK)
PR	Public Relations
PRM	Prezzi, Rimborso e Mercato (Italy)
PTOA	Prontuario Terapeutico Ospedaliero Aziendale (Italy)
QALY	Quality Adjusted Life Years
QOL	Quality Of Life
R&D	Research and Development
RBP	Reference-Based Pricing
RBP-I	RBP Phase I
RBP-II	RBP Phase II
RENAME	Relação Nacional de Medicamentos Essencias (Brazil)
Rx	Prescription

SCHIP	State Children's Health Insurance Program (US)
SF-36	Short Form 36 (QOL questionnaire)
SMC	Scottish Medicines Consortium (UK)
SMR	Service Médical Rendu (France)
SNRI	Serotonin-Norepinephrine Reuptake Inhibitor
SNS	Sistema Nacional de Salud (Brazil)
SSN	Servizio Sanitario Nazionale (Italy)
SSRI	Selective Serotonin Reuptake Inhibitor
SU	Sulfonylurea
SUS	Sistema Único de Saúde
TCC	Therapeutic Class Comparison
TOP	Target Opportunity Profile
TPP	Target Product Profile
tPA	Tissue Plasminogen Activator
TPD	Therapeutics Products Directorate (Canada)
TR	Therapeutic Referencing
TRIPS	Trade-Related Aspects of Intellectual Property Rights
Tx	Treatment
TZD	Thiazolidinedione
UK	United Kingdom
UNCAM	Union National des Organismes d'Assurance Maladie Complémentaires (France)
US	United States
VA	Veterans Administration (US)
VBA	Value-Based Assessment (UK)
VBP	Value-Based Pricing (UK)
WAC	Wholesale Acquisition Cost (US)
WAWP	Weighted Average Wholesale Price (Japan)
WHO	World Health Organization
WTO	World Trade Organization

Foreword

I first met Ed in 2012 when I was working in hematology and had to find new ways to demonstrate the value of a second generation drug in comparison with the existing standard of therapy. On this occasion, Ed presented the core content of his book and methodology, and for the first time I could clearly see all the market access processes and key success factors of a product launch laid out neatly in front of me. This book not only addresses health economics, but it specifically focuses on how to build a value story, effectively present it and finally negotiate it.

The book, of course, goes well beyond that, illustrating how the market access function can drive the success of a new brand launch: How do you engage with your stakeholders? How do you identify the key success factors for your product? What hurdles will you encounter? What kinds of risks will you have? What organizational set-up would be able to overcome those hurdles and risks? How do you build a customized value story for your markets, globally? What will be the right price for your product? How will you successfully negotiate your price?

I think Ed—for the first time in this relatively new field—has achieved an outstanding result with his book: putting down a clear methodology to help you understand the basics of market access. Moreover, this book allows you to easily understand the complexities beyond each and every activity you should be doing for a successful rollout of a great market access strategy.

Needless to say, after my initial meeting with Ed, I asked him to start working with us on a key challenge that was (and is) heavily discussed around the globe: the increasing pressure of oncology drug costs on healthcare systems. From that day onward, I have worked extensively with Ed and his well-prepared team in Europe, in order to build the basis for the development of a new value story for a key hematology product, not forgetting to map risks and benefits, hurdles and future scenarios for every key European market; and ultimately to understand what would be the best pricing strategy for the markets at greater risk. This has been a long journey, but I believe I have learned a lot from the experience and Ed's book, and the team's support has been invaluable in helping me to understand what the key success factors were, what risks were coming and how we could tackle them.

Overall, the outcome of this relationship has been great because I believe we both learned from each other, possibly bringing in new food for thought for the new version of his book, where you will find more concrete examples, more illustrative cases and an overall improved approach to what I believe is the key to the success of each market access function: demonstrating clearly and easily the value of a new drug (or new indications) in order to have it reimbursed in any market and healthcare system, at the right time and at the right price.

I believe this book is a must-read for any market access professional around the world who wants to be successful. This new edition provides important substantive improvements and additional materials. It is a well-balanced book in terms of methodology, theory and practice. Theory is not easy to put into practice. Ed and his team can truly help you achieve results.

Andrea Mantovani
Head of Value and Patient Access, Sanofi Italy
Former Market Access Lead, Hematology Franchise
Novartis Oncology Europe

Acknowledgments

There are a lot of people that I want to thank for their general support in my personal and professional development, which have been the basis for this book, as well as specific support to the actual book itself. Yet, with any name that comes to mind mentioning, I realize that I will fail to mention at least 10 others, who have contributed in equally important ways.

I owe gratitude to many colleagues and friends from the pharmaceutical industry and consulting firms that I have worked with over the last 22 years, as well as clients that I have had the pleasure of assisting in their strategic and supporting research needs. The contents of this book have been shaped over the last 10 years, since I first considered writing the book, as colleagues and clients have endorsed or challenged the individual ideas that have gone into this work.

I would like to thank colleagues from ZS Associates who have enthusiastically supported me in finalizing this book, as well as Gower Publishing, who recognized the value in bringing it to you.

Last, but certainly not least, I want to thank my wife Hana and children Liron and Kevin for their enthusiasm, support and patience during various stages of idea conceptualization and actual writing of this book.

For the second edition, I would like to thank my ZS Associates team and colleagues for their support and suggestions to further build on the first edition and incorporate updates on the many changes that have occurred in the global marketplace.

Preface to the Second Edition

I am delighted to present this second edition of *The Price of Global Health*. Reactions to the first edition have been overwhelmingly great and heartwarming. It frankly has made me wonder why I did not write this book earlier.

Why a new edition? In the last three years, there has been an amazing amount of change in the prescription drug environment and particularly in payer systems. The US has seen a large transformation under the Patient Protection and Affordable Care Act (ACA) or Obamacare. Economic recession and resulting Euro-crisis and fiscal austerity measures have transformed the European environment. Individual countries have seen major change, such as AMNOG in Germany, the introduction of Medico-Economic requirements and the impact of the Mediator scandal in France, the Value-Based Pricing debate in the UK. Emerging markets continue to grow rapidly, with China now taking the third spot in global prescription drug sales.

The second edition has been updated to reflect all the above and many more changes in payer systems. I have also taken the opportunity to add some content on a number of important topics. Essentially, these are the changes in the second edition:

- Four chapters were added:
    - Payer Value Story Development. How do we structure and formulate a high-level compelling argument to convince payers, that can form the basis for our Market Access & Pricing (MA&P) strategy, payer value dossier and individual payer negotiations?
    - Oncology and Orphan Drugs. Two top-of-mind challenge areas in MA&P. Both are growing rapidly and are drawing attention from payers and the public.
    - Market Access and Pricing Negotiations. Negotiations with payers are very different from other negotiations. Some great

> negotiation frameworks are available, but how do they translate to the MA&P negotiation world? What should we specifically consider to be successful?
>
> o South Korea. As an important market in Asia, I thought that it would be useful to add South Korea to the country system descriptions.

- The book content has been divided into five sections (A–E) instead of the previous four to better emphasize strategy implementation aspects;

- Updates were made to reflect substantial health care system changes in the United States, France, Germany, UK and many smaller changes in all other countries;

- The Pricing Research chapter was updated with more US specific materials;

- The Payer Segmentation chapter has been significantly updated and expanded;

- A detailed example of the impact of international price referencing was added in Chapter 12;

- Throughout the book, more clarifications and examples were added and large numbers of updates were made;

- All illustrations were updated.

I hope that this second edition will continue to be helpful to many in building a strong understanding of payers and the Market Access and Pricing discipline. I do appreciate any feedback, both positive and critical.

Preface to First Edition

Many people have asked me to recommend a book about global drug pricing. I never had an answer. Others have suggested that I write that book. Well, here it is …

It is puzzling that there are hardly, if any, books written about global drug pricing. The topic is certainly garnering interest and emotion from politicians, healthcare professionals, drug industry professionals and the public. Also inside pharmaceutical companies there is a great need for a better understanding of the topic. As a client recently noted, many drug marketing people are not really proficient in pharmaceutical market access and pricing.

Global drug pricing is a very complex topic, partly because patents give companies a period of market exclusivity. It is also different from most other industries due to the fact that government payers have a lot of buying power. In economic terms it could be typified as "monopoly versus monopsony" that causes a very unique and interesting dynamic, particularly when considering the situation on a larger global scale. Payers and politicians sometimes complain about lack of competition for a new drug category. Drug manufacturers complain about government controls in drug pricing. In any case, in the pharmaceutical market dynamic, general pricing principles do not directly apply without significant customization. This is why general pricing textbooks are essentially useless for application in pharmaceutical pricing cases.

In contrast to drug pricing, many books have been written about health economics, a discipline that provides a systematic methodology to make health resource decisions under budget constraints. Health economics is used, for example in the United Kingdom, to decide whether a new anti-cancer drug should be included in their drug formulary or whether liver transplants should be reimbursed for every eligible patient. In most countries, however, payers and politicians are struggling to strictly base drug coverage decisions on a calculation that is only understood in detail by academics. In reality, only few payers strictly use health economics principles in pricing and market access decision making. Global drug pricing includes health economics and health outcomes considerations, but is in reality even broader and more complicated.

As a leader in global pricing and health outcomes and economics disciplines in three large global drug companies and serving as a consultant to many others, I have had the privilege of observing the evolving roles of pricing and health economics over the years. It is particularly interesting that the two disciplines that focus on payer decision making are usually reporting into different corporate branches, that is commercial and research and development. It makes successful collaboration of the two areas heavily dependent on having similar viewpoints among the leaders of both fields, in a setting where even a joint textbook on best practices did not exist until this present work.

Healthcare is a matter that is and should be near and dear to all of us. In times of a health scare, for example caused by H1N1 or Anthrax, we call for miracle solutions to protect ourselves from harm. Whether during recent debates on US Health Care Reform or previous ones on pricing of HIV/AIDS drugs or patient co-payments in a European country, the public seems to be very engaged, yet very poorly informed about the topic. Politicians who go to bat for drug pricing issues are often equally poorly informed and are driven by short-term political motives rather than a long-term societal perspective. Welcome to the age of the sound byte.

The drug industry is often mentioned for its lobbying muscle. However, with all its capabilities, it has certainly not managed to gain the heart of the public. For an industry that is saving lives and improving patient wellbeing, to be outperformed in gaining public sympathy by the gun and tobacco industries is remarkable. Yes, there are a number of factors that make the pharmaceutical company story complicated. These are outlined in this book. However the full story is worth telling, as the interested public deserves more than sound bytes.

High prices for new biotechnology drugs can create a lot of issues for individual patients, as they may not be able to afford the cost of co-payment for the treatment. There are patient assistance programs in place to offset some of that pain, but these cannot eliminate the issue entirely, particularly not in emerging countries, such as China. However, the ability to charge these prices within reason, is essential to ensure that we are able to address future healthcare challenges, such as the next H1N1 epidemic, emerging resistant MRSA infected patients, multi-drug resistant HIV/AIDS patients, to continue to improve treatment and compliance of common conditions such as diabetes, and to find new treatment approaches for rare diseases that currently don't have drug solutions.

Unfortunately, our dietary and sedentary lifestyle and our litigious nature are likely to further increase the cost of healthcare. Any healthcare reform in any country is unlikely to address that effectively without fundamentally changing the underlying factors or significantly reduce healthcare coverage. Many governments are choosing price control mechanisms to address their funding issues. History has shown that failing controls lead to more controls, resulting in a patchwork of government bureaucracy, which is creating more problems rather than restoring a market mechanism. I have frequently challenged, and will continue to challenge government payers to explore ways of restoring market mechanism rather than putting another layer on all existing controls. It is in the interest of all of us, to find acceptable solutions to healthcare funding, while securing sufficient innovative research efforts to be ready to battle the next healthcare challenge in addition to all the existing ones.

Hopefully this book will make a contribution in the ability to educate professionals, students, policy makers, politicians and the broader public about global drug pricing, its challenges and potential solutions. If anything, it would be great to at least achieve a common understanding on the issues. For the pharmaceutical industry, this book will hopefully form a basis for a more structured approach to addressing market access and pricing challenges and to build a solid working relationship between the pricing and market access function and other commercial and scientific functions. A good understanding of this field is critical for the survival of any pharmaceutical company.

About the Author

Ed Schoonveld is a renowned global expert on global market access and pricing for pharmaceuticals with experience in global, regional and local market access and pricing strategy formulation and implementation through various positions in industry and consulting over more than 20 years.

Ed is currently Managing Principal of the Market Access and Pricing Practice with ZS Associates in New York, NY. He has gained extensive experience in the pharmaceutical industry through various sales, marketing and general management positions for Lederle, Wyeth, Eli Lilly and BMS in the United States and Europe. He has gained deep expertise in Global Pricing and Reimbursement both on an affiliate level as a general manager of a European affiliate and at corporate headquarters as the responsible leader for global pricing and health economics groups in Wyeth, Eli Lilly and BMS.

Prior to his recent leadership position at BMS, Ed has been leading pricing and reimbursement consulting practices in Cambridge Pharma Consulting/ IMS, the Analytica Group and his own consultancy firm. During this time he has advised many large drug companies on product market access and pricing strategy, global pricing policy and internal organizational and process challenges. Most of these projects involved global payer and pricing research through a host of qualitative and quantitative methodologies.

Ed has also served as an expert pricing consultant in a WHO/WTO-sponsored dialog on differential pricing of drugs between governments, industry, consumer organizations and NGOs.

Ed Schoonveld can be reached at ed.schoonveld@zsassociates.com.

Introduction

Three years ago, I wrote in the introduction of the first edition of this book: "Global drug pricing is one of the most debated yet least understood aspects of the pharmaceutical industry." Some recent events show that this is even more pertinent today than it was three years ago:

- Governments in the US, France, Germany, Italy and the UK have all recently adopted major healthcare system overhauls that heavily impact market access and pricing for prescription drugs.

- Recent public objections regarding pricing for high cost oncology, hepatitis-C and orphan drugs have spurred a lot of debate in pharmaceutical and health insurance industries. US health insurance companies have called for greater transparency in drug company pricing practices and economics.

- European government payers have threatened to jointly negotiate prices for Sovaldi (sofosbuvir) and a US payer has announced a ban on Sovaldi from formulary immediately after launch of a second drug in the category.

The above events suggest that the debate about global drug pricing is intensifying rather than abating.

> *How did the drug industry, with its life saving innovations, manage to earn a public image that is much worse than industries with products that kill, such as the gun and tobacco industries?*

> *How will stricter controls over pricing and patient access to drugs evolve as a new generation of expensive biotech drugs threatens to bankrupt pharmaceutical budgets?*

How can pharmaceutical companies avoid wasting billions of R&D dollars through adjustment in their drug development process in favor of emerging payer information needs?

The Price of Global Health is the first book of its kind: an in-depth but straightforward exploration of the pricing process and its implications. The book is designed to help a wide range of audiences gain a better understanding of this complex and emotionally charged field.

This book is an invaluable resource for anybody who is interested, involved in or affected by the development, funding and utilization of prescription drugs. In particular, it is of critical importance to pharmaceutical company executives and other leaders and professionals in drug development and commercialization, including marketing, business development, market access and pricing, clinical development, drug discovery, regulatory affairs, market research and public affairs.

Consumers will

- gain an understanding of drug company behaviors and how they impact the emergence of new and innovative therapies;

- better appreciate how pharmaceutical prices are determined and what factors influence the process;

- form an opinion on how various healthcare reform proposals may impact their ability to obtain future drug treatments.

Legislators will

- understand reasons for differences between global healthcare systems and drug pricing and market access controls;

- grasp the advantages and pitfalls of seemingly attractive control mechanisms employed in various countries;

- be able to propose healthcare legislation that ensures appropriate healthcare coverage of patients and allows for future exploration of new therapies.

Pharmaceutical company leaders will

- learn how to optimize their drug development efforts and avoid hundreds of millions of dollars in misdirected drug development investments, by ensuring that they are optimally directed at today's critical decision makers: government and private payers in global markets;

- be able to identify real commercial potential of development compounds and licensing opportunities, thus allowing for better decisions and avoiding investments in compounds with poor commercial prospects.

Market access and pricing professionals will

- gain insight into how to analyze pricing and market access opportunities for new drugs with some well-structured analytical frameworks, thus enabling them to bring blockbuster and specialty drugs to their full potential;

- understand how to develop a meaningful value story for payers, thus enabling broader market access and avoiding large discounts and rebates that can eliminate profit margins;

- avoid common pitfalls in payer and pricing research that is done to optimize and validate pricing and market access strategies.

This book consists of five parts and 31 chapters. There is a logical sequence to the chapters, but each can be read individually to suit each reader's particular interests. Readers with a general (non-specialist) interest in pharmaceutical pricing issues are recommended to read Chapters 1, 2 and 7 for an initial overview and then select further chapters depending on their specific interest.

Part A provides a basic overview of the pharmaceutical market access and pricing discipline. It describes the main issues and challenges for payers, drug industry and other stakeholders and discusses some of the most commonly used approaches in the field.

Chapter 1 provides a general overview and background of the challenges and issues of global drug pricing. It explains why the industry is so different from other industries and why governments deem it necessary to exert control over its marketing and pricing practices.

Chapter 2 gives an overview of the main global payer systems and provides a good perspective on the payers' considerations and views.

Chapter 3 discusses some fundamental microeconomic principles as they apply to pharmaceutical pricing in a free pricing and price controlled environment. Willingness-to-pay and price-elasticity of demand concepts are discussed in relation to drugs with multiple indications for patients in different disease states.

Chapter 4 examines the increasingly utilized payer management technique of reference pricing and its application for multi-source products, as well as the more controversial use of therapeutic price referencing and the challenges that it is posing in its daily operation and with respect to securing future pharmaceutical innovation.

Chapter 5 gives an in-depth view and analysis of the common principles in health outcomes and health economics and its application in MA&P decision making. A view is given on the current practices and the likely future role of health outcomes and health economics in key healthcare systems and its implications for MA&P requirements.

Features, benefits, value and price, the topic of Chapter 6, gets to the fundamental evaluation of customer value and appreciation of an innovation and related willingness-to-pay and price. Demonstrating fundamental healthcare value is the core requirement for success of drugs and other healthcare products. However, what constitutes value, from what perspective and how it is measured is vastly different across the globe, which has important implications for drug development. In this chapter, benefits of drugs are systematically examined and tested with respect to preferences of payers and other customers in the context of the need to deliver value.

Part B outlines a number of new structured approaches and frameworks towards the creation of an optimal global market access and pricing strategy. The approaches and frameworks are helpful in aligning efforts and strategic thinking between the increasing number of functional and geographic teams that get involved with drug market access and pricing activities and decisions today.

Drug development decisions are increasingly influenced by market access and pricing considerations next to regulatory considerations. The change in trade-offs and dynamics is covered in Chapter 7. A detailed discussion is included on MA&P trade-offs for each of the three main stages of a drug's life cycle.

Chapter 8 discusses payer segmentation and provides an approach to address the variety of global payer systems by considering them in terms of four global payer archetypes or segments. Addressing the global segments helps to analyze the fundamental payer requirements in most payer systems even though no market may be the perfect example of a described segment. With the four global payer segment models, a practical tool is obtained to perform a global payer analysis for any prescription drug.

Chapter 9 provides a methodical "PODiUM" approach to evaluate the situational context in a specific therapy area. The approach helps gather and evaluate medical, competitive and economic data that sets the stage for innovative new drug treatment options.

Chapter 10 introduces an evaluation framework for MA&P opportunities and strategies. The BEST PRICE framework is an easy to implement approach that aids the systematic evaluation of payer-related needs in key payer segments and systems. It helps identify early development guidance on key benefits, enabling the definition of a target opportunity profile, as well as key Phase III evidence needs, payer value story and optimal global pricing strategy.

Chapter 11 provides a detailed analysis of payer value stories and introduces the TEMPLE framework to build a payer value story that is compelling and addresses payer needs in a structured way.

Part C helps to structure an integrated global market access and pricing strategy, building on the concepts explained in Part B in light of ethical and financial considerations and validated through payer and pricing research.

Chapter 12 shows how to put it all together in an integrated global market access and pricing strategy addressing some complex international pricing issues, such as international price referencing, parallel trade and pharmaco-political issues.

Chapter 13 further examines drug industry issues and particularly issues related to global drug pricing and pricing differentials highlighted earlier in this introduction. Differential pricing is discussed as an option to provide better access to healthcare in developing and middle-income countries, and its issues and challenges are addressed.

Chapter 14 is devoted to two specialty areas that are under increasing attention: Oncology and Orphan Drugs. Payer perspectives and the impact for MA&P are discussed for both specialty areas. Risk sharing in oncology is discussed, as well as a typical oncology-specific benefits analysis. For orphan drugs and ultra-orphan drugs the formal status for MA&P purposes is discussed, as well as the attitudes of payers towards the acceptability of their often high prices.

Even the best thought out strategies, based on deep customer understanding and experience in the field require customer validation through Payer and Pricing Research. Chapter 15 provides a fundamental review of drug pricing analyses and research techniques. This chapter is very important reading for pricing and marketing professionals as it provides guidance into acquiring reliable payer insights and techniques for optimal price setting in various payer systems and situations. It is particularly important for market researchers, as payer and pricing research has its own set of requirements and potential pitfalls.

Part D focuses on all implementation-related aspects of MA&P, including building a functional organization in the global drug company. How to prepare for and structure payer negotiations, as well as an in-depth discussion of Risk Sharing deals and Managed Entry Agreements should further help in getting the business.

The corporate market access and pricing function and organization are discussed in Chapter 16. The role of the market access and pricing function in the drug development process is increasingly essential as payers are exerting an increasing influence on prescribing. How should a pharmaceutical company organize to most effectively address payer and market access and pricing needs and formulate effective strategies that can be implemented?

Chapter 17 provides insights on how to use and customize some known negotiation techniques in the prescription drugs and payer negotiations setting.

Risk sharing and managed entry agreements, the new buzzwords in global pharmaceutical pricing, are evaluated in detail in Chapter 18. Key examples and case studies of deals are analyzed and categorized in deal types, thus enabling the development of a policy with respect to these deals. Which deals are meaningful and which ones are just disguised price reductions without any risk sharing element? Which deals are really innovative and are useful in addressing some global market access and pricing hurdles? These questions are methodically addressed and answered.

Part E provides a high-level description of the payer systems in the United States, Canada, France, Germany, Italy, Spain, the United Kingdom, Japan, Australia, Brazil, China, India and South Korea. In each chapter, the healthcare system structure, as well as decision-making process and requirements for successful market access and pricing approval are discussed. These descriptions are intended as a reference and foundation for more in-depth discussions in Parts A through D.

PART A

Drug Market Access and Pricing Basics

1

The Drug Pricing Challenge

The pharmaceutical industry has been under a lot of public pressure, facing criticism over promotional practices, direct-to-consumer (DTC) advertising, and drug pricing. Particularly in the United States the drug industry reputation has been deteriorating over the last decade, resulting in a public image that seems worse than that of the gun and tobacco industries. It is a stunning observation, particularly for an industry that has, and continues to bring, important health benefits as it offers alleviation and cure for the many devastating diseases, compared with two industries whose products kill people.

Drug pricing in particular, is a topic that has captured the attention of many people, including pharmaceutical industry professionals, payers, healthcare providers, politicians and patients. The topic causes emotion and difference in views as people's lives and general well-being are dependent on access to the drugs that they need. In this chapter we will discuss some fundamental aspects of drug market access and pricing and the reasons why drug pricing is so different from other industries. Many of the observations in this chapter provide a basis for understanding the host of issues covered in the rest of this book

Drug Pricing

Global drug pricing is highly complicated in comparison with pricing for most other products. It is subject to a lot of political debate, government intervention and public dissatisfaction.

Many governments have a very strict approval process in place for pricing and/or reimbursement decision making for drugs. For reasons explained later, governments in many countries feel the need to control drug pricing. It is obviously a nearly impossible task to design effective, but reasonable, pricing and reimbursement controls that take individual patient situations into consideration. As a result, many of these systems have become very complex and cause many unintended "side effects."

In many cases in the past, governments have also mandated price reductions across all drugs, usually to address drug budget shortfalls. This is an interesting aspect of the drug monopsony privilege of government system buyers. Imagine that you go to your oil or gas supplier at the end of the year and demand a refund for going over your household heating budget. Your supplier would be in doubt whether you were pulling a prank on him or you were an escaped patient from a mental institution. Only governments can get away with this and have done so and will continue to do so frequently in many countries!

Over the last few decades, we have seen waves of political and public dissent over drug pricing. Price differences between countries have frequently been the basis for complaints and initiatives to control. In many countries, governments have instituted international price referencing laws on that basis. This will be further discussed later in this chapter. In the United States, price differences with Canada have particularly been subject to media coverage in the days leading up to Medicare reform and the institution of Medicare Part D. Bus trips to Canada for the elderly to purchase cheaper drugs were effectively advertised to gather support for drug coverage for senior citizens and to complain about high prices of drugs in comparison to Canada.

International price differences have probably been one of the most contentious of the issues that the industry has faced. It is not surprising that global price differences of drugs are a contentious issue. It can be hard to evaluate what should be a reasonable price for a product. For a gallon of milk it may be relatively easy as it is considered a commodity with a sufficient number of similar options in the store. For some branded products it is very hard. What is a reasonable price for a Porsche, a high-end brand perfume, or a ticket to a World Cup soccer game? Sitting on an airplane, we would be shocked to find out what the prices are that each passenger on the plane has paid for his or her ticket. It is hard to put a reasonable value on each product feature or benefit. How much is the brand image of a Porsche worth, the "hope" that is bought with the exclusive perfume or the exclusivity of attending a unique sports event. This is hard to say and it will be different from individual to individual. We have a hard time to identify a correct price for a product, but we are all upset when we find out that someone else paid substantially less. Why would we pay more than someone else? This is the question that is posed for international pharmaceutical pricing and the industry has been struggling in providing an acceptable answer. In this chapter, I will make my own attempt to explain the complexities of global drug pricing.

Market Access

Market access is the new buzzword in the pharmaceutical industry. Companies re-focus, restructure and add staff to their organizations to better address today's market access needs. More disciplines and people get involved in an already complex multidisciplinary process to further optimize development and commercial strategies aimed at preparing fewer new chemical entities for an increasingly demanding payer environment. However, there is a lot of confusion over the term "market access."

As with every new term, individuals from different disciplines translate a meaning, sometimes twisting it in the context of their own functional specialty, particularly when it seems to be the new hot trend. This reminds me of an analogy from the aircraft industry, which uses the functional perspectives and priorities discussed above, but applied in an aircraft design setting. The wing design group sees the aircraft as a wing with a small fuselage attached, the service group emphasizes all the access panels to reach their service items, whereas the armament group merely sees the plane as an opportunity to hang weapons.

In an attempt to eliminate some of the confusion, this chapter starts with a definition of market access as it is used in this book. Each reader can be the judge which one of the caricatures fits the description and perhaps distorted view of the author.

Pricing, reimbursement and access or market access are terms that are used in any set of combinations to describe the activities related to setting a drug price across markets that addresses third-party reimbursement or cash pay affordability in the context of each payer system and segment. The term pricing is usually well understood to be the activity of evaluating willingness-to-pay among key customers, resulting in an assessment of the optimal price.

For most consumer goods, pricing involves the assessment of customer price elasticity of demand. Not considering middlemen for now, the two key players are the seller and the buyer and the micro-economics laws of supply and demand drive optimal price. In the drug market, the purchasing process is much more complicated due to the involvement of third-party payers such as insurance companies. Depending on country and healthcare system, the payer acts as a gatekeeper in order to control drug and overall medical cost of treatment in some way or form. In some cases, for example in the United States, payers decide on a co-payment (fixed dollar amount of say $25) or co-insurance (fixed percentage of cost of say 20 percent). In markets such as China and Mexico, there is very limited insurance coverage for prescription drugs. Patients frequently pay for drugs cash out-of-pocket as they can afford it. Issues related to full or partial reimbursement by a payer, or patient affordability, are usually all captured under the term "market access."

A broader set of activities can be considered part of market access. For instance, it is important for a drug to be included in clinical treatment guidelines as they are frequently agreed upon and published, for example, in the US for hypertension, by the Joint National Committee on Prevention, Detection, Evaluation, and Treatment of High Blood Pressure. Some argue that gaining marketing authorization by the FDA is part of market access. I would argue that this is a bit of a stretch.

The term "access" is also used to address the ability to reach patients in developing countries or even the ability for the sales force to speak to physicians. In this book this is not considered part of the market access definition. Obtaining regulatory market authorization by the FDA or a similar foreign body is not considered market access either. Healthcare technology assessments and health economics evaluations, frequently used in reimbursement decision making, is part of market access.

In this book, the following definition will be used for market access:

> Market access is the discipline that addresses any financially based consideration or hurdle to drug prescribing and use, whether imposed by public or private third-party payers, or experienced as a consequence of patient affordability.

Regulatory and Other Drug Approval Systems

In every healthcare system, drug companies must obtain regulatory approval or market authorization before they can promote prescription drugs.

Regulatory approval is contingent on demonstrating drug efficacy and safety for the proposed indications and at the proposed dosing regimen to the Food and Drug Administration (FDA) in the US, the European Medicines Agency (EMA) in Europe and to the appropriate national authorities in other countries. Balancing speed of approval with safety concerns has been a contentious issue over the years, and has once more become a hot issue over the market withdrawal of Vioxx and emerging side effect concerns for Avandia a number of years ago. Drugs go through a robust efficacy and safety evaluation over years of research preceding the approval, however unfortunately it cannot completely guarantee that no additional side effects and rare toxicities present itself after treatment of millions of patients. For most drugs, these side effects are unfortunate, but they do not change the risk-benefit trade-off of using the treatment for the underlying patient condition. However, in a number of cases, serious health concerns have emerged a number of years after launch, resulting in market withdrawal of the drug or the inclusion of "black box" warnings on the product label.

A key factor in our legal society is whether anybody can be blamed for a potentially debilitating effect of an unknown and previously unreported side-effect. Clearly, drug companies are and should be held to the highest ethical standards with respect to transparency in reporting clinical outcomes for all company sponsored trials, as well as any other third-party results that they become aware of. Drug companies only very rarely violate this principle, but when they do, they certainly deserve to be legally pursued to the fullest extent of the law. Beside these legitimate cases, there are a lot of "ambulance chasing" frivolous class actions initiated, which will eventually only end up benefiting lawyers, thus further increasing the cost of healthcare and limiting opportunities for much needed new treatments to reach patients. It is actually puzzling that the responsible approval agencies, such as the FDA and the EMA, who write the approval requirements and implement them, don't seem to have any accountability for their decisions.

REGULATORY APPROVAL – WHAT'S NEXT?

Obtaining regulatory approval or market authorization for a new chemical entity is an important milestone in gaining the entry ticket for launch and promotional activities in most markets. In the United States, a company can start marketing and selling a new drug within its approved labeling immediately after regulatory approval by the FDA.

In most healthcare systems, effective market entry is not possible without pricing and/or reimbursement approval. Pricing and reimbursement approval is handled after regulatory approval. Process and requirements are very different between the various payer systems. In Europe, contrary to the regulatory process, pricing and reimbursement is not approved by the EMA on a European level, as the individual EU member countries have insisted on maintaining national control over healthcare expenditures. Healthcare funding and the pricing and reimbursement approval process for drugs are very different between countries such as France, Germany, Italy and the UK. Figure 1.1 is giving an illustrative listing of agencies and terms that are encountered in the payer space in contrast to the regulatory environment.

Differentiation between regulatory and pricing and reimbursement approvals is important in the context of the information and evidence needs in each of the two processes. Demonstrated efficacy and safety are crucial conditions for registration. For market access and pricing they are also important, but there are important commercial and budgetary objectives that play a role in decision making. Questions that may rise during these discussions may be:

Figure 1.1   Key global pricing and market access players

- What is the anticipated use of a new drug, what is the impact on the healthcare budget and, in the context of budget limitations, is this deemed an appropriate use of funds?

- What is a reasonable price of the drug, in the context of alternatives already available and the innovation demonstrated?

- What share of the cost or up to what amount should drug cost be reimbursed?

- Should any limitations be imposed on drug prescribing?

- What are the potential consequences if a drug at agreed–upon prices, exceeds its anticipated (or agreed upon) sales volume or average daily dose?

Depending on the payer system, a mix of the above questions will have to be addressed during the pricing and reimbursement approval process in each country.

Information needs for pricing and reimbursement negotiations have important implications for the drug development process. Clinical end points required to demonstrate drug efficacy and safety to the FDA or equivalent non-US agency, generally do not meet evidence requirements for pricing and reimbursement discussions. Placebo-controlled trials and non-inferiority claims, frequently sufficient for registration approval, will generally not impress public and private payers. This will be further discussed in Chapter 7: Pricing and Drug Development.

Market Access and Pricing Controls – Why?

What is different in the pharmaceutical industry that entices many governments to build controls related to price, reimbursement and drug company profitability? Market access and pricing controls are not very common in any product category other than drugs and are usually only introduced where national authorities are concerned over the lack of a natural market mechanism, insufficient competition and potential for price gouging by the industry. Examples of price controls can be found in the utilities industry, where governments have either put specific price controls in place or have brought the service completely under direct government management. Fear of bureaucracy and inefficiencies due to these controls have led to a search for revision of market mechanisms, for example in the US in the electrical power industry, where private enterprises have been encouraged to build supply sources to the public network and bid for supply prices, thus offering consumers choice. It is an interesting experiment, although it is questionable how much it will enable a sustainable competitive market structure, as the infrastructure is shared and consequently the consumer cannot be offered any meaningful service differentiation beside price. One can argue that if market mechanisms can be restored in the utilities with all its infrastructure limitations, it certainly provides a basis for trying harder in the drug industry, where controls have been both complicated and ineffective with respect to cost control.

In a competitive market, buyers and sellers are balancing supply and demand at a "market price." Consumer reactions to price can be characterized through price elasticity relationships. In a market with relatively high returns on investment, additional sellers are attracted, provided that there are no insurmountable regulatory hurdles or other barriers to entry. Thus, it is reasonable to expect that industries that make excessive profits will, over time, face more competition, resulting in squeezing of margins and bringing the industry in line with a "normal" return on capital.

Most international governments have in some form exerted control over market access and pricing of drugs. As a result, when trying to gain favorable market access and pricing decisions, we have to be prepared to deal with a myriad of healthcare agencies and national and regional regulations.

Why do governments feel the need to interfere in drug pricing? Why is drug pricing so contentious and subject to public scrutiny? What is the cause of the poor reputation of the industry despite the life-saving character of many of its products?

To better understand the perceived need by government to interfere in drug pricing, we should consider the main factors that cause this complexity:

- Drugs are subject to an unusual *purchase decision model* as payer, prescriber and patient engage in an increasingly complex tripartite product selection process.

- *Industry cost structure* is different, as high and risky upfront investments in research and development are offset by relatively high margins during commercialization.

- Heavy reliance on *patent protection* to allow for a pay-back period of development cost.

- Governments partly or entirely act as **monopsony** payers in many countries with socialized healthcare systems, such as in Europe, Japan, Canada and Australia.

- Social complexity related to what many consider to be the *right to affordable healthcare*.

These pharmaceutical industry characteristics, particularly in conjunction, create a very complicated environment with a lot of temptation for government involvement as natural market mechanisms are deemed to be impaired. Unfortunately, government involvement on a national basis only creates further problems, as most of the issues are global in nature. Frequently, new rules are introduced to tackle unwanted side effects and market reactions from existing rules, thus causing an increasingly complex web of rules and regulations. For example, therapeutic referencing systems in The Netherlands were recognized to cause substantial increases in prices of generics. By creating fixed reimbursement limits, generics manufacturers were incentivized to increase price up to the reimbursement limit rather than lower them under competitive pressures. Any price competition that did take place did not benefit the healthcare system, but flowed to the pockets of entrepreneurial pharmacists. Unintentionally, the cost containment system went completely contrary to the universally adopted European intent and policy of using savings through use of inexpensive generics to fund for innovative new therapies, also referred to as the "Headroom for Innovation" principle.

Changes in the environment naturally impact the drug industry's strategies, as they try to optimally adjust to the new customer requirements. Unfortunately, it may take 10 years before a change in strategy sees its impact in market performance. Rapid and frequent changes in healthcare systems are hampering the ability of drug companies to plan for success.

PURCHASE DECISION MODEL

For most consumer goods the decision maker, payer and user are the same, thus providing the basis for a natural balance between product benefits and willingness to pay. Micro-economic theory explains how in a free market economy a natural balance will occur between supply and demand at a market price.

A prescription drug purchase is very unusual, as it involves the writing of a prescription by a physician and, frequently, funding by a third party. Most characteristically different for the drug selection process is that payer, decision maker and consumer are three different entities. Since each of the players has different perspectives, responsibilities and preferences, the purchasing process is complicated in nature. Payers are likely to argue that patients, in absence of a substantial co-pay or co-insurance, are not sensitive to drug cost. Consequently, they will favor expensive therapies more than would be the case in a natural market system where payer and consumer are the same.

Payers, whether a US Managed Care organization or the Italian government, tend to be less sensitive to patient benefits than the patients themselves, particularly where convenience and non-life-threatening side effects are concerned. Naturally, payers judge drug performance on a statistical basis where individual patients have a more emotional relationship to their health, which leads to a higher aversion for risk. Governments and insurance companies are frequently faced with budget trade-offs to apply limited resources to competing causes. Health economic cost-effectiveness calculations can be used to make trade-offs in terms of cost per life saved and other similar measures. Although rational, these considerations run into difficult ethical discussions, as it is hard to value a life. This is further discussed in Chapter 5. Patients will obviously insist on any life-saving treatment, regardless of cost.

Co-pays and co-insurance rates are a means of raising patient involvement with drug funding and creating at least some price elasticity towards a natural market mechanism. In the United States, insurance companies have drastically increased co-pays and deductibles for drugs. Due to the fragmented nature of the market and lack of transparency on behalf of physicians and patients, these mechanisms have probably been relatively ineffective. Fixed co-pays, rather than a percentage co-insurance also do little towards achieving a higher awareness of drug cost with the patient. Co-insurance rates for high-cost biologics have a great impact on patient cost, but may in many cases only frustrate a patient when he or she has no other choice. In these cases it creates an ethical dilemma for the physician, who has taken an oath and has some legal liabilities to provide the best possible care for a patient, but may be tempted to choose a less favorable choice for the patient on the basis of patient co-pay or co-insurance.

The drug purchasing decision is an interesting situation once described to me as an unusual "dinner for three." Imagine three people, Bob, Ben and Betty going to a restaurant, where Bob makes a meal choice from the menu, Betty is consuming the meal and Ben is paying the bill. Sounds ridiculous? In drug terms, Doctor Bob prescribes the drug, patient Betty takes the drug and insurance agent Ben pays the bill. Common practice! Is it surprising that Ben has issues? He pays for what he perhaps perceives to be extravagant dishes that he can only hope that Betty will appreciate and benefit from. For Ben, the cheapest meal would certainly have done the job. Bob may be sensitive to Ben's pleas to order something less expensive, but he has his own responsibility to help Betty and wants to make sure that she is happy with the treatment. The absurdity of the situation illustrates the issue with respect to the role of the payer/insurance in drug prescribing (see Figure 1.2). Preferences between each of the three with respect to quality and cost of the ordered meal can be seen to be very different from each of their perspectives. It illustrates the importance of examining each healthcare system with respect to its ability to provide reasonable healthcare coverage to its citizens, while providing effective incentives to be cost conscious and avoid waste. Decisions of healthcare funding are both economically and ethically complex as they force a value to be placed on improvements of human life.

This "dinner for three" phenomenon is the cause of what many government healthcare agencies refer to as a lack of market mechanism. To address this apparent lack of market mechanism in the drug purchase model, they have felt it necessary to take action through the institution of price and/or reimbursement controls. These systems have grown into very complex sets of measures, each aimed at correcting "imperfections" in another control. Payer Ben has taken charge of the menu decisions, which is creating a new set of issues, particularly when the payer is a monopsony, a single payer with control over all government drug expenses. It is not surprising that national healthcare systems with monopsony purchasing power have chosen to push for control of drug prices as a mechanism to correct market imperfections. A better model would probably have been the institution of patient co-insurance (percentage co-pay) rates, as they restore a natural market mechanism, provided that open

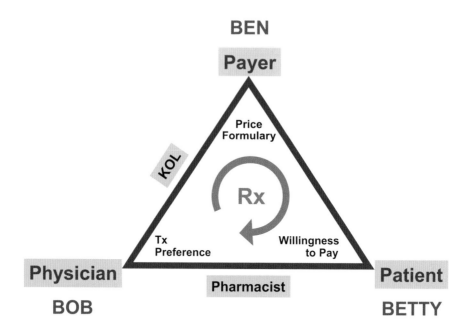

Figure 1.2 **"Dinner for three" analogy**

communication of the value of drugs is permitted. However, in most (at least somewhat socialistically spirited) price and/or reimbursement controlled markets this was deemed unacceptable, as it would potentially allow for a better medical treatment for people with higher incomes. Resistance to co-insurance rates have perhaps relaxed somewhat over the last few years; perhaps there is still hope for more market-driven solutions, as it becomes more and more apparent that increasingly complex sets of government controls have some toxic "side effects."

INDUSTRY COST STRUCTURE

The cost of development of a new drug was estimated to be in excess of $1.3 billion in 2006 (DiMasi, 2007). Given the past steep growth curve in the cost of drug development, today's average cost of drug development is probably much higher than $1.3 billion dollars. See Chapter 7 for more discussion on drug development cost. Payback of drug investments is very uncertain and only starts after successful completion of a 10- to 15-year development program.

The cost of drug development is likely to continue to rise, as the FDA and drug companies are increasingly under scrutiny for having approved and marketed drugs which only show unacceptable side effects after years of patient use. The market withdrawal of Vioxx has significantly added to this concern and pressures on the FDA to intensify safety drug reviews.

Due to the high cost of development and small probability of success for each compound, drug companies have worked extensively on work processes for early identification of promising compounds and an early failure of problematic ones. Drug revenue forecasts need to be substantial to justify a billion-dollar investment and companies that do hit the "pharmaceutical jackpot" need to employ significant marketing muscle to ensure their share of voice in a very competitive fragmented market.

Whether even a successfully approved drug delivers payback and potentially profit to the innovating company depends on the ability to claim a reasonable price and sufficient sales volume over its limited patent life.

Due to the high cost of drug development, the industry has a cost structure that is much different from most other industries. Let's look closely at the cost structure shown in Figure 1.3. The illustration shows a comparison in cost structure between a drug and a "widget," an average consumer product. The numbers are fictitious and not representative of any specific drug company and are just intended to illustrate differences with typical consumer goods.

The drug company cost structure has some remarkable characteristics:

- Very high upfront R&D and other fixed cost. Global R&D and commercialization cost is essentially sunk, independent of the actual number of countries that launch the drug;

- Relatively low marginal cost of goods (manufacturing materials and labor) and local marginal marketing cost;

- A high contribution margin to help offset the high upfront cost of R&D and other fixed cost of development and commercialization.

In this illustrative example, the contribution margin towards profitability is much higher for the drug than for the widget, as the marginal cost is 25 percent for the drug versus 70 percent for the widget. This implies that any price above

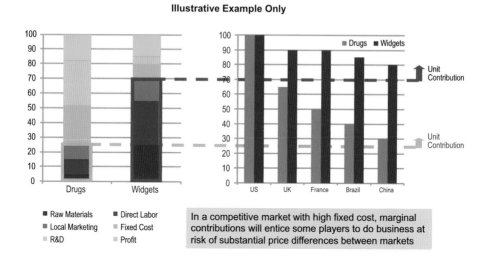

Figure 1.3   Drug industry cost structure implications

25 percent of total allocated cost will contribute to company payback of its upfront investments.

When a drug company is making price concessions in one or more countries, it will help to offset its investments. However it does need higher price levels for the majority of its sales to ensure overall profitability of the business and sustainability of the firm.

What happens if a customer (or a monopsony government) insists that it is only willing to pay a relatively low price for a drug? When the price is at a sufficient level above the marginal cost of manufacturing and marketing the drug, one of the market players is likely to take the deal, knowing that if it doesn't, it may put itself at a competitive disadvantage versus companies that do accept the deal. This is the reason why the United States is indeed subsidizing monopsony governments. Under competitive pressure, companies accept the risk of downward price cascading to other countries and potential public criticism in the United States.

From the government's perspective it is tempting to demand a company to make its innovation available at a very modest price level that everybody can afford. But what does that mean for the future? Will we be able to continue to convince Biotech and traditional Pharma companies to develop new drugs? Or do we think that we do not need next generation drugs to treat HIV/AIDS, cancer and other diseases?

For our widget example, the situation is fundamentally different. At the much higher cost of goods, only an irrational company would sell a widget at a substantial discount, as it would give a negative contribution to corporate profits.

PATENT PROTECTION

The pharmaceutical industry is heavily dependent on patents to pay for its innovation and provide a return on investment for its shareholders. This is how pharmaceutical products can command relatively high prices. Without patent protection, companies would not be willing or able to invest more than $1.3 billion to bring a product to market. Generic manufacturers would be able to make copy products available at much lower prices, since they don't have to engage in a 10-year risky development program where perhaps only one in a 1,000 products see commercial daylight. The theoretical patent life of a molecule is 20 years in most countries. However the real effective patent life from the moment of first sale to patent expiration is usually not much more than 10 years, as evidence needs of efficacy and safety take a large portion of its protected life cycle away. At least 10 years market exclusivity after launch is usually guaranteed in the US and Europe through patent and related exclusivity laws, such as the Hatch-Waxman Act in the US. Setting a reasonable, but adequate, price for a new product is therefore crucial for the survival of a pharmaceutical company. If the price is set too low, the return on investment is not sufficient to fund continuing business; if the price is set too high, customers may decide not to use the new product, leading to equal financial problems for the company.

GOVERNMENT MONOPSONY

In most countries, the government is responsible for the funding of healthcare. Organizations such as the National Health Service in the UK are directly funded by the government. In Germany, sick funds play an intermediary role, but are also funded by federal taxes. Employer-sponsored insurance programs, such as the Mutuelles in France, fund part of the drug bill, but the government is the main payer.

Facing budget pressures, governments have historically been tempted to interfere in the drug markets with pricing and reimbursement control measures by using their monopsony buying power. Government interference on drug market access and pricing has already been discussed in detail earlier in this chapter. However there are many other ways of interference beyond these systems. In many instances, governments have dictated drug price reductions to resolve budget problems. Price reductions were enforced in Germany as part of their healthcare reform and in the UK as part of a PPRS renewal. It is a bit ironic that the industry has to accept a 7 percent price cut in order to continue the profit control scheme. Similar price cuts have occurred, sometimes multiple times, in a list of countries that is too long for this book. The latest round of steep price cuts in Greece and other EU markets, following recession-related economic problems in 2010, illustrate the magnitude of this problem.

Monopsony power can result in significant market distortions in the international arena. It is much debated that the US is subsidizing healthcare in other markets with lower prices. The cause of this is at least partly found in monopsony power.

RIGHT TO AFFORDABLE HEALTHCARE

The right to affordable healthcare is a difficult and sensitive topic. Should everybody have equal access to the best healthcare, independent of personal affordability? Idealistically that sounds right to many of us. Within many healthcare systems in individual countries this also may be the case to a large extent. Many countries have universal healthcare coverage that is available and affordable for everyone. Prior to President Obama's Affordable Care Act (ACA), more than 15 percent of the United States population was uninsured. Under US law, hospitals are obliged to provide emergency care to any patient, independent of insurance coverage or personal financial conditions. Lack of insurance and unwillingness or inability to pay for preventative or early treatments left many inner city emergency care units overcrowded. Unfortunately, lack of insurance coverage thus resulted in much more expensive care in the emergency room, as important treatments were postponed.

What if we look at this internationally? This is obviously much harder, as solidarity tends to not reach as far across borders as it does within the borders of a country. Who would pay for a heart transplant for a patient in Nigeria? The Nigerian healthcare system is likely to have different priorities, as it can save more lives with other, less expensive interventions. Lack of hospitals, training and critical supplies cause the quality of care to be at a lower standard than it would be, for example, in the United States or Italy and this is generally accepted as part of reality.

The World Health Organization (WHO) has for many years now, maintained a list of "essential drugs." These drugs, which are mostly generically available compounds, should in WHO's vision be available to anyone in need as part of its philosophy that healthcare should be accessible to all, independent of income. Challenges arose, when as a consequence of the world crisis on HIV/AIDS, several patented drugs became crucial for developing countries healthcare needs. Given the price of these drugs and the inability to fund for large amounts of drugs that were required to address the emerging needs, huge issues emerged related to pricing for these drugs. Drug companies ultimately responded to pressures to engage in "differential pricing" practices and made the drugs available to the least developed countries at essentially cost of manufacturing, and dramatically reduced cost to lower- and middle-income countries.

It is notable that drug companies are subject to so much criticism and pressure over international pricing. Emerging and middle-income markets use threats of compulsory licensing, that is TRIPS (Trade-Related Aspects of Intellectual Property Rights) agreement based emergency-driven overruling of a patent right, to obtain drugs at a fraction of its cost. It creates complicated issues with respect to international trade and price referencing that are further discussed in Chapter 2.

A COMPARISON WITH OTHER INDUSTRIES

When considering the differentiating elements, described in the preceding sections, it may have become apparent that the drug industry is different from other consumer product industries. This is probably the main reason why drug pricing is a unique discipline that is hard to compare with price optimization for other products.

Which other industry has the same mix of complexities as the drug industry. None come to mind. The utilities industries have some similarities in terms of investments and cost structures, but are very different in every other aspect. The software and DVD movie businesses have similar intellectual property and cost structure aspects. DVD markets are regionally divided through regional zones in DVD players and DVDs, an interesting way of segmenting markets and allowing for price differentiation. This industry does not have the social aspects of life-or-death needs or the government monopsony aspects.

One wonders if the regionalization of DVDs would have been challenged if it was a high government expense item in European countries.

Global Pricing Issues

Price differences between markets can be substantial for any product, not just pharmaceuticals. For consumer goods, such as cars, DVDs and books, we sometimes find substantial price differences. For some goods, such as for example milk, price differences can be justified by local cost differences. Also most services are priced at local labor rates and as such, are likely to be much lower in a village in Argentina, than they are in, for example, Manhattan. For consumer goods that can be easily transported, such as batteries, computer software and memory chips, international price differences can result in legal or gray market importation. For products with natural or legal trade hurdles, such as water with transportation cost, price differences are less of a commercial threat.

The Economist publishes an annual Mac Index overview, which compares prices of a McDonald's Big Mac in a large number of countries (*Economist*, 2013). Interestingly, *The Economist* draws parallels between the price differences of the Big Mac and the over- or undervaluation of currencies. In most non-American minds, the use of a hamburger as an economic standard may be a bit of a stretch, however the index does demonstrate the wide variety in retail prices for a product which is identical in every market. With the increasing number of open borders, resulting from trade agreements, price differences for many goods may disappear as a consequence of arbitrage.

Figure 1.4 shows the distribution of Big Mac prices across countries. The highest price in Norway ($7.51) is five times higher than the price in India ($1.50). The US and European markets are at the high price range; lower-income countries have prices that are at the low end of the range. Differences in mainly local cost of production seem to allow McDonald's to address differences in willingness-to-pay and affordability between countries. If it was possible to practically ship a Big Mac from India to Norway without losing its appeal, price differences for the Big Mac would probably be smaller than they are today.

Figure 1.5 shows a similar price comparison for the iPad Retina (16Gb Wi-Fi model), as reported by CommSec (2013) in their CommSec iPad index. Interestingly, the US price is almost the lowest in the selection of countries.

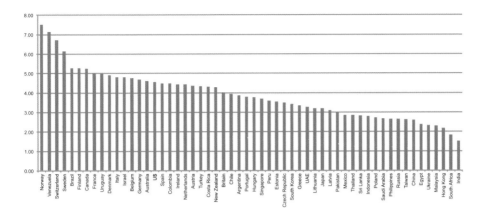

Figure 1.4   Global Big Mac prices

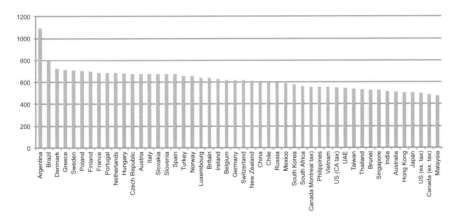

Figure 1.5   Global iPad prices

With the exception of Argentina and Brazil, most prices are actually within a relatively narrow band between $500 and $700. The most important observation to make is that Apple did not feel a need to provide its iPad at a lower price to the less affluent populations in developing countries. The chosen, higher than US prices seem to be local profit optimizing prices. Obviously, Apple need not be too concerned about political consequences of high-priced iPads in developing countries; an iPad may not be high on the list of needs of a relatively poor population. Figure 1.6 shows a comparison of the Big Mac and iPad prices, indexed to the US price.

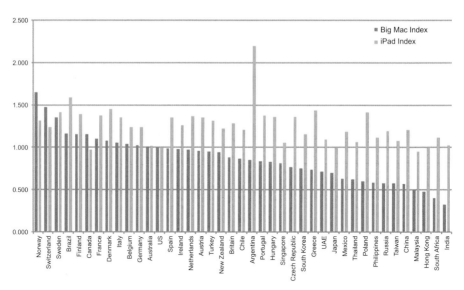

Figure 1.6   Global prices indexed to the US for iPad and Big Mac

Beside freshness-related considerations, such as with a Big Mac, there are other barriers to trade which enable the sustainability of international price differences. The movie industry has successfully introduced global zones for DVDs making Chinese or Spanish retail DVDs practically unusable in the United States and vice versa. It is hard to think of any reason besides market segmentation that justifies this industry-wide agreement. The zones clearly allow the DVD manufacturers to charge vastly different prices between countries.

Global price differences for drugs have increasingly become an issue for the pharmaceutical industry. Ethical issues prevent drug companies from adopting global pricing strategies similar to the one adopted by Apple for iPad. It would not be right to sell an anti-cancer drug or HIV/AIDS drug at double the US price in Malaysia. Financially, Apple may be able to sell its iPads at US prices in developing countries. However, the cost structure of an iPad will prevent Apple from adopting the relatively very low prices in developing countries that have been given for HIV/AIDS drugs.

The HIV/AIDS pandemic has globally raised concern about drug pricing issues. Affordability of new and innovative drugs for diseases such as AIDS has motivated many developing countries and new economies such as Brazil and South Africa to introduce generics under compulsory licensing provisions.

Compulsory licensing threats have further complicated an already complex global pricing and trade environment. This topic is discussed more extensively in Chapter 13.

Government payers have used international price differences to negotiate better terms with companies by introducing price referencing laws. Starting in Europe, but now expanding to other countries, companies have also been encouraged to engage in international trade or "parallel trade" for pharmaceuticals. Also on the political arena, international price differences have caused many issues around the world. Since 1994, every few years and again recently, the United States has seen a flurry of political attention concerning global price differences for drugs, resulting, increasingly, in support for initiatives with respect to importation legislation for drugs.

INTERNATIONAL PRICE REFERENCING

Starting in Europe about 20 or so years ago, countries have increasingly introduced international price referencing laws to take advantage of lower prices in other countries. These mechanisms put a cap on in-market prices (ex-factory or retail) on the basis of the price in the country of origin, the average price of a list of countries or in some cases even the lowest price of a list of countries. This trend is still expanding rapidly with, for example, now Brazil and Mexico adopting such measures.

Figure 1.7 shows that considering just two major countries, an already complex picture develops. As an example, in Canada a price for a new drug cannot exceed the median level of prices for the same compound in the United States, France, Germany, Italy, Sweden, Switzerland and the United Kingdom. Japan's "Foreign Price Adjustment" rule can adjust the approved price either upward or downward through a relatively complex formula based on the price difference compared with the average of the US, the UK, France and Germany.

Many countries have international reference pricing laws in place. Figure 1.8 gives a more complete picture of all global price referencing laws in existence. The black lines represent countries that reference one or more other countries as part of their price approval process. Figure 1.8 does not, however, take into consideration that many pricing authorities engage in informal price comparisons, thus further adding to the mix. For example, national payers in Europe have many informal contacts, which give them a good lay of the land with respect to actual net prices in other countries.

Figure 1.7   International price referencing in some key countries

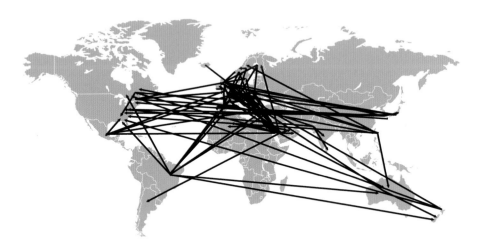

Figure 1.8   Global price referencing network

It may become clear from Figure 1.8, that local pricing decisions have regional and global implications. Forced price reductions or concessions in negotiations for launch can have far-reaching global implications and should be carefully assessed before implementation.

PARALLEL TRADE/IMPORTATION

In Europe, the Middle-East and parts of Asia, trading companies are actively purchasing pharmaceuticals in low-priced countries and shipping and selling them in higher-priced countries. When a prescription drug, for example Januvia, is €30 per pack cheaper in Greece, than it is in the UK, easy arbitrage opportunities are created for wholesalers. These wholesalers, parallel trading companies, file for a relatively simple to obtain approval for parallel import of a branded drug. In the European Union, parallel trading companies are authorized by law to re-package in a local language pack and print a local language package insert. Even small price differences between countries, frequently caused by currency exchange fluctuations over time or government forced price reductions, are sufficient to create a very profitable arbitrage opportunity for parallel traders. In the EU, pharmacists can substitute branded products with their parallel trade equivalent. In some countries, such as The Netherlands, pharmacists are actually incentivized to make the substitution by allowing them to pocket a substantial share of savings achieved.

Parallel trade is not unique to the pharmaceutical industry. In any other industry, a company can price its products across countries, best meeting local market conditions, without any interference by the government. Also, a company can adjust prices upward or downward to reflect cost changes or market conditions. When for example Toyota decides to sell its Corolla model at a higher price in Belgium than in Italy, an arbitrage opportunity is created for anybody, either for personal use or for financial gain, to purchase a vehicle in Italy and sell it in Belgium. Since the adoption of the Euro there is very little risk associated with this form of parallel trade. It is also simple to do as it essentially only requires financing and transportation. Now consider the same car situation with a price that is much higher in the UK than in Belgium, Italy and perhaps some other EU markets. The UK has not joined other EU markets in the common Euro currency. Currency exchange rate fluctuations between the British Pound and the Euro can impact relative price levels between the countries, which can further increase any existing price differences to a level where it becomes an attractive opportunity for a parallel trader. When deemed unacceptable to Toyota, they have the ability to adjust their prices in either of the countries to eliminate price differences. In this case, Toyota may effectively be protected from trade due to the fact that British cars drive on the left side of the road, thus requiring a driver's seat on the right side.

Let's return to our pharmaceutical case. Even when a drug company is able to negotiate exactly the same price in all EU countries, currency changes between, say the British Pound and the Euro can cause substantial price differences between the UK and other EU markets. Since a drug company cannot increase prices in virtually every EU market, its only option is to reduce price in the UK or accept parallel trade. If subsequently the Swedish government mandates a price reduction or the Swedish Krone value slides relative to the Euro, a next round of price cascading is introduced.

Not only is parallel trade legal in Europe, it is actually illegal to engage in any preventive activities. As part of the efforts to eliminate trade barriers between EU markets, strict rules have been put into place limiting differentiation between countries on brand name, product form and other trade limiting features. Some "reasonable" supply restrictions based on local needs have been allowed. Through this mechanism, companies have been allowed to limit supply to lower-price countries to avoid shipping to other countries. Since it is hard to control whether drugs go to patients or to foreign warehouses, this mechanism of control has serious issues, as patients may be withheld access to much needed drugs when a wholesaler decides that he can make more money in trading it to a higher-priced country. In June 2009 an Opinion was issued that a "dual pricing" practice, charging wholesalers in a country more for an export drug than for domestically used drugs, is an infringement of the EC Treaty. This ruling is just another step in a long and complicated ongoing legal battle regarding parallel trade in the European Union.

How well allowing parallel trade has served society is debatable. Allowing parallel trade in the EU has been the result of a highly dogmatic implementation of the EU free trade principle. The combination of government price intervention and free trade simply doesn't make any sense from any reasonable perspective. European bureaucracy has no doubt withheld useful drugs from patients in some lower-priced countries, as companies have been forced into all-or-nothing decisions on government set prices with relatively unrestricted arbitrage opportunities for parallel trade companies. It has also resulted in a proportion of the proceeds of patented pharmaceuticals going to parallel trade companies that essentially add no value, rather than funding new research for innovative drug treatments. It has had some impact on the cost of drugs, but the question is at what price. Parallel trade causes the market to deal with imbalances between the separate EU markets, thus stimulating the creation of a single European market. However there are very few "markets" for prescription drugs in Europe as government have taken control of price either directly or indirectly.

The European Union has largely been unsympathetic to the industry's complaints and has been very dogmatic in upholding its free trade principles. The fact that pricing freedom is blatantly absent in most European markets has not softened their position.

Discussions and legislative initiatives in the United States to allow wholesale importation of prescription drugs can have a substantial impact on the global drug market. Price differences between the US and Canada, caused by decades of Canadian government interference in drug marketing and compulsory licensing, favoring the local generics industry, are substantial for many drugs. A typical Canadian price may be 60 percent of the US price, although the difference is actually smaller when considering Medicaid and Federal Supply Schedule (FSS) prices. In some cases the differences are bigger. Many attribute the large price differences to the greedy behavior of pharmaceutical companies. In reality, prices in Canada are artificially low due to the lasting impact of a period of compulsory licensing in Canada, where Canada in effect enabled a now strong generics industry through the drug industry-wide government-forced licensing of their technology to these local generics companies. Upon the abolition of this practice, the industry was limited in its pricing through the establishment of the PMPRB agency, which ensured that prices could not easily exceed the prevailing generic price levels.

Over the last 10 to 15 years there have been many US bills to authorize wholesale importation of drugs into the US from Canada and other countries. In a number of bills, the number of authorized source countries is fairly large as it includes all EU countries, Switzerland, Canada, Australia, New Zealand and Japan. Safety concerns over imported drugs have withheld the implementation of previously approved legislation, but as the political pressure is high, this seems only a matter of time. Since October 16, 2013, Maine residents can directly buy imported prescription drugs from Canada, the United Kingdom, Australia or New Zealand in local retail pharmacies. Court battles are likely to endure for a while before the legality of this measure is clarified. Prior to this new broader (re-)importation initiative, Maine municipalities and companies were already operating importation initiatives from Canada through organizations such as CanaRx.

The US name "re-importation" suggests that it is a US-manufactured drug that is imported back into the US after export to international markets. In some cases this may be true, but since the drug is sold in these international markets, it will have to comply with their requirements on for example excipients and dyes, not necessarily the US ones. Where the rules are different, this will certainly be importation rather than re-importation.

In this Chapter ...

It has been shown how drug pricing is uniquely different from pricing in other industries due to a number of reasons, including the "dinner for three" phenomenon and its competitive market implications. We learned that global drug pricing is highly complex as government controls and international trade aspects make for difficult trade-offs. The industry cost structure and humanistic considerations related to access to healthcare further add to sometimes emotional reactions to trade-off decisions.

2

Payers

Understanding payers and payer systems is the key element to understanding global pharmaceutical market access and pricing. Payers are people with personal objectives, opinions and emotions that drive their daily actions and interpret rules as they see best fit given their charter and guidance from health plan or department of health and political leadership.

The goal of this chapter is to give a better understanding of the wide variety of payer systems, as well as to show the role of decision-making bodies and key budget holders in this process. We will discuss the most important drug coverage philosophies, cost control mechanisms and decision-making processes used by payers.

Global Payer Systems

Payer systems are designed to achieve certain policy objectives and to provide a rational set of rules to fairly decide on pricing and coverage of a variety of drugs and medical benefits. Internal consistency is extremely important to maintain an image of fairness to individual patients, which is particularly important as healthcare coverage decisions can mean life or death to an individual patient. Cost of healthcare continues to increase due to advancement of technology and availability of sometimes very expensive new medical treatments and drugs. Payers are challenged to provide healthcare coverage to their customers, while staying within their medical and/or drug budget.

The world has a wide variety of payer systems and methods of market access and price control by governments. In most countries, the national department of health has the responsibility of providing healthcare to its citizens. In the United Kingdom, there is a large healthcare system that provides all controlling aspects of healthcare, including regional Clinical

Commissioning Groups (CCGs), that set and control expenses within that region and subject to National Health Service (NHS) funding and guidelines. In Germany and The Netherlands, a large number of independent sick funds control much of the implementation of healthcare management, but also here there is a very tight national funding and control structure. In Canada, national authorities control aspects of drug pricing, but leave the management of budget and related formularies to regional provinces. In Italy and Spain, national authorities always tightly control drug pricing and reimbursement; however both countries have authorized regions to exert (additional) controls over drug utilization and within their regional healthcare budget.

It may be apparent from the above, that each country has its own way of utilizing various drug market access and price control mechanisms to conform to local preferences. The concepts and tools that are used in each of the countries have a high degree of similarity, as governments tend to copy elements of each other's systems. This is why, today, global market access and pricing seems like a complicated and confusing world. Hopefully, this chapter will provide some structure and an effective way to navigate the global pricing maze.

In Chapter 8, systems will be categorized and segmented by their main underlying management principle. Let's, however, first examine the perspectives and motivations of payers in order to better understand the systems that they have created.

The Payer Perspective

Put yourself in the shoes of a payer, responsible for a drug or broader healthcare budget. How would you weigh the responsibility of ensuring availability of drugs that treat debilitating diseases against the need to stay within the assigned budget?

In evaluating a payer's preferences and actions, it is first of all important to verify the true "perspective" of the payer in terms of his or her area of responsibility. Is a payer, for example, responsible for a drug budget or an overall medical budget? When claiming benefits of the lower cost of reduced or no hospitalization as a result of the use of a new, more expensive drug, a holder of an overall medical budget is likely to be more genuinely interested. Similarly, better compliance means higher drug cost and potentially lower overall medical cost. An insurance plan that only covers pharmacy benefits, such as a Medicare Part D plan, will not be clearly incentivized to improve compliance and adherence. Another important consideration is the time horizon for a payer. Payers in US Managed Care will carefully consider patient plan switch behaviors in evaluating the financial return of long-term benefits, whereas a European government is more likely to accept a longer-term time horizon. The National Institute for Health and Care Excellence (NICE) may consider a 25-year time horizon in their effectiveness and cost-effectiveness considerations, but the local Clinical Commissioning Groups (CCGs), which make formulary decisions on the basis of NICE advice, are cash strapped and are often not willing to spend more in favor of significantly larger future-year savings.

The way in which payers are generally handling their decision making is probably best illustrated through a number of successive questions that can be asked:

Medical Need   How strong is the need for a new drug treatment?

                      Is the disease area and indication high on the priority list of unmet needs? Will there be a lot of excitement over any new treatment solution for the patients under consideration?

Effectiveness   Does the new drug treatment work and address the unmet medical need in a substantial way? Will the treatment effectiveness claims have a substantial impact on patient lives when proven?

Evidence   Is the evidence of effectiveness and safety compelling? Are there any remaining doubts with respect to real-life efficacy or safety that temper the "clinical hunger" for the new drug? Are there any flaws in the clinical package that can challenge the improvement claim? Are there any substantial safety issues or concerns that negate the benefit claims?

Economic Impact   How will the approval impact the drug budget? Will it cause a substantial increase in overall drug cost or is it negligible? How does the budget impact compare against the likely cost of other healthcare priorities?

Ability to Control   Does the government or private payer have any control over expenses once pricing and reimbursement is approved? How well is the approval defined to avoid on or off label unintended use? Will this pose a budget risk and how can this be handled?

Political Importance   Particularly in government controlled systems, the happiness of political leadership and their constituencies has a large impact on decision making. Most drug pricing and reimbursement decisions do not have a level of impact and urgency that make political intervention likely. In selected cases, such as for example the MS drug decision making in the UK (see risk sharing case study in Chapter 11), the department of health can decide to intervene to address specific public health issues, often influenced by the direct impact of the decision on public opinion and coverage in the news media. In reality, the political importance will be on the drug budget manager's mind in addressing his/her question on whether they can decline reimbursement.

Making market access and pricing decisions for pharmaceuticals can be very difficult, as it impacts people's well-being and even life or death. Affordability of healthcare is oftentimes considered a basic human right, but how far does this right go when the community can simply not afford the most expensive new technologies for all situations? How does a payer weigh the relatively limited cost per patient of for example pre-natal vitamins with the high cost of the use of an orphan drug for a single patient? This challenge is not unique to pharmaceuticals as, for example, the decision to pay for a liver transplant is equally difficult. Many ethical issues arise when for example patient age is taken into consideration in the funding decision.

Given the potential emotional character of a healthcare funding decision, it is important to have a robust and fair process to make the trade-offs. As part of this process, payers find it usually important to have the actual medical evaluation done by independent key opinion leaders and experts who, within pre-defined healthcare system rules, make an evaluation of the new drug treatment and its supporting evidence. Most US healthcare plans will make a coverage decision on medical grounds, followed by a formulary tier placement decision, which may involve contracting. In France, the Economic Committee (Comité Economique du Médicament, CEPS) makes a pricing decision after a clinical evaluation by the Transparency Commission (Commission de Transparence, CT), with advice from the recently created Economic Evaluation Committee (Commission Evaluation Economique et de Santé Publique, CEESP).

The remainder of this chapter is used to describe the philosophies and rules that key global healthcare systems around the world are using to rationalize and guide drug market access and pricing decision making.

Drug Budget

As mentioned in the previous section, the payer's perspective is an important consideration in our expectation of the reaction of a payer to our value story. However, even within healthcare systems that take a broad medical perspective and are open to reward for medical and public health innovations, the drug budget impact is an important aspect of decision making.

In the United States, almost all discussions around contracting and formulary acceptance have a close relationship to impact on the drug budget. Particularly for step-wise innovations or "me-too's" it is important to analyze this carefully from the payer perspective through budget impact analysis tools.

In France, the estimated sales volume becomes an integral part of the "accord cadre" with the price-setting Economic Committee (CEPS). When the budget is exceeded, penalties apply, usually through a rebate or price reduction. Accurate forecasting of product uptake in France is a critical success factor in sustaining a profitable business.

In many other countries, budget impact is very important as an aspect of payer decision making, although not necessarily to the same extent as in France.

As mentioned earlier in this chapter, it is very important to understand the budget holder's responsibilities and perspective, i.e. what falls under the payer's budget: outpatient prescription drugs, inpatient prescription drugs, medical benefits, long-term care, etc.

Overview of Payer Cost Control Mechanisms

In most countries the government in some way or form controls market access and/or pricing for pharmaceuticals. Very few countries, if any, truly have free pricing. The degree of price control is vastly different between countries and the number and types of control systems in place is high.

Payers have generally used three fundamental mechanisms to control drug cost:

1. Direct price control;

2. Indirect price control;

3. Utilization control.

A brief outline of the various control mechanisms is given below. Most healthcare systems are using multiple mechanisms to control market access and/or price. A more elaborate description of the main healthcare and pricing and reimbursement systems is found in Part E.

Most countries have direct price controls, indirect price controls or both. It is important to realize that each country has its own distinct pricing and reimbursement system and acts independently, although they do like to learn from each other and opportunistically take advantage of lower prices in other systems. The European Union has a central regulatory review agency (EMA), but pricing and reimbursement is not handled on a European level.

DIRECT PRICE CONTROL

Government agencies are directly setting drug prices in many countries, including large markets such as France, Germany, Italy, Spain and Japan. Common to all of these systems is that premiums are not easily obtained and require thorough and early preparation on behalf of the pharmaceutical company. Each healthcare system requires submission of a dossier in a local standardized format through which the company can argue how the product should be priced within the bureaucratic pricing system. The ultimate decision is solely at the discretion of the government agency. Considering that the government is also trying to control its healthcare and drug budget, the bias towards lower prices is evident.

To illustrate how governments engage in direct price control, let's consider France, Japan and Canada as three examples. More detailed descriptions of these and a number of other healthcare systems are found in Chapters 8 and 19–31.

The French and Japanese systems are probably most notorious in assigning an existing drug comparator or reference and allowing an innovativeness premium that is established on the basis of the demonstrated improvement over the reference treatment. These systems are based on a principle of therapeutic referencing, which is further described in Chapters 4 and 8.

In Japan, most new chemical entities are evaluated for pricing on the basis of an existing drug comparator and an innovativeness premium. The rules for establishing a comparator are well defined and based on an evaluation of drug indication, chemical structure and mechanism of action. The innovativeness premium awarded is usually small, although it can theoretically reach 120 percent. Few drugs qualify for a "cost-plus" evaluation, which does not sound very enticing, but in reality is an opportunity to achieve much more favorable price levels. The conditions to qualify for cost-plus are very restrictive, thus limiting it to only a few drugs for which a comparator cannot reasonably be assigned. In cases where the Japanese price is much above or much below the average of prices in the United States, France, Germany and the UK, a "foreign price adjustment" calculation kicks in with a substantial impact on the finally approved market price. Generic drug pricing is very restrictive as well, with growing discounts over existing market players, depending on the number of available compounds.

The French system is also based on assigning a reference drug, usually either a gold standard for treatment or a very similar previously launched compound. The method of assigning a reference in France is much less rigidly defined than in Japan and is more directly linked to clinical use. The "Transparency Commission" decides on the appropriate comparator, as well as an ASMR (Amélioration du Service Medical Rendu) rating, which reflects the rate of treatment improvement over the comparator. The ASMR rating, from I to V, is generally clearly correlated to a relatively narrow range of potential price premiums or discounts. The actual price is established on the basis of the ASMR rating and contractual arrangements with the manufacturer by the Economic Committee (CEPS). Pricing contracts in France frequently include limits and penalties which, for example, trigger a price decrease or rebate when sales volume is higher than agreed upon or an average dose is exceeded.

Some may argue that the French system does not control price directly, since the manufacturer has the option to sell the drug without reimbursement. However, since this is not a realistic option for most therapy areas, it should be considered a direct form of price control for all practical purposes.

In Canada, one of the many controls in place is the price control mechanism used by the Patented Medicine Prices Review Board (PMPRB). Under this scheme, "excessive pricing" for patented drugs is retroactively pursued. As an example, sustained release formulations are not allowed a price premium over their original formulation as this is deemed an exploitation of patent rights under Canadian law. Similarly, drugs with only minor healthcare improvements over the existing standard of care are allowed only slightly higher prices. In addition, prices of drugs cannot exceed the median price of the same drug in the United States, France, Germany, Italy, Sweden, Switzerland and the UK.

The examples of these three countries give a sense of the kinds of price control systems that are used by governments around the world. Many other similar systems exist in other countries.

INDIRECT PRICE CONTROL

In indirect price control systems, reimbursement is controlled through one or more mechanisms. An increasingly prevalent reimbursement control system is that of "therapeutic referencing," where groups of drugs that are deemed similar in therapeutic effect are assigned an equal fixed reimbursement amount. For drugs that are priced above the reimbursement level, the patient has to absorb the difference between price and reimbursement limit, which in almost all cases leads to strong patient objections, as they have been educated by the government that all medically necessary options are fully reimbursed without patient co-payment. Therapeutic referencing has been used in direct controls as well, although price controls based on this system allow for some price differentiation on the basis of demonstrated improvements.

Probably the best known example of a therapeutic referencing based reimbursement system is the German system with its "jumbo groups," in which all brand and generic drugs in the same therapy area are used to establish the reimbursement limit for the class. The reimbursement limit is calculated on the basis of the average cost of all drugs in the class at a fixed historical time point. Therapeutic referencing has had a large impact on prescribing. Probably the most widely discussed example is the impact that it had on sales for Lipitor after the creation of a jumbo class with statins, including generics. Pfizer was unsuccessful in demonstrating sufficient differentiation from other statins under the tight regulations in the system. As they were unable or unwilling to slash Lipitor prices to the established reimbursement limit, Lipitor sales rapidly dwindled to a fraction of its original levels. The German Act on the Reform of the Market for Medical Products (Arzneimittelmarkt-Neuordnungsgesetz – AMNOG) of December 22, 2010 has further implemented the philosophy of therapeutic referencing by automatically pegging prices for new drugs that are ruled to not offer additional benefit to the prevailing prices of existing drugs. At the same time, AMNOG changed the system from reimbursement control to price control. Therapeutic referencing, which is a widely used indirect price control mechanism, is further discussed in Chapter 4. The German healthcare system and details of its therapeutic referencing practices and guidelines are found in Chapter 22.

Another example of indirect price controls is the use of health economically driven reimbursement such as used in the UK, where guidelines are prepared by the National Institute for Health and Care Excellence (NICE) based on proven cost-effectiveness. Each of the National Health Service (NHS) regions in England have a Clinical Commissioning Group, which decides on formulary and hence patient access for each drug. Since price is one of the direct factors determining cost-effectiveness, there is inherent pressure on manufacturers to lower price when cost-effectiveness is not realized within the unofficial range of acceptability. More detail about the NHS, NICE and cost-effectiveness requirements is found in Chapter 25.

Besides cost-effectiveness-based price controls, the UK also limits pricing freedom through its Pharmaceutical Price Regulation Scheme (PPRS) profit control system. Return on investment is subject to regulation for all pharmaceutical companies through this system. Initial price setting is free for the first five years after launch of a new chemical entity, but after that period, price changes are subject to approval on the basis of a financial evaluation.

In reality, the difference between direct and indirect price controls is very small. Indirect price controls can only be overcome by drug companies by convincing patients that they should pay more for their drug than the one that is deemed equivalent. In the case of "life style" drugs, whole categories are excluded from reimbursement. Patient use may be somewhat hampered by this and differences in price between options are likely to have a larger impact on drug selection than in the case of reimbursed classes of drugs. When one or two drug options in an otherwise reimbursed class are excluded, the burden of a strong value message is upon the drug company. In only a few of these cases have drug companies been successful in overcoming the patient cost hurdle. One example where this has been done successfully is the case of third-generation oral contraceptives in France. Women have been prepared to pay the cost of this newer generation of birth control drugs where the older generation drugs are fully reimbursed. This example clearly is an exceptional case in that drug companies have been successful in marketing non-reimbursed options in an otherwise reimbursed market.

UTILIZATION CONTROL

Payers are generally not just concerned about price, but also about sales volume of drugs. Particularly after approval of expensive drugs, they are concerned that these will be used "inappropriately" for patients that can be effectively treated with less expensive alternatives.

One example of utilization control is the well-known "envelope agreement" in France, under which companies are bound by a multi-annual contract, which among other things specifies an agreed-upon maximum sales volume for each drug. When exceeding volume, agreed upon price reductions or rebates are applied. The negotiated sales volumes are usually tied to epidemiologic data, indicating which volume is in accordance with the agreed-upon patient types for which evidence demonstrated benefits from the new drug treatment.

Another example of utilization controls is the use of limitations on length of therapy, such as used in many countries for anti-platelet therapy with clopidogrel for up to one year following a cardiovascular event. Beyond one year, the health risk of these patients has reduced substantially, thus changing the basis for justification for the use of clopidogrel over a much cheaper aspirin. In cases such as this, reimbursement limitations are usually linked to the medical treatment guidelines and their underlying clinical (and sometimes health economics) evaluations.

The use of health economics controls is in effect a form of utilization control as well. A drug treatment may be cost-effective for one kind of patient, but may not be cost-effective for patients who, for example, are only suffering from a mild stage of the disease. In the UK, the NHS only reimbursed Aricept for moderate to severe Alzheimer's disease patients until a few years ago. The basis for this decision was the fact that the advising "National Institute for Health and Care Excellence" (NICE) had ruled that the treatment was not cost-effective for mild Alzheimer's disease patients.

FREE PRICING

This category seems to be suffering from a threat of extinction. As such, the United States is perhaps the only industrialized country with true free pricing for drugs. It is the only country that allows pharmaceutical companies to make competitive choices without government interference and no doubt the most desirable system in a free market economy. Over the last 15 years, even in the US there are pressures for price controls, particularly for Medicare and Medicaid programs. Perhaps it is just a matter of time before calls to provide the Center for Medicare and Medicaid Services (CMS) with the power to negotiate drug prices for government-funded programs, such as Medicare Part D, become reality.

Free pricing can be found in a decreasing number of other countries in Latin America and Asia. These countries usually do not have a government-funded healthcare system, which in many cases is the fundamental basis for perceived need of control. However even in these countries governments increasingly impose international price referencing laws and other price controls to address or pre-empt local concerns related to the high cost of drugs.

Similarities and Differences between Payer Systems

In complex situations, it is tempting and often useful to simplify things. However it can also be dangerous to ignore key differences between individual country payer systems. To address this, I have taken the following approach in describing global payer systems to help the reader understand its implications:

- Payer cost management techniques are discussed in this chapter, as well as in Chapter 4: Reference-Based Pricing and in Chapter 5: Health Outcomes and Health Economics.

- Payers are segmented by general payer management philosophy in Chapter 8: Payer Segmentation.

- Individual country payer systems are further described in detail in Part E: Key Healthcare Systems.

With this approach, I hope that a high level of understanding about the strategic implications can be obtained, while offering the opportunity to study each country system in more detail, where needed.

In this Chapter ...

We examined preferences and behaviors of payers and payer systems. In particular, we both analyzed the questions that payers ask themselves as part of a review process and the types of control they use to ensure that drug spending stays within their budget.

3

Fundamentals of Pricing

What increased the value of a cup of coffee from $0.80 to over $3.00 when Starbucks built its franchise? Why does parking cost $50 a day in Manhattan? How did water become an expensive beverage?

What motivates consumers to pay a large amount of money for a product? How do we judge the value of a product and how is this different from person to person? How are these considerations the same or different for pharmaceuticals in comparison with other consumer goods?

In this chapter we will examine some basic principles of pricing and assess how they apply to drug pricing under various conditions and under reimbursement restrictions.

Importance of Setting the Right Price

Product pricing has a more direct impact on profits than most other elements of the marketing mix. When considering fixed cost, even a slight decrease in price can significantly reduce or even eliminate the profit margin.

In the example in Figure 3.1, a 10 percent decrease in price results in a 50 percent reduction in profit margin, whereas a 10 percent increase in price adds 50 percent to profits. In reality, price changes can have consequences in terms of changes in unit sales. In the example, a 10 percent price reduction may result in significant increases in market share and sales, but since the margins were cut in half, a doubling of sales volume is required to match the original profitability without the price decrease. There are few cases, where a 10 percent price cut will double sales. Cases where it will are characterized by a high price sensitivity or high "price elasticity of demand," such as is particularly the case with undifferentiated products or commodities.

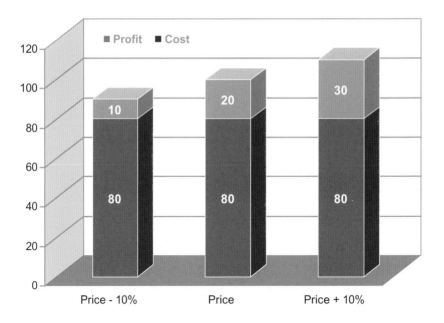

Figure 3.1   Price and profit

Relationships between price, sales revenue and profits are studied in micro-economic theory. Drug pricing is different from pricing for most consumer goods due to reasons discussed in Chapter 2. Nevertheless, as a starting point, let's examine the micro-economic concepts on their applicability to the free and government-controlled drug markets. Figures and calculations are intended to serve as illustrations for enhanced understanding rather than to suggest a practical means of solving pricing challenges. Actual research methodologies and analyses to support price decision making are discussed in Chapter 15.

Pricing in a Free Market Economy

Figure 3.2 shows the price–volume relationships for demand and supply for a typical industry in a free market economy. Willingness to supply increases as price increases. Customer demand decreases with increasing price. Supply and demand are in equilibrium at a market price P_A. In industries with an above average return on investment, new entrants cause supply to increase (for example from supply line A to supply line B in Figure 3.2) with a resulting decrease in equilibrium price from P_A to P_B. This process continues over time with companies entering and exiting the industry until profitability is in line

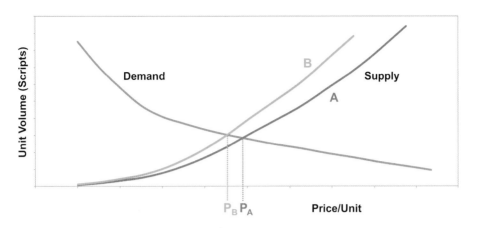

Figure 3.2   General supply and demand relationships

with what can be expected for the industry on the basis of its business and financial risk profile.

Pharmaceutical companies have a relatively high risk of R&D investments and liability issues related to potential adverse events. DiMasi (2007) states an estimated investment cost in excess of $1.3 billion for each drug reaching market authorization. The cost of marketing drugs in a very competitive environment can also be very high, and sudden loss of compound value at patent expiration is limiting the time horizon to earn back investments. This explains why powerhouses such as Merck and Pfizer can suddenly be faced with financial trouble due to issues related to pipeline strength or safety issues for a single drug.

How much supply and demand fluctuates with price (elasticity of supply and demand) depends very much on the manufacturing cost structure, barriers to entry, the uniqueness of the product and purchaser needs and preferences. On the supply side, the generics market will show a very steep price–supply relationship, as manufacturing processes and sales opportunities are more clearly defined than for a new and risky development track for a new chemical entity.

Price elasticity of demand or willingness-to-pay is of prime importance when determining whether to fund for a promising development candidate. Figure 3.3 shows some illustrative examples of varying degrees of price elasticity. In the top blue line in the figure, unit volume changes only slightly as a result of

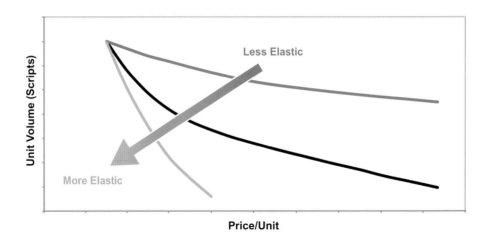

Figure 3.3   Price elasticity of demand

price so that demand is considered to be relatively price-inelastic. Examples of relatively inelastic goods are generally found in the most innovative products within a category, for example the latest high-end digital camera, imported luxury food, a Lamborghini car and some brand name clothing. The orange line shows a much steeper curve and is considered more elastic. Small changes in price have a relatively strong impact on demand. High elasticity of demand typically occurs in markets where close substitutes are available. Examples are gasoline, milk and many other consumer goods.

In the pharmaceutical market, price elasticity is different between products as well. Innovative drugs tend to show much less elasticity than me-too or generic drugs. Gliptins are likely to have much more sensitivity to price than a new cancer vaccine or cancer treatment like Avastin or Erbitux. In the US, when Bristol-Myers Squibb (BMS) launched Erbitux, price elasticity at the chosen price point was not as high as it was when Amgen launched Vectibix a few years after. As a first entry, BMS was free to choose a price point which was much higher than the largely generically available group of chemotherapy agents used for colorectal cancer, based on an expected improvement on long-term patient outcomes. When Vectibix was launched with a generally similar profile, its price elasticity was much higher and Amgen chose to offer a discounted price versus Erbitux. When in the future a bio-similar or bio-generic version of Erbitux is launched, price elasticity is likely to be even higher. Expectation of a high willingness-to-pay motivated BMS to deeply invest in the development of new biotechnology agents for cancer treatment. Amgen was faced with a slightly different market situation and somewhat higher price elasticity around the Erbitux price point. Similar situations to the one described for Erbitux and Vectibix are occurring in other therapy areas as well. In some therapy areas, price elasticity for a second entry is much higher than for oncology, where treatments continue to be challenging and individualized to patients. Other examples are Vioxx after Celebrex in the COX-II market or Galvus (ex-US) and Onglyza after Januvia in diabetes. To truly assess the impact on pricing strategies, one should consider competitive simulation.

Price elasticity may also vary considerably from patient to patient. Depression patients, not responding to an SSRI, may be much less sensitive to a high price (or co-pay) for Abilify or Seroquel XR, than a treatment naive patient. More severely ill patients may also have a higher tendency to accept a doctor's suggestion irrespective of price or co-pay. When patients have no co-pay or co-insurance, their behavior is likely to be very inelastic relative to price as they will simply want the best treatment at any cost. This is of obvious concern to payers. We will discuss this aspect later in this chapter.

How does a price–volume relationship translate into an optimal price in a free market? Let's consider the example illustrated in Figure 3.4. Let's assume that in this example all customers or customer segments collectively demonstrate a price–volume relationship as indicated in the figure. Volume of demand gradually declines with increasing price, however there is no

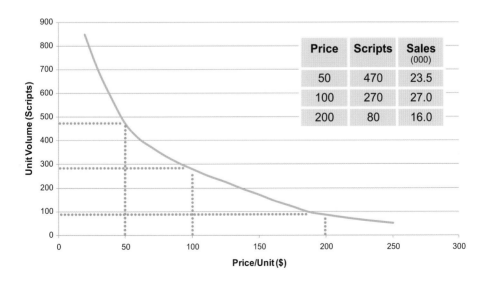

Price	Scripts	Sales (000)
50	470	23.5
100	270	27.0
200	80	16.0

Figure 3.4   Example of a price–volume relationship

particular price point at which demand particularly drops off. This is typical for a relatively innovative drug without close substitutes.

In order to identify the optimal price for our product, we need to calculate how profits depend on price. Figure 3.5 shows how, with some variable and fixed cost assumptions, one can construct a profit–price relationship. It should be realized that this is a highly simplified picture, as in reality, production and marketing costs are dependent on a complex number of variables and choices. For example, manufacturing costs may be variable within a range of volume only. Team-related expenses may be variable in the long run, but fixed in the short run due to labor contracts.

The number of prescriptions is declining continuously with increasing price (Figure 3.4). Figure 3.5 shows that at prices up to about $120 per unit, decreases in volume are offset by the higher price, thus causing the revenues and profits to increase with price.

Profitability, as derived in this example from a very simple cost relationship, is maximized at a price somewhere near $120 per unit. At prices above this point, profitability is declining as utilization is dropping more rapidly than the increased price can compensate for. Below $120 the increase in sales volume does not justify a lower price. In this example, small pricing "mistakes" do not

Price	Scripts	Sales (000)	Profit (000)
50	470	23.5	4.8
100	270	27.0	7.3
200	80	16.0	0.7

Profit = (Price – Var. Cost) × Scripts – Fixed Cost

Figure 3.5   Profit maximization: example A

have a devastating impact on profits. For products with higher price elasticity around the chosen price point, the price–profit relationship will show a more distinct profit peak. This situation, illustrated in Figure 3.6 is typical for a situation where one or more other poorly differentiated competitors are on the market in a similar price range. A slight increase in price will result in switch to the cheaper alternative option and as a result a sharp drop in profits for our brand.

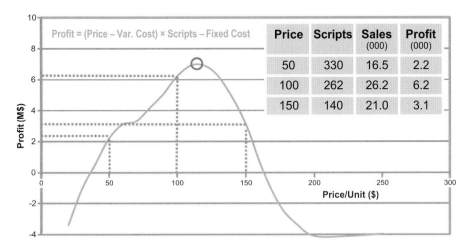

Price	Scripts	Sales (000)	Profit (000)
50	330	16.5	2.2
100	262	26.2	6.2
150	140	21.0	3.1

Profit = (Price – Var. Cost) × Scripts – Fixed Cost

Figure 3.6   Profit maximization: example B

Price elasticity of demand can be very different from customer to customer. Income and personal preferences are two of the obvious parameters that impact price elasticity. Imagine that the curves in Figures 3.4 and 3.5 are actually the summation of a larger number of curves for every distinct customer group. Market segmentation is essential in evaluating buying behaviors and preferences of key customer groups. Product positioning and the choice of target customer segments should be prime considerations when evaluating pricing strategy options. Only then can a pricing strategy truly support the marketing and commercial strategy of the product and the company.

Drug Pricing

Micro-economic principles and price optimization analyses discussed above are generally applicable for any product in a free market economy. To further illustrate the considerations that play a role in drug pricing analyses, let's consider some examples in the drug industry specifically. Consider the development of a new drug, which has two potential indications – A and B. Practical examples that may come to mind are:

- Prevention and treatment of osteoporosis;

- Major depression and treatment resistant major depression;

- Hepatic cancer and breast cancer;

- First line and second line Non-Hodgkin Lymphoma;

- Antibiotic treatment or prophylaxis for surgical infections in a hospital setting.

In any of these examples, willingness-to-pay is likely to be different as the presented value and the cost of current treatment alternatives may vary significantly. Figure 3.7 illustrates a potential price–demand relationship for this example. Indication A seems to have a higher incidence, as prescription volumes are very high at relatively low prices. At higher prices demand is declining considerably. This kind of pattern is typical for a preventative treatment with low likelihood of disease or a treatment for which multiple

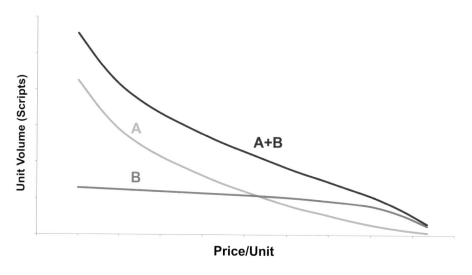

Figure 3.7   Elasticity under multiple indications

lower-cost options can be considered. Indication B is relatively inelastic for demand, that is demand does not change much as price increases. This type of curve can be expected for a treatment resistant patient or a similar patient situation with fewer treatment options.

An analysis of the profitability of this product, illustrated in Figure 3.8, shows that the optimal price points for indication A and B are very different. In this example, indication B has an optimal price point which is about double that of the optimal price point for indication A. Interestingly, the optimal price point for the combined product with indications A and B puts it at a price level

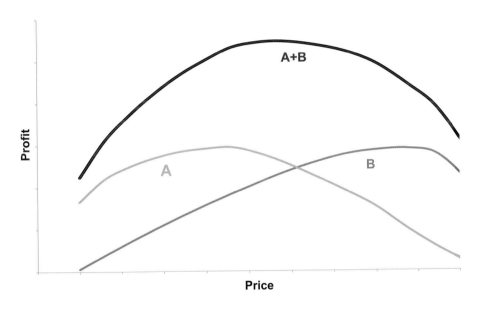

Figure 3.8   Profitability under multiple indications

which is somewhat overpriced for indication A and somewhat underpriced for indication B.

We can learn some things from this example:

1.   It is important to consider the impact of different segments of a market, as they may have important differences in their price–volume characteristic and resulting optimal price. Different optimal

prices are frequently driven by differences in existing treatment options, unmet needs and health outcomes consequences of poor treatment.

2. Since different indications frequently have different clinical development timelines, it is important to consider the drug indications and resulting ability to set price at launch. A drug which is initially indicated for hypertension and subsequently gains approval for the treatment of congestive heart disease is posing a difficult choice. The company can either overprice the drug at launch with a resulting limited initial uptake and perceived commercial failure, or underprice it with a resulting reduction in profit margin. These trade-offs are typical in drug development decision making.

Government Control

How do micro-economic theory and our examples stack up in an environment where a government is interfering through pricing and/or reimbursement controls? Let's consider a simple example of a drug with one indication to analyze the situation. Assume that the government sets a price at a level which is lower than the profit maximizing point (otherwise price control would be moot). The situation is illustrated in Figure 3.9.

At prices up to the "price limit," the maximum price that the government allows, demand is flat as every patient qualifies for full reimbursement independent of price. For every price point that exceeds the price limit, demand decreases sharply, as characterized by the vertical line. As illustrated in the example, only relatively few physicians/patients choose to use the drug at the higher price.

This is typical for countries, such as France, where the government has taken complete market control and leaves the physician and patient indifferent of actual price as long as the drug is reimbursed. It may be clear from Figure 3.9 that price elasticity studies for drugs are a waste of money in this situation, unless a non-reimbursed option is considered. The most important aspect of

Figure 3.9   Price elasticity under price controls

price setting in France is the ability to negotiate price with the government and how this is influenced by the chosen clinical indication and outcomes data associated with the drug. In reality, most drugs have multiple potential indications with, as a result, different potential levels at which the government may set the price.

In some countries, a private free pricing option exists next to a government-controlled public option. Canada is a very complex example of this situation, where a national CDR cost-effectiveness evaluation dictates a maximum price at which most provinces will accept the drug on formulary. However above this price, reimbursement can be potentially secured independently in the private market or for Quebec, which does not use CDR evaluations.

Over the last few years the trend in Europe has been towards a composite control model, as governments in Italy and Spain increasingly decentralize pharmaceutical budget management. In both countries, the central government agency still controls price, but allows for regions to introduce cost containment programs, initially for generics and now for branded drugs.

Price Sensitivity under US Managed Care

Over the last decade, patient co-pay and co-insurance (percentage co-pay) rates have increased dramatically in the United States. In some drug categories, for example gliptins, co-pay differentials between treatment options have had a large impact on prescribing. In these cases, differences between drugs are not deemed critical to most physicians and patients objecting to high co-payments tend to be switched to lower co-pay options. Switch can happen either as the patient returns to the physician or after the pharmacist contacts the physician for a switch authorization for the patient when he or she complains at the pharmacy. Understanding real prescribing behavior and switch is important, particularly in these therapy areas where drugs are regarded essentially equivalent. The emergence of high co-insurance rates, particularly in Medicare Part D can impact prescribing as well, as patient co-pays of typically 33 percent for specialty drugs cause patient affordability issues.

To evaluate the use and impact of co-pay and co-insurance tiers on prescribing, we start by linking price and coverage decision making. For each individual payer, when provided with the information, we can construct a relationship between price and coverage decision. When aggregating this for a representative sample of the total US Managed Care world, we obtain a relationship as illustrated in Figure 3.10. The figure shows some clear price sensitivities at around $55 per course, where many plans shift from listing at second tier to third tier, and in a range around $110 per course, where restrictions become commonplace.

For patients that are covered under one of these insurance plans, we should consider some form of *co-pay elasticity*, rather than price elasticity, as patients face co-pay only rather than the actual price of the drug. Past experience has shown that patients respond particularly to co-pay differentials, that is how much more they have to pay for one drug option versus another one. Figure 3.11 shows the results of an evaluation of impact of co-pay differential on a drug's market share. In this example, there is a remarkable shift in market share of 2 to 12 percent between a co-pay advantage versus the competition of $15 per script to a co-pay disadvantage of $15 per script. It is obvious that in this example the product and its competition are considered very similar, such that at high co-pay differentials most patients are switching to the lower co-pay option.

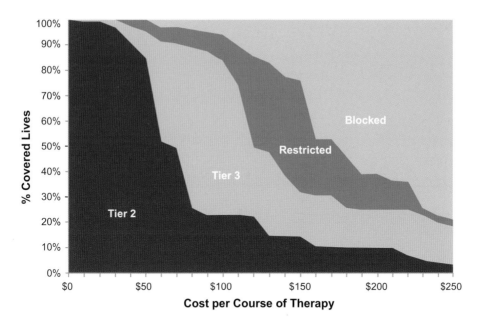

Figure 3.10   Price elasticity in US Managed Care

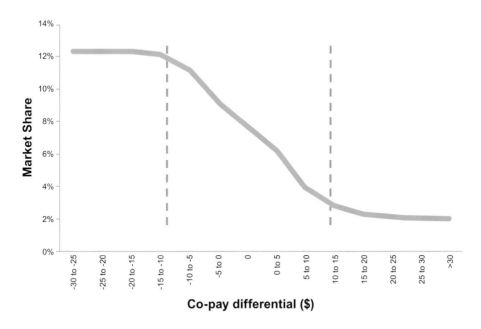

Figure 3.11   Co-pay impact on market share – high co-pay sensitivity

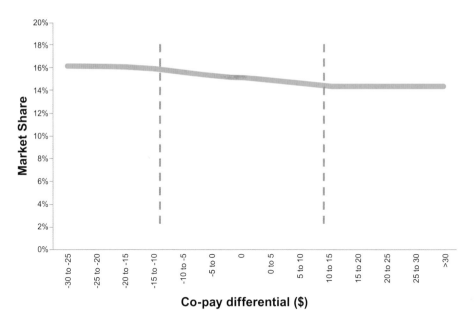

Figure 3.12　Co-pay impact on market share – low co-pay sensitivity

In many cases, there are important reasons for physicians to prescribe and for patients to fill a prescription for an option with a higher co-pay. Examples are patients who don't respond to one treatment option, or who have certain tolerance issues. Figure 3.12 shows an example of a relationship between co-pay differential and market share for a differentiated drug option. Market share shows only little dependence on co-pay, which is in large contrast to the example from Figure 3.11.

The previous examples of co-pay impact on market share can be obtained through analysis of patient level claims data, which capture the results of prescribing, as well as switch behavior due to co-pay and other reasons. For a drug that is on the market, this data allows us to optimize contracting strategies. For new drugs we don't have the benefit of in-market data; however we can use in-market analogues to supplement market research data.

Patient Impact

In most industries, price elasticity of demand is measured through consumer preferences and behaviors. How is this different for drugs? How do we evaluate the impact of patient preferences and how do they impact the physician's prescribing decision? To better understand this, we need to address this in the context of each individual healthcare system and the patient's clinical condition. Let's consider a few situations to illustrate the point.

NON-REIMBURSED LAUNCH IN PRICE CONTROLLED MARKETS

Earlier in this chapter, we discussed the situation in France, where the government decides on a price above which the manufacturer only has an option to launch without reimbursement. In some cases it may indeed be worthwhile to assess the ability to promote a drug as a non-reimbursed treatment option to physician and patient. Oral contraceptives for example have a large non-reimbursed market in France, as women are willing to pay for the newer generation products. For most drug categories patient preferences are less strong and non-reimbursed marketing options are usually not commercially attractive in price controlled markets.

EMERGING MARKETS

In most emerging markets, patients do not have healthcare coverage and as a consequence pay for drugs out-of-pocket. The absence of an insurance carrier simplifies the situation somewhat from the "dinner for three" situation outlined in Chapter 1. However, the absence of the insurance carrier still does not result in a normal consumer purchasing decision model, as the physician plays a central role in decision making. Depending on the local culture, disease area and patient condition, the prescribing physician may discuss treatment options and cost with the patient. Alternatively, patients may find out at the pharmacy about cheaper treatment options and return to the physician to prescribe a less expensive option. In some cases the patient may fill the script, but not or only be partially compliant due to cost.

How the actual decision process occurs needs to be evaluated for each particular situation. See Chapters 12 and 15 for more discussion of emerging market pricing strategies and supporting market research.

MEASURING PRICE ELASTICITY

The concepts discussed in this chapter are intended to provide insights in the mechanisms that underlie price-setting considerations. In many cases, a good understanding of the preferences and behavior of the various customer groups is more valuable than a detailed quantitative research project to establish price–volume relationship curves. However a targeted program can be very important to verify the validity of qualitatively established pricing assumptions and further establish optimal price in a pre-determined range. How to practically go about the evaluation of optimal price through market evaluation and pricing research is further discussed in Chapters 12 and 15.

In this Chapter ...

We have discussed the theoretical pricing concepts in the context of their application in drug pricing. Price elasticity relationships and price optimization analyses were discussed in the context of various forms of payer control, such as payer price controls and Managed Care formularies.

4

Reference-Based Pricing

As a consumer, when we look at a new product, we automatically compare it on its merits with a similar existing product, most likely the one that we are using today. A new car model we tend to compare with the car we drive or another model that we have been considering for purchase. Whether an accounting service, dry cleaner, bakery or other product or service, we tend to calibrate our expectations, requirements and willingness-to-pay this way.

Whether informal or formal, most payers will also compare a new drug offering to the current gold standard of treatment for the proposed place in therapy. Formulary reviews for US Managed Care and any other healthcare system, such as a hospital, will systematically review the benefits and costs of the new treatment in light of patient unmet needs and healthcare funding priorities and limitations.

A number of government payer systems, starting in The Netherlands and Germany in the early 1990s, have introduced a highly formal Reference-Based Pricing (RBP) system of evaluating new drugs versus existing options. Under these systems, a new treatment is evaluated versus a "reference" drug or treatment.

ATC Classification System

The most common methods of referencing are based on the WHO Anatomical Therapeutic Classification (ATC) system. The ATC system classifies drug groups on the basis of their therapeutic activity and chemical structure.

Figure 4.1 shows how lipid lowering agents are classified with the cardiovascular group C. ATC Class C10AA includes all statins, such as simvastatin, lovastatin and so on. Drug classes indicated in this manner are

C	CARDIOVASCULAR SYSTEM
C10	LIPID MODIFYING AGENTS
C10A	LIPID MODIFYING AGENTS, PLAIN
C10AA	HMG CoA reductase inhibitors

C10AA01	simvastatin
C10AA02	lovastatin
C10AA03	pravastatin
C10AA04	fluvastatin
C10AA05	atorvastatin
C10AA06	cerivastatin
C10AA07	rosuvastatin
C10AA08	pitavastatin

Figure 4.1   WHO ATC classification of drugs

frequently referred to as ATC Level 4 classes. ATC Level 5 classification only includes one chemical entity and its generic substitutes.

Under RBP systems, drugs within one category are assumed to be interchangeable and hence get the same approved price or reimbursement. If the manufacturer's price exceeds the reference price or reimbursement limit, the patient has to pay the difference. The calculation of the price or reimbursement limit can be very complex, but usually results in a limit that is at the lower end of the price range of drugs in the reference class.

Today, many countries have adopted some form of RBP in their market access and pricing approval systems. The level of impact is highly dependent on the choices with respect to the breadth or narrowness of a reference class. From this perspective, there are essentially two groups of RBP systems, Phase I and Phase II RBP systems.

RBP Phase I (RBP-I) systems have groups (often called clusters) of drugs, based on identical chemical structure, thus encouraging generic substitution. In our example of lipid lowering agents, all drugs within, for example, the ATC C10AA01 (simvastatin) class Level 5 would have one price or reimbursement limit. Generics with a lower price can pull down the price or reimbursement limit substantially so that, unless the brand price is reduced substantially, generics will build significant market share. In our example, Zocor and generic simvastatin drugs are clustered together and reimbursed at one level, which for example in Germany would be at about one-third of the range of prices of drugs in the class, that is €1.00 if prices range from €0.50 to €2.00 for one particular tablet form. Most healthcare systems with RBP systems have liberal pharmacy substitution rules and sometimes pharmacist incentives to substitute, so that generics with prices at or below the price or reimbursement limit are widely used.

CASE STUDY: LIPITOR, GERMANY

The impact of RBP-II type reference systems is perhaps best illustrated with the Lipitor case in Germany. In 2003, Pfizer's Sortis (German tradename for Lipitor) was placed in a "jumbo" reference group together with other statins, including simvastatin, the generic version of Merck's Zocor. Because of the impact of generics, the maximum reimbursement was set by the government at a fraction of the Sortis price.

Lipitor lost 75 percent of its German market share between 2003 and 2005. Pfizer chose not to lower the price of Lipitor to match the new reimbursement rates. As a result, its customers were faced with substantial out-of-pocket costs for Lipitor if they didn't switch to its less costly substitute.

There is fairly substantial evidence that Lipitor is showing additional efficacy benefits for patients, particularly at higher doses where other lipid-lowering agents no longer achieve higher response rates. However, within the German reference system, which largely focuses on average patients, the benefit was not deemed sufficiently large to warrant the creation of a separate reimbursement class.

One might wonder why Pfizer did not lower its price to maintain market share. The answer is probably that, besides policy and profit margin reasons, there would be potentially large consequences of a lower German price on prices in the rest of the world, particularly in Europe. Potential for parallel trade and international price referencing continue to complicate the global pricing arena for drugs.

RBP Phase II (RBP-II) systems have clusters of drugs which can contain both identical chemical molecules and "similar" molecules, thus encouraging both generic and therapeutic substitution. In the case of lipid lowering agents, a reimbursement class will usually include all of the C10AA drugs, including simvastatin, lovastatin, atorvastatin and so on. In some systems, such as Germany, patent expiration for any of the drugs in the class will have a large impact on the whole category. See the Lipitor Germany case study (previous page) as an example.

Under RBP-II systems, drugs receive the same price or reimbursement as previously approved drugs in the same ATC Level 4 class (the class that is formed by the first four elements of the ATC code, that is C-10-A-A). Vildagliptin, saxagliptin and aldogliptin, all members of the same chemical family of DPP4-inhibitors that Januvia (sitagliptin) is leading, will likely have a similar reimbursement based on classification in the A10BH ATC class.

It may be obvious by now that the treatment of follow-on drugs in an already existing chemical class is fairly straightforward in RBP-II systems. Depending on the healthcare system and the demonstrated benefits of the new drug over existing drugs in the class, a price premium, parity or discount is obtained. In countries such as Germany and The Netherlands, reimbursement will be at parity as only a single reimbursement limit is used, but in France, Italy, Spain and Japan an innovativeness evaluation will drive the actual price within a narrow range of the comparator.

For a new anti-cancer agent the reference may be an existing compound frequently used in a similar chemotherapy treatment or a payer may consider the new drug together with its likely chemotherapy protocol in comparison with existing protocols for patients at similar treatment stage. Most payers don't have the ability to track complex combination regimens, hence usually individual drugs are chosen as a reference.

References can change over time. When Januvia was launched, branded and generic TZDs, such as Actos and Avandia, were the most logical reference. For the subsequent launch of Galvus, Januvia was the reference. Similarly, while Viagra has been a reference for Cialis, no such direct reference was available for Viagra. When Enbrel was launched, the gold standard and logical reference was methotrexate; for Humira it was Enbrel. However, not only direct clinical comparisons play a role. Enbrel and Remicade were the first biotech drug launched for the treatment of rheumatoid arthritis. Biotech drugs were a new phenomenon at the time and there was a universal awareness of the complexity and cost of this new technology. Therefore nobody expected a biotech drug to be available at a cost similar to the older generation treatments, thus elevating the reference to a more general level of cost and price expectancy for biotech drugs as a group.

The above examples illustrate that new, innovative drugs are expected to command premium pricing in comparison with current treatment options, whereas me-too drugs will mostly have to be priced at parity, a small premium or a discount, depending on marketing objectives, dynamics of the market and the value claims of the compound.

Problems with Referenced-Based Pricing Systems

Reference-based pricing systems have been contested by many, but despite that it is the basis for many drug reimbursement systems. It is favored by payers because of its relative simplicity, hated by most others also because of its simplicity and lack of appreciation for differences between individual patients.

The WHO ATC system is fundamental to many RBP systems. The key for differentiation of a new drug is the creation of a new ATC Level 4 class. New drug classes are decided upon by the WHO on the basis of a scientific evaluation of a request by the innovator. However one of the requirements by the WHO is that there are at least two new molecules of a certain chemical family before a new ATC Level 4 class can be created. *In other words an innovative drug must have a competitor before it allows a new ATC class to be created.* Uniqueness will only be recognized after its key features have been copied. This goes beyond any logic and is in total violation of the frequently stated intent to encourage innovation in healthcare. Of course payers are not responsible for the ATC classification decision making. The WHO in turn makes its scientific decisions for other than drug pricing and reimbursement reasons.

The role of the ATC system in pricing and reimbursement determination becomes even more questionable when considering the determination of comparable doses between "interchangeable" chemical entities in an ATC Level 4 class. Comparison of doses is highly complicated due to dose variations between indications and differences between patients. Governments that use

---

WHO COLLABORATING CENTRE FOR DRUG STATISTICS METHODOLOGY ON THE USE OF ITS DDD DATA FOR REIMBURSEMENT PURPOSES:

"Basing detailed reimbursement, therapeutic group reference pricing and other specific pricing decisions on the ATC and DDD assignments is a misuse of the system. This is because the ATC and DDD assignments are designed solely to maintain a stable system of drug consumption measurement, which can be used to follow and compare trends in the utilization of drugs within and across therapeutic groups."

Source: Website WHO Collaborating Centre for Drugs Statistics Methodology http://www.whocc.no/atcddd/

RBP systems have found a convenient way to compare doses between drugs in the Daily Defined Dose (DDD) as defined by the WHO Collaborating Centre for Drug Statistics Methodology (WHO CCDSM), based in Oslo, Norway. However WHO DDD's were designed to provide statistical guidance on drug usage, irrespective of the distribution and nature of patient conditions within the data pool. The WHO CCDSM organization is clearly stating that use of their data for pricing and reimbursement purposes is an inappropriate misuse.

Why are the WHO DDD data not suitable for pricing and reimbursement decision making? The answer is very straightforward. It only measures average doses for each drug, irrespective of indication, treatment stage and patient condition. It does not compare similar patients, as is rational for any cost comparison.

Adoption of RBP-II Systems

As mentioned earlier in this chapter, The Netherlands and Germany were among the first countries to introduce RBP systems. The Netherlands introduced its "Geneesmiddelen Vergoedings Systeem" (GVS) in 1991. The system was a full RBP-II system with therapeutic reimbursement categories for the large majority of available drugs. A review of the system's savings (Pronk et al., 2002) shows that initially the system reduced drug expense growth rates, probably due to delay of introduction of new drugs. Immediately following the removal of a blockage of listing of new drugs steep expense growth rates resumed. GVS also introduced some unwanted side-effects, such as the increase in cost of generics, as incentives for lower prices were effectively removed, and a phenomenon called cluster hopping, where physicians move to more expensive drug categories when their preferred option is not fully reimbursed (*Pharmo Report*, 2004).

After an intention to introduce an RBP-II system, Germany limited its initial system in 1995 to an RBP-I with generic substitution only, as patented drugs were excluded. It was about ten years later when the system evolved from RBP-I to RBP-II through its famous jumbo groups. So far, only a limited number of therapy areas have been moved into the RBP-II system. See the Lipitor Case Study for an illustrative example. Under AMNOG, the German government has extended the therapeutic referencing principle to all new drugs that have not demonstrated additional benefits over existing treatments.

Norway abandoned its RBP-II experiment in 2000 after concluding that savings since the start of the system in 1993 were negligible in consideration of the program's expenses. Limited success is also reported with the introduction of the system in Canada's British Columbia (Graham, 2002).

Experience in New Zealand illustrates the potentially devastating effect of RBP systems. The system was introduced, offering full reimbursement for fluvastatin, while demanding patient co-pays for simvastatin and pravastatin. Thomas (2005) reports that 94 percent of patients that switched because of co-pays suffered from increases in triglycerides or LDL and significant increases in thrombotic cardiovascular events.

Experience with RBP systems overwhelmingly points to problems in effectively implementing such a system while avoiding system "side effects," some of which can be very harmful to patients, as illustrated by the New Zealand experience.

In this Chapter ...

We have discussed reference-based pricing, which is one of the most frequently applied methods of pricing and reimbursement control. We reviewed technical aspects related to reference based pricing, such as ATC classes and Daily Defined Doses (DDD), as well as its challenges and impact on incentives for innovation in drug development. Lastly, we discussed some safety problems related to the introduction of reference-based pricing and reimbursement systems.

5

Health Outcomes and Health Economics

The relatively young discipline of health outcomes, health economics or pharmaco-economics is increasingly used in pricing and reimbursement decisions. There are however many misconceptions about its exact role in key healthcare systems. As a result, the use of health economics frequently results in wrong pricing assumptions for new drugs. The goal of this chapter is to outline the way in which health economics and health outcomes can be meaningful and should be used to optimize market access and pricing decisions for global markets. At the end of this chapter a section is included to discuss Value-Based Pricing, a seemingly innovative way to address some of the issues that have been encountered particularly in the UK with cost-effectiveness-based reimbursement decision making.

What Is It?

The terms health outcomes, health economics and pharmaco-economics are all used in a similar context to cost-related decision making in allocation of healthcare resources. Interestingly, few resources define all three terms in a consistent way to illustrate the differences. The National Institute of Health (NIH) provides definitions for each of the terms as indicated in Table 5.1 (NICHSR, 2009).

The definitions provided by the NIH are also adapted from various sources and don't specifically clarify the differences between the terms. For purposes of clarity, overleaf in Figure 5.1 are the definitions that are used in this book.

The health outcomes discipline broadly focuses on economic and humanistic outcomes of a healthcare intervention. Pharmaco-economics and health economics are focused on cost and the economic consequences of healthcare interventions, with pharmaco-economics focusing particularly on drug cost.

Table 5.1   NIH Definitions

Health Outcomes	In health economics, the term 'outcome' is used to describe the result of a health care intervention weighted by a value assigned to that result
Health Economics	The study of how scarce resources are allocated among alternative uses for the care of sickness and the promotion, maintenance and improvement of health, including the study of how healthcare and health-related services, their costs and benefits, and health itself are distributed among individuals and groups in society
Pharmaco-economics	Economic aspects of the fields of pharmacy and pharmacology as they apply to the development and study of medical economics in rational drug therapy and the impact of pharmaceuticals on the cost of medical care. Pharmaceutical economics also includes the economic considerations of the pharmaceutical care delivery system and in drug prescribing, particularly of cost-benefit values

Health Outcomes and Economic Research

Figure 5.1   Domains in health outcomes and economics research

Health Outcomes and Quality of Life

Clinical improvements as measured during clinical trials have been generally defined and accepted for each major therapeutic area, whether HbA1c for diabetes, HAM-D for depression or partial and complete tumor response rates for oncology. Health outcomes are usually expressed in long-term patient outcomes and patient quality of life measures or a mix of these.

Long-term patient outcomes are of crucial importance in evaluating the beneficial impact of a treatment. For the three above examples for clinical outcomes, some meaningful long-term patient outcomes are shown in Table 5.2. For diabetes, HbA1c levels are closely monitored in expectation of reduced long-term health complications with significant mortality and morbidity consequences. Similarly, unsuccessfully treated major depression can result in progression of the disease to a point where the patient is at high risk of suicide or where long-term institutionalization or even the severely debilitating electroconvulsive therapy (ECT) or electro-shock therapy is deemed necessary.

Besides the hard health outcomes, such as survival and reduction in cardio-vascular events, there are softer end points related to a patient's well-being or "quality of life." The term quality of life has gained a relatively poor reputation among many payers, as in its generic form it is very vague. Health outcomes data gathering in studies frequently includes an SF-36 Health Survey with general questions related to the patient's feeling of well-being. Questionnaires such as the SF-36 and more specific questionnaires for specific disease areas, also referred to also health outcomes instruments, are used to measure health improvements and to rate the relative value of life extension. Increased survival for patients such as cancer patients is weighed by QOL measures through use of the Quality Adjusted Life Years (QALY). Through this concept, treatments that extend life, but cause patients to be only partially functional are of lesser significance than treatments that results in better patient functionality and well-being.

Table 5.2   Examples of clinical and long-term patient health outcomes

Disease area	Clinical outcome	Long-term patient outcome
Diabetes	HbA1c reduction	Rate of long-term cardiovascular and microvascular events
Depression	HAM-D score	Rate of progression to Tx resistant depression; rate of suicide; rate of institutionalization
Oncology	Partial and complete tumor response	Progression-free survival; long-term overall survival

Importance of Health Outcomes and Health Economics

Health outcomes improvements can be very compelling to patients, family and physicians. Health outcomes can be instrumental in demonstrating a positive impact of a new treatment on patient well-being and as such has a strong value in supporting classical clinical trial end points. Demonstrating the value of a new treatment is important in any situation, even when absent of any economic considerations or claims.

Some typical examples of health outcomes improvements are:

- Ability for schizophrenia patients to return to work and interact with family;

- Ability to keep rheumatoid arthritis patients out of a wheelchair or enable them to write a letter;

- Ability to save depressed patients from the consequences of electro-shock therapy or avoid suicide;

- Ability to avoid the serious mortality and morbidity consequences of sepsis.

Health economics can be a very helpful approach in aiding resource decisions between different interventions where resources are limited. It may, for example, be helpful to make policy choices for liver transplants or the therapeutic use of a new drug on the hospital formulary. A positive and credible health economic story may excite a payer, as it provides a rational way of making trade-offs between competing medical interventions on the basis of health outcomes related to cost. Health economic arguments will only seldom form a selling argument to clinicians.

Health economic analyses are focused on the evaluation of cost impact of clinical and health outcomes consequences of a drug or medical treatment. Depending on the situation and evidence requirements in a particular payer system, one or more of the following types of health economic analyses may be required: cost-minimization analysis, cost-benefit analysis, cost-effectiveness analysis and cost-utility analysis.

PERSPECTIVE

Before we engage in detailed calculations related to cost-minimization, cost-effectiveness or other, we need to realize what the responsibility and area of concern is for the payer that we are in discussion with. In health economics this is referred to as the "perspective" of the payer.

Perspective is the formal viewpoint that the health economic evaluation considers in its assessment of benefits and particularly cost. Table 5.3 shows some typical examples of a perspective that can be chosen for a health economic evaluation.

The societal perspective is the broadest perspective of all as it considers costs and benefits to all parties. In reality a societal perspective is often not considered, but can be important when considering for example missed income due to sickness and other expenses that are typically not covered by the healthcare system.

The healthcare system perspective is most frequently used by central bodies responsible for healthcare, such as single payer government-run health insurance providers. In these cases the healthcare system perspective is the same as the government perspective.

Table 5.3   Health economic perspectives

Perspective	Description
Drug Budget	Considers only drug cost. This is a natural perspective for a payer who only holds the drug budget, such as a Pharmaceutical Benefit Manager (PBM) or Medicare Part D Plan in US Managed Care or government drug budget holder
Institutional	Only considers cost from a hospital perspective in relation to its reimbursement and any treatment quality data that may be gathered and published
Healthcare System	Approaches cost and benefits from the perspective of its formal system and responsibility, as frequently applicable in universal healthcare systems
Government	Government budget perspective, not considering privately born cost
Societal	Broad overall societal perspective, considering cost and benefits to all players, including employers, patients, and so on
Patient	Only considering aspects that directly impact the patient, such as co-pays, lost income, non-reimbursed treatments. Unusual perspective for a health economics evaluation, but appropriate in, for example, cases without insurance coverage such as in emerging cash markets

COST MINIMIZATION

A new drug, device or treatment may result in cost savings in other healthcare areas. Examples are: reduction in hospital stay (antibiotics, Neupogen), avoidance of surgery (GI drugs), and less nursing time (wound products). Cost avoided can partly or completely offset the additional cost of the new drug or treatment, thus providing a more favorable economic case for utilization.

In some instances, payers insist that the new drug is cost-minimizing, that is the additional cost incurred for the more expensive drug should be more than offset by realized savings. This may be the case when a payer is not sufficiently convinced of the added clinical value of a new treatment, but is willing to accept it at a neutral impact on cost. Generally speaking, payers' wishes to contain cost increases are understandable, particularly where budgets are controlled on a silo basis. However, this raises many issues, as it denies any value for stepwise innovation that is not supported with the kind of evidence required because it is usually not available for these drugs at time of launch.

Cost offsets may be helpful in making the additional cost of the new drug or treatment acceptable to the budget holder. The "perspective" of the payer is a key consideration. Whether the payer is only interested in the drug budget or is interested in overall hospital budget or national healthcare budget has a large impact on the willingness to consider various kinds of cost offsets. A drug which is cost neutral due to demonstrated reductions in cost of nursing staff may not create sufficient excitement with a pharmacy director. Another important issue for payers is whether they can actually realize the savings. Savings in nursing time can only be realized when staff can actually be reduced.

Some typical examples of cost offsets:

1.   Reduced need for anti-emetics due to a lower incidence of severe nausea in cancer chemotherapy.

2.   Reduction in patient hospitalizations through effective cardiovascular disease prevention programs or more effective treatment of infections with antibiotics.

3.   Higher employee productivity and lower work absenteeism due to a more effective flu vaccine.

The three examples all concern a claim of cost-offset versus the (usually additional cost) of a new drug treatment. However each of the examples involves a trade-off with a different "perspective."

The first example shows an offset in *drug cost* due to the avoidance of drug treatment requiring nausea as part of a cancer patient's chemotherapy course. The additional cost of the new drug and the cost savings are both part of the drug budget, keeping the cost offset claim simply within the drug budget holder's perspective.

The second example involves a cost-offset in the form of *non-drug medical expenses*. General medical expenses, such as hospitalization expenses, are a cost to the government agency or insurance company that is responsible for the patient under consideration. The cost trade-off may make perfect sense from an overall healthcare cost perspective, just like in the first example, but for the individuals responsible for the drug budget, the additional drug cost comes at no benefit within their responsibility.

The third example involves a case where a new drug treatment can help improve *employee work productivity* by allowing the employee to go to work sooner or otherwise reduce absenteeism. A condition like flu may cause some increased medical expenses, but the main claim in this example is related to the non-medical cost to the employer and employee. The perspective in this case is the societal perspective, which is broader than the healthcare system cost perspective, as it considers cost other than cost to the insurance company or government department of health.

COST-EFFECTIVENESS

The relationship between the achieved health improvement and cost is best measured through cost-effectiveness. What is the additional cost required to, on average, save one life or avoid blindness or deliver any other important humanistic value? In other words, what is the cost per unit of demonstrated health improvement? What is an appropriate measure of health improvement differs from condition to condition. Some events, like death, are easily defined. Others may be more difficult to measure. Quality-of-life scales can be helpful in carefully assessing health improvements. Payers are often unfamiliar and more often skeptical of these measures and do not always feel that health outcomes measures are sufficiently meaningful to justify additional expense. Frequently used cost-effectiveness measures are cost-per-life-year-saved or cost-per-quality-adjusted-life-year-saved (cost/QALY).

Cost-effectiveness measures are only practically meaningful in conjunction with a specific cut-off or comparative trade-off. Should a government or health plan cover a liver transplant for a 70-year-old? Approve an Avastin containing chemotherapy regimen for a cancer patient? Reimburse annual mammograms for women between 40 and 50 years of age? Cost-effectiveness evaluations can provide theoretical answers to each of those questions, provided there is a comparator or an established limit. However what is a reasonable cost for an avoided amputation, a life saved or a stroke episode avoided? This is a very difficult question with a lot of emotional, ethical and legal hooks. What is the value of a life? Is the value of a life different depending on age, economic situation, nationality? Ideologically it would be very hard to justify a different value for different individuals; it also seems a very inappropriate discussion for most of us. However, in reality these choices are made as technologies are approved and access restrictions imposed. Some healthcare systems utilize cost-effectiveness cut-offs, but are frequently uncomfortable to state the cut-off criteria.

Legal issues can also play an important role in the ability to use cost-effectiveness criteria. Healthcare agencies or insurance plans may be obliged to provide any care deemed medically appropriate, irrespective of cost. In Germany for example, access to healthcare and choice of physician are constitutional rights. Denying access to proven therapies and drugs is difficult under this system, although it does not prevent the government from imposing reimbursement limits and mandatory drug price cuts.

Consider a technology A, the added costs of which are $5,000,000 for the treatment of 5,000 eligible patients and which saves the lives of 10 percent of these patients, that is 500 lives. A simple cost-effectiveness calculation yields a cost of $10,000 per life saved, which by most standards would be considered highly cost-effective. Now consider a technology B which for the same patient population would save 11 percent of these patients at a cost of $11,000,000. Technology B saves 550 lives at a cost of $20,000 per life saved, which is still considered cost-effective in most healthcare systems. However the adoption of technology B instead of A results in 50 additional lives saved at an additional cost of $6,000,000. The incremental cost-effectiveness of technology B over A is therefore $120,000 per life saved, certainly a less favorable cost-effectiveness ratio. By many cost-effectiveness standards it would not be justified to standardize technology B. An interesting question is whether a subset of patients can be defined for which B is more effective. When these subsets can be defined and selected through for example a test, the incremental cost-effectiveness can be substantially improved and may warrant adoption of technology B for these patients.

Figure 5.2 shows the relationship between added cost and improved patient outcomes in a graph that is commonly known as the cost-effectiveness plane. On the lower right quadrant of the graph, cost is reduced and outcomes are improved. Since acceptance of a new therapy with these characteristics has no disadvantages to anybody, cost-effectiveness is referred to as "dominant." As cost increases, a trade-off needs to be made between the improved outcomes and its associated additional cost. The figure illustrates how the National Institute for Health and Care Excellence (NICE) tends to address this issue, although it is not formally stated anywhere. Cost increases are acceptable, provided that improvements in outcomes justify it.

NICE considers treatments cost effective when their incremental cost is below £20,000 per QALY. Between £20,000 and £30,000 per QALY, treatments are considered marginally cost-effective. Above £30,000 treatments are considered not cost-effective by the unwritten rules of NICE.

In reality, health economic evaluations are much more complicated than the example given previously. Since every patient has a different prognosis and

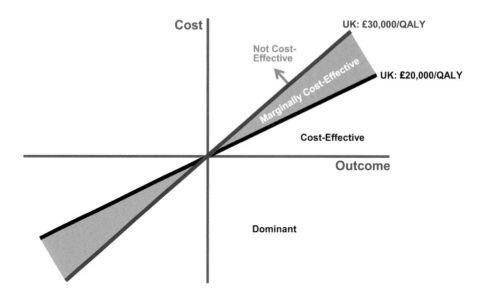

Figure 5.2   Cost-effectiveness plane

reacts differently to various treatment options, statistical analyses of outcomes across patient groups is very important for a good assessment of health improvements and associated costs. Payers are also frequently concerned about their ability to control for use outside the indications for which it is authorized and proven once they have approved reimbursement.

Role of Health Outcomes and Health Economics in MA&P

A key consideration in planning for health outcomes and health economics-related trials and analyses is how the information is used by healthcare systems around the world for for market access and pricing decision-making. In reality there are huge differences between countries on this aspect. In addressing this, we need to distinguish clearly between health outcomes and health economics.

HEALTH OUTCOMES

The use of health outcomes to better show the impact of a treatment on a patient's wellbeing can be beneficial in any payer system. The general debilitating nature of an untreated or insufficiently treated condition or the toxicity and side effects of older treatment options are frequently underestimated. One reason is that physicians tend to not embellish on issues with current treatments unless there are better options. After all, why raise an issue and upset a patient when there is no solution available?

Showing improved long-term outcomes, such as a reduction in cardio-vascular events or improved overall survival, are particularly powerful in payer discussions. In general, long-term outcomes are much more important than shorter-term surrogate end points in its impact on overall patient health and associated long-term medical cost.

Softer health outcomes end points, such as a non-specific QOL improvement claim, better compliance and fewer side effects are frequently met with skepticism by payers, unless the claim is clearly linked to long-term outcomes and/or cost savings and supported with strong data.

HEALTH ECONOMICS

Health economic data are required by some healthcare systems, but certainly not by all. National Health Service England (NHS England) bases many reimbursement decisions in an evaluation by the National Institute for Health and Care Excellence (NICE). Within NICE guidelines, drugs are typically not recommended for formulary inclusion unless they are both effective and cost-effective, as defined by their standards. For more information on the UK, NHS England and NICE, see Chapter 25. Australia, Canadian provinces and some smaller countries use health economics in a similar way in reimbursement decision making. A more detailed description of this group of markets is found in Chapter 8.

Most countries will consider the impact of a drug or treatment on medical and/or drug budget, even if they do not evaluate cost-effectiveness. New drugs that are selectively used for appropriate patients and don't "break the bank" tend to be reviewed in a much more lenient fashion than new potential blockbuster drugs. For these drugs, the discussion frequently focuses on the identification of "appropriate patients" for the new treatment. By selecting only a fraction of the population for which a drug is approved in the FDA or EMA label, a payer can allow a new treatment, while securing the use of less expensive, perhaps generically available treatment options first. In reality this can work well, when a payer has the ability to control utilization, for example through the use of step edits, as is done frequently in the United States.

The drug industry generally experiences health economic requirements as an additional (fourth) hurdle to patient access. It is practically impossible to have strong naturalistic study data for inclusion in a health economic dossier before launch. As a result, health economic requirements are often perceived as an additional hurdle to overcome, both in terms of time and resources required to satisfy rigidly formulated health economic requirements. On top of that, payers tend to mistrust or even reject any health economic data gathered by drug manufacturers.

Health economic evaluations probably make more sense when applied at a later stage, say 3–5 years after a new product launch. Doing so will allow for a more robust evaluation of a drug's benefits in a real treatment setting.

VALUE-BASED PRICING

The latest buzzword in pharmaceutical market access and pricing is "Value-Based Pricing." Under PPRS reform discussions in the United Kingdom (UK) from 2010 to 2013, Value-Based pricing (VBP) was to be the new method by which drug prices would be pegged to real value. The sound bite immediately gained great traction with health economists around the world. Who after all can argue with "value" as a basis for establishing a reasonable price? It sounds so logical, that one might questions why it was not done before? In reality, the name is misleading with respect to actual intent of the VBP reform in the UK and not offering anything really new in a global context. Every drug company with innovative drugs will try to establish a price that is based on the value that is demonstrated to customers and the resulting willingness-to-pay.

In the UK, VBP was brought to life to address some of the apparent shortcomings of the reimbursement systems in England, Wales, Scotland and Northern Ireland. The initial proposals included the following essential elements:

1. Flexibility to establish value by incorporating burden of illness and societal benefits as a modifier to the cost-effectiveness cut-off criteria operated by NICE.

2. Price control at the government-established value of the new drug instead of a limit on reimbursement at that established value under the existing system.

Creating more flexibility with respect to the cost-effectiveness cut-off criteria highlights a longstanding issue with health economics-driven systems. Particularly for oncology agents, the need for more latitude versus the general cost-effectiveness criteria has been an issue that has led to higher cut-off criteria for oncology in Australia and the institution of end-of-life approval criteria and the Cancer Drug Fund in England.

NICE rulings have been often heavily criticized by patient groups and medical specialists. Any reimbursement decision creates tensions, as it can hardly ever address the variety of patient conditions, needs and potential benefits of a treatment. NHS England and the UK Government have been painfully aware of this and have been intending to deflect the problems of the reimbursement decision making by shifting to price control. Under the original version of VBP, companies would be forced to explain to patients why they are not willing to provide for a drug at what the government designates as its "value-based price." This is clearly a flawed government strategy, as drug companies can simply not afford to agree to much lower pricing in a country with high per capita income levels that only represents 2.5 percent of the global pharmaceutical market.

Value-Based Pricing, or rather "flexible cost-effectiveness thresholds" provide more flexibility in coverage decision making, but also introduce additional criteria that can easily be perceived as arbitrary and further complicate an already "out of touch" academic evaluation system. Most global payers and clinicians simply feel uncomfortable to use intuitively incomprehensible QALY-related funding metrics to make life-and-death decisions. This is particularly problematic since data that is required to make a reliable assessment of real-life long-term patient outcomes is practically not available at or near time of drug launch when only FDA- and EMA-mandated controlled clinical trials are available. As such, Value-Based Reimbursement may make sense, but probably not within at least five years of launch.

At the time of publishing of this book edition the future of VBP in the UK was still largely unknown. Terminology seems to have shifted to "Value-Based Assessment" rather than Value-Based Pricing, to reflect that it will not be pricing that is controlled, but reimbursement decision making.

In this Chapter …

We have discussed health economics and its application in pricing and market access. Budget impact analyses and cost-minimization are applied to support stepwise innovations, and cost-effectiveness analyses to support innovations with substantial drug cost consequences.

6

Features, Benefits, Value and Price

What is the monetary value of a new drug? As with any product, value is in the eye of the beholder, and it will be different from customer to customer due to different uses and willingness-to-pay. What is the value of a new Toyota Corolla? For most people it will be largely determined by prices of comparable cars in the same class. Particular features may give some benefits to the purchaser, which can change willingness-to-pay for the customer up or down from the competitive benchmark price. In cases where differentiation is not valued very highly, we are in essence looking at a commodity situation, where there is likely to be little motivation to pay more for a certain brand. As a purchaser, there are strong advantages to commodity situations, since it increases competition, as the lowest-price product wins the order. This is why purchasing organizations try to commoditize their purchases as much as possible. For perfect commodities and a well functioning economic market, cost of a product will be close to the cost of efficient manufacturing plus a reasonable return.

Brand value is much harder to estimate. Quality perceptions and elements such as warranty can lead to a higher willingness-to-pay for a brand. In the case of perfumes, this is even more obvious, where the product is often said to offer "hope" rather than a chemical formula.

As with many other products, there is a value to the brand. The brand value can be based on company reputation, evidence supplied through clinical studies and promotional efforts, endorsement by key opinion leaders and treatment guidelines and other factors. But how does this relate to the product's features and benefits? Let's examine this.

Benefits

"Our brand has a unique chemical structure and mechanism of action." The payer yawned. "It has a very long half-life and can be dosed once a day." More yawning. "The drug is very potent." Who cares! Why do we always expect that a customer falls immediately in love with our new drug with stories about product features, which by themselves are totally meaningless?

Product features only add value if they have functional consequences that result in meaningful benefits. Figure 6.1 shows the relationship between product features and its benefits. Features can at best raise interest, but benefits will always need to be demonstrated to sell to a rational payer.

What kind of benefits are there? How do customers value these? First let's look at categories of benefits. We generally consider four categories: clinical, humanistic, economic and public health benefits. We will explain each of them and any interrelationships in the following sections.

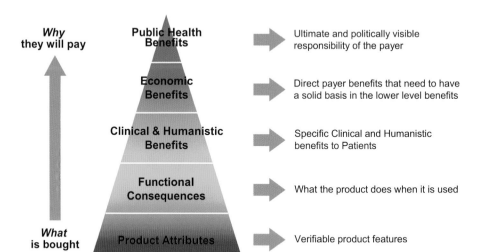

Payer Goal: Public Health, Economic and Compelling Clinical Benefits

Why they will pay	**Public Health Benefits**	Ultimate and politically visible responsibility of the payer
	Economic Benefits	Direct payer benefits that need to have a solid basis in the lower level benefits
	Clinical & Humanistic Benefits	Specific Clinical and Humanistic benefits to Patients
	Functional Consequences	What the product does when it is used
What is bought	**Product Attributes**	Verifiable product features

Figure 6.1   The payer benefit pyramid

CLINICAL BENEFITS

A broad range of efficacy and safety measures fit into this category. Whether HbA1c or LDL lowering surrogate end points or long-term cancer survival or avoidance of fractures in prevention of osteoporosis, these are all clinical efficacy and effectiveness measures and clinical benefits. Reduction of certain toxicities or elimination of safety concerns also fit into this category.

Clinical benefits are generally considered to be the most compelling benefits that convince physicians to prescribe a new drug. Improvements in efficacy and/or safety are also the focus of review and approval criteria for the FDA and other regulatory agencies around the world. Meaningful clinical benefits are also valued by payers. After all they represent the ultimate goal of the medical treatment and the reason why we want to fund drugs in the first place. Payers value clinical benefits even more, when they result in cost savings through avoidance of costly health complications.

HUMANISTIC BENEFITS

These benefits include what is generally referred to as "quality of life" measures. This can be very vaguely expressed in an improvement of scoring on an SF-36 quality of life survey instrument, where patients are asked about their well-being through a serious of questions. It can also be a specific improvement, such as reduction in hospitalization, fewer patients requiring a wheelchair, or other non-clinical patient improvement measures. Quality of life benefits are frequently met with skepticism by payers, unless they have economic implications that impact their budget or are otherwise significant in nature. In most health economics-driven systems, humanistic improvements are measured in quality-adjusted-life-year (QALY) improvements, which are incorporated in their cost benefit criteria for approval.

ECONOMIC BENEFITS

Benefits that are always valued in a purchase are economic benefits. Who doesn't like to save money? Particularly when economic benefits outweigh the cost of purchase, a purchase becomes tempting from a budget perspective. For physicians and patients, economic benefits tend to be less important unless it affects them directly, for example through a patient co-payment. As part of the "dinner for three" phenomenon explained in Chapter 1, patients and physicians tend to choose the best treatment option, irrespective of cost to the payer. Payers are obviously more sensitive to cost, but we should also not assume that cost is the only thing that payers care about. Providing healthcare is the prime task of any health department of a health insurance company. Ignoring this aspect and only focusing on cost minimization is not prudent for either a government budget holder or pharmacy budget manager.

PUBLIC HEALTH BENEFITS

The highest category with respect to its impact on payer behaviors is the public health benefit. Benefits in this category are most likely to get attention from health department leadership, as it touches on the ultimate responsibility of the department. Significant improvements in key public health aspects, such as the reduction in mortality of a disease or a reduction in occurrence of preventable infections will quickly rise above other benefits, with a less compelling impact. Politicians will be much more tempted to make extra budget available for a visible public health improvement than any of the other benefit categories.

It should be kept in mind however that, just like economic benefits, public health benefit claims need to be supported with strong clinical evidence in order to be compelling. In many cases, these benefits will only become apparent during post-marketing studies, thus creating a challenge during market access and pricing negotiations.

The benefit pyramid is extremely useful to identify meaningful customer benefits and linking them to the product features.

Value

What benefits do customers value? How does that differ across customers? Should we consider value in terms of economic value and willingness-to-pay or perhaps "willingness-to-demand-coverage" for a drug treatment?

Physicians may value a drug that requires less patient education and therefore does not take time away from treating other patients. Patients and payers may value an oral version of a drug that does not require as many physician office visits. Physicians may not like that when they want to ensure patient compliance with the treatment. Prescribing oral drugs can also be financially unattractive to physicians, as they lose revenues due to the lower frequency of patient visits.

Value is directly linked to the degree to which the drug is addressing unmet needs. A thorough assessment of unmet needs is frequently the best starting point in the assessment of opportunities in a disease area. Sedation and danger of addiction were unmet needs in the treatment of anxiety before SSRIs and SNRIs obtained anxiety indications. Every disease area has its unmet needs whether in terms of better efficacy, tolerance/side effects or ease of administration. Clearly identifying and prioritizing them is important when one is assessing value or the potential value of a new drug treatment.

The most important and least measurable contributor to willingness-to-pay for a patient is that of humanistic or emotional value. The cost of laser surgery to temporarily postpone or avoid blindness for a diabetes patient may only be $1,000 to the health insurance company, however the value of continued eye-sight and a reduction of risk of blindness would clearly be much higher for most people. The value of avoiding nausea or alopecia associated with chemotherapy is certainly of higher value than its economic cost. An effective erectile dysfunction drug can be of great individual value as can be a treatment to resolve infertility for a couple wanting to raise a child. Each of us may assign a different value to a health improvement or avoidance of a health risk. The value of avoidance of flu through an influenza vaccination is particularly important for high risk age groups (infants, elderly), but may also be of particular economic value for people that potentially face tough economic hardship in case of illness.

For most consumer products, value and personal preferences go hand in hand. Willingness-to-pay for these goods is dependent on a trade-off between personal preferences and cost. This is not always a rational process, as it is sometimes hard to compare products. In some cases, a higher price may give an impression of better quality (tools) or exclusivity (perfume).

For medical devices and drugs, the judgment of regulatory authorities and medical opinion leaders play a major role. Brand awareness through DTC advertising does impact choice, as patients ask physicians about a treatment. Physicians may also have a higher awareness of a new brand through promotional activities and advertising. Some argue that drug companies spend too much money on DTC advertising, thus causing unnecessary demand for high cost drugs. However, one can also argue that there would be substantial opportunities for better information to patients, if the rules for communication to patients were not so restrictive that DTC advertising can effectively only aim at brand awareness. Patients are clearly looking for more information, illustrated by the fact that medical information is the number one reason for people to consult the internet. Physicians are busy and rarely have sufficient meaningful materials for patients to consult after a visit.

Well-informed patients, most frequently found in chronic disease categories, are better able to hold a meaningful dialog with the physician about the treatment choice and are better able to influence trade-offs between drug choices. Absent financial incentives, patients will obviously prefer the newest treatments with the best efficacy, lowest risk and fewest side effects.

Customer Preferences

From some of the above examples, it is probably clear, that preferences can be somewhat different between our key customer groups of physicians, patients and payers. It should also not be assumed that there are no preference differences within each of the groups, but these are likely to be of a lower magnitude and will be considered later. Let's consider the likely preferences and behaviors of each of the three customer groups and then evaluate their impact on a drug pricing decision.

PHYSICIANS

Physicians are trained to select the therapy which best assists the health of the particular patient in the doctor's office. Involvement of payers in the treatment selection is extremely bothersome for most physicians and increasingly puts physicians in conflict with what they feel is appropriate for the patient. Payer involvement in treatment decision making is a contentious issue everywhere, it is considered acceptable in some healthcare systems and taboo in others.

In the United States, physician gag orders, instituted by Managed Care in the 1990s, limiting physician communication on non-reimbursed treatment options, were abolished after court challenge. This re-established a physician's right or duty to inform the patient of their most suitable treatment options, even when the insurance does not or only partly covers its expense.

In Germany, the issue of government control on drug prescribing has arisen again recently during healthcare reform discussions, where the government has been seeking to provide more guidance and restrictions related to physician prescribing in order to halt the rate of growth of the national healthcare budget.

German physicians are generally sensitive to drug cost in prescribing decisions, caused largely by a system of drug budget controls introduced in the early 1990s, but are very sensitive towards the right to healthcare that is guaranteed under the German Constitution. The introduction of a NICE-style "Qualitäts Institut" – IQWIG – to impose health economics prescribing guidelines was significantly toned down to a more general advisory role without teeth. The subsequent introduction of AMNOG focused more on price negotiation with manufacturers rather than limiting physician prescribing options.

In France, prescribing volumes are a prime concern of payers. French physicians are generally rapidly adopting new drug treatments, once approved for reimbursement, causing a perceived need by the government to impose limitations on sales volumes under monopsony style "agreed upon" pricing conditions with the manufacturer.

In every healthcare system, physicians try to prescribe the best possible treatment for their patients within the limitations and bureaucratic authorization hurdles posed upon them. Increasing patient contributions towards drug cost and improved awareness of treatment options have made the physician a bit more of an authoritative advisor than the sole decision maker that he or she has been in the past. In emerging markets, patients usually pay all or a large share of the cost of prescription drugs. Patient affordability is a key consideration for physicians, who try to evaluate how they can best prescribe the most suitable option for each patient, considering the patient's condition, related good treatment options and affordability.

PATIENTS

Consumers/patients will generally simply want what is best for their health, particularly when the product is paid by the healthcare insurance. Patients are usually heavily relying on the physician in determining the best treatment option, although over the last decade patients have become increasingly informed and educated on medical treatment options through the Internet. Patient co-pays have started to influence patient involvement in drug prescribing in the United States, particularly in some drug categories such as TNF inhibitors for Rheumatoid Arthritis, where various treatment options are available and physicians may be willing to switch prescribed brand over patient objection to sometimes substantial co-pay differences. Patients with chronic diseases are increasingly taking on an important role in their treatment decisions. Hemophilia patients, for example, are generally extremely well informed about the benefits and risks of various treatment options, particularly after scandals related to HIV virus contaminated blood products that have been used in the production process of blood-derived Factor VIII drugs.

However also for other chronic diseases with a less burdened safety issue, patients have increasingly taken advantage of Internet access to medical data to be educated on their disease and treatment options.

In the United States, the last decade has been characterized by "increasing patient responsibility" or actually cost shifting from employers and health insurance companies to patients. Increasing employee contributions towards health insurance, choice options for lower premiums in exchange for higher deductibles, physician visit co-pays and higher co-pay and co-insurance rates for drugs have made healthcare cost a bigger issue for many people. As the cost for a family for health insurance can now easily exceed $1,000 per month, many small business owners and employees with limited or no job benefits are choosing to forego health insurance, thus effectively becoming a cash-paying patient. Under President Obama's Affordable Care Act, implemented in 2014, the uninsured population has started to decline, but particularly for the Bronze Insurance Exchange plans, co-insurance rates may be as high as 50 percent and high deductibles remain.

Patient co-payments have long been considered undesirable for most European governments, as the element of income dependent access to healthcare is not deemed appropriate from the dominantly socialistically oriented political base. However, as governments are struggling to contain healthcare cost, it seems that co-pays and co-insurance schemes have become more viable political options and play an important role in countries such as Spain.

As long as patient co-pays are non-existent or nominal, patient cost sensitivity will continue to be very low in these markets and governments will have to continue to play the unpopular role of gatekeeper for new and innovative drugs.

PAYERS

As indicated in Figure 6.1, payers tend to generally favor public health benefits, economic benefits and meaningful clinical benefits. After all, they feel compelled to use their limited budget to make meaningful improvements with respect to public health. What is meaningful, is difficult to define, but simply speaking it can be defined as any health improvement opportunity that, when rejected, will cause potential public and political backlash. In more positive terms, it means any improvement that will give positive endorsement by Key Opinion Leaders (KOLs) and patient organizations and that will reflect well upon the department of health's funding policies. In order to more specifically evaluate individual payer preferences, we need to identify better who the payer is that we are considering for a situation.

In many healthcare systems, the central government carries a large proportion of the cost burden. Although different in many ways, the healthcare systems in European countries, Canada, Australia and Japan are all centrally funded by the government. In all these markets, their role as payer has provided governments an incentive to actively intervene in price setting of drugs through either direct or indirect price controls. Lowering the approved price results in direct cost savings to the government without any impact on patient treatment, provided that the drug manufacturer does not withdraw its application and intention to market the drug.

Southern European countries, Canada and Japan have instituted direct approval processes for prices for drugs. Northern European markets, such as the UK, Scandinavian markets and The Netherlands have generally sought control through limitations on drug reimbursement. These reimbursement controls have been put in place in a way which strongly discourages use of drugs with a price that exceeds comparable drugs for a therapeutic area. For example, in The Netherlands, reimbursement limits are set for groups of therapeutically "equivalent drugs". Prices set above the reimbursement limit result in a patient charge for the balance, which in many cases result in patient objections and potential switch.

Reimbursement controls have in reality had the impact of price controls in most markets. The impact of withholding reimbursement, frequently assisted by government initiated communications programs, tends to result in rejection of the choice as a treatment option for most patients. In many of these markets patient co-pays form a real hurdle to prescribing, as physician awareness of co-pays is generally high and patient willingness to accept co-pays is very low. The latter is illustrated by the fact that in the 1990s in The Netherlands the government was forced to resign over the introduction of a $1.50 patient co-pay requirement per script.

In considering reimbursement controls, the issue is often not whether a drug is to be reimbursed, but rather for which patients? Payer concerns over high cost of drugs can sometimes be addressed by ensuring that only particular patients are treated, thus delivering the claimed benefits without unnecessary use in patients for which other, less expensive, options work well.

In many countries, regional payers take on an increasingly meaningful role. While initially only making decisions for purchasing of multi-source generics, regional payers in Italy, Spain and Sweden now make regional formulary and treatment protocol decisions that impact access to all drugs for patients.

In the United States, prices are not controlled, but certain reimbursement limitations are imposed by Managed Care organizations and government programs (Medicaid and so on). Co-pays have dramatically increased over recent years. The introduction of Medicare Part D has further accelerated that trend with higher fixed co-pays and widespread use of fourth tier co-insurance, say 33 percent co-pay, for biologics that are over $600 per month. The Insurance Exchanges under ACA have further added to high co-insurance rate plan offerings. Switching of prescriptions due to patient co-pay and co-insurance has been increasing, particularly in categories where drugs are deemed relatively similar and where there are no significant safety concerns.

Interestingly, co-pays have until recently been viewed by Managed Care more as a means of offsetting cost, rather than a tool to change behaviors and encourage switch to alternatives with a lower co-pay. In their formulary decisions, Managed Care payers will compare overall drug cost between contracting and related tier placement options on the basis of financial forecasts, unless the drug has a very strong medical rationale for inclusion on a favorable tier. The ability to shift share under co-pay differentiation differs from plan to plan and region to region.

Hospital payers are a separate category of payers that are important to consider in the evaluation of preferences and ultimate decision making. Hospitals make decisions with respect to drug formulary inclusion on the basis of treatment outcome in relation to direct cost of treatment and their reimbursement. For example a new treatment that reduces the number of days of hospitalization, may raise some obstacles from hospitals if they are reimbursed on a daily basis rather than a cost per diagnosis for which a standard number of hospital days are reimbursed. In some countries, including Italy and

Spain, hospitals also play an important role in budgeting and market access to high-cost pharmaceuticals in the outpatient setting.

Setting the Right Price

What is the right price for a new drug? At what price does a drug reach its commercial potential, allowing for a sufficient return over research, development and manufacturing expenses, but is affordable and deemed reasonable for its target patients? In the previous chapters, we have discussed price-elasticity relationships in free pricing markets and pricing and reimbursement control mechanisms and rules in key markets with government control on access for pharmaceuticals. However, how do all these elements translate into a pricing decision, so that the company's marketing objectives are supported?

The interactions between the payer, physician and patient can be considered as a "negotiating triangle" (Figure 6.2), in which each of the parties needs to consider their responsibility and the impact and response from the other players. Payers will generally consider physician and patient preferences and reactions in access decision making. Physicians will consider reimbursement and prescribing decisions imposed by payers, as well as patient preferences and potential objections to co-pays or lack of reimbursement.

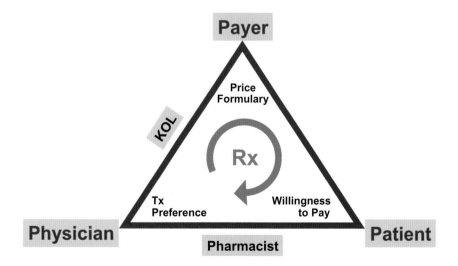

Figure 6.2   The negotiating triangle

Whether or not there are actual negotiations between the parties or not, does not affect the need for consideration of the arguments and the impact that each of the players have in the decision-making process, as defined in each healthcare system. What is important is the fact that all three parties always have a direct or indirect impact on the decision.

A good understanding of the perspectives of the three main players of the negotiating triangle and the nature of the interaction between the parties is important in evaluating the optimal value and pricing strategy for a drug. Assembling the evidential data that suits the preferences and needs of each of the players in the negotiating triangle will further enhance probability of success in securing market access at a reasonable price.

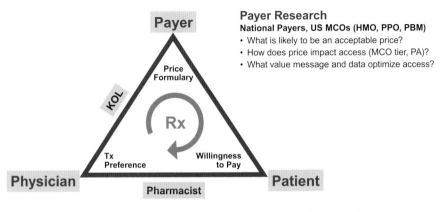

Payer Research
National Payers, US MCOs (HMO, PPO, PBM)
• What is likely to be an acceptable price?
• How does price impact access (MCO tier, PA)?
• What value message and data optimize access?

Physician Research
Specialists, PCPs
• How do drug profile and clinical/health outcomes data impact intent to prescribe and for which patient type(s)?
• How strongly are specialists (KOLs) willing to push for reimbursement?
• How does reimbursement status (tier, PA, step edits) impact prescribing across patients?
• How does patient preference play a role?

Patient Research
Mainly US and Cash Markets
• How does price or co-pay impact patient behavior at physician and pharmacy office i.e. likelihood of patient initiating switch?
• What is the impact of physician communication (reason to accept price or co-pay) on likelihood of switch?
• How effective is a co-pay offset program for the particular drug and disease area (US)?

Figure 6.3   **Sample questions to evaluate perspectives and likely behavior of key players in the negotiating triangle**

Figure 6.3 indicates the areas of focus that each of the key customer groups are likely to have in their decision making for a US example. The questions are merely a sample of important general questions that need to be considered in assessing the impact of price on payer decision making and ultimately on drug prescribing. We need to consider many more in-depth questions for each specific situation in each payer system for a complete understanding of the situation.

In this Chapter …

We discussed elements related to value in relation to drugs and their impact on the key stakeholders: physicians, patients and payers. Benefits analyses are used to identify important benefits and related value messages. The importance of benefits is analyzed from the perspectives of each of the stakeholders.

PART B

Structured Market Access and Pricing Approaches

7

Pricing and Drug Development

Drug development is expensive, time consuming and very risky. From first discovery to launch and commercialization the process takes from 10 to 15 years of pre-clinical and clinical testing, as is illustrated in the "Uphill Battle" of Figure 7.1. Finding promising drug candidates is preceded by extensive fundamental research that tries to build an understanding of the disease and its biochemical processes. Once a theoretical approach is identified, it needs to go through extensive and expensive pre-clinical and clinical testing with a very high failure rate.

The Research and Development (R&D) investment cost for new drugs is much debated. A frequently quoted source (DiMasi, 2007) estimates average R&D cost per successful development over $1.3 billion. Some critics of the DiMasi analysis claim that it is much lower, but Forbes (Forbes, 2012) shows in an analysis for the largest pharmaceutical companies that the number ranges from $3.5 billion for Amgen to almost $12 billion for AstraZeneca, just by dividing the reported R&D costs over the few approved drugs from 1997 to 2011. Depending on your political agenda, the high cost of drug development can be either seen as a supporting argument for high drugs prices, or as proof that there are large opportunities for efficiency improvement in drug R&D. As noted by Forbes, both are false premises. Drugs should be judged on their value in treating disease, not cost of development. Companies that can devise more efficient processes to develop new and innovative drugs will do well; laggards will cease to exist in our highly competitive financial markets.

Traditionally, clinical trials are designed to meet the requirements set by the FDA and equivalent non-US regulatory agencies, such as the EMA for Europe, to demonstrate efficacy and safety in the treatment for the indication that is sought for approval. Figure 7.2 shows a typical development program for a drug as it has been practiced by most pharmaceutical companies. The process is focused on the regulatory approval and subsequent launch event. In a world

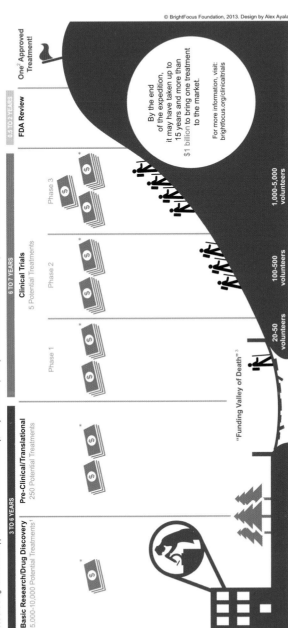

Figure 7.1 Challenges of the drug development expedition

Source: © 2014 BrightFocus Foundation. Reprinted with permission from BrightFocus Foundation, 22512 Gateway Center Drive, Clarksburg, Maryland, 20871. All rights reserved by BrightFocus Foundation. Unauthorized reprints not allowed.

Figure 7.2   Drug development sequence

without payers, this process works well, however it is no longer suited for today's environment, where payers are increasingly demanding evidence of effectiveness and value if not cost-effectiveness. Where a placebo controlled trial may be a perfectly legitimate instrument to obtain FDA approval, it is not likely to impress payers unless there are no existing treatment alternatives for the ailment under consideration. Many pharmaceutical companies are still struggling to recognize and act on the importance of thoroughly understanding the payer's perspectives and needs.

As global drug markets are increasingly cost sensitive and government and private payers are instituting various market access and price control systems, it has become critical to alter the drug development approach to one which takes better notice of the requirements of payers. In Europe and Japan the awareness of the need to consider payer perspectives in drug development has been more evident than in the United States, where this is still further evolving with the changing market.

Figure 7.3   Updated drug development sequence

Figure 7.3 shows a modified activities sequence, recognizing that in most payer systems an approval is required for price or reimbursement. Some may think that this change is either obvious or trivial, but in reality it is far from that in many payer systems. Clinical trial designs and data that are meaningful to regulatory agencies are not necessarily meaningful to payers. Payers can, for example, require substantiation of superiority claims through appropriate randomized double-blind trials with a statistically significant demonstration of the superiority claims. Superiority in efficacy on surrogate end points and other predictive short-term measures are not necessarily accepted as evidence for anticipated long-term health claims, particularly when cost to the healthcare system is substantial. In oncology, payers increasingly want to see long-term patient Overall Survival (OS) data and may not accept having only tumor response or Progression-Free Survival (PFS) data for reimbursement approval.

Since the publication of ENHANCE trial data for Vytorin in January 2008, payers have been much more hesitant to accept LDL lowering data to honor claims related to reductions in cardiovascular events, thus creating substantial hurdles for new generation cholesterol lowering agents, particularly when many lipid lowering agents are available as generics. Providing statistically significant mortality reduction data takes many years to execute and is likely to be cost-prohibitive for many drug companies, particularly when the remaining patent life beyond launch does not provide for an adequate risk-adjusted return on investment. Similarly, disappointing data for Avastin in breast cancer showed no overall survival in contrast to earlier proof of PFS, further increasing payer skepticism over PFS-related claims.

From the above it should be clear that market access and pricing considerations need to be incorporated in decision making regarding the drug development program. The nature of the input changes over the development and life cycle of the asset. Figure 7.4 shows three distinguished stages of MA&P input.

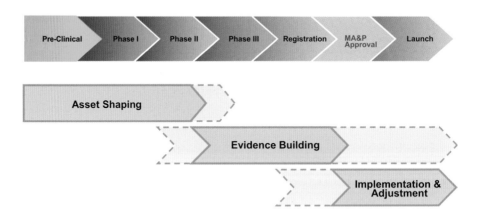

Figure 7.4   MA&P management stages

The "Asset Shaping" stage involves all activities starting at the earliest disease area strategy and Target Opportunity Profile (TOP) discussions up to and including the Phase III go/no-go decision.

The "Evidence Building" stage starts immediately following the Phase III decision and extends through to regulatory approval, that is up to the start of MA&P negotiations with payers.

The "Implementation and Adjustment" stage extends from the start of MA&P negotiations through the rest of the drug's life cycle, including competitive adjustments and generic defense strategies.

Asset Shaping Stage

Figure 7.5 shows some, although not necessarily all, of the key decisions that need to be supported during the asset shaping stage of development. We will discuss MA&P input on each of these in general terms. Individual compounds may need additional customized support. MA&P support needs tend to be highly dependent on the experience in the therapy area. Entirely new treatments for previously untreated diseases may require intensive evaluations and supportive payer research as early as Phase I; others can be based on experience assumptions until preparation for the Phase III program.

The following are some typical examples of questions that arise during the asset shaping stage:

- My forecasted profits are heavily dependent on achieving pricing and reimbursement. Are my assumptions realistic?

- What will tomorrow's payer environment look like? How does it impact my pipeline potential?

- What should my launch indication be?

- What should be the comparator in our Phase III trial?

- Is a superiority trial necessary? The FDA only requires non-inferiority!

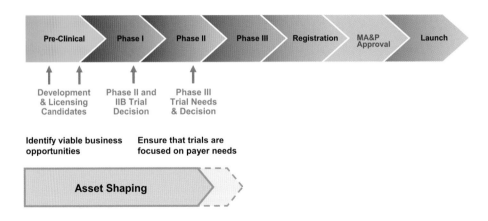

Figure 7.5   Asset shaping stage

In the following sections we will consider specific needs for various decisions in this stage.

DEVELOPMENT AND LICENSING CANDIDATES

In early development, it is important to build consensus on the minimum requirements for both internal development and external licensing opportunities. What does a good opportunity with commercial potential look like? For this purpose, many companies define a Target Opportunity Profile (TOP) or Target Product Profile (TPP), which specifies what claims are to be pursued. Some companies also use a Minimally Acceptable Profile (MAP), indicating that unless certain key claims can be made, development should be discontinued. Arriving at meaningful TOPs and MAPs requires thorough analysis of unmet needs, technical feasibility and risk and market attractiveness, which can all be reflected in forecasts and risk-adjusted NPV calculations.

TOPs can play an important practical role in business development decision making as an internal contract or benchmark for opportunities to be pursued. Having a clear consensus on a TOP can be important in business development, as decision making sometimes needs to be very rapid.

Each transition to the next development stage is important, as choices are made and the drug's value proposition at launch is more clearly defined. During early stages of development a proof of concept is pursued, dosing is established, and target indications are selected.

PHASE II AND IIB DECISIONS

Phase II and IIB decisions can be of particular importance for two reasons. First, these decisions may lock us in to choices that have implications for the Phase III program. If, for example we decide to only pursue a certain indication for Phase II or IIB, we may not have enough data to confidently power a Phase III trial for a different indication. Phase II and IIB trials can lock us in, leaving only a limited set of choices for realistic Phase III options. For this reason, it is important to not only consider choices in Phase II and IIB decision making, but also the choices that are excluded for consideration.

Secondly, particularly for oncology, Phase IIB trial data are sometimes used in getting an expedited regulatory approval. In these cases, the Phase IIB trial data form the basis for MA&P reviews and approvals and become crucial for commercial success. It can be important to get the "endorsement" that goes with qualifying for approval on the basis of Phase IIB data, but this does not mean that payer requirements are relaxed as well. This should be taken into serious consideration when deciding to capitalize on an opportunity to file early. Advantages of entering the market earlier can be very important, particularly when competing compounds in the same class are in development.

When considering filing early with Phase IIB data only, it is important to evaluate the opportunity on that basis, that is evaluate the market impact as described in the following Phase III discussion.

PHASE III DECISION

A key decision point during the drug development process is the Phase III trial decision point. The Phase III trials form the basis for all regulatory and market access-related submissions and negotiations. Preparation for a Phase III trial decision requires a thorough assessment of the payer environment, its reactions to the potential drug profiles that may emerge from Phase III data, and choices and decisions that are related to the emerging profile. Phase IIB data can play a critical role in enabling a well-informed decision for a Phase III program. A large Phase III trial program and its required investments always carry some risk of failure, as claims that are pursued need to be meaningful both in the eyes of regulators and payers.

Changing the decision-making process in pharmaceutical companies to better incorporate payer information needs is particularly important for

Phase III decision making, but has proven to be difficult in many pharmaceutical companies due to some substantial hurdles:

- Clinical and regulatory teams have collaborated in drug development for many years and have established work processes and a common understanding on development needs and trade-offs.

- Many pharmaceutical company executives and other employees are relatively unfamiliar with the payer environment and its implications for drug development needs.

- R&D incentives are encouraging rapid development progression, irrespective of the commercial value that compounds ultimately realize as they come to market.

- Development programs with increased focus on payer value messages tend to be more expensive, more risky and require more time.

All of these changes form a difficult trade-off as they create resource challenges for other development priorities and increase the risk of compound failure. Educating researchers is critical in changing their attitudes with respect to incorporating payer needs.

Critical decisions for the Phase III trial design are:

- Choice of indication or indications;

- Improvement claims over standard of care;

- Clinical end points chosen to demonstrate and measure the claim;

- Trial design structure, that is double blind versus open label, comparative versus non-comparative, number of arms, active comparator versus placebo controlled;

- Choice of comparator in the trial;

- Patient pre-treatment;

- Superiority and non-inferiority testing and related claims, underlying statistics;

- Choice of patient population or populations;

- Patient exclusion criteria;

- Patient outcomes data collected;

- Length of patient follow-up.

Many of these choices have an impact on the value of the claims that become part of the payer value story. A thorough assessment of the impact of the various Phase III design aspects and expected trials results on MA&P is critical. Let's consider a few examples to better understand the trade-offs that need to be made.

Oncology example

A new chemotherapy agent for breast cancer can provide additional curative potential when used in a first line setting, or palliative quality-of-life improvements in end stage metastatic patients. The value of the drug, as hard as it is to put a number on it, is likely to be perceived as much higher in earlier lines of therapy, where patient survival is impacted. So why not immediately initiate trials to obtain approval in first line breast cancer? There are actually a few complications that need to be considered carefully. First, it may be unethical to initiate clinical trials on breast cancer patients with an unproven and relatively unknown new chemical agent, particularly when drugs are available that offer some prospect of cure. Particularly for breast cancer, prospects for early treatment have improved dramatically over the last few decades, which makes it harder for new treatments to qualify for experimentation. In patients who have failed earlier curative lines of treatment, fewer options tend to be available. Particularly, patients who have metastases in other organs after failure of various chemotherapy options, can be helped with new treatments that can reduce tumor burden, improve quality of life and offer some modest survival benefits. New chemical entities tend to be tried first in late-stage cancer patients for the reasons described above. As mentioned earlier, the impact on patient survival prospects is relatively limited in these settings. Over time, as these drugs are introduced to earlier treatment settings, curative potential is improved and the healthcare contributions and willingness-to-pay for these agents will increase. Unfortunately, price is set at product launch, and can usually not be increased when more value is demonstrated through curative potential in earlier lines of therapy. This is how price control mechanisms hold up the process of stepwise innovation in healthcare. Changes in the UK, to allow for less restrictive cost-effectiveness requirements in end-stage cancer patients are a step in the right direction, but no more than an inadequate band-aid on a lethal healthcare wound.

Besides ethical considerations, commercial and risk arguments play a role in the choice of line of therapy for launch indication trials of anti-cancer agents. Demonstrating survival benefits in a first line treatment requires long and expensive trials and is more risky in terms of success in demonstrating statistically significant patient outcomes. Even if it is financially prudent to make the time and financial investment for a curative indication and a higher price, a competitive launch of a competitive compound with the same or similar characteristics can eliminate premium price potential when that competitor chooses to launch earlier with a late treatment stage indication and hence lower value.

This example illustrates the need to identify and evaluate all options with respect to market access and pricing opportunities, as well as other elements that impact the forecast and net present value of the asset.

Diabetes example

Diabetes is an intriguing therapy area from a market access and pricing perspective. The following example is perhaps a bit dated, but it nicely illustrates the development choices that a drug developer needs to make in the context of payer behavior and broader commercial potential. Ten years ago, oral therapy options for early treatment such as Avandia suffered from a number of safety issues. Outside the United States, the Thiazolidinedione (TZD) category, with Actos and Avandia, originally suffered from extremely slow uptake at least in part due to payer restrictions. Prices for Actos and Avandia are much lower in Europe than they are in the United States, despite the fact that unmet needs and concern for compliance are very high in diabetes. With any brand introduction in diabetes, payers are very concerned that generic first line agents, such as metformin and sulfonylurea are displaced, thus causing large increases in drug spend. This continues to be true today, as for example the German G-BA continues to be extremely tough in ruling on new generation diabetes drugs, favoring broad use of metformin and sulfonylurea.

Let's contemplate what the considerations may have been for Merck when it developed Januvia (sitagliptin) and was facing critical Phase III decisions. As with every compound in the category, when seeking market differentiation, a choice has to be made between a measure in efficacy or in safety. It looks like Merck decided to focus on safety differentiation, perhaps because of the concern that efficacy superiority either in monotherapy (versus standard of care metformin) or in combination with metformin (versus Actos or Avandia), would have a risk of failure. Alternatively, perhaps Merck decided that safety issues with TZDs would provide for good opportunities for market entry by demonstrating similar efficacy and improved tolerance. Let's consider the two options with respect to their implications on the Phase III trial program.

Efficacy option

When considering an efficacy claim in, for example, combination therapy with metformin, most payers will insist on seeing a direct comparison versus standard of care add-on therapy, either sulfonylurea or Actos/Avandia. Powering a trial to show statistical significance can be both expensive and risky, particularly when the differences are not expected to be large. Failure of such a trial is likely to result in discontinuation of development efforts, unless a pre-defined non-inferiority test is included in the data analysis plan and significant value remains due to other product advantages and related claims.

Safety option

Given concerns on some of the side effects of sulfonylurea and TZDs, demonstrating safety improvements over existing add-on options to metformin is another viable strategy. Willingness-to-pay is generally higher for efficacy improvements, but safety claims can be effective if they are particularly compelling or do not add significantly to cost. A clinical trial would have to demonstrate statistically significant safety advantages, while showing non-inferiority with respect to key efficacy measures. Compelling non-inferiority data are important, as the perception of a drug with a good tolerance can easily be one of efficacy inferiority, that is it does not only have the safety, but also the efficacy profile of a placebo.

In hindsight we know that Merck chose the safety option with respect to its clinical development program. This has been successful because cost to the payer was not higher than TZDs in second line use with metformin. In Canada, where generic TZDs were available at the time of Januvia approval, payers have largely been able to block out Januvia. This illustrates that a safety claim versus a generic comparator can pose challenges for payer approval.

Biomarkers

Biomarkers and personalized medicine have become much talked about topics in drug development. Biomarkers can be extremely valuable in identifying certain patient characteristics that inform about a patient's suitability for a treatment. As such they are indeed helpful in "personalizing" a treatment for an individual patient.

It is important to realize that there are fundamentally two kinds of biomarkers:

1.   Biomarkers that help pre-determine whether an individual patient is likely to positively respond to a drug therapy, that is a *diagnostic*.

2.   Biomarkers that act as a *surrogate end point* for efficacy during the actual treatment of patients.

Both types of biomarkers can be very important in optimizing patient treatment. For particularly the diagnostic biomarker (sometimes referred to as "companion diagnostic"), it is very important to work on an early identification of candidates and to have the biomarker operationally available and reimbursed at the time of product launch. A biomarker that is identified after launch will not enable the establishment of an optimal launch price and will potentially reduce the eligible patient population for the drug, although obviously the patient outcomes are still going to be better.

Evidence-Building Stage

The evidence building stage involves a number of pre-launch decisions that have an important impact on our ability to implement a successful commercial strategy. When we enter the evidence building stage, key asset decisions have been made and the Phase III trials are typically underway. Examples of typical questions that may arise during this stage are:

- What is the impact of a new post-launch indication on MA&P?

- My label is more restrictive than I had anticipated. Should I increase price?

- I have a 1,000-page health economics dossier. How do I get payers to review our data and analyses?

- What price should I launch my drug at? Should my price be the same in the United States, France and China?

- Should I set a lower price to obtain a better US Managed Care reimbursement tier or should I set price high and contract?

- Should I contract for a lower co-pay tier or should I rely on patient coupons to address co-pay concerns?

- Our management wants us to be more innovative with "risk sharing" deals. How should I approach this?

Figure 7.6 shows the most important decision points and activities during this stage. We will discuss each of these in the next sections.

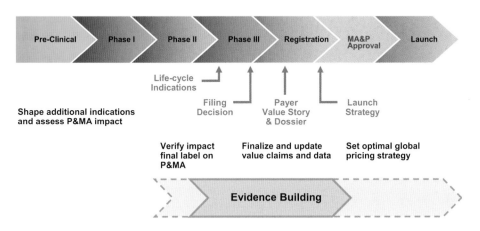

Figure 7.6   Evidence building stage

LIFE-CYCLE INDICATIONS

Ideally, all planned indications are extensively analyzed and debated prior to a Phase III decision for the first indication. In reality this hardly ever happens due to time pressures to get Phase III trials for the lead indications underway, as well as the fact that the competitive environment continues to evolve and the team continues to sharpen its insights after the Phase III decision.

In most payer systems new line extensions, indications or other, will lead to a re-negotiation of price and/or reimbursement. There are a couple of reasons for this:

1.   A new indication may have a different value and competitive benchmark, leading to a challenge on price when the existing price seems higher than reasonable for the new indication.

2.   Increased volumes will further add pressure to the payer budget. Payers will want to control reasonable use for the new application of the drug.

3.   Because they can ... In some payer systems, payers will use any available opportunity to re-negotiate price, particularly when a drug is used extensively and has a noticeable impact on the budget.

Because of the above, new indications should be considered as a new launch from a MA&P perspective in many markets.

In the United States the situation is slightly different, but also needs close consideration. Assume for example, where a drug has achieved reasonable market share in its first indication, partly because of a broad acceptance on a second co-pay tier in Managed Care. Suppose a new indication is launched, which is expected to draw higher utilization, and for this indication the drug is not very different from an existing generically available standard of care. In this situation, Managed Care might seriously consider to either move the drug to a higher tier, or to institute use restrictions, typically step edits, to enforce a generics-first policy. Payers generally do not distinguish between indications in reimbursement policies, that is a tier is the same for every patient. Through this situation we are running the risk of complicating thus far unrestricted use in the primary indication.

In Canada, a new indication is not subject to review by the Patented Medicines Price Review Board (PMPRB), which reviews pricing for every new patented drug (see Chapter 20). This can be a great advantage in situations where as a stand-alone indication, PMPRB would be likely to challenge. A typical situation would be where current standard of care is very inexpensive. In reality though, each new indication will have to be endorsed by the Common Drug Review (CDR) with respect to relative effectiveness and cost-effectiveness, and by each of the provinces' formulary decision bodies.

Interestingly, in the UK the situation is practically opposite to the Canadian one with respect to price approvals for line extensions. Under the British Pharmaceutical Price Regulation Scheme (PPRS), companies can price a New Chemical Entity (NCE) freely in the first five years (see Chapter 25). After five years, newly introduced product forms with the same active ingredient are subject to strict control by the government agency.

New formulations and drug presentations, such as a new tablet strength, will have a less substantial impact on MA&P, but need to be negotiated in each system as well.

FILING DECISION

When the Phase III trial results become available, teams go in overdrive to analyze the data, evaluate the impact on strategy and prepare a dossier for the regulatory submission to FDA, EMA and other regulatory agencies. At this phase of activity it is particularly important to ensure that MA&P considerations are incorporated in decision making. Filing decisions and proposed labeling are frequently decided upon before any final payer research data are available. Therefore it is important to have key insights on trade-offs readily available at the time of this analysis.

Particularly important elements of the filing decision are the final choice of indications, claims included in the label and any data that can be referenced from the label. Endorsement of claims and related data through inclusion in the formal label carries a lot of weight in payer discussions. Many drug companies still attempt to use "Data on File" as a means of convincing payers of the legitimacy of a claim. It should be realized that there are important benefits for inclusion of claims in the label, or alternatively as a publication in a reputable peer reviewed journal.

In some cases, it may actually make more sense to accept or even propose more restrictive labeling. Doing so will no doubt require extensive discussions with the marketing lead, as from a marketing perspective we tend to strive for as broad a labeling as possible to have a strong platform for promotion and resulting utilization. In some cases however an overly broad label will raise concerns with payers and may entice them to refuse reimbursement, force price down, or put in place severe use restrictions. As an example, when biologics Remicade and Enbrel were first introduced for the treatment of rheumatoid arthritis, their label was restricting both drugs for use after failure of one or more Disease Modifying Anti-Rheumatic Drug (DMARD). Despite the (then) very high cost of $10,000–$15,000 per year, both drugs have had good uptake. If labeling had been much broader, severe restrictions would have been put in place for fear of earlier use. Addressing payer concerns over broad use of expensive drugs is an essential element of pricing for many specialty drugs, particularly orphan drugs. It illustrates that many payers feel that they have insufficient control over appropriate drug use within label.

In some cases the team can be surprised by a regulatory approval that is different from what was included in the chosen strategy. It is important to try to anticipate these occurrences, as they can impact payer evidence requirements and can result in an inconsistent strategy and launch delays.

PAYER VALUE STORY AND DOSSIER

Creating a strong payer value story and ensuring the availability at launch of good supportive evidence of all key claims should be an area of focus throughout the drug development and commercialization process.

After availability of Phase III data and the filing decision, launch preparations accelerate. For the market access and pricing team this means a finalization of the MA&P strategy and the global payer value story and dossier. These two activities are described sequentially in this chapter, but in reality go hand-in-hand. During this stage detailed payer and pricing research is usually done in the key global markets.

As explained earlier, marketing and market access strategies need to be perfectly in sync. Payer messages need to be consistent with messages to other customers, although some messages may be emphasized more with payers than with other customers. Many physician messages will not resonate well with payers as payers tend to strongly discount any claims that are not well supported with direct comparative data versus the standard of care. Also payers tend to focus on universal claims for a reimbursed population, whereas physicians can focus on benefits to individual patient cases.

A useful way to link payer messages to the brand's messaging is shown in Figure 7.7. It combines two dimensions that are important in identifying key payer value messages:

- Differentiation versus standard of care. How does this message help in claims to replace current treatment practices with our newly proposed drug or drug regimen?

- Importance to payers. How much does a claim resonate with payers in terms of its significance with respect to the payer system decision criteria?

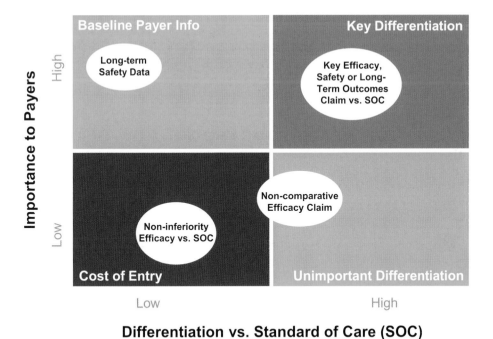

Figure 7.7   Identifying key payer messages

As illustrated with the general examples included on the grid in Figure 7.7, we can place each of the marketing team's core messages on the grid. The ones that are captured on the top right quadrant are differentiating messages that are of importance to payers. These are important messages for inclusion in our payer value story and dossier. Wherever feasible, we need to make sure that these messages are convincingly supported with evidence.

Once we have decided on a high-level value story and are comfortable with its supporting claims and evidence, a robust value dossier needs to be prepared to assist formulation and implementation of local MA&P negotiation plans. This is further discussed in Chapter 11. To support this process, we should be continually searching for opportunities to strengthen the value story and verify sufficiency of data support from the clinical and health outcomes trial programs.

LAUNCH STRATEGY

Reaching organizational consensus on an integrated launch strategy is of obvious importance for commercial success. How to go about this technically and organizationally is discussed in Chapters 12 and 16. Building an optimal MA&P strategy is an ongoing point of concern during the drug development program, starting in its earliest stages.

Implementation and Adjustment Stage

After regulatory approval is obtained, all the preparations for MA&P negotiations are rolled out market by market. After successful negotiations and product adoption in the market, there are several events that further require attention of the MA&P team (see Figure 7.8). The introduction of a line extension and the launch of a competitive compound may require a strategy adjustment. Timing and number of occurrences of these events can obviously be very different from drug to drug. As an appropriate completion to this chapter, we will discuss the impact of patent expiration and generic defense strategies.

Examples of typical questions that may arise during this stage are:

• What are the most important preparations for payer negotiations?

- The Italian government is only approving a much lower price than our global pricing strategy allows for. Should we allow an exception?

- The German healthcare system is likely to change significantly. What impact will this have on my portfolio and key drugs?

- A new competitor is about to launch. Should I proactively change my strategy? Should I ignore until after their launch?

- I am preparing for the launch of a new formulation. How will payers respond to this? Do I have to re-negotiate price? Do I have enough evidence?

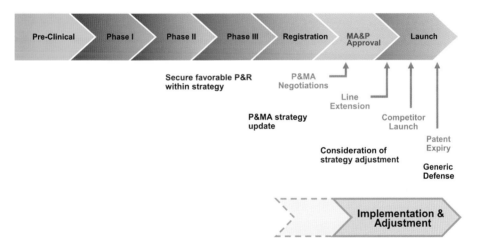

Figure 7.8   Implementation and adjustment stage

Covering all the implementation-related issues is going beyond the scope of this book, particularly since there are so many aspects related to individual countries. We will discuss the most important ones at a high level.

MA&P NEGOTIATIONS

The ultimate negotiation for price and/or reimbursement is where all preparations over the years of drug development need to come to fruition.

Price negotiations take a lot of preparation, most of which is done long before the actual launch.

A positive result of the negotiations is dependent on effectively shaping a compelling evidence-based value story that is supported by key influencers and that addresses payer preferences within the established payer system rules. The value story and evidence dossier are discussed extensively in Chapter 11 and earlier in this chapter. Payer negotiations are discussed in Chapter 17.

Having a deep understanding of the payer system rules, payer preferences and factors that influence their decision making within these rules forms the basis for all MA&P considerations (Figure 7.9). Building this understanding through a mix of direct interactions with key decision makers and payer research is important for both strategy formulation and implementation.

The critical implementation element that has not been previously discussed is the one of key influencers of payers. Payers don't make decisions in isolation, but rely on a number of supportive bodies, committees and advisors to enable them to make an informed decision that is likely to find support in the medical and political community. In Chapters 19 through 31, the payment systems

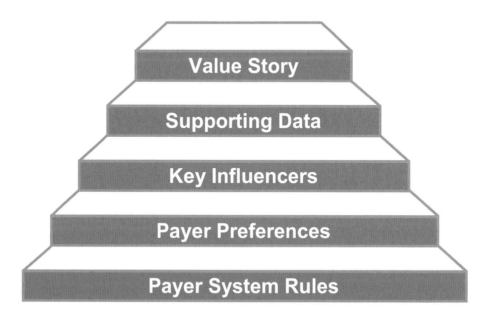

Figure 7.9   Key steps to MA&P approval

and supporting bodies and committees are described in more detail. Beyond these organizations there are a large number of national and international organizations that influence decision making for each individual therapy area. For example for oncology, we need to consider national cancer networks, organizations such as the European Organization for Research and Treatment of Cancer (EORTC) in Europe and other local and international organizations. In some cases it can be useful to engage in an organized "influence mapping" effort to help identify key influencing organizations and individuals for a particular therapy area.

LINE EXTENSION

A new drug is usually launched with a limited number of formulations and dosage strengths. Over time there can be a number of reasons to introduce line extensions. Some of the most common line extensions are:

- *New formulation for a new use*, such as suspension for pediatric use, a rapidly dissolving tablet or injectable form for acute patients;

- *New dosage strength*, for a new indication or more practical form for currently approved use;

- *New pack size*, for example to accommodate use of chronic use for a drug that was launched for acute use.

The justification for a new use is a very important consideration for MA&P decision making. The factors that play a role in that consideration are whether use is expanded for a new use and whether that use has an impact on overall drug and healthcare cost. A new indication requires a separate approval on the basis of its own merits and in a proper comparison to the standard of care for that particular use. When the new drug use is adding to drug cost, a good justification will be required, just like it would in the case of a new drug application. If the evaluation leads to justification of price at a lower level than the approved price, many payers will insist on a price reduction, probably on a weighted basis for the new use.

New formulations that are easing the use of a drug for an already approved indication, can usually obtain a relatively easy approval, provided that cost is the same. When a premium price is targeted, payers are likely to seek a strong justification beyond convenience. Convenience and soft compliance claims generally will not find an enthusiastic audience with payers, unless evidence is presented that shows a real-life impact on clinical outcomes.

COMPETITOR LAUNCH

The launch of a new competitor can cause a drastic change in the competitive environment. Considerations in preparation for a competitor's launch involve the same key elements as an owned new compound, although obviously from an opposite perspective. As challenging as it may be to make assumptions with respect to the clinical characteristics of a new compound in development, it is even more difficult to do so for a competitive compound in development, where information is limited to what the innovator chooses to share prior to launch.

In preparation for a competitive launch, it may often make sense to perform analyses and supporting market research as if the compound is your own and assessing what from the owners' perspective is the best development and marketing strategy. This can be done by a specially assigned "competitor team" composed of experienced staff in various disciplines.

PATENT EXPIRATION

It has been said that patent expiration is the only clear milestone in a drug's planning horizon, yet many companies are ill prepared for it. Once patent has expired, profitability declines rapidly in many markets, particularly for blockbuster drugs which attract a lot of interest from generics companies. Particularly in markets with a highly competitive generics sector, such as the United States, the United Kingdom, Germany and The Netherlands, profitability is declining rapidly at patent expiration.

There are some exceptions, where the effective patent life has been extended with new formulations. Examples are Neoral, the improved oral cyclosporine formulation of Sandimmune and Nexium (esomeprazole) as an isomer of Prilosec (omeprazole). In the past, many companies have attempted to extend their effective patent life with sustained formulations, providing for a once daily and sometimes a weekly administration (Fosamax, Risperdal). To be successful, these strategies usually need to be implemented long before patent expiration.

In this Chapter ...

We have evaluated the impact of market access and pricing considerations and needs on the drug development process. We considered three key phases of the development and commercialization process: asset shaping, evidence building and implementation and adjustment. For each phase we identified the impact on market access and pricing and the required activities to best support optimal development in the light of market access and pricing results.

8

Payer Segmentation

Every national, regional and local health care system is uniquely different from others. How can we make sense of the global patchwork of hundreds of national health care systems when none of them are identical? How do we address small and large differences between about 1,300 hospitals in Italy, hundreds of health plans in the US Managed Care market or 17 autonomous healthcare regions in Spain? Since devising a market access strategy for each payer is impractical and since a general one-size-fits-all strategy is likely to be sub-optimal, we need to consider how we define a manageable number of payer segments that require a meaningfully different strategic approach.

Segmentation Dimensions and Archetypes

How we segment a market, needs to be driven by the asset under consideration and how it will "fit" into the healthcare system. Inpatient specialty drugs will face a somewhat different payer environment than an outpatient oral diabetes drug. Drugs with generic competition may be treated differently across markets than drugs without generic competition. It is important to define the dimensions that are the strongest drivers of differentiation between payers for the situation at hand. A few illustrative examples of such potential dimensions are:

- Priority of a disease area by geography, for example Hepatitis C prevalence by country;

- US Managed Care Plan design, for example 3-tier versus 4-tier or 5-tier;

- Local Tx characteristics that drive relative value and required evidence, such as: standard of care drug/regimen, dosing;

- Use of cost-effectiveness based approval criteria in national pricing or reimbursement determinations;

- Formal ability to market without reimbursement;

- Expected number of Tier 2 drugs accepted from same drug class (for example gliptins) in US Managed Care plans.

The above are just examples to illustrate that the dimensions of segmentations can be highly specific to the drug and therapy area under consideration. The typical high-control versus low-control segmentation in the US can be helpful at times, but we often need to look deeper to identify a meaningful segmentation for our situation.

In many cases it makes sense to at least start with a more universal segmentation that is derived from more general dimensions. One that is often used is the global segmentation example that is described later in this chapter.

PAYER ARCHETYPES

In order to simplify the classification of payers we can create a number of characteristic archetypes that show fundamental differences in payer approaches. You may want to think of them more as caricatures rather than complete healthcare systems with the main purpose to describe fundamental choices in approach. This is often helpful, as it helps to overcome a typical hurdle in segmentation that "nothing fits perfectly in the box." Examples of a national payer archetype can be:

- All decisions are driven by cost-effectiveness evidence" versus other payer management principles;

or

- "Specialty drugs are budgeted and distributed through hospital channels" versus through regular retail pharmacy channels.

We need a complete set of archetypes to form a meaningful tool. The specific examples above are not meant to fit together as a comprehensive description of the payer environment, but just illustrate the concept. The simplicity of archetypes helps to analyze the potential of a drug in the payer environment.

It helps for example to focus on typical hospital formulary approval criteria in countries where this is the primary way to get access to specialty drugs.

SEGMENTATION EXAMPLES

The following examples are intended to serve as examples of payer segmentation. Each of them is founded on characteristics that are fundamental to the specific situation at hand and that are important in consideration of likely payer actions with respect to MA&P decision making:

HOSPITAL ANTI-INFECTIVE EXAMPLE

We are defining a hospital strategy in adopting a new antibiotic therapy on formulary. Some potential segmentation dimensions may be:

- Restrictions placed on treating specialists in antibiotic prescribing;

- History with respect to occurrence of antibiotic resistance issues (for example for MRSA);

- Current formulary policies and use of high-cost antibiotics.

DIABETES DRUG IN US MANAGED CARE EXAMPLE

We are launching a second or third in class oral diabetic drug in the United States. Criteria for segmenting the employer-sponsored managed care environment may be:

- Number of drugs in class accepted concurrently on second tier (one, two or more);

- Willingness to accept market share criteria in contracting;

- Urgency to address special patient needs (such as specific side effects or renal/liver excretion sensitivities).

These are just illustrations of specific dimensions of payer control that can be of interest in analyzing expected differential payer behaviors with respect to our situation or value proposition. The main message with these examples is that payer segmentation can be very different for each specific situation.

Global Payer Segmentation

The global payer environment is highly complex. Because of that it is tempting to resist efforts to segment payer systems. The answer to this challenge lies in looking at important similarities rather than differences. At a macro level, the global payer environment is characterized through four main payer management principles or archetypes that are used to manage market access and price for drugs. We can segment global payer systems on the basis of the most dominating payer management principles or archetypes. The segments do not eliminate the need to eventually consider the detailed characteristics and market access and pricing rules in each of the individual countries. There are differences between countries within the segments. However the segments play an important role in understanding market access and price requirements and their impact on clinical development needs and optimal strategies.

Table 8.1 describes the global payer environment in terms of four payer archetypes that typify the world.

Table 8.1   Global payer archetypes

Payer Segment	Description	Typical Issue	Typical Countries
Health Economics-Driven	Cost-effectiveness drives price or reimbursement approval	Real-life effectiveness and cost-effectiveness	Australia, Canada, S. Korea, Sweden, UK
Therapeutic Referencing	Price or reimbursement based on demonstrated value over comparator (health economics can play a secondary role)	Choice of high price comparator; demonstrated meaningful benefits over comparator	France, Germany, Italy, Japan, Spain
Competitive Insurance-Based	Free market environment with competing private insurance	Preferred tier placement, co-pay impact on prescribing and adherence; PA's, step edits	United States (except some Medicaid states)
Emerging Cash	Primarily cash-paying patients, public and private reimbursement still relatively small or limited coverage	Affordability, patient willingness-to-pay	China, India

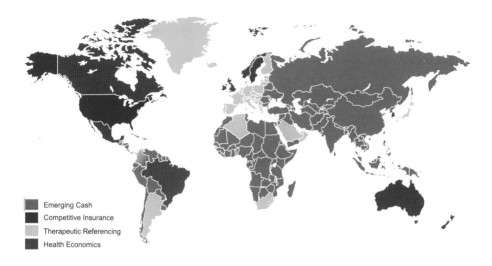

Emerging Cash
Competitive Insurance
Therapeutic Referencing
Health Economics

Figure 8.1   Global payer segments

Figure 8.1 classifies the world into four global payer segments, based on similarity to the archetypes from Table 8.1. Therapeutic referencing systems are the most common market access and price control systems among industrialized countries, as most European markets and Japan are based on this principle. Because of its market size the US Competitive Insurance-Based system is equally influential in terms of pharmaceutical sales that are subject to this control mechanism. The key health economics-driven markets are Australia, Canada and the UK. The system has also made inroads into Sweden, South Korea, Taiwan and in Colombia. Germany was frequently quoted as moving towards adoption of health economics control mechanisms through its Institut für Qualität und Wirtschaftlichkeit im Gesundheitswesen (IQWiG), but with the introduction of AMNOG, cost-effectiveness evaluations are rarely a basis for reimbursement decision making. The Netherlands and recently France are taking health economic data into consideration for pricing of particularly innovative high-cost drugs. Payers in the Netherlands have argued that they should be marked orange, appropriately reflecting the royal family color.

The developing world is largely a cash market for branded drugs. In markets such as China and India, only a small portion of the population is benefiting from any meaningful healthcare coverage. This coverage usually includes no or mostly generically available drugs. The intensity of green on the map in Figure 8.1 is not really reflecting the fact that in each country there is usually a government-run universal healthcare system. However, in most cases, these systems do not cover drugs or operate a largely generic drug formulary.

It should be realized that not each country fits perfectly in one segment for every situation. Also, markets such as Canada and Australia, which are classified as health economics-driven markets, have elements of therapeutic referencing control. However, since the health economics criteria tend to be more restrictive against pricing and market access objectives, they are classified as health economics-driven markets. Brazil today is a dual system with a large private healthcare sector that has been classified as a Competitive Insurance-based and a slightly smaller public sector SUS, which bases its decisions largely on CONITEC's health economic evaluations. China has been classified as an Emerging Cash market, although there are both public reimbursement and private coverage opportunities. However, from the perspective of the multinational branded drug company, the cash option is more often the logical opportunity. This will certainly differ from drug to drug and will change over time. **As such, the segmentation is merely an illustration of what should be a close evaluation for each individual drug opportunity.**

From Figure 8.2 it is apparent that there is wide discrepancy between population and pharmaceutical sales shares among the global payer segments. The US Competitive Insurance-based segment represents 40 percent of global pharmaceutical sales for only about 4 percent of the world population. Emerging cash markets only represent about 11 percent of global pharmaceutical sales for 86 percent of the world population. However, as pharmaceutical market growth

Figure 8.2   **Global payer segments by sales and population**

in developed markets has recently been slowing down, emerging markets are receiving increasing attention. Actually, over the last three to four years, since the last edition of this book was published, the emerging cash markets have been growing from 5 to 11 percent of global sales, reflecting virtually stagnant or declining US and European markets and rapid growth in countries such as China. Growth of the emerging cash market segments would have been higher if some countries had not been re-classified to therapeutic referencing and health economics-driven systems.

The following sections contain descriptions of the four key global payer archetypes that form the basis for our global segmentation. The archetypes were chosen to represent and explain key management principles that characterize payer systems around the world. Understanding these principles is extremely helpful in understanding the methods by which innovations are measured and recognized, as well as how they are "rewarded" in terms of potentially more favorable market access and pricing. Most of the healthcare systems around the world may be mainly characterized by one of the archetypes, but may contain elements of other payer archetypes for all or some areas of its healthcare system. As an example, Canada is characterized as a health economics-driven market. When examining the Canadian healthcare system, it has some national control systems, executed through the PMPRB agency, which very much limit prices for new drugs on the basis of price comparisons with existing drugs in the same therapy area. In addition, in British Columbia, few therapy areas have a reimbursement limit across therapeutically deemed "equivalent" drugs, typical for therapeutic reference systems. The most restrictive elements of the Canadian healthcare system are formed by its health economics controls, as guided by CDR reports and implemented by the provinces. As mentioned earlier, this is why Canada has been classified as a health economics-driven system although it has some elements of the Therapeutic Referencing archetype.

For a more detailed analysis of each of the largest global healthcare systems, please refer to Part E: Chapters 19–31.

Competitive Insurance-Based System

The United States today is one of the few, if not the only large healthcare system, where drug pricing is to a large extent uncontrolled by government intervention. The private Managed Care organization is managing its offerings and related formulary decision making in an environment where it is competing with other

Managed Care organizations without any direct government control on drug market access and pricing-related decision making.

The US does have a number of government-controlled sectors, such as Medicare, Medicaid and a number of large institutional customers, such as the Department of Defense (DoD) and the Veterans Administration (VA). These customer groups and related government agencies generally don't follow the behaviors of the competitive insurance-based payer segment, but rather behave more like therapeutic referencing systems. For a further discussion of these customer groups and market access and pricing opportunities in these US market segments, see Chapter 19, as well as a discussion of the therapeutic referencing payer segment later in this chapter.

US Medicare Part D and the Healthcare Exchanges (Marketplace) instituted under the Affordable Care Act (ACA, Obamacare) are handled by Managed Care organizations in a very similar way in which they manage private offerings. As funding for Part D and the Exchanges tends to be less rich than private offerings, the actual formularies are much more restricted and patient deductibles and co-pays may be higher, but the principles of formulary management tend to be very similar.

There are some other healthcare systems around the world, for example Germany and The Netherlands, where medical care is managed through private or semi-private plans. However in each of these cases, pharmaceutical market access and pricing is subject to specific governmental control mechanisms.

Brazil has a large and growing private health insurance sector, which may be the closest ex-US equivalent to the Managed Care environment. It co-exists with the largely health economics controlled public sector (SUS) and a still large cash market sector. When creating a global segmentation map, Brazil can thus appear in green, red or blue, depending on the drug opportunity under consideration.

MARKET ACCESS

Managed Care and Medicare distinguish between medical and pharmacy benefits in determining coverage. Medical benefits generally refer to any procedures that medical staff conducts, but it also includes physician administered drugs, which are often directly reimbursed to the physician's office or clinic, unless it is included in an overall fixed treatment reimbursement group, such as is the case for most hospital inpatient treatments. Medical benefits include drugs such as Benlysta (belimumab), Jevtana (carbazitaxel) and other infusion drugs, as well as items such as pediatric vaccines that are administered intra-muscularly. In Medicare, medical benefits are covered under Medicare Part B and usually reimbursed at 6 percent above the average selling price (ASP), as periodically reported to CMS by the drug company. Pharmacy benefits are prescription drugs that are mostly dispensed through retail pharmacies.

Obtaining market access for pharmacy benefits is subject to negotiations. US Managed Care organizations and PBMs maintain drug formularies for pharmaceutical benefits, placement on which can be subject to an agreed-upon discount or rebate. Private plans, Medicare Part D plans and Healthcare Exchange plans mostly manage pharmacy benefits through three-tier, four-tier and some five-tier formularies with co-pay and co-insurance rates that have increased significantly over the last decade. Plans can negotiate discounts with pharmaceutical companies for a preferential co-pay tier or to avoid prior authorizations, step edits or other formulary restrictions.

Managed Care organizations are motivated to contract with drug companies for drugs which have a relatively large market share in the treatment category. Placement of these drugs on a preferred drug tier can deliver significant budget savings, which would be foregone without the contract unless the plan is able to shift share to an existing preferred drug. As such, preferred brand status is much easier to negotiate for a brand with a specific unique characteristic and significant demand for its claims.

OPTIMIZING MARKET ACCESS IN A TIERED FORMULARY SYSTEM

For most brands, the main consideration for manufacturers is whether they should try to contract for a second-tier preferred formulary position. Required rebate concessions for preferred formulary placement differ greatly from situation to situation. Particularly in situations where differences between drugs in the same class are perceived to be small, such as for gliptins, switch due to co-pay is commonplace. In some other therapy areas, such as in mental health, switch due to co-pay is less common, as physicians are more concerned about differences between treatment options in terms of its desired therapeutic effect. In the latter case it makes less sense to make substantial rebate concessions to the healthcare plan than in the former case. After all why pay for a better formulary position if it does not affect physician and patient behavior. As co-pay and co-insurance rates have risen substantially, particularly for Medicare Part D patients, contracting for these plans is becoming more important. For employer-sponsored private plans, drug companies can choose to issue coupons in co-pay offset programs. Particularly in situations where patients can be reached and physicians are motivated to collaborate in such a program, this can be an effective way to circumvent high rebate demands or unwillingness to contract by payers. For Medicare Part D coupons cannot be issued as they would be in violation of US Federal Anti-Kickback Statute. In October 2013, the US Department of Health and Human Services (HHS) declared that Anti-Kickback Statutes would not be applied with reference to Healthcare Exchanges, thereby opening the doors for the use of discount coupons by drug companies. At time of writing of this second edition there was still considerable confusion and disagreement between HHS and Congress on this point.

The first tier on drug formularies is uniquely reserved for generics. Upon patent expiry and placement of a first generic on first tier with a very low patient co-payment, the branded originator drug is frequently automatically moved to third tier, whereby the incentive to switch to the generic is maximized.

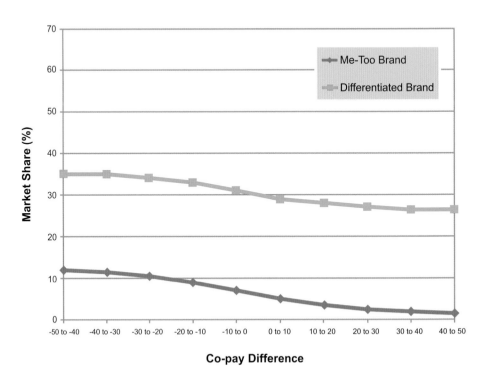

Figure 8.3   Examples of impact of co-pay on market share

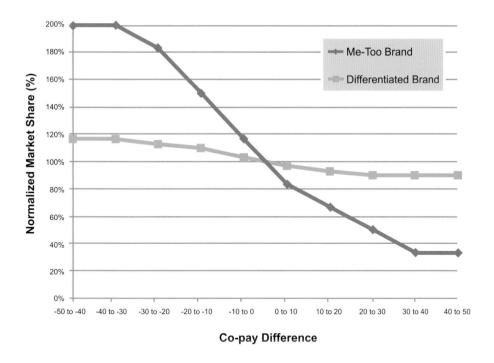

Figure 8.4   Normalized impact of co-pay on market share

A good way to assess patient behavior and the benefits of contracting is by considering the relationship between co-pay differential and market share. Figure 8.3 illustrates two examples of such a relationship which represent situations, such as the ones discussed above.

In this illustrative example, the absolute market share changes relatively little for both drugs, but as can be seen in Figure 8.4, the relative change in share is much larger for the me-too brand, as it declines to 34 percent of its co-pay neutral market share. For the differentiated brand in this example, the additional marginal income from a higher price may very well outweigh the 10 percent share loss associated with a co-pay-related switch. Only case-specific analysis will tell.

For a drug that is on the market, relationships between co-pay and market share can usually be established through analysis of prescribing data. In a pre-launch situation, such data is obviously not available. In that situation the use of analogs, supplemented with payer and physician research, can provide the answers. This is further described in Chapter 10 (under Price Evaluation).

Therapeutic Reference Systems

Therapeutic referencing is used as a MA&P control principle in the great majority of healthcare systems with universal healthcare coverage. Countries that use therapeutic referencing as their guiding principle include Japan, France, Germany, Italy, Spain, as well as Medicaid coverage in some key US states.

Essential to the therapeutic referencing markets is a two- or three-step approach in guiding MA&P decisions:

1. Comparator selection;

2. Price premium determination;

3. Definition of qualifying patient population (not in all systems).

COMPARATOR SELECTION

The selection of the comparator is the element which in most cases has the highest impact on MA&P determination. Most healthcare systems have a very well defined process by which a comparator is assigned. For example in Germany, the WHO Anatomic Therapeutic Classification (ATC) system is used to identify therapy classes for the determination of reimbursement limits. In Japan, a systematic evaluation of indication, mechanism of action and chemical structure is used sequentially to determine the closest comparator.

Generally speaking a comparator selection can be based on one or more of the following:

- Standard of care, that is the proposed position in clinical treatment guidelines;

- Similarity in drug profile, indication;

- Chemical similarity (ATC class or other);

- Latest launch in the therapy area class;

- Least expensive treatment option;

- Comparator in pivotal clinical trials.

Each of the above criteria tends to be a variation on the assessment of similarity, either in chemical properties or, in the likely or proposed place, in therapy. Any first in class drug is generally assessed against current standard of care, as a close chemical comparator is not available. Later entries in a chemical class are subsequently referenced to the "first in class" compound. As mentioned earlier, the comparator selection is a critical component of a favorable MA&P assessment. The combination of a low price comparator with a low innovativeness premium is obviously a recipe for disaster for a new chemical compound, implying that any drug which is chemically differentiated should come with adequate clinical differentiation in order to stand a chance of successful commercialization on most global healthcare systems. Follow-on compounds have the luxury of a good price reference and, even with a discount, will generally be priced at a much higher level than some of the lower-cost drugs in the category. Obviously there are many other later-entry marketing disadvantages that complicate success for these drugs.

In some cases, it is very difficult to select an appropriate comparator, for example because there are no current treatment alternatives for the condition. In Japan, some compounds qualify for a "cost-plus" designation for this reason. As scary as the cost-plus term sounds, it is usually a very favorable situation to be in, as price can generally be set at higher levels than feasible under the outcome of the comparator method. It should be realized that it is generally not easy in any system and in some cases impossible to be accepted as not having a comparator.

> Many assumed cases of "lack of appropriate comparator" are based on wishful thinking rather than rational analysis of the situation.

PRICE PREMIUM DETERMINATION

The determination of price premium over the selected comparator is generally based on a systematic assessment of clinical added value in terms of efficacy and safety by typical therapy area specific measures. Clinical need and breadth of indication will play a role as well, particularly for drugs that are likely to have a substantial impact on the annual payer drug budget. Probably the best known system of innovation based price premium determination is the French ASMR classification system. In this system the Transparency Commission, a committee of primarily clinical experts, decides on an ASMR rating of 1 through 5, representing the demonstrated clinical value of the innovation. The ASMR rating is later used by a different "Economic Committee," which assigns a high price premium versus the comparator for a rating of 1 and a price discount versus the comparator for an ASMR of 5. A more detailed description of the French ASMR system is found in Chapter 21.

The ability to get a respectable price premium in therapeutic referencing systems is usually very limited. Price premiums of 25 percent or higher are very rare in Japan, despite much political gesturing and suggested intent to improve this. Japan and France have used different ways of dealing with some of the problematic situations resulting from limited price premiums for highly innovative drugs. In Japan, the government has introduced the Foreign Price Adjustment (FPA) calculation, which allows for a higher price when the locally referenced price is much below the average of France, Germany, the UK and the US. In France, any drug with an ASMR rating of 1, 2 or 3 was allowed to be priced in line with its approved price in other European markets, but is subject to medico-economic review since October 1, 2013. In analogy to the cost-effectiveness plane shown in Figure 5.2, we can illustrate the relationship between benefits/innovation rating and the price premium obtainable within therapeutic referencing systems. This is shown in Figure 8.5 for the French ASMR based system. The system tends to control prices tightly for drugs that get minor innovation ratings (ASMR 4 or 5). As discussed above, it is for the higher innovation ratings that payers struggle to exert control and often rely on either international referencing or some form of health economic guidance, although usually not with a strict cost-effectiveness cut-off.

DEFINITION OF QUALIFIED PATIENT POPULATION

Particularly for high cost drugs, payers are concerned about its prescribing for patients where less expensive treatment options are deemed more appropriate. To address this, payers are increasingly linking price approvals for expensive drugs to utilization controls or prescribing volume agreements. Utilization controls can have the character of a US prior authorization, where physicians need to seek approval for each patient treatment with a drug, which is only granted when confirmed that the intended scripts are in line with labeling and reimbursement approval criteria. Prescribing volume agreements are very tricky for drug companies, as they penalize a company for its success

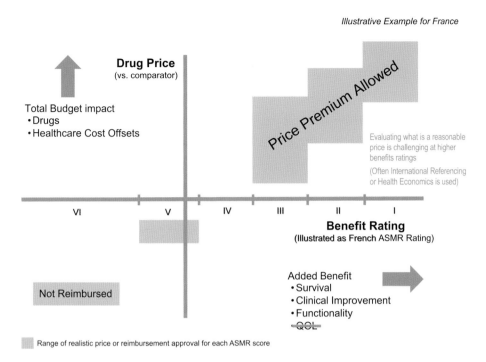

Figure 8.5   TR markets: price premium vs. innovation rating

in convincing physicians to prescribe a drug, even when all prescribing is appropriate and within the agreement.

This element of MA&P control for therapeutic reference-based systems is highly variable between countries. Also, volume controls and other patient restrictions are not unique to these systems, but can be found in other global payer segments.

Health Economics-Driven Systems

Health economics (HE)-driven systems have grown in importance over the years, although their role is not nearly as significant as many health economists claim or would like it to be. In reality, many healthcare officials and governments are struggling with its implicit trade-off between money and patient lives. In the United States and Germany, the role of health economics is relatively limited, as the public is not ready to accept the simplicity of its decision making to withhold innovative drugs to, for example, terminal cancer patients. In many countries, the study of comparative or relative effectiveness has found a more accepting audience.

Health economics has been the established basis for national and regional healthcare funding decision making in Australia, Canada and the UK for many years. In Scandinavian markets and selected other markets, including South Korea, health economics has played a central role as well. In most other markets, the role of health economics is generally limited to, for example, hospital inpatient cost evaluations or national funding trade-offs for large low-probability prevention programs such as vaccines.

An important factor to consider in health economics evaluations is the "perspective". It makes a big difference whether a pharmaceutical budget, total medical cost or societal cost perspective is assumed in the evaluation. For example, when taking the pharmaceutical drug perspective, medical cost offsets do not favorably alter the assessment. Most healthcare systems take a medical cost perspective, allowing for medical cost offsets to count favorably in a health economics evaluation, but not allowing for societal cost other than medical cost, such as work absenteeism, forfeited income or non-reimbursed patient cost to count towards the evaluation. In reality, many drug budget holders are only focused on their area of responsibility and thus take on a pharmaceutical cost perspective. As an example, a drug budget holder in the Canadian province of Alberta will take on the pharmaceutical drug budget perspective, while a provincial health administrator will take on a broader medical cost perspective. In England, Clinical Commissioning Groups (CCGs) will need to see budget increases before they happily endorse a NICE recommendation. This also plays a role in other global payer segments. For example, a US PBM will take a pharmaceutical drug budget perspective, while an HMO will take on a broader medical cost perspective.

The principles of health economics and considerations with respect to its applications are discussed in detail in Chapter 5.

The two essential aspects that typify a health economics review are:

- Budget impact analysis;

- Cost-effectiveness assessment.

Each of the two elements will be discussed with respect to their application in HE-driven systems.

BUDGET IMPACT ANALYSIS

Introductions of new drugs and medical treatments are frequently accompanied with claims of reductions in cost for medical interventions or other drugs. As most healthcare officials and pharmaceutical MA&P decision makers have primary responsibility for the pharmaceutical cost, budget impact analyses play a key role in the assessment of a new drug. Important considerations in the budget impact analysis are the overall impact on the budget and the magnitude of any cost offsets. Budget impact analysis is the first evaluation to consider for a new drug, since it directly addresses the prime concern of any drug budget holder. The Australian healthcare system addresses this in a simple and clear way. If a new drug has no compelling evidence of improved clinical performance, then its price will be evaluated on the basis of cost minimization, that is zero added cost. Cost-effectiveness assessments are only granted for drugs that have been accepted to offer significant clinical improvements.

Payers are generally not happy with "surprises" in the form of an unanticipated additional cost of a new drug launch with significant prospects of use. Early communication with payers with respect to an impending launch is usually appreciated by any payer, not just in HE-driven systems; however, such early communication needs to be balanced against the fact of doing so in the light of limitations on "pre-launch promotion" and concerns of strengthened resistance of a forewarned critical payer.

In most health economics-driven systems, budget impact analyses play an important, but usually not clearly defined role. We know from experience that drugs which are likely to have a large budget impact are getting closer scrutiny than drugs that have a minimal impact on the drug bill. This is also true for many healthcare systems with other than health economics-driven approaches. In early 2009, the National Health Service of England decided to show more lenience in assessing cancer drugs for smaller end-of-life indications, such as Renal Cell Carcinoma. From a patient perspective, it seems odd and unfair that patients with a less prevalent disease receive better drug reimbursement conditions, through reduced cost-effectiveness requirements, than other patients who are suffering from an equally devastating similar disease with a higher prevalence rate. Nevertheless, many systems look at the magnitude of budget impact for pragmatic reasons, allowing them to focus on innovations that form a larger problem to drug budget management.

COST-EFFECTIVENESS

As explained in more detail in Chapter 5, cost-effectiveness assessments provide a means of comparing treatment cost to patient outcomes improvements. Survival benefits are usually measured in Quality Adjusted Life Years (QALY), thus linking survival improvements and quality of life in a single measure. The cost-effectiveness measure, usually expressed as Cost per QALY, allows for a comparison of effectiveness of medical investments across therapy and drug areas.

In key health economics-driven systems – Australia, Canada and the UK – cost-effectiveness evaluations are the core of the MA&P approval process. The requirements and principles used in the evaluations show a high degree of similarity, however the way in which evaluations are commissioned and MA&P guidelines are linked to it are different.

In England, the National Institute for Health and Care Excellence (NICE) is tasked by the National Health Service (NHS) to undertake cost-effectiveness evaluations for a class of drugs (multiple technology appraisal (MTA)) or individual drugs (single technology appraisal (STA)). NICE is increasingly pushing for STAs for drugs immediately after launch. NICE is probably one of the most debated MA&P institutions in the world. There is an interesting paradox in the fact that NICE management considers itself to be at the forefront of market access management and is extremely active in providing its insights and services to other countries and health technology assessment (HTA) agencies, and the fact that the NHS is struggling to reform its system through Value Based Pricing, with more flexible cost-effectiveness criteria. Particularly the poor access to anti-cancer treatments under NICE has been much criticized, as the methodology used creates particularly high hurdles for new agents unless compelling long-term survival data is available. This blocks opportunities for many new drugs, as cost-effectiveness data are particularly hard to obtain at time of launch with the FDA- and EMA-driven clinical trial protocols

A positive recommendation by NICE is supposed to lead to additional funding for implementation of the treatment recommendations at a regional level.

Emerging Cash Markets

Emerging cash markets represent the fastest growing global payer segment. Rapidly growing new economies in Brazil, Russia, India and China, often referred to as the BRIC markets are increasingly drawing investment from multi-national pharmaceutical companies, particularly as growth is stagnating in the traditional developed markets. BRIC and most other emerging markets have only very limited healthcare insurance coverage for their citizens. As a consequence, most drugs are paid for by patients and their family.

In most emerging cash markets, drugs marketed by multinational pharmaceutical companies are only practically accessible for patients from the upper- and upper-middle-income classes. Local low-priced generics dominate the rest of the pharmaceutical market. Multinational drug companies have had some issues in reaching middle- and lower-income classes, to some extent because lower prices would lower marginal income levels below levels that allow for feasible commercialization. However, even in cases where this is not an issue, drug companies have been concerned with global price differences between countries and its potential price cascading effect into key industrialized markets.

One of the markets that have been creating huge concern for drug companies is Mexico. Until recently, companies would generally not price drugs in Mexico far below the US levels out of concern for political fallout. Prior to the implementation of the Medicare Modernization Act with Medicare Part D, elderly patients going to Mexico for cheaper US made drugs, similar to the Canadian drug bus stories, dominated global drug pricing policies.

In 2007 Merck made an interesting decision to depart from their previous strict global pricing policies in allowing Januvia to be priced at a substantial discount relative to the US and also much cheaper than the Mexican TZD prices (Actos and Avandia), thus allowing access to Januvia to middle-income populations. This policy has been extended into other Latin American and Asian markets. This decision perhaps reflects the fact that emerging markets represent an increasingly important segment of the global prescription drug market, as growth in the US, Europe and Japan have declined to single digits. As a result, prices in markets such as Mexico and China are increasingly based on local market analyses, rather than a consideration for the US or Europe.

Most of the BRIC markets are described in Part E: Key Healthcare Systems.

In this Chapter …

We have discussed payer segmentation and have engaged in a detailed segmentation of the global payer environment on the basis of common underlying principles and cost management philosophies. We described the essential characteristics of competitive insurance-based systems, therapeutic referencing systems, health economics-driven systems and emerging cash markets.

9

Key Situation Factors: The PODiUM Approach

Customer attitudes towards a drug and its price are directly dependent on the drug's value proposition. However what constitutes an attractive value proposition is determined by the specific situation or context in the particular therapy area and healthcare setting.

Many factors determine the situational context for a drug. To assess them systematically, the "PODiUM" approach has been developed. This analysis helps, so to speak, to explore the stage for the performance of a new drug and its claims. Each of the PODiUM components is described in detail in this chapter. The importance and impact of each of the elements is very different from situation to situation. In some cases the analysis may be very straightforward, in others highly complex. There is no strict order in which they need to be addressed, as they all complement a picture. You may for example argue that unmet need is a key driver of opportunity, but we need to know where in the treatment pathway this unmet need is most evident, what the currently available treatment options are for that stage of treatment and what the realistic promise options are. The PODiUM approach may also be somewhat different between global regions and countries. To avoid an unnecessary level of complexity for global analyses, it is recommended to first focus on the big picture through one or a few important countries. A broader evaluation of countries, their differences and its impact on the global strategy can be evaluated later.

The elements of PODiUM are set out in Figure 9.1.

The actual PODiUM analysis can be relatively broad, for example in the very early stages of development, or very detailed, for example pre-launch for a complicated situation. How much detail is required is hard to exactly define, as it is dependent on individual situations and preferences.

Figure 9.1   The PODiUM approach

Some of the PODiUM elements are further illustrated with two examples:

1.   A typical physician office treatment situation with mostly pharmacy dispensed drugs, prescribed by the PCP or specialist; a fictitious new oral diabetes drug is used as an example.

2.   A typical hospital inpatient situation, where a drug (oral, IV or other) is dispensed through the hospital pharmacy and administered to the patient. A fictitious new stroke drug is used as an illustrative example.

Patient and Treatment Flow

In identifying opportunities for value added treatment opportunities and related willingness-to-pay for a new drug, we need to analyze the prevailing way, in which patients are currently treated in the healthcare system. How are physicians treating patients for each indication, depending on severity and stage of disease? Which physician specialties are treating in what setting (hospital inpatient, outpatient, clinic, physician's office, home care)? When do they refer to (other) specialists? What are the treatments that are typically used at various disease stages and by each provider? How does drug treatment fit in with other treatment alternatives, such as surgery, radiation, or, for our diabetes example, diet and exercise?

Most disease areas have defined treatment standards and practices that are built on the basis of consensus building among key opinion leaders in the field. Medical treatment guidelines can be different in different countries. In addition, payers have mechanisms to control, particularly the use of high-cost drugs, through guidelines or other approval barriers such as step edits. In the US, prior authorizations are used to verify that a patient is appropriate for the drug treatment, based on label and various drug compendia. Similar systems are in place in other countries.

Figure 9.2 shows an illustrative example of a recommended treatment algorithm for diabetes. As in most, if not all, diabetes treatment guidelines, recommended first line treatment is diet and exercise with metformin. Medical guidelines tend to favor proven therapies for which efficacy and safety is well documented. Payers tend to favor them even more, since they tend to be less expensive, particularly when patents have expired and generic versions are available.

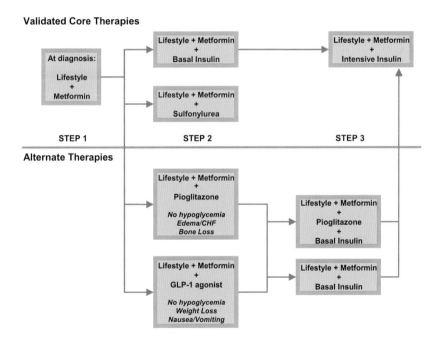

Figure 9.2   Example of a diabetes treatment algorithm

Promise Options

What are the opportunities for treatment improvement that may offer potential for a new drug? What place in therapy (indication, line of therapy, patient status and so on) can be targeted for inclusion in the medical treatment and reimbursement guidelines? What are the potential patient improvement claims in each of the options in comparison with current standard of care?

The following are some typical concepts for treatment improvement opportunities:

- Replacement of a medical treatment, such as was the case with Zantac in replacing surgery for ulcers;

- Augmentation or add-on to a medical treatment, for example where chemotherapy is added to radiotherapy for cancer treatment;

- Replacement of another drug, which is the most common situation with new drugs competing with existing ones in categories such as hypertension drugs, antibiotics, anti-depressants and so on;

- Used in combination with an existing drug treatment as an add-on, for example as a second hypertension drug added to a diuretic in uncontrolled hypertension, or Januvia added to metformin in uncontrolled diabetes;

- Used instead of no treatment besides general supportive care as is the case for many new late-stage cancer treatments after all older generation agents fail to give a response.

In each of the above cases it is important to consider the potential or proven performance versus the appropriate comparative treatment and its clinical and health outcomes. For any replacement of a drug or medical therapy, the formal price comparator will usually be that replaced therapy and any benefits will be assessed against any additional direct or indirect cost from the new drug treatment.

For a new combination therapy and any other additive treatment, the new drug and any administration cost will be an additional cost to the payer.

The benefits of the new drug treatment, measured against placebo, will have to justify its additional cost.

In many cases a drug will be approved and proposed for reimbursement for various indications or places in therapy. Since payers are likely to evaluate each proposed use on its own merits, a separate analysis should be done for each.

For any new treatment, drug or other, to be accepted and paid for, it needs to bring new benefits in comparison with the existing treatment standard. The improvement needs to also be sufficiently convincing to offset any doubts resulting from a lack of experience with the new drug. Some of the improvement opportunities that may justify the use of a new treatment are discussed under the following headings.

EFFICACY

Efficacy improvements, such as a more effective reduction in hypertension, avoidance of an infection with a vaccine or prophylactic antibiotic, or increased long-term survival of a lung cancer patient, are generally the most compelling means of clinical improvement. The value of the improvement is strongly dependent on the importance and general value that is placed on the efficacy measure. For many diseases, surrogate efficacy measures are used to predict long-term outcomes. Examples are bone mineral density in osteoporosis, tumor response rates in oncology and HbA1c levels for diabetes. Actually, in the cardiovascular therapy area, many of the treatments are aimed at maintaining blood pressure and cholesterol at levels which are believed to be associated with a lower risk of cardiovascular events. However this is not always evident, as illustrated with the Vytorin case, where long-term health outcomes studies did not show long-term mortality benefits for Vytorin despite better management of the surrogate clinical measure of cholesterol. Whenever a surrogate end point is considered, usually because it is impractical or cost-prohibitive to measure more meaningful direct outcomes, it is important to validate the acceptability of the data with KOLs and payers.

SAFETY/TOLERABILITY

Safety or tolerability improvements can be very important in cases where side effects are debilitating and require treatment or in cases where tolerability is causing a barrier to reaching the required efficacy levels. Generally, the value placed on safety and tolerability improvements tends to be much lower and more intensely challenged than the value placed on efficacy improvements. The reason is probably that in many cases the drug industry has claimed benefits in terms of a better patient compliance, which in reality has not always translated into higher effectiveness. In some payer systems, for example in Canada, sustained release formulations and other dose regimen improvements are not rewarded in terms of a price premium, as health-related claims due to compliance through dose regimen simplification are rejected as unproven.

This does not mean that safety and tolerability improvements cannot lead to broad access at premium pricing. It does mean however that more scrutiny on any claims can be expected. Also, for example for a claim of less nausea, payers can argue that the new treatment should be reserved for those patients that have this particular tolerability issue. Safety claims can certainly be compelling when they are significant. For serious diseases, treatment options with safety risks can still be good options as a trade-off between risks and benefits is made for every patient or patient type. However, when a safety issue is not present in a new drug, everything else being equal, it becomes an important consideration and can be of high value and lead to premium pricing.

PRODUCTIVITY AND ECONOMICS

Productivity and economics claims can be important, but are usually the result of the impact of an efficacy claim. For example a reduction in days of hospitalization can result from a more effective treatment for almost any condition that requires hospitalization. Again, the evidence needs to be clear for the claim to be compelling. Similarly, what is the value of a 15-minute versus a 4-hour infusion, particularly when considering that reimbursement rates to the physician or clinic may be different?

There may be other types of claims that can lead to viable opportunities. The key condition is that they lead to demonstrated value in the eyes of the decision maker.

Direct Competition

Existing and future drugs that are expected to compete with our new drug at or around the time of launch, considering the anticipated indication and use of the drug.

An overview of existing treatment options, their benefits and concerns, and an overview of daily and treatment cost is usually not difficult to obtain, particularly when dosing is clearly defined in the labels. Comparing daily treatment cost can be tricky when there are substantial dose variations between patients and between indications. Particularly when the patient mix is different between drugs, average dose comparisons can be misleading. In oncology, where drugs are mostly part of a multi-drug treatment regimen, the cost of regimens should be compared. In many cases this is very complicated and, in reality, payers are comparing the cost for key branded drugs. Apart from the case where two expensive branded (particularly biotech) drugs are used in one regimen, this is a practical approach, particularly since payers may not be able to track the use of multi-drug treatment regimens.

It is considerably more complex to estimate characteristics and performance of competing pipeline products. Comparisons can only be made on the basis of early clinical data, when publicly available, and considerations related to the chemical characteristics of the molecules, mechanism of action and so on. Obviously the cost of these drugs is not yet known. This creates extra uncertainty when competitive compounds are launched prior to the drug under consideration. The most practical solution to this is to estimate competitor pricing on the basis of assumed rational behavior.

Unmet Needs

What are the remaining needs for the patients under consideration in terms of clinical performance and related consequences and concerns? The most customary unmet needs are better efficacy and fewer side effects. The nature and level of unmet needs can vary substantially over the course of the disease and across patients.

In diabetes, there are still a large number of unmet needs, as many patients keep progressing to more severe disease stages where cardiovascular and other complications cause increased mortality and morbidity. Long-term HbA1c control and compliance, particularly, are key improvement areas that increase clinical effectiveness. Weight control is an important issue, as some treatments cause weight problems thus potentially further complicating patient health and related risks. At later disease stages, micro-vascular complications can lead to blindness and complications in the extremities, such as the "diabetic foot" which frequently leads to amputation.

Despite intensive efforts by many scientists and pharmaceutical companies, the treatment of stroke has a lot of limitations and, hence, patient unmet needs are substantial. Many companies have tried unsuccessfully to develop drugs that offer hope for patients after the critical initial three hours following a stroke.

In order to help guide efforts to address unmet needs, we need to identify specific clinical, humanistic or economic benefits that improvements would ideally exhibit, as the current standard of care is sub-optimal. See discussion of benefit analyses later in this chapter.

Money Flow

Who is paying for the treatment that the patient requires and how the money flows between the various players is of key importance in pricing and market access evaluations. What are the cost considerations from each of the key constituents that play a part in the treatment funding?

In the case of a retail drug that is prescribed by a physician and dispensed at the local pharmacy, the payment flow is rather uncomplicated. In most payer systems, the pharmacist may be incentivized to substitute a multi-source drug for a generic version, but will not interfere in the brand choice for financial reasons. For generics, the pharmacist and his/her margins can play a significant role in the selection of the dispensed generic version in many countries.

In our diabetes example, drugs are generally covered by the health insurance program; whether a private US Managed Care organization with tier-based co-pays and other controls, or a government-sponsored program in, for example, France. In emerging cash markets, most patients will pay out-of-pocket, as they mostly don't have universal healthcare coverage that covers prescription drugs.

Money or payment flows are particularly important for drug treatment in hospitals and physician offices. Reimbursement in these situations is frequently a fixed rate for a medical treatment, where the drug cost is only one of the components. Hospitals are frequently reimbursed under a Diagnosis-Related Group (DRG), leaving the institution at risk for drug and all other medical costs for one fixed daily or overall diagnosis-related fee. DRGs have been used to standardize reimbursement rates for inpatient treatments in the US and a number of other healthcare systems, such as Australia and Germany, and it is beginning to appear in Japan.

DRG rates can play a determining factor in the adoption of new high-cost drug treatments such as our hypothetical new stroke drug. They can form a strong disincentive to adopt new drugs, unless they produce significant savings that offset the cost of the new drug. In some cases, additional reimbursement can be obtained, particularly when a compelling clinical improvement can be demonstrated. For important clinical improvements, a hospital or other provider may simply accept a loss because of its importance on patient outcomes, particularly when it impacts some of the formal treatment quality metrics that are monitored nationally.

In the situation of a hospital or clinic with a fixed treatment reimbursement rate, the situation of the decision maker needs to be carefully considered with respect to their own preferences in pursuing his or her medical and financial goals. Let's consider a few examples to understand this.

A new hospital antibiotic that has been demonstrated to shorten hospital stays of certain patients can save a hospital a considerable amount of money while the reimbursement amount may be the same. The hospital may be willing to pay more for the antibiotic, provided that it leaves attractive savings under the most conservative assumptions. It is important to carefully consider the real impact on hospital practices and the ability to realize the claimed savings in a real life setting.

A new anticoagulant, used to avoid cardiovascular complications of surgery, may help the hospital achieve better patient outcomes statistics. Even when it does not affect the length of hospitalization, the additional cost may be acceptable in light of the improved outcomes statistics and related reputation of the institution. Alternatively, the hospital may be concerned about adopting a new treatment when this may lead to liabilities in case of patient complications.

> For a new stroke treatment, hospitals are likely to want to use any new treatment that can improve the generally poor prognosis for stroke patients. Particularly new treatment options that offer hope beyond the three-hour timeframe after onset that the use of tPA is generally restricted to, will meet a high demand. When the cost of the drug is not deemed "excessive", hospitals and insurers are likely to want to find ways to fund the treatment for patients where the benefit is clearly demonstrated.

Hospitals are in the business of treating people and saving lives. Generally, problematic margins for individual treatments will raise concerns when cost is exceeding reimbursement for a noticeable patient population, as it will threaten the ongoing viability of the institution. It is important to carefully consider the institution's decision making in the context of the importance assigned to the claimed innovation and the hospital's willingness to honor specialist requests despite a short- or long-term loss in income.

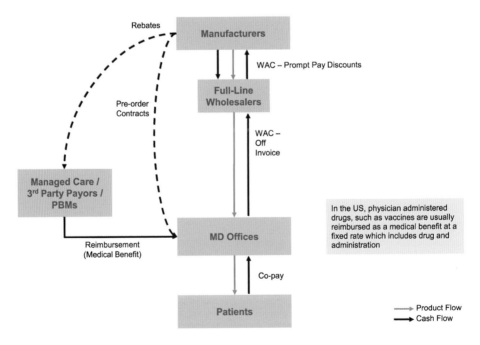

Figure 9.3   Example of a simple money flow evaluation

Physician administered drugs are frequently reimbursed at a fixed rate. As an example, consider a drug administered by infusion, such as Remicade or Orencia. Physicians will be reimbursed for the treatment at a fixed rate for the drug and a standard administration fee for the infusion. Figure 9.3 illustrates the payment flow for this situation. For high-cost drugs, physicians and their provider organizations usually have the choice to either purchase and stock a drug that falls under a medical benefit (Buy-and-Bill), or to have the drug delivery (and any patient co-pay) handled through a specialty pharmacy. Efficient provider organizations may choose to engage in Buy-and-Bill, but they are exposed to risk of non-reimbursement for individual patients as a trade-off to any margin that they may be making over drug cost. In Buy-and-Bill situations it is critical to evaluate the impact of price and price increases versus reimbursement on provider group and individual physician decision making.

In this Chapter …

We have used the PODiUM approach (**P**atient and treatment flow, promise **O**ptions, **Di**rect competition, **U**nmet needs and **M**oney flow) to evaluate some key situational context elements that are important in the assessment of pricing and market access opportunities for a new drug. It is shown how each of the elements are of high importance in considering opportunities to create value in the eyes of payers, physicians and patients.

10

The **BEST PRICE** Framework to Market Access and Pricing

Pricing is a multidimensional discipline. A perfect pricing strategy enables meeting company-specific marketing and financial objectives and matching of product-specific claims to the perceptual, economic and humanistic values of the customer groups. A price must be perceived as reasonable and not cause major surprises to clients for a product to be purchased. However what is reasonable and justifiable depends on a host of factors and can change over time as customers learn more about the product and consider it in the context of other purchasing options.

What makes a price for a new drug reasonable or not? How may the perspective on reasonable price be different for a payer, a physician or a patient? How may it be different across indications or patient types? To evaluate this, it may be helpful to use the BEST PRICE framework (Figure 10.1). The BEST PRICE framework is a stepwise evaluation of a number of elements that are important in the evaluation of market access and pricing. It builds on some of the concepts that have been covered in earlier chapters of the book, such as the global payer segmentation (Chapter 8) and the "PODiUM" approach (Chapter 9).

The BEST PRICE framework is designed to help us explore potential and strategy for market access and pricing for a drug by following the following steps:

1. Perform detailed **B**enefits analysis;

2. Assess **E**vidence needs;

3. Build and test payer value **ST**ory;

4.   Determine optimal **PRICE** and market access.

Each of the steps builds on the previous one in terms of identifying value and willingness-to-pay of payers. In the first part of this chapter we will explain how each of the steps can be executed successfully, leading to key answers with respect to market access and price approval potential and its impact on the business opportunity. In the last part of the chapter we will discuss how the framework fits into the drug development and commercialization process.

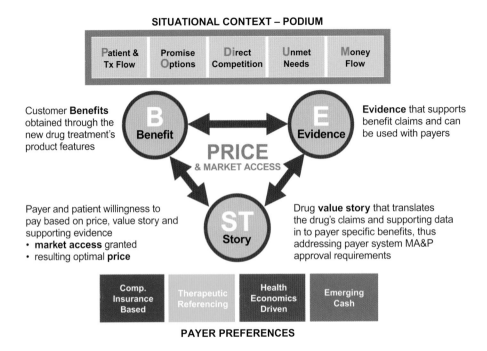

Figure 10.1   BEST PRICE Framework

Benefits Analysis

Product features, benefits and value have been discussed in detail in Chapter 6. The benefit pyramid is a useful tool in linking product features and related functional consequences to clinical, humanistic, economic and public health benefits. For the development drug opportunities under consideration, we need to identify what the most compelling benefits are to payers and their advisors, given current treatment standards and unmet needs in the therapy area under consideration (as identified with PODiUM).

A customary approach to identify drug benefits is the bottom-up approach, starting with the drug's chemical attributes and, through a consideration of its functional consequences, determine benefits that may be of significant importance to payers, physicians and patients. Some illustrative examples:

- A molecule's chemical structure may give reason to believe that it is highly potent in its desired pharmacological effect in, say anxiety, while avoiding certain debilitating side effects;

- Early animal model data may offer promise of very strong efficacy against Hepatitis C;

- Bio-availability data may help expectations of a particularly rapid onset of action, allowing for schizophrenia treatment start with an oral drug and avoiding an initial IM booster;

- Long half-life of a drug may offer promise as a once a week hypertension treatment.

The above examples are representative of a wide array of potential value. In reality, a new drug can offer multiple potential benefits, for example higher efficacy with comparable tolerance levels or similar efficacy with much improved tolerance. Particularly in the earliest stages of development, it is challenging to identify magnitudes of potential improvements in clinical measures, thus making it tempting to create a relatively "safe" profile, with clinical requirements that the drug is likely to meet. The problem is that these profiles have very little commercial potential. Balancing risk between "killing" a compound due to overly optimistic assumptions and missing blockbuster opportunity by failing to show impressive benefits is a difficult part in the drug development and commercialization decision process.

Figure 10.2 shows some typical examples of attributes and benefits that may be applicable. Identifying meaningful benefits that are linked to product features is obviously difficult. Predictability of benefits is one of the main causes of the challenge. For this, and some other reasons, only about 1 in 1,000 new chemical entities makes it to market. Frequently, benefits related to product

ATTRIBUTE/BENEFIT	TYPICAL EXAMPLE
Product Attribute	Mechanism of Action
Functional Consequences	High bio-availability Short half-life
Clinical Benefits	Improved efficacy Better tolerability
Humanistic Benefits	Quality of Life improvement Social functioning Ability to live at home
Economic Benefits	Cost-effectiveness Reduction in hospitalization cost Avoidance of cost of events Reduced nursing time
Public Health Benefits	Reduction in disease incidence Higher average cancer survival Reduced stroke mortality Reduced absenteeism

Figure 10.2   Examples of product benefits

attributes are not deemed very important in the customer's eyes or may only be attractive to a very small patient population, making it commercially unattractive to invest and risk resources.

A way of increasing focus on a strong benefit, that is meaningful to customers, is to take a top-down approach, as is illustrated in Figure 10.3. At least theoretically, by knowing which public health benefits are important, we have a higher probability of finding a drug that will be able to realize these benefits. In reality however, a top-down approach may not always be practical, as technology has not (yet) reached a stage where a drug can be designed to exactly deliver a cure to any disease. This approach does however help to focus on differentiation options that are meaningful in the eyes of payers.

Most large pharmaceutical companies are focusing on a limited number of disease areas as part of their corporate strategy. This has obvious advantages in building up scientific experience in key therapy areas, but it also allows having "multiple shots at goal" for any one area. When this is the case, a mix of top-down and bottom-up approaches in shaping key assets is likely to be very beneficial.

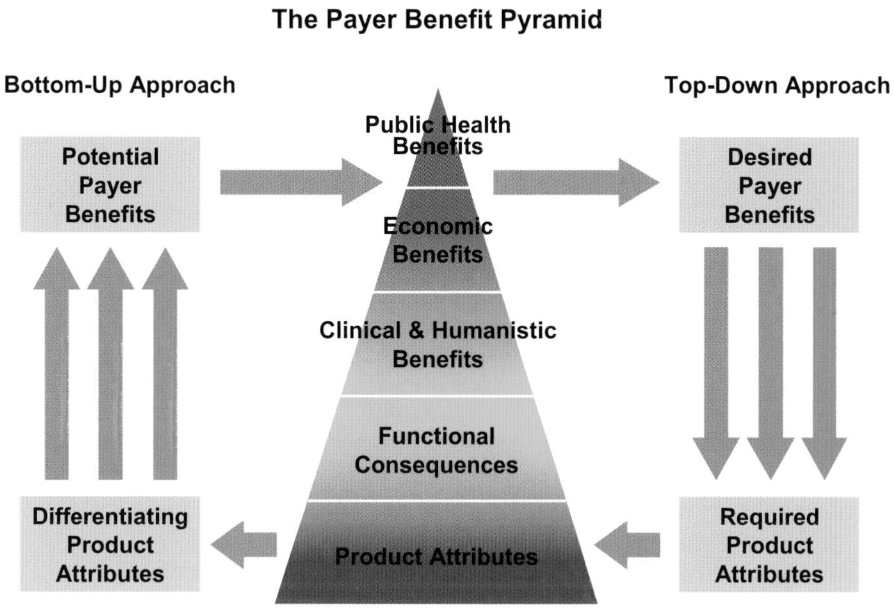

The Payer Benefit Pyramid

Figure 10.3   Bottom-up and top-down approach with the payer benefit pyramid

How can we evaluate the potential and attractiveness of a specific drug and make the appropriate trade-offs between multiple potential benefits claims?

Figure 10.4 shows a simplified example of a stepwise assessment of benefits for a new diabetes drug. It is important to use this sequential approach to evaluate benefits, relative importance and expected or measured drug performance. In this example, both customer preference and drug performance are rated on a scale from 1 to 5. The information contained in the Figure can be derived from an internal assessment with a cross-functional team. Such an exercise can be of great value in promoting dialog and building consensus with respect to key benefits claims, particularly in early stages of development. In those cases it usually makes sense to use a more qualitative measurement, such as high/medium/low (H/M/L) rather than a numerical scale. An internal assessment holds some risk with respect to a team's bias. Parents tend to always think of their babies as beautiful and certainly never ugly. For development drugs there tend to be some parallels, as the team may view the world through rose-colored glasses.

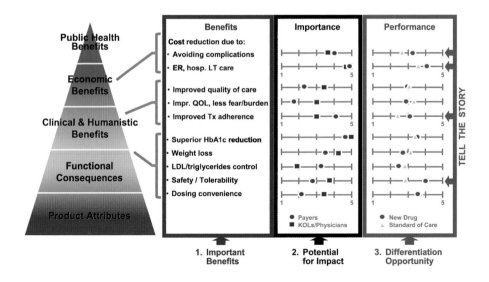

Figure 10.4   Illustrative example of a detailed benefits assessment

Market testing with payers, physicians and patients is an important validation, first to test whether the right benefits are identified and second to get a quantitative measurement of the relative importance and perceptions on current standard of care with respect to performance on key benefits.

SELECTION OF BENEFITS TO BE EVALUATED

Based on both the perspective of market needs and potential benefits related to the product's attributes, we need to select benefits for inclusion in the analysis. It is important to include the most important benefits for the disease area, irrespective of the compound's premise and supplement the ones that result from potential improvement opportunities for the compound under consideration. In the example in Figure 10.4, HbA1c reduction is clearly viewed as the most important efficacy measure in diabetes. However, as in many cases, it is not that easy to differentiate on demonstrated HbA1c efficacy improvement. Therefore it may make sense to consider the ability to differentiate on other benefits, such as safety and tolerability, as was successfully done for Januvia in this market. For an oncology drug, clinical benefits could include a number of clinical response rates, such as tumor response rates, progression-free survival (PFS) and five-year survival. Since, practically, it is difficult to show five-year survival at time of launch without a major launch delay, it is important to know whether surrogate end points such as tumor response rate and PFS help to sufficiently differentiate the drug to warrant earlier launch. Robust discussions with KOLs and payers are important in any example to inform the importance and trade-offs between these measures.

The humanistic benefit category is frequently contested with respect to its real value. In general terms, quality of life is accepted as important, but very specific improvement claims are required to really have an impact. Being bedridden for many months is a quality of life issue, but so are less severe inconveniences, such as a slight headache. Alopecia for a cancer patient can be devastating; however a payer may look upon it as the cost of a wig. For a pulmonary hypertension patient the ability to walk up the stairs and for an asthmatic child the ability to participate in sports can be important quality of life aspects for which it is hard to assign a specific value. Given that the term "quality of life" is very generic, with a very broad range of impact, we need to be very specific and compelling in how we use the term when we want to sway skeptical payers.

Economic benefits are of natural interest to payers. It is obviously very compelling to offer a new and better treatment and save money at the same time. Whether this is a meaningful argument towards the payer, depends on the perspective of the payer. Does the payer have responsibility over the drug budget or a broader medical budget? Obviously, the underlying assumptions of the economic claim will be closely scrutinized and need to be supported with detailed analysis and modeling. This is discussed more in detail in Chapter 5: "Health Outcomes and Health Economics." It is important to realize that economic benefits need to be closely tied to robust clinical claims. If they are not, then the economic benefits can only be achieved through a lower price.

Public health benefits are simply benefits that are of sufficient magnitude to impact population health statistics and, as such, rise to the level where it attracts the attention of public health officials. Most innovative drugs have a dramatic impact on individual patients, but relatively few have a significant impact on public health. Examples of drugs with a public health impact may be the Gardasil cervical cancer vaccine, H1N1 vaccines, Sovaldi for Hepatitis C, as well as less publicized improvements, such as Plavix.

CUSTOMER IMPORTANCE RATING

We can differentiate our drug versus standard of care on a particular benefit, but does anybody care? To ensure appropriate assessment of the impact of our benefit, we need to evaluate the relative importance of the benefit for key customer groups. In Figure 10.4 an illustrative example is given for our diabetes example.

The example shows a clear difference in preferences between the customer groups. Payers tend to emphasize economic and long-term clinical benefits and tend to be more critical of short-term surrogate data. It is important in each case to consider how much the payer is educated about a specific condition and treatment at the time of evaluation. Large differences between physicians and payers can indicate a need to engage in early communication and obtain KOL engagement as advocates.

PRODUCT PERFORMANCE RANKINGS

An important evaluation is the assessment of how our new treatment is likely to stack up versus the standard of care treatment, illustrated on the right side of Figure 10.4. Early in development, this is particularly hard to do and it may make more sense to use a H/M/L rating, as discussed earlier in this chapter.

As a result of the analysis, we should be able to focus on differentiating benefits versus standard of care that are of significant importance to key customers. In our example, the new drug has some compelling advantages in terms of safety and tolerability improvements that may result in improved adherence and economic benefits. The example is simplified, but the idea is hopefully clear. In reality, this analysis is usually done with multiple indications or patient types and validated through payer and KOL market research. An additional example for an oncology drug is found in Chapter 14.

Assess Evidence Needs

No matter how compelling the benefits may seem, payers and prescribing physicians are likely to want to see evidence before they are willing to endorse a new drug. Particularly payers will generally have high standards for evidence requirements, as any new drug they will accept tends to add to budget pressures.

A key moment during the drug development process is the decision making for the Phase III trial program. Phase III trials form the basis for regulatory

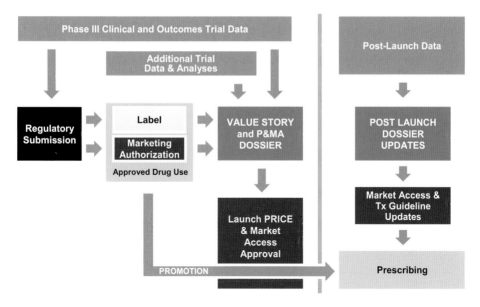

Figure 10.5   Role of evidence in market access

submissions to the FDA, EMA and other regulatory agencies, but it generally also forms the basis for justification of launch pricing and reimbursement.

Figure 10.5 gives an overview of the use of clinical and health outcomes trial data for regulatory and market access and pricing purposes. Obtaining market authorization and an approved label is essential for a drug company's ability to promote a new drug to prescribing physicians. However, Phase III data also forms the basis for approval of market access and/or price. Phase III trial design should therefore be based on a thorough analysis of both regulatory and market access requirements.

PAYER VERSUS REGULATORY REQUIREMENTS

Many pharmaceutical companies are still basing Phase III clinical trials decisions mainly on regulatory requirements. *In today's environment this can easily be a huge mistake.* To further illustrate this, let's compare and contrast regulatory and payer requirements in general terms. Exact requirements will be different from payer segment to payer segment and from country to country.

Placebo controlled versus direct comparison

Particularly in the United States, placebo-controlled trials are acceptable and considered appropriate evidence in regulatory submissions. It is generally not required to show improvements over the existing standard of care treatment.

Payers would generally consider placebo-controlled trials to be meaningless. A drug being better than placebo is assumed as a given. The only meaningful test is versus an existing treatment option, usually standard of care. A new oral diabetic drug should probably be compared against Januvia if it is intended for use with metformin after monotherapy failure. If first line treatment is argued, significant improvements will have to be demonstrated in direct comparison with metformin in order to justify a probably much higher cost than generic metformin.

The only exception is a situation where the standard of care is limited to supportive care, that is there is no real comparator. For example in late-stage cancer treatment, where patients' tumors have become resistant to existing treatment options, a new treatment can legitimately be compared to a placebo.

Non-inferiority versus superiority

Imagine going to the car dealer to trade in your old clunker for a brand new car. You have been saving money for a while now, as you insist in paying cash for the new car and you are starting to carefully compare car options within your budget.

You enter a dealership. A sales person comes up to you immediately and gives the following sales pitch: "This car is just as good as your clunker." Ready to write the check? So what is different about a non-inferiority trial, showing that a new drug is equivalent to an existing, perhaps even generically available existing drug? Nothing really!

LABELING

The content and exact wording of a drug's labeling can be of very high importance to market access and pricing decision making for two reasons:

1.   Labeling constitutes a stamp of approval on any evidence and claims that are made as part of the regulatory submission. Claims

in the labeling generally form a convincing and necessary basis for any evidence of economic benefits.

2.   In most healthcare systems, labeling determines what a pharmaceutical company is authorized to say to any customer as part of its promotional efforts.

Pharmaceutical companies are frequently focusing too late on operational limitations imposed by the outcome of labeling discussions with the regulatory authorities. Therefore it is important to thoroughly examine labeling claims that are likely to be approved based on the clinical trial program and its options that are under consideration at an early stage of Phase III trial decision making.

Generally, reimbursement is restricted to uses that are approved in the drug's labeling. Each market system may have its own sets of rules on that matter. For example, in the United States, listing of a drug use in one or more "compendia" such as the National Comprehensive Cancer Network (NCCN) Drugs & Biologics Compendium, American Hospital Formulary Service – Drug Information (AFHS – DI) or Thomson Micromedex Drug Points, is generally sufficient to qualify for reimbursement under the drug's formulary status and related co-pays. Many anti-cancer agents are reimbursed as a result of a compendium listing for uses that are not or not yet approved in label. A compendium listing does not necessarily lead to widespread use of a particular drug indication, as drugs companies are not authorized to actively promote this unlabeled use and hence these treatment options tend to not be widely communicated.

Pharmaceutical companies can choose not to delay their regulatory approval for key data that is of critical importance for certain labeling claims. Although label claims are a strong basis for payer negotiations, companies can decide to use clinical data that has not been part of the regulatory filing. In many countries, pricing and reimbursement filings to governments are not subject to the same restrictions as promotional efforts to physicians. However, unless the data is endorsed through publication in reputable peer reviewed journals, this strategy may be very risky, as the credibility of the data and related claims may very well be called into question.

EVIDENCE REQUIREMENTS FOR MARKET ACCESS AND PRICING

As explained in previous sections in this chapter, pricing or reimbursement approvals typically require strong supportive data. Submitted evidence needs to compellingly support the claim in a way that is credible in the eyes of the customer. Let's consider the key categories:

Clinical trial data

Clinical trial data, usually obtained from Phase III trials, are most convincing as evidence in support of claims. However there is a broad spectrum of potential ways of structuring a trial. Double-blind randomized trials are generally a minimum requirement for a claim to be honored. But even then, the results need to have statistical significance to overcome skepticism.

There are still many situations where clinical teams propose to engage in non-inferiority trials against a much cheaper, for example, generic comparator. That puts a lot of pressure on the team to find alternative ways of demonstrating value and supporting critical claims to payers. In some cases, committing to a double-blind comparative trial to prove statistically significant efficacy improvements can be commercially unattractive. The level of investment required, when for example 40,000 patients are required in order to reach statistical significance, can substantially reduce the commercial attractiveness of a drug opportunity. Required time to enroll for such a trial can also cause loss in leadership as a first compound in a new class when a competitor chooses a less ambitious level of evidence.

In some cases, when Phase II data are particularly compelling, Phase III is omitted and registration is obtained on the basis of relatively limited evidence. This happens frequently in oncology. There are obvious timing advantages of obtaining an accelerated approval on the basis of Phase II clinical data, but it can also cause some challenges for a payer submission. Compelling data from a regulatory perspective are likely to have a positive impact of an initial medical review of a new drug treatment, but is it sufficient to overcome the inherent lack of evidence in support of claims to payers, particularly when a drug is expensive? It is important to consider these aspects in the design of a Phase II trial in situations where there is a chance of regulatory approval on the basis of that data.

Naturalistic trial data

Clinical data are typically designed to show relative performance of a new drug in comparison with a reference treatment. The protocol requires close control and monitoring of a treatment, to the extent that it no longer is representative of typical "real life" treatment of patients. Comparative naturalistic trials are designed to show how a treatment performs outside the controlled clinical trial setting. Naturalistic trials are usually not suited for regulatory filings and are ethically difficult to defend prior to regulatory approval, making it practically unworkable to implement them prior to launch.

Registries are an increasingly popular form of gathering post-launch treatment data. In Chapter 18, a case study is discussed for multiple sclerosis in the UK, where a registry was used to settle a dispute over three new drugs and a negative NICE ruling. The case also shows that registries can be very difficult to set up.

Epidemiologic data

Epidemiologic studies and data can provide important evidence in support of budget impact assessments, for example by demonstrating actual usage patterns for the current standard of care. Epidemiologic data can provide answers and reassurance in these cases.

Economic data

The role of economic data is very different between countries and payer segments. In health economics-driven markets, the economic data need is fairly obvious and spelled out in detail in Chapters 5 and 8. However in other situations and settings, economic data can be of importance. For example in a hospital setting where a drug is paid for through a DRG fixed reimbursement rate, a detailed analysis of the impact of the drug on the hospital's P&L may be important. What is the added cost? what are the cost-offsets? and if the new drug adds a significant cost burden, are there opportunities for additional reimbursement from the government or private payer through means of a separate reimbursement code?

Budget impact data are of importance in many situations. Although not necessarily included as a formal factor in the pricing or reimbursement decision making, the overall budget impact tends to be an important factor in the level of scrutiny and the amount of resistance that is exhibited in payer discussions and negotiations.

TRADE-OFFS IN TRIAL DESIGN

It is very important to make rational trade-offs between various options that emerge in trial design discussions. Pricing and market access considerations should be closely evaluated as part of the decision, but will not always drive the optimal solution for the company. In other cases, not addressing the MA&P needs will lead to a dreadful failure. A structured approach towards identifying the optimal decision for a development approach should include:

1.   Identify a number of options, including preferred options by key team members and functions.

2.   Analysis for each option with respect to impact on clinical feasibility, requirements and risk, regulatory impact and label, market access and pricing and physician preference share.

3.   Evaluation of revenue, cost, timing, risk and resulting Net Present Value (NPV) for each opportunity.

Figure 10.6 provides a very simple template for a trade-off analysis between various clinical trial program options.

After a qualitative evaluation of options, it is important to evaluate more detailed business forecasts for the most attractive options. Pricing and market access assumptions can be validated through payer and pricing research.

Payer Value STory

The goal of the payer value story is to present a compelling rationale for payers to accept a drug's value proposition and allow broad market access, that is provide the opportunity for utilization of a drug for its target population at a favorable price. The payer value story has to present key benefits and related evidence in a way that is meaningful and important to each of the key global payer segments, as illustrated in Figure 10.1. The exact focus of a value story needs to be driven by each individual situation and potential anticipated payer objections.

	Option 1	Option 2	Option 3
Regulatory US/EU/J Approval Prospects Labeling			
Clinical Feasibility Cost Length of trial program Probability of Success			
Pricing & Market Access Comp. Insurance Based Therapeutic Referencing Health Economics Driven			
Promotional Power Differentiation vs. SOC Peak Market Share			

Figure 10.6   Template for qualitative evaluation of trial options

A compelling payer value proposition is essential to the commercial success of any new drug. What is the most compelling reason to use the drug versus standard of care? The benefits analysis, discussed earlier in this chapter, should have helped identify benefits that are appealing to physicians, patients and payers. Ultimately, we are obviously limited by the availability of compelling clinical data in what we can communicate and claim. We also need to make sure that the company's legal department is equally convinced about our ability to communicate our messages and claims.

Payers are the customers who ultimately need to approve market access and/or price in each healthcare system. Payers will usually consult with key opinion leaders in the field, but it is still important to provide the payer an opportunity to educate him or herself on the particular issues and unmet needs in the treatment of patients that we are targeting. Shortcomings of existing treatments are usually not heavily communicated unless a solution is available. Physicians tend to naturally play down medical issues for which there is no solution available. Why upset the patient? When a solution becomes available to an existing medical issue, it becomes essential to clearly communicate the problem with the support of key opinion leaders and subsequently introduce the solution. Pre-marketing can be as essential for payer marketing as it is for marketing to physicians.

To be successful, the payer value story needs to present claims and supporting evidence with a logical connection to the payer system requirements. For example, in a therapeutic referencing system it needs to compellingly argue for a favorable comparator selection, a possible price premium over that comparator and authorization for relatively broad use in the target patient population. As a specific example for an inpatient drug, the goal may be to convince a hospital payer to pay a higher price for a drug in order to reduce length of stay in a hospital or reduce 30-day re-hospitalization rates. Chapter 11 will provide more detailed frameworks to design and test payer value stories.

PRICE Evaluation

Defining the optimal pricing strategy is the central activity that brings all the analyses in the previous chapters together. The pricing strategy should be designed to support the marketing strategy that was determined to best capitalize on the local opportunity in each market. The set price will need to obtain the necessary approvals and allow for a level of market access that is considered optimal in the light of the drug profile, the approval requirements in a key payer system and the positioning strategy.

LOCALLY OPTIMAL PRICE

The optimal price for each country is determined by evaluating the trade-off between options within the rules of the local payer system, following the analytical steps as outlined in the BEST PRICE framework as they apply within the rules and logic of the local healthcare system. Usually the locally optimal price is expressed in terms of a relative price versus a competitive benchmark. For a new oral treatment for Type II diabetes it might be a price premium, parity or discount versus Januvia or another most appropriate agent given the molecular structure and indication.

The **PRICE** Evaluation is essentially a three-step approach:

1.   Assess potential market access status and price levels;

2.   Determine impact of market access on prescribing;

3.   Optimize market access and pricing, by combining 1 and 2.

In the remainder of this chapter, we will examine how to go about identifying the optimal price in each of the four global payer segments. In Chapter 12, we will consider an optimal global pricing strategy, given analyses and determined optimal prices in each global payer segment and key country and a number of other considerations.

COMPETITIVE INSURANCE-BASED SYSTEM

First, let's consider optimal pricing for an oral drug in US Managed Care. As discussed in Chapter 8, Figure 10.7 shows an example of a relationship between price, expressed as a cost per course of therapy, and Managed Care tier status. The information is obtained from market research with Managed Care pharmacy directors, validated with demonstrated behaviors in a number of analogues.

In this example, at prices above $50 per course, the number of plans that cover the drug in tier 2 drops dramatically, many of them switching to tier 3.

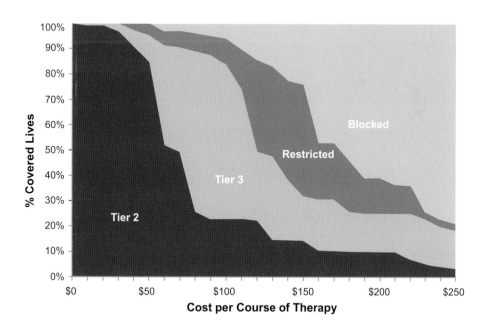

Figure 10.7   Price impact on US Managed Care tier status

Above approximately $110 per course restrictions kick in rapidly. Whether tier status impacts sales revenue, is heavily dependent on the attitude of physicians and patients to the resulting change in co-pay and (if the patient qualifies) to the hassle in dealing with restrictions, such as prior authorizations.

Figure 10.8 shows two very different scenarios with respect to the impact of tier placement on prescribing. Scenario 1 shows a clear impact of price on market share as, for example, the market share is only one ninth for the restricted case of what it is on tier 2 placement (2 percent versus 18 percent). Under scenario 2 prescribing is relatively inelastic with respect to tier placement, unless it is blocked, at which point a dramatic decline in share takes place.

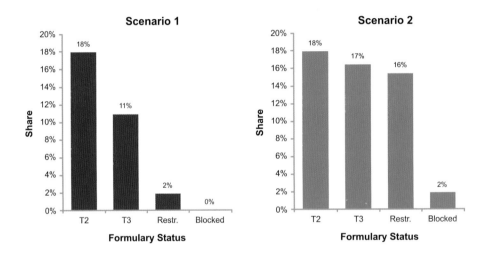

Figure 10.8   Scenarios for impact of tier placement on prescribing

Scenario 2 reflects a situation where the drug under consideration is fairly unique for a relatively well-defined patient population, resulting in a nearly constant share for every covered scenario, independent of co-pay and prior authorization hurdles. Figure 10.9 shows the combined effect of Managed Care coverage decision making (Figure 10.7) and the two scenarios of physician prescribing behavior (Figure 10.8). The drop off in prescribing at higher tiers for scenario 1 results in price maximization at about $55 per course of treatment. For scenario 2, with its lower cost sensitivity, the optimal price is in excess of $80 per course of treatment. The example shows that it is important to carefully analyze and quantify behaviors of each of the players that influence

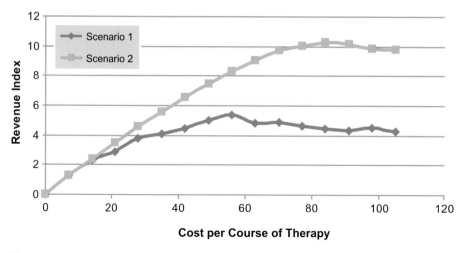

Figure 10.9   Price–revenue relationship

the prescribing decision as a result of cost variations. Market players who do not act differentially on the basis of price can be excluded from consideration.

THERAPEUTIC REFERENCING SYSTEMS

The evaluation of optimal price for therapeutic referencing systems is very different from other systems. As explained in Chapter 8 (under Therapeutic Reference Systems), we need to consider a stepwise approach to the price determination:

1.   Comparator selection;

2.   Price premium determination;

3.   Definition of qualifying patient population.

Let's consider a few examples to illustrate the way in which a number of important therapeutic referencing systems review pricing and reimbursement for drugs. As examples we will consider France, Germany and Japan.

France

Januvia received price approval in France in 2007. In accordance with the French system, a comparator was selected, presumably pioglitazone and the

Rating	Improvement in Clinical Benefit
ASMR I	Major Improvement (new therapeutic area, reduction in mortality)
ASMR II	Significant improvement in efficacy and/or reduction in side-effects
ASMR III	Modest improvement in efficacy and/or reduction in side-effects
ASMR IV	Minor improvement
ASMR V	No improvement

Figure 10.10   The French ASMR Innovativeness Rating System

French Transparency Commission (Commission de Transparence (CT)) made a determination of Januvia in comparison with the reference drug. Figure 10.10 shows the ASMR Innovativeness Rating System (see Chapter 21 for a detailed description of the French market access and price approval system, including ASMR).

The *Official Gazette* announced an ASMR of IV which, generally, translates to a comparable price of small price premium in comparison with the reference drug Actos (pioglitazone). When awarded a price, manufacturers have the option to either accept the price (and obtain full reimbursement), or set a higher uncontrolled price without reimbursement. In most cases a non-reimbursed option is not commercially viable, as patients are not used to paying themselves for pharmaceuticals.

Today, the new Medico-Economic requirements in France would not apply to our case, unless the company were to argue for an ASMR of III. With the awarded ASMR of IV, the analysis of that dossier would likely not have impacted the CEPT pricing decision.

Figure 10.11 illustrates the impact of drug reimbursement on market share. It provides obvious support to the statement that non-reimbursed launches in France are rarely commercially successful. Without needing a lot of detailed quantitative research, it is clear that in most cases the maximum achievable reimbursed price is the most attractive commercial option, particularly, since in France the actual price has no further impact on market share, that is French doctors are not price sensitive for reimbursed drugs.

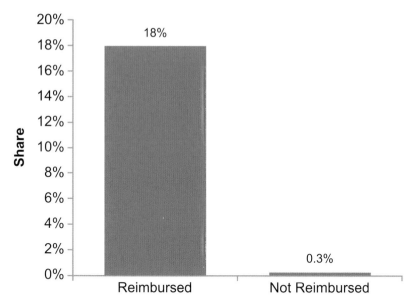

Figure 10.11   Impact of French reimbursement on prescribing

French price approval always goes together with a multi-annual contract, which includes a maximum sales volume and depending on the particular drug and situation, elements such as average dose or for example required length of therapy, thus contractually holding the drug company to key factors that impact cost to the department of health. Penalties of exceeding sales volume or another utilization metric are defined in the contract.

Through the contract, a French price approval is clearly linked to a therapeutic use of a drug. For our Januvia example, approval was clearly only granted for use after failure of single agent metformin therapy. Surely, if Merck wanted to pursue a first line use instead of the much cheaper metformin, and assuming that data would support that use, metformin would have been the treatment comparator and very compelling evidence versus metformin mono-therapy would have been required to gain a premium price.

Germany

For a number of high-cost therapy areas, the German government has introduced formal reimbursement classes with a reimbursement limit applying to all drugs in the class. The reimbursement limit is calculated through consideration of all compounds in the class, whether patent protected or multi-source. Any portion of a price that exceeds the reimbursement limit is to be paid by the patient out-of-pocket which, as in most European countries, is both unpopular and considered unnecessary.

Pricing for new drugs in Germany is driven by two key factors:

1. Does the new drug fit into any of the therapy areas of the existing ATC-based *reimbursement groups*? If we would introduce a new hypertension drug, it would likely be subject to the same reimbursement limit as the other branded and generic drugs in the class. The only way to create a commercially attractive launch proposition is to qualify for a separate reimbursement class. The German reference price system has somewhat clearly defined guidelines with respect to efficacy and/or side-effect improvements to qualify for separate classification.

2. Does the new drug offer benefits improvement over existing drug treatment options? Since the introduction of AMNOG, every new drug that is claimed to not fit an existing reimbursement group is evaluated by IQWiG and the G-BA on the additional benefits that it provides versus the existing standard of care. When a benefit is demonstrated, negotiations between the drug company and the Spitzenverband are held to finalize pricing. An in-depth description of the AMNOG procedure is found in Chapter 22.

The introduction of AMNOG has had a large impact on the gliptin drug category specifically. Trajenta, the fourth gliptin to enter the market, and the first in the category to qualify for an AMNOG assessment, was found to not bring additional benefits over generic metformin and sulfonylurea. Trajenta was subsequently withdrawn from the market. The case illustrates the importance of having Head-to-Head comparative trial data versus an appropriate comparator with meaningful end points.

Cost of treatment plays a role on physician prescribing at several levels:

a) Physicians have cost *"richtgrössen"* or guidelines that indicate how much they can prescribe annually by patient. Exceeding the cost guidelines can result in prescribing audits and ultimately financial penalties when a physician is found to excessively prescribe overly expensive drugs.

b)   Regional physician groups, holding drug budget responsibilities, increasingly issue guidelines and prescription quota for the use of branded drugs where generic equivalents are available.

A clear and compelling value proposition is essential in convincing physicians to prescribe a new drug. As a result of various cost-containment measures, German physicians have become much more cost conscious than most of their European counterparts. Physicians, who see a value in a new drug, will carefully consider whether the drug is needed for each patient, or only for those that do not qualify for other, cheaper treatment alternatives.

Besides an evaluation of pricing under AMNOG, it is very important to support a pricing strategy with detailed payer analysis and physician research. Physician acceptance of a drug's price in relation to its differentiation of treatment alternatives is crucial for a successful strategy. For our Januvia example, there has been no reason to expect a me-too classification for the drug at the time of launch. The clean side-effect profile of Januvia offered an alternative for the TZD category, of which particularly Avandia has been suffering from concerns about its side effects. At Januvia's price setting, with a similar daily cost to Actos and Avandia, physicians considered it an appropriate alternative for combination therapy where they would have considered TZDs. There are strong disincentives to displace metformin monotherapy.

If Januvia were launched today, it would likely struggle much more with gaining G-BA endorsement. As written above, Trajenta was ultimately withdrawn from the market over the AMNOG evaluation. It seems doubtful though, that G-BA would have rejected Januvia in the same way. We will never know. What is clear however is that the same issues that appeared in the Trajenta evaluation should be a more serious point of consideration in clinical trial design discussions in drug companies:

•   Definition and choice of proper trial population(s);

•   Representative background therapy;

- Head-to-Head superiority demonstration versus a meaningful comparator;

- Selection of end points that payers will endorse (usually long-term outcomes versus response rates or other surrogate end points).

Japan

As described in detail in Chapter 26, the Japanese drug approval system is very structured. For most drugs, therapeutic referencing is the foundation of an approved price, usually some moderate innovativeness premium over an existing reference drug. The reference drug is determined through a structured process, in which the following steps are performed to identify a most suitable candidate:

1.   Drug indication;

2.   Mechanism of action;

3.   Chemical structure.

Since the method is implemented under the strictest interpretation of the rules, it is important to evaluate impact of, for example, an additional or narrower indication.

Carefully evaluating options prior to finalization of the Phase III clinical trial program can have important price implications, as a resulting selection of a different price comparator may substantially change price without any impact on prescribing volume. For some rare cases, where a comparator is not easily assigned, a drug can be priced using the "Cost-Plus" method, which is actually much more favorable than any comparator.

HEALTH ECONOMICS-DRIVEN MARKETS

The three largest health economics-driven markets (UK, Canada, Australia), use very similar ways of reviewing cost-effectiveness for new drugs. In some cases the outcome can be different, as we will see in the Januvia discussion later in this section. In addition, each country has its own additional requirements, such as for example the UK has a PPRS profit control (see Chapter 25) and Canada has a PMPRB price control (see Chapter 20).

United Kingdom

In England and Wales, the National Institute for Health and Care Excellence (NICE) evaluates new and existing treatments with respect to effectiveness and cost-effectiveness, both as a class of drugs and (increasingly) as a single technology assessment. For Scotland, the Scottish Medicines Consortium (SMC), is doing the same. For many anti-cancer agents, NICE approval has been an insurmountable hurdle. Even drugs such as Gleevec, which has almost universally been lauded for its added clinical value for CML patients, were initially not deemed cost-effective under NICE rules and criteria. In 2009, NICE has softened its requirements for late-stage "end-of-life" treatments, however only for small patient populations (under about 3,000 patients). In the case of Januvia, NICE ruled that it was cost-effective as an add-on to metformin, resulting in a recommendation to add Januvia to PCT formularies. It is intuitively easy to understand that it makes sense to approve Januvia given its similar price and use in comparison to Actos and Avandia, and with its clean side effect profile.

The optimal price in England and Wales is likely to be the price that is endorsed by NICE as cost-effective. However in many cases, companies are not prepared to reduce prices in the UK to the required level, out of concerns for international price implications, such as parallel trade and international price referencing. This will be further discussed in Chapter 12.

Under Value-Based Pricing/Assessment discussions, the cost-effectiveness criteria are likely to be more flexible on the basis of societal factors. However that does not change the essence of the points made above.

Canada

Canadian drug prices are of great concern for most US-based global pharmaceutical companies. Since the days of compulsory licensing, drug prices in Canada have been artificially depressed to control cost of healthcare. As described in Chapter 20, Canadian market access and price approval involves a number of separate steps:

1.   PMPRB (Retrospective) Price Approval, verifying that patent is not "abused" by referencing price to range of prices of current therapy alternatives and international median price for a basket of countries;

2.   Common Drug Review (CDR) evaluation of effectiveness and cost-effectiveness;

3.   Provincial Formulary Approval, primarily based on CDR for most provinces (exception Quebec);

4.   Provincial Listing Agreements (PLAs) or pan-Canadian price agreement where an agreement is reached after CDR rejection on confidential terms.

PMPRB price reviews are problematic in that they severely limit the ability to charge premium prices for stepwise innovation, as price levels cannot exceed the existing range of prices within a therapeutic area. Exceptions to this rule are only granted to select drugs with a recognized high level of innovation, however very few compounds (one to two drugs per year) qualify for this designation.

Common Drug Reviews have been negative in more than 50 percent of the reviews since the inception of CDR. Januvia has also been rejected by CDR. As reasons for rejection, effectiveness data have been indicated, but a positive review would have been unlikely in any case due to patent expiration and related cost differences with generic TZDs.

Canadian prices have caused many issues in relation to its proximity to the United States. Many drug companies have a problem accepting a much lower Canadian price given the magnitude of the market of about 4 percent of the US market, and concerns over reimportation and other pharmacy-political issues related to price differences between the US and Canada.

EMERGING CASH MARKETS

Patient affordability is a major issue in marketing pharmaceutical products in emerging cash markets. Pharmaceuticals from multi-national pharmaceutical companies are usually only affordable for a small segment of the population in emerging cash markets, such as India, China and Mexico. In the recent past, many pharmaceutical companies were not prepared to differentiate in drug prices between markets because of fear of impact of international price differences on price referencing and parallel trade. This topic is discussed in detail in Chapter 12. In the last few years, particularly as pharmaceutical companies have come under increasing financial pressure and as focus on growth prospects of emerging markets has taken hold, pricing for emerging markets has gained increasing attention. Interestingly, both Merck and Novartis have decided to market their DPP4s, Januvia and Galvus, at prices in Mexico and Brazil below the prevailing TZD prices, thus stepping away from previous policies to not allow large price discrepancies versus the United States. As price differences with US and other developed markets don't dominate prices in Mexico and BRIC markets, optimization of the local business becomes more viable. Various techniques have been used in Latin American and Asian markets to discount price while maintaining a higher list price. This can help to selectively use discounts for patients who need it most and can be helpful in improving compliance through a well-designed patient discount card program. These programs can also be helpful in addressing concerns of cross-border trade with lower-cost product.

Expensive biotechnology products will continue to pose patient access issues in emerging markets. First, cost of manufacturing is very high for these products, thus offering only limited room to reduce price in addressing patient affordability issues. Second, lowering price for these drugs in emerging markets exposes pharmaceutical companies to potential criticism of high prices for these drugs in the United States, Europe and other developed markets.

Price elasticity of demand for a product such as Januvia can be tested in quantitative market research. In cash markets, pricing research needs to be focused on both physicians and patients. Ultimately, the price sensitivity of the patient will decide whether the patient will fill the prescription and be compliant. Depending on the severity of the condition and the treatment choices available, the physician may engage in a dialog with the patient or base his/her prescription decision on an expectation of patient willingness and ability to pay. It is important to carefully model the behavior of physicians, pharmacists and patients for the therapy area under consideration through qualitative research. Subsequently, we should determine optimal price and related product positioning through quantitative research. See Chapter 15 for a more detailed discussion of pricing research techniques.

In this Chapter ...

The BEST PRICE Framework is used to provide structure to market access and pricing analysis. The framework systematically examines Benefits, Evidence, value STory and subsequent PRICE determination within each of the global payer segments. For each segment we analyzed various country-specific examples to illustrate the relationship between demonstrated evidence of key benefits and the market access and price negotiation process.

11

Payer Value Story

In Chapter 10, we discussed how the Payer Value Story is used to rationally translate benefits and related evidence to the payer system requirements for Market Access and Pricing. In this chapter we will describe more in detail how we can effectively structure and communicate our payer value story for maximum impact in payer negotiations.

How do we convince a payer to make a Market Access or Pricing decision that is favorable to our strategic objectives? How do we make sure that our payer audience is

1. interested to even listen to, or read our proposal and claims;

2. sufficiently concerned about the clinical challenges in the disease area under consideration that provides the basis for the treatment solution that we will offer now or in the future;

3. inclined to have a positive mindset with respect to our specific offering, so that he/she is open to consider our claims and give us some benefit of the doubt where the supporting evidence is not perfect;

4. willing to engage in dialog and a practical deal to address or overcome any evidence gaps and other concerns that the payer may have, rather than outright reject our proposition over skepticism against a budget concern background?

The framework in this chapter will provide a structured solution to addressing the above questions, building on the BEST PRICE framework that was discussed in Chapter 10.

Value Dossier

Many companies are putting significant efforts in creating a Value Dossier. This dossier is intended to provide guidance to national and local teams on the value strategy that should be followed and provides the supporting data to strengthen the brand's claims and hopefully enable positive negotiation results. The American Academy of Managed Care Pharmacy (AMCP) has structured a proposed design of a new drug dossier for the purpose of Managed Care formulary review. The "AMCP Dossier" is very comprehensive in its inclusion of all relevant clinical and economic data. However it is also structured so as not to allow the manufacturer to "tell the story." As such, the AMCP dossier format is designed to minimize the probability of success in convincing a payer of added value of a new treatment. It ignores the fact that Managed Care management is able to critically judge the value of an offered innovation without imposed limitations on what can be submitted. The AMCP dossier format should, where possible, be ignored and at least not serve as our framework for value communication and company dossier structure. Certainly there are more suitable structures that allow us to tell the story and build the supporting arguments with clinical evidence.

So how can we make sure that we provide a compelling story and ensure that we have a willing audience to listen to us or read a dossier? Our TEMPLE Framework may be helpful in achieving that objective.

TEMPLE Framework

The TEMPLE Framework is based on the concept that we need to create both an early interest and a strong rationale for meaningful claims that our new drug brings to payers and other important players in the drug prescribing decision process. Most of us like to read a good book, but dread reading a poorly written, less than compelling "dossier." A benefits dossier for an AMNOG submission in Germany easily counts 30,000 pages, hardly a Stephen King novel. The mindset of anybody who starts to study a dossier is probably not one of great expectation and enthusiasm. Therefore, relying on a collection of unstructured information and data to instill payer enthusiasm is not a great strategy. Short of hitting a payer over the head, it is not easy to impress a payer with a 1,000+ pages dossier. Therefore we need to create a well-structured and credible story that ties into payer concerns and interests. Further, we need to use pre-payer marketing strategies to carefully prepare the audience for our ultimate claims and actual dossier for review. The TEMPLE Framework clearly distinguishes between branded messages that can only be communicated after FDA/EMA approval and unbranded messages that can be communicated much earlier. Starting the process early is important, since many of the improvement claims are dependent on a thorough understanding of the unmet needs and shortcomings of existing treatments.

Figure 11.1 shows the TEMPLE Framework for Payer Value Messaging and its components: Elevator Message, Pillar Messages and Detailed support messages and evidence. The philosophy is that the elevator message is to be a high-level succinct statement that creates interest and launches the claim. The pillars form the essential support to make the elevator claims "stand," considering the anticipated general understanding of the typical payer. Detailed messages create more robustness for each of the pillars to support the claims with scientific data.

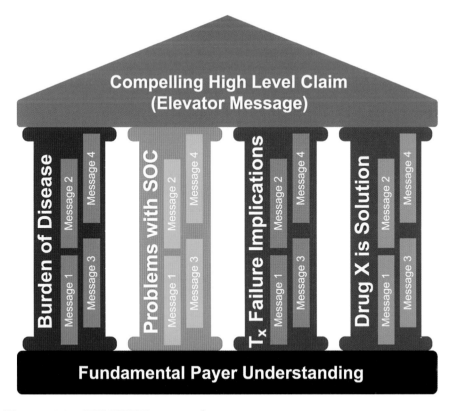

Figure 11.1   TEMPLE Framework

ELEVATOR MESSAGE

A brief and compelling "elevator message" style value proposition is essential to a good value story. The notion is that if you cannot raise interest in a brief statement, then a lengthy dossier will certainly not do it. The elevator message needs to communicate the essential claims of the drug that are of interest to the payer and that address an unmet need. We cannot expect that the message alone will be enough to sway a payer into a positive market access or pricing decision, but should rather peak their interest to hear or read the full story. The elevator message needs to be a reasonable high level summary of the claims made and supported in the pillar messages. Overstating a claim in an elevator message is a short lived victory.

Creating a strong elevator message is an iterative process. It is useful to consider from the start what the most compelling claims are, based on the benefits analysis, but it also makes sense to review after creating the more detailed pillars and supporting messages. At that stage we should consider whether we have really built a strong case or whether we have left compelling claims out.

Particularly in early stages of the story development, we should not get hung up on exact wording, but rather focus on having the most important elements in place. Engaging in wordsmithing too early can detract from considering the bigger picture. This is not just true for the elevator message, but for all elements of the payer value story.

PILLAR MESSAGES

It is unlikely that an elevator message in itself will create sufficient buy in from a payer to support a favorable decision. However that is also not the intent. A more realistic goal is to create genuine interest and/or get an endorsement that if a claim can be met, this would be a meaningful improvement, hence warranting a closer review of the dossier.

Payers are very different from treating physicians in their decision-making process and evidence requirements. A physician who hears 10 different messages related to a new drug, may be intrigued by one or two of them. If these messages are highly relevant for specific patients and if the physician has no other concerns, then he/she may try the new drug on appropriate patients. When successful he/she may expand usage to a broader set of patients. National and regional payers are much less likely to "try" new drugs. They expect a complete dossier that will enable them to make a balanced decision for price and/or reimbursement based on the evidence provided by the manufacturer and experience of consulting KOLs. Therefore a Payer Value Story and Dossier needs to provide a complete picture of the appropriate use of a new drug, not just an incentive to "try." Hospital payers have some more flexibility. When good reasons exist, they can organize a pilot program in a hospital and make a more formal formulary and treatment protocol decision later.

The TEMPLE Framework example in Figure 11.1 uses the following typical Pillar Message Topics:

1.   What is the Burden of the Disease?
     Why is this disease area one where I should be concerned about having effective treatment available to patients? What is the financial and human cost of suffering because of this condition? Is or should this be considered a public health priority?

2.   What are the Problems with the current Standard of Care?
     Why are the current drugs and other treatments not sufficiently effective or safe to provide an effective treatment to patients? Why should I consider new treatment options?

3.   What are the Implications of Treatment Failure?
     What are the health consequences of treatment failure with the current options available? How do these consequences impact patient (drug and medical) treatment and care requirements and cost?

4.   What solution does Product X provide?
     What is the impact of Product X on the treatment problems for the disease? How do clinical, humanistic, economic and public health benefits provide a favorable proposition to payers, their healthcare systems and the general public?

The four pillar messages provide the high-level flow of the payer value story in support of the elevator message. They bridge the gap between the foundational understanding of the payer and the elevator message that we are trying to support. There is no particular reason why there could not be three or five pillars, but four seems to generally work well to outline the high-level value story in logical steps. It is important to note that pillars 1, 2 and 3 are unbranded and therefore are to be communicated prior to launch (within certain legal constraints). This is very important, since building support for the recognition of an unmet need is a process that will take time; more time than may usually be available between market authorization and launch of our new drug. Pillar 4 is the branded message for which communication is commonly restricted to post-marketing approval timing.

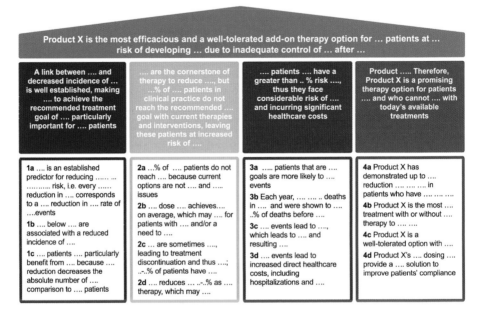

Figure 11.2   Example of a payer value story

Below each pillar we require more detailed messages and supporting evidence to make the story credible and address the obvious evidence requirements for each message and its sub-messages. Many of these messages may refer to substantial data packages. Despite the ultimate need for detail, it is important to thoroughly consider a simple format for the high-level messages. Dossier weight is a poor substitute for substance and unfortunately, many value dossiers ignore this important aspect. Of course a value dossier can only be as good as the asset value that it represents. Great innovations make creating a payer value story easier, but a poor value dossier can harm even the best drug innovation. An example of a payer value story with Elevator Messages, Pillar Messages and Sub-Messages is shown in Figure 11.2. Unfortunately, this real-life example had to be significantly blinded to honor client confidentiality, but the intent of the example is to show the structure of the payer value story, with a short elevator message, four pillar messages and usually three to six sub-messages for each pillar that link to the data and references.

KOL AND PHYSICIAN ENDORSEMENT

Probably the most important step towards gaining payer endorsement is to gain support from key opinion leaders (KOLs) in the field with respect to the medical necessity of the new treatment. KOLs will not be able to comment on cost issues, but they can influence payers by informing them of the importance of a new treatment, the impact on individual patients and the impact on patient prognosis of not allowing the treatment. In order to achieve this, it is crucial to work closely with KOLs to define data and other information needs to come to this conclusion.

Physicians are primarily interested in medical value. Price and cost usually only play a role in absence of reimbursement or at high patient co-pay, although medical societies such as ASCO and AHA have stated an intent to incorporate cost or "financial toxicity" as one of the perspectives in guideline development. In some markets, for example Germany, physicians have become more cost-sensitive as a result of practices in the healthcare system. German drug budgets of the 1990s have created a lot of anxiety among physicians because of the potential impact of over-prescribing on the physician's retirement benefit. Although only few, if any, cases exist where physicians have actually been penalized, the drug budgets (nowadays called "cost guidelines") and prescribing audits have been very effective in creating some cost-sensitivity among the physician community.

Absent of cost-driven guidelines or budget incentives, most physicians tend to want to prescribe the best treatment option for the patient, irrespective of cost. In the United States, increases in co-pays and co-insurance rates have altered the situation for some therapeutic areas. For Medicare Part D and Exchange plans, co-insurance rates of 33 or 50 percent are not unusual. Specifically drug categories with relatively close substitutes, such as gliptins in diabetes, have seen increases in substitutions as a result of patients' complaints, sometimes aided with pharmacists' suggestions. Specialty drugs have traditionally seen less substitution, but high co-insurance rates and the imminent emergence of biosimilars have created large incentives for substitution, particularly for TNF inhibitors, where multiple options are now available.

An important question to answer is related to patient selection. "What is the right patient for this new treatment?" "Given cost, should every patient within an indication be a candidate for the new treatment?" Often, a new treatment is crucial for a selection of patients (for example, treatment resistant), but not for others. Before banking on a KOL endorsement for "medically necessary" coverage of a new drug, one should carefully evaluate for which patients the support would stand under pressure from payers.

PAYER VIEWS ON THE VALUE STORY AND DOSSIER

What are payers looking for in a dossier? Payers, as holders of the budget, tend to resist new more expensive treatments, particularly when they don't see a strong push from the community. The natural stance for payers will frequently be: "Why would I pay more?" Some of the controlled payer systems, such as in France and Japan, link the approved price to a selected reference drug, with an awarded price premium based on the demonstrated innovation and patient benefits. Since the government regulators are also paying the bill, and are rewarded on the basis of their budget control results, innovativeness premiums tend to be hard to obtain unless compelling arguments are delivered. Hospital payers will often feel squeezed between capitated reimbursement rates and the value of an improved treatment. In that setting they likely demand to see an impact on their performance metric, such as for example re-hospitalization rates, since they impact US Medicare reimbursement.

Whether skeptical vis-à-vis a new drug treatment or not, payers normally follow an agreed-upon path for reviewing a drug. The review path is very consistent with the system's formalized ways of awarding market access and price. This is why it is important to address the fundamental elements of the approval process in each of the payer systems and the global payer segments that characterize them.

Figure 11.3 gives an overview of considerations and information needs by customer group in global payer segments and representative key countries. Payers universally make their decisions on the basis of unmet needs and either "value" versus a reference standard or cost-effectiveness. In any case, they have a mechanism to evaluate the value story in the context of existing treatment alternatives. Since reimbursement to patients and US patient co-pays are important to physicians, payers need to take reactions to their decisions by physicians and leading KOLs into consideration, as they will try to avoid controversial situations. There is no standard recipe towards assessing payer

Global Payer Segment Example	Comp. Ins. Based US	Therapeutic Reference Based France	Health Economics Driven UK	Emerging Cash Markets China
Payers	• Unmet Needs • Reference • Budget Impact	• Unmet Needs • Reference Innovativeness Rating – ASMR • Budget Impact	• Unmet Needs • Budget Impact • NICE: Cost-Effectiveness	• N/A
Physicians	• Value vs. SOC • Restrictions • Patient co-pay	• Value vs. SOC • Reimbursement	• Value vs. SOC Reimbursement	• Value vs. SOC • Patient • Affordability
Patients	• Value • Co-Pay	• Value • Reimbursement	• Value • Reimbursement	• Value • Affordability

Figure 11.3   Examples of prime customer perspectives in some markets

reactions to a value story and dossier. Past behaviors, examined through case studies can be helpful, but specific testing of the value story remains crucial. This is discussed later in this chapter.

HEALTH ECONOMIC DATA

Cost and budget impact is a prime concern for most new drugs or treatments. Particularly as healthcare cost has been rising rapidly in most countries, payers are struggling to find ways to fund broad access to healthcare at a reasonable cost. When considering cost, the payer may be interested in both the drug budget impact and an overall assessment on the treatment cost per patient. Many payers are responsible for management of a drug budget only. Particularly in many pricing and reimbursement controlled systems, drug budgets are managed as a silo, separate from other healthcare costs. P&R authorities are held responsible for controlling drug cost, regardless of the new therapies available or savings achieved in other healthcare sectors. Within the available budgets, they seek to negotiate access for compelling new treatments at the lowest cost and try to realize budget savings in competitive areas through voluntary or forced price concessions, discounts and rebates. New and innovative drug treatments can cause budget issues for drug budget holders, sometimes motivating them to delay negotiations and cost increases that are associated with reimbursement approval. Some healthcare systems have been notorious to do so in the past, resulting in European Union legislation to control pricing and reimbursement decision-making timelines. In most systems, payers feel compelled to provide access for truly innovative treatments and want to avoid access restrictions, both for reasons of PR and workload associated with tight access control (such as a prior authorization and its equivalent in international markets).

Assessing the budget impact for a new drug is a difficult task as it is strongly dependent on the actual utilization patterns and physician acceptance of the drug. A common payer concern is the use of an expensive drug for patients for which it is not deemed medically necessary. For these expensive drugs, payers are increasingly enforcing use restrictions on the basis of the formal clinical indications and evidence-based guidelines, as they feel that pharmaceutical companies are promoting the use of its drugs beyond the indications where it has demonstrated its core value. Most national payers feel that they have little control over use of a drug within its approved label. They are then faced with the choice of either finding a way to contractually link overutilization or "inappropriate use" (France) or relying on regional payers to impose additional control measures (Italy, Spain).

The health economics discipline provides a rational way of allocating limited resources across a high number of needs. Unfortunately, it has also been used as an easy way for payers to delay or deny access for lack of demonstrated economic rationale. The two most important ways in which health economic evaluations tend to be used for pricing purposes consider cost-minimization and cost-effectiveness. Each of these is discussed in depth in Chapter 5.

Strong evidence of cost-minimization should make the access decision for a new drug a no-brainer, provided that the drug has a benefit and that the negotiating payer has a perspective and budget authority that is in line with the cost perspective used in the cost-minimization analysis. To illustrate this, a hospital administrator will be interested to see cost savings due to shorter hospital stays (when not affecting reimbursement), whereas the Australian drug budget holder may be less swayed. Whether the evidence is strong is a natural point of contention. Payers tend to distrust any health economic data provided by drug manufacturers, contending that promised savings in the past have often not materialized. For this reason, many payers want to see claims supported with real-life (naturalistic) data rather than claims that are only supported with clinical trial data and economic models. The real dilemma is that at launch it is usually impossible to have meaningful real-life data as clinical programs need to adhere to strict protocols prior to market authorization. FDA and EMA don't tend to focus on a real-life data setting for regulatory evidence.

Cost-effectiveness measures are particularly useful for compelling health improvements that require additional spending. However not every healthcare system accepts cost-effectiveness as a formal evaluation instrument. Australia, Canada and the UK probably have the most established healthcare systems with respect to the use of cost-effectiveness measures as part of pricing and/or reimbursement approvals. In the UK, the National Institute for Care Excellence evaluates drugs and other treatments on cost-effectiveness and provides recommendations for treatment practices and healthcare coverage on that basis.

Depending on the individual healthcare system and depending on the particular clinical and economic benefits of a drug proposition, health economic data may be beneficial in improving willingness-to-pay. However this is not a given for every situation and a thorough evaluation is warranted before making any claims. Actually, the majority of healthcare systems has no way of assessing health economic data or chooses not to do so, because it is not consistent with its chosen approach towards pricing and reimbursement approval for prescription drugs. As shown in Chapter 8, only about 10 percent of global pharmaceutical sales take place in a system where market access decision-making is primarily driven by health economics.

More detailed discussions are found in Chapter 5: "Health Outcomes and Health Economics."

VALUE STORY TESTING

It is extremely important to thoroughly test a drug's value story. We must avoid making critical development and launch strategy decisions solely based on our perhaps rose-colored view of the world. Whether at a higher level, prior to Phase III clinical program decision making, or in all detail prior to launch, we need to ensure that the key points in our value claims are well in line with the KOL and payer customers' priorities and frame of mind.

In testing our value story and its high level and detailed messages, we need to consider the dynamic interactions between payers and their advising clinical KOLs. Therefore it is advisable to ensure that any value message can rely on the support of KOLs. Without a proper analysis of KOL input, we will be left with a distorted view on the acceptability or potential rejection of a message by payers.

A value message needs to be clear, relevant, credible and compelling/ unique in order to be effective in affecting someone's opinion. Let's consider each of these dimensions separately in detail.

Clear

How easily can the message be read and understood? If multiple readings are required to understand the message, it will lose most of its power. We don't need to show our literary strength to impress the reader. Keep sentences short. There is no shame in our children understanding the messages.

Relevant

Is the message content important for drug pricing or reimbursement decision making? Would our audience care about this point? Does it concern their responsibility?

Credible

Is the claim credible or can it be easily rejected? Is it likely in line with the customer perspective and logic? Are there any flaws in the reasoning or is it "water tight"?

Compelling/Unique

How convincing is the argument? Will it strongly support the decision at hand? For branded messages: Is it unique and differentiating versus existing and other emerging treatment options?

When carefully implementing these four dimensions in structuring our value messages, we should be able to prepare the most compelling argument possible, of course within the constraints of the available evidence package. Clever messaging cannot be a substitute for appropriate and convincing clinical and health outcomes data. It merely provides an opening for the data to make its way for serious consideration in the process and to help overcome initial emotional objections towards a new proposition.

Actual testing of a payer value story and its messages can be done in various ways. Interviews with payers and KOLs can be extremely useful, particularly in exploring receptivity to elements of a value story. It is important for the final high-level version to be tested in a mixed audience of payers and KOLs. When not exposed to KOL opinion, payers may act differently from a real-life formulary review process. Therefore we need to ensure that we test story and messages for KOL acceptability and endorsement. Where the dialog between KOLs and payers is expected to be critical for the final evaluation, a mixed payer/KOL advisory board is often useful.

Payer/KOL research or advisory boards should ideally be organized by global payer segment, that is one for the US Managed Care, one for therapeutic referencing markets and one for health economics-driven markets. In reality it is difficult to entice payers from, for example, the UK, Canada and Australia, to meet for an adboard meeting. Having adboards for each individual country is usually cost-prohibitive as well during drug development. Frequently one US and one EU-5 adboard is the most pragmatic alternative, but it is important to consider differences between the review criteria and approval systems in the valuation of the results. Separate evaluations may be useful to address the acceptance of health economic arguments and models with health economists in markets where this is critical.

OBJECTION HANDLING

Objection handling is an important component of payer value story development. It is extremely important to be well prepared for a wide range of objections. With a good understanding of payers, we can anticipate most if not all of the objections and be well prepared for them. If recognized early enough in the process, we can still try to further strengthen our objection handling with additional data analyses or even some targeted trials prior to launch.

In some cases it makes sense to consciously address an issue through objection handling rather than in the actual value story. This is for example the case when this is not of importance for every payer. To illustrate this, we may have a comparator in our trials that is not the standard of care in each country. For some countries this is obviously not a challenge, for others we have to use the objection handler. Similarly, budget impact and cost-effectiveness will be different across countries, potentially resulting in different outcomes with respect to economic claims.

Whether to address some obvious objections immediately in the value story or to tackle them in the objection handling is often a part of strategy and to some extent preference. "Give a payer something to shoot at" may be an approach that can work, but by leaving a weakness in the general story we may be risking an opportunity to get it right from the start. Most payers are very structured in their analysis, so trickery like this, with the intent of leaving other weaknesses uncovered, is not likely to work with many payers. A better reason to leave it somewhat open may be that it is simply not feasible to address this in the general value story and the objection requires a thorough evaluation in each case, for example with specific analysis of the environment of the specific payer questioning.

HOW DO WE USE THE VALUE STORY?

The payer value story is not just intended to be a document that is shipped to a payer. Rather it should be a much broader guidance to all pre-launch and peri-launch communications to payers and their influencers in each market. To illustrate the point, here are some examples on how the value story can be used:

- For a Pre-Phase III version of the payer value story: Help guide the design of the Phase III clinical and health outcomes trials, including patient inclusion/exclusion criteria, background therapy, trial comparator(s), primary and secondary end points, superiority (or non-inferiority) claims, length of patient follow-up, economic and other supplemental data gathered.

- Strategic guidance for the development of a Value Dossier and subsequent local P&R submission documents.

- Identify key medical facts and opinions that need to be supported by KOLs and directly or indirectly communicated to payers through articles, consultations, consensus meetings or other.

- Initiate additional data gathering work through clinical data searches, data registries, clinical trials, etc.

- Educate and train company staff to ensure preparation of the appropriate marketing and selling materials.

- Work with local country affiliates to "translate" the story and messages to the local environment and approval requirements and identify any specific local gaps to address.

- Prepare and execute regional or local mock negotiations sessions to validate the approach, test specific messages in a real-life situation and practice objection handling.

The above list is intended to be illustrative rather than all-inclusive. It is hopefully apparent that the payer value story is a very powerful and important aspect of the preparation of a drug asset for commercialization success.

VALUE DOSSIER CONTENT AND STRUCTURE

There is not a single correct way to structure a value dossier. Earlier in this chapter, we discussed the AMCP dossier format and its less than ideal structure to convey our value story. However, in many cases we cannot choose the format of our submission. In those cases it is important to consider other additional means of communicating our messages to our target customers, such as: press announcements, investor-focused communications, medical congress events, KOL discussions, peer-reviewed articles, etc.

A way of logically structuring a dossier that communicates the value story and provides supporting evidence is included below:

Executive summary

High-level value story and overview of dossier content.

Burden of disease

Medical and economic consequences of the condition, including direct and indirect medical cost and broader societal cost. Most payers will want to see direct medical expenses separated from indirect and broader societal cost.

Tax Practices and unmet needs

Prevailing treatment practices, shortcomings in current treatment alternatives and medical and economic consequences of shortcomings in current treatments.

Value proposition and improvement claims

Concise value proposition, that is elevator message with key improvement claims and supporting statements.

Clinical and health outcomes data

Complete overview of clinical and health outcomes data, logically structured to support value proposition and claims.

Health economics data and models

Budget impact models and cost-effectiveness models, as required to support value proposition and related claims. Data in this module should be entirely driven by payer-segment-based evidence needs.

Objection handling

Summary of most likely questions and objections to the value story and its related claims. Concisely formulated responses to each question.

Appendix

Detailed overview of all the available data and references clearly linked to the earlier dossier components where the data is referenced.

In this Chapter ...

The TEMPLE Framework is used to develop an easy to understand and compelling payer value story for our drug. We discussed elevator message, pillar messages and detailed supporting messages and data as the components of our value story, as well as testing the story to be clear, relevant, credible and compelling/unique. Lastly, we discussed how to use the value story, handle objections and how to structure a value dossier.

PART C
Developing an Integrated Global Strategy

12

Developing a Global Pricing Strategy

In this chapter we will look at pricing strategies from a global perspective. We will evaluate the need for a global strategy and discuss, step by step, how we should go about defining the right strategy for the drug's global business opportunity. Global drug pricing is complicated due to international referencing, trade issues and political sensitivity with respect to price differences between countries.

Objective of a Global Pricing Strategy

Why do we need a global pricing strategy? Why not let each country optimize its business opportunity and decide on a pricing strategy that best supports that? There are two somewhat related good reasons to maintain a fairly strict global pricing strategy:

1. *A global pricing strategy will consistently support the global marketing strategy and other supporting medical and operational strategies.*

   A consistent global marketing strategy with strategic product positioning and supporting claims and messages is important for commercial success. Opportunistic local pricing strategies that are inconsistent with the global strategy can form a risk of confusing an increasingly global customer base. Also, by nature these local strategies can only gain sub-optimal support from HQ functions and, as a result, are less likely to be successful.

2.   *Prices between countries and over a drug's life cycle need to be closely
      managed in order to avoid a negative impact on company profits.*

      As explained in Chapter 1, international price differences can have
      a major impact on local pricing through product diversion/trade,
      international price referencing and pharmaco-political issues.

In formulating a global pricing strategy we need to trade-off between the
importance of having the optimal local price and avoiding global cascading
from lower-priced markets to higher-priced ones through a kind of price
domino effect. Consider the example shown in Figure 12.1. Optimal local prices,
derived from detailed local analyses and pricing research, vary dramatically
from country to country. The optimal price is much higher for the United States
than for other countries. Canadian and European prices are much lower and
also within Europe there are substantial price differences. Asia has the lowest
optimal prices from the set of markets considered in this example. In this
example the Japanese price is relatively high.

Only larger countries are indicated in Figure 12.1. However, these markets
probably constitute over 95 percent of the global market.

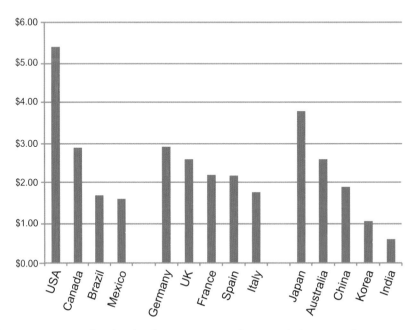

Figure 12.1   Optimal price by country: a characteristic example

Economic theory tells us that profits would be maximized when we price at the optimal price level in each country. There is one caveat: each market must be totally separated. In reality, separation of markets is not even nearly true. We will discuss this more extensively in the next section of this chapter. As a consequence of our inability to separate markets, we need to find a compromise between the need to locally optimize price and the avoidance of international price cascading. As graphically illustrated in Figure 12.2, price cascading initially occurs on a regional basis; however global effects take place as well, for example for Canada and Japan.

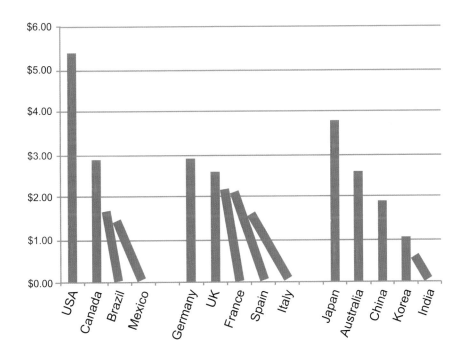

Figure 12.2 **Price cascading due to international referencing and trade**

Impact of Price Cascading on Profits

Estimating the actual impact of price cascading on profitability is not always an easy task. In some cases, price referencing mechanisms are easy to predict, but in other cases, where it involves softer references and trade, it is harder to predict and it becomes a judgment call whether the risk is acceptable to the corporation. To illustrate the impact of international price differences, let's consider a simple example.

Today, prices in the United States are only occasionally impacted by Canada. In some cases, however, companies may have decided to not allow an optimal Canadian price level out of concern for political problems in the United States or even an expectation of reimportation in a not too distant future. Figure 12.3 shows how in the two-country world of the US and Canada we would need to trade-off between local optimal price setting and avoidance of price cascading. The orange line shows a price–profit relationship for the United States. For the purpose of this example, consider that this profit curve has been appropriately obtained through a robust market research program. The optimal US price would be close to $160. In Canada, if we could price freely, the optimum price would be about $75 (blue line) in this example. The red line is simply the sum

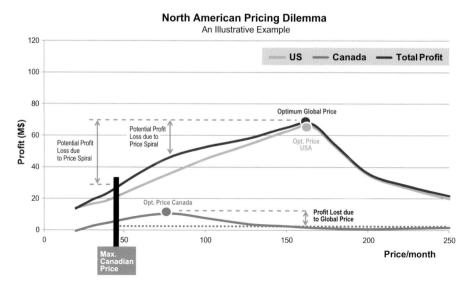

Figure 12.3   Simplified example of global pricing trade-offs

of the US and Canadian profit opportunities with a maximum which is just below the optimal US price point.

Now consider the ideal situation, where we are not concerned about price differences and market our drug in each market at its optimal price. Total profit would be about $79 million ($67 million in the US and $12 million in Canada). Let's consider two cases:

1. We are very concerned about price differences and decide to set one global price, that is $160 per month. US profits remain almost the same, but Canadian profits drop from $12 million to about $2 million. Global profits have dropped by $10 million to $69 million.

2. What happens if we launch at each market's optimal price, but by some mechanism, US price slides down to the Canadian level. Between the US and Canada this, today, would be a far-fetched scenario. However if it does happen, US profits slide by about $20 million, bringing total profits to $59 million.

In this simple example, our belief of the danger of Canadian pricing impacting the US should drive the decision of either one of the two options or a compromise option in between. Choices between the options constitute a certain $10 million profit reduction at one global price versus a risk of a $20 million profit reduction if and when the US price would be forced down.

The existence of price controls in Canada actually makes the situation worse. In many cases, a company is not free to set its price at the optimal price point due to interference of the PMPRB (see Chapter 20). This results in a price which is even below the $75, for example $45, as illustrated in Figure 12.3. It can easily be seen that a forced price decline in the US to Canadian price levels would now have an even more dramatic impact on profits, actually about $40 million. Today, these examples seem very far-fetched. Any threat of price reductions in the US due to lower Canadian prices would probably result in immediate withdrawal from the Canadian market. However these kinds of trade-offs have been very real in the rest of the world. In Europe, prices have been impacted by international prices for many years. In Japan, the price of the same drug in the US, France, Germany or the UK may have a bigger impact than the value story-based innovativeness premium.

The US–Canada example illustrates the importance of considering international price differences as part of global pricing strategy decision making. In the real world, larger than just the US and Canada, it becomes even more obvious.

Global Strategy Development

Establishing the optimal global pricing strategy involves five key steps:

1. Identify *locally optimal price in each key strategic market*, optimizing profitability for each local organization without any consideration for international pricing mechanisms and issues;

2. Analyze the potential impact of *price referencing and international trade* on the global pricing strategy;

3. Evaluate *pharmaco-political concerns* and its impact on the strategy;

4. Identify *global strategy options*, reflecting the need to compromise between the impact of international pricing mechanisms and local profit maximization;

5. *Select the optimal solution*, given analysis with respect to options and corporate preferences.

LOCALLY OPTIMAL PRICE

The evaluation of local pricing in each country is discussed in detail in Chapter 10. Let's assume that as a result of this evaluation, we have determined a rationale for a pricing strategy in terms of a price relative to an appropriate comparator, and an actual price in local currency. For our Januvia example that may have been a price relative to Actos or Avandia.

Figure 12.4 shows some illustrative examples of the global picture including the most significant global pharmaceutical markets. On the left side is a typical drug representing a stepwise innovation. In those cases, local pricing is typically strictly bound by existing drugs in the same category. As a result, large differences in price between countries have to be accepted in order to enable launch. On the right side of Figure 12.4 is an example of a more innovative drug, which to some extent can set a new price reference on the basis of its inherent value and is less limited by historical evolution of existing price levels.

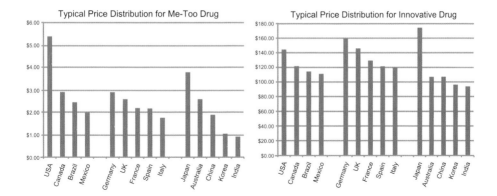

Figure 12.4   Typical examples of locally optimal prices

IMPACT OF INTERNATIONAL PRICE REFERENCING

A key aspect of determining the optimal global pricing strategy is the evaluation of the impact of international price referencing and parallel trade. Both mechanisms result in reductions of profits and a downward cascading of price, although in somewhat different ways. Most price referencing mechanisms are very simple and its results are easy to predict, as the method of calculation is always clearly defined. The most common methods of reference calculations are:

- Lowest price from a basket of countries;

- Average price from a basket of countries;

- Median price from a basket of countries.

Calculations of lowest and average prices are usually straightforward, but it is important to know how each price level is defined. Usually an official list price, such as the "Vidal" for France and the "Rote Liste" for Germany is used, but not every reference system will necessarily make the same choice. It is also important to know what is done when a certain presentation or strength is not available in one market; this is always clearly defined.

The Canadian PMPRB uses the median price of France, Germany, Italy, Sweden, Switzerland, the UK and the United States as a reference. The median price is calculated by ranking specified price levels in each country from low to high and selecting the middle value.

Many other international price reference systems are some variation on the basic ones shown above. For example, Japan's Foreign Price Adjustment (FPA) uses the average of prices in the US, France, Germany and the UK in a complicated formula with the local reference price to arrive at a price. The complexity in international price referencing is not in each individual country's evaluation, but in the large number of countries that have these rules in place. Figure 12.5 shows today's network of international reference price connections. Every line represents a country that compares its price to another country, usually as a part of a basket of countries. Many countries are referencing each other as part of their basket, so that launch sequencing becomes an important strategic factor in a global strategy. Let's discuss a simplified example to illustrate the way in which international price referencing should impact our decision making.

Imagine we are preparing for launch of a very innovative drug "CureAll" in the United States, Canada, Japan, France, Germany, Italy, Sweden and Switzerland. To not overcomplicate this case, let's exclude all other markets from consideration for now. Table 12.1 gives an overview for each of the countries of the expected commercial results in post-launch.

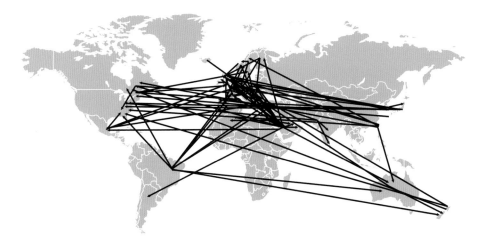

Figure 12.5   Global price referencing network

Table 12.1   Case Study: Optimal local price without international referencing

Year 5 Revenue in US $ (Millions)								
Price per 100 mg Tablet	$3.00	$4.00	$5.00	$6.00	$7.00	$8.00	$9.00	Locally Optimal Price
US	230	300	370	430	480	510	525	525
Canada	25	30	35	36	38	39	12	39
Japan	84	110	135	0	0	0	0	135
France	30	40	50	60	3	3	3	60
Germany	42	55	70	75	0	0	0	75
Italy	25	30	37	44	0	0	0	44
Sweden	13	15	18	21	7	6	5	21
Switzerland	7	10	12	13	14	13	10	14
UK	30	40	49	32	27	21	12	49
Total	486	630	776	711	570	593	568	962

Normally, we would do a more complete forecast and Net Present Value comparison, but for the purpose of this example let's consider Year 5 sales revenue as a proxy for that. Revenues at optimal prices at each individual country in isolation are indicated in red in the table. The optimal prices by country are just illustrative and can be very different for each situation. No revenue is booked at prices above what is assumed as the maximum approved price. US prices are optimal at the highest level that the company felt comfortable with ($9.00) for generally policy reasons. Japan has poor pricing due to a very low cost comparator due to a poor choice of indication many years ago. Other prices range from $5.00 to $8.00 based on research-supported evaluations. If every country were able to launch at its optimal price, total revenue would be $962 million. Please note that if the company were to decide on a single global price, total revenue would be substantially less at $776 million.

How can international price referencing change this picture? Within Europe, the low UK price will likely cause some problems in other European countries; either through international referencing or parallel trade (see next section in this chapter). In the example we are assuming that the low UK price will negatively impact negotiations in France, Germany and Italy where prices will drop to $5.00. The risk for Sweden and Switzerland has been assumed to be lower and no price cut is projected.

Canada is referencing price to France, Germany, Italy, Sweden, Switzerland, the United Kingdom and the United States by maximizing the Canadian price to the median of the reference country prices (see Chapter 20). For the US the Federal Supply Schedule price is used for referencing. In our example, the median price would be $6.00, which implies that in Canada we cannot launch at the projected $8.00 per day. In our example there is little downside for Canadian revenue, probably because some provincial formularies are already reacting to a high price. In reality there may be some upside, depending on exact launch timing in Canada in comparison with the other higher-priced countries from their reference country list. The lower Canadian price does have implications for the price differences between the US and Canada, which can become a sensitive issue in the US.

Japanese calculations are a bit more complicated. See Chapter 26 for a detailed discussion on Japanese Foreign Price Adjustment (FPA) rules. The internally calculated price, based on comparator choice and innovation premium expected is $5.00 in this example. Since the average price for US, France, Germany and UK is $6.50, we do not qualify for the FPA. We would only qualify for FPA if the average foreign price were $6.67 or higher (internally calculated price must be equal or less than 75 percent of the average foreign price). Therefore after price referencing our business picture looks like that illustrated in Table 12.2.

Table 12.2   Case Study: Prices adjusted with international referencing

Year 5 Revenue in US $ (Millions)								
Price per 100 mg Tablet	$3.00	$4.00	$5.00	$6.00	$7.00	$8.00	$9.00	Locally Optimal Price
US	230	300	370	430	480	510	525	525
Canada	25	30	35	36	0	0	0	36
Japan	84	110	135	0	0	0	0	135
France	30	40	50	3	3	3	3	50
Germany	42	55	70	0	0	0	0	70
Italy	25	30	37	1	1	1	1	37
Sweden	13	15	18	21	7	6	5	21
Switzerland	7	10	12	13	14	13	10	14
UK	30	40	49	32	27	21	12	49
Total	486	630	776	536	532	554	556	937

Our total business declined by $25 million due to price referencing in Canada (due to its basket of countries), as well as in France, Germany and Italy (due to the UK). The result is just illustrative; every situation will be different.

What else could we have done to optimize our business case?

1.   Could we have avoided price referencing in France, Italy and Germany by increasing price in the UK or by delaying launch in the UK?
      Probably yes. Without the lower price of $5.00 in the UK, we would have avoided the price reduction in these other EU markets. However, we would also have lost revenue in the UK due to presumably a negative NICE advice. In this case the UK loss of launching at $6.00 instead of $5.00 is $17 million and may have been worthwhile. Launch sequencing would have helped in Germany and, at least in the short run, in France and Italy. If we could have negotiated a patient access scheme in the UK (see Chapter 18), thus maintaining a high list price, that would have helped even more.

2.   Could we change the situation in Japan so that we qualify for the FPA?
      Yes we could. By increasing price in the UK to $6.00 (which hurts the UK business) we can achieve an average international price of $6.75, which brings the Japanese affiliate in the range where it qualifies for FPA. The impact on Japanese price would be marginal however. If we increase the UK price further to $8.00 and launch in France and Germany after Japan, we could even increase our Japanese price to $5.92 (I rounded to $6.00 in the analysis).

Table 12.3 shows how our case would change as a result of our adjusted strategy. Total revenues increase from $937 million to $967 million, a gain of $30 million due to avoidance of price reductions in France, Germany and Italy, as well as a higher price in Japan. This is just an example to illustrate the mechanics. It is obviously a tough decision to price higher in the UK and forego the opportunity there. It may be obvious that it requires a global perspective to make a rational decision. For every situation the result can be different. In many cases Japanese prices are higher, in which case another dynamic will influence decision making.

Table 12.3   **Case Study: Prices adjusted with international referencing; UK price increased to qualify for FPA in Japan**

Price per 100 mg Tablet	$3.00	$4.00	$5.00	$6.00	$7.00	$8.00	$9.00	Globally Optimal Price
US	230	300	370	430	480	510	525	525
Canada	25	30	35	36	0	0	0	36
Japan	84	110	135	160	0	0	0	160
France	30	40	50	60	3	3	3	60
Germany	42	55	70	75	0	0	0	75
Italy	25	30	37	44	1	1	1	44
Sweden	13	15	18	21	7	6	5	21
Switzerland	7	10	12	13	14	13	10	14
UK	30	40	49	32	27	21	12	32
Total	486	630	776	871	532	554	556	967

Year 5 Revenue in US $ (Millions)

Modeling of the impact of international price referencing is very useful in evaluating a global pricing strategy. It usually makes most sense to do so in conjunction with the evaluation of parallel trade or potential re-importation in the US, which is discussed in the next section.

INTERNATIONAL TRADE

There are many forms of international trade for drugs. The most important ones for us to consider are parallel trade and re-importation, which are different titles for what is essentially the same thing, a legal trade between countries of a product.

DEFINITION: PARALLEL TRADE

Parallel trade is the practice to engage in import and export of prescription drugs on a wholesale level between countries for which this is authorized. Parallel trade is engaged in to take advantage of arbitrage opportunities created though international price differences between countries.

In Europe the term parallel trade is used. The term parallel is intended to express that it is a trade that is parallel to the pharmaceutical company's distribution to each of its country affiliates. It is an extensive practice for drugs in Europe, but also for other products, such as cars. Re-importation suggests that it is US-manufactured product that is exported to a lower-priced country and then "re-imported" to the US channels. The term is very misleading, since it suggests that only US-manufactured drugs are involved. At the time of publication of this book, US re-importation was generally not legal. In discussions on the topic, parallel trade and re-importation represent the same identical practice. Other forms of international trade in drugs that are commonly occurring are:

- International mail order, usually for personal use;

- Drug importation of limited quantities for personal use;

- Product diversion, that is organized illegal international trade between countries.

Mail order trade has become very common, particularly for life-style drugs that are not covered by insurance. In the United States, mail order and personal imports were very common practice in the past, as the elderly did not have drug coverage for self-administered (for example oral) prescription drugs. Much publicized bus tours to Canada, allowing senior citizens to buy expensive drugs at much lower prices across the border have been used to create a lot of tension on US drug pricing. Medicare reform and the related introduction of Medicare Part D have provided partial coverage of drugs for seniors, thus taking incentives away to import discounted drugs that don't qualify for coverage. Since the introduction of Medicare Part D, mail order and personal imports of non-life-style drugs have fallen to very low levels.

The European parallel trade case study provides more background on the historical development of parallel trade in Europe. It is interesting to consider the European events over time in light of the developments in the United States. A large number of bills have been passed in both the US Senate and House of Representatives in support of re-importation of prescription drugs. In most initiatives, source countries for re-importation are all US FDA-approved regulatory regimes, including all EU markets, Canada, Japan, Australia, and New Zealand. So far, implementation of these laws has been held up over safety concerns regarding imported drugs. This is not so much

CASE STUDY: PARALLEL TRADE IN EUROPE

Parallel trade has been a common practice in Europe for many years. Whether it has brought any benefits to patients is a much contested issue. Answers to that question are different depending on the personal interest of the one who gives the answer. Parallel import companies and governments argue that they have been able to bring lower prices to patients and thus have added value. However fundamentally, the act of arbitrage does not bring any value beyond the enrichment of the parallel import companies. Monies that could otherwise have benefited clinical research for new treatments are now re-directed to companies that do not spend a single penny to that purpose. Creating arbitrage to punish companies for overcharging in one market seems reasonable on the surface, but certainly not so when government controls are causing the arbitrage opportunity in the first place. European bureaucracy has certainly played a dubious role as it enforced its dogmatic free trade principle, which is intended to stimulate a European "market", in a situation where individual monosponistic government purchasers are preventing this market from existing.

Since the introduction of parallel trade in the 1970s, additional EU laws have been enacted to block attempts to discourage trade, such as differences in trade names, formulations, strengths and so on.

The role of the European Medicines Agency (EMA) as a central European regulatory authority has further synchronized European drugs and enabled parallel trade. In addition, parallel trade companies have been legally enabled to re-package drugs in a local language pack with the originator's brand name on it and the approved local package insert. To engage in parallel trade, a license needs to be granted by regulatory authorities. The process is relatively simple and fast.

Preventing parallel trade is illegal under EU law. In a landmark case in January 1996, Bayer was found in violation of EU Article 81(1) and fined €3 million. The Bayer case concerned the question whether Bayer had engaged in agreements with distributors to limit trade for its product Adalat after Spanish and French health authorities set Adalat price at 40 percent below the UK price and significant parallel trade developed. Bayer refused to meet the rapidly increasingly supply from Spain and France and limited supply to a 10 percent annual growth rate over previous years. In October 2000 the Court of First Instance reversed the EU ruling against Bayer. The European Court of Justice (ECJ) dismissed an appeal by the European Commission and others in January 2004. Subsequent cases involving GSK in Spain and Greece have further served to clarify the ability of drug companies to limit supply to wholesalers in countries beyond what they deem reasonable supplies for local use. In Spain, GSK introduced a policy, where product to be exported from Spain was sold at a higher price, and limited supply to the local Spanish market at the government approved price.

The challenge with this practice is to estimate what the requirements for local use are. Also, how can you avoid the situation where a wholesaler uses product for parallel export purposes anyhow, thus preventing necessary drugs from reaching the local market. Supply restrictions have been used as a tool to manage the impact of parallel trade by many companies. The practice continues to be under legal challenge, but so far it continues to have support from the highest courts.

In Greece, GSK stopped supplying its Greek wholesalers with its products because the wholesalers exported a substantial proportion of GSK's products to other, higher-priced Member States. GSK alleged that the export of its products by the wholesalers was leading to significant shortages on the Greek market.

Eventually, the European Court of Justice (ECJ) ruled that non-dominant companies can unilaterally limit the supply of their products to wholesalers within a Member State in order to prevent them from exporting the goods to another Member State, provided this policy does not become part of the agreement with the wholesaler.

related to concerns over quality standards of drugs in these countries, but more to a potential lack of control over counterfeit drugs seeping into the system undetected. Counterfeit drugs have been a major concern, particularly since the large number of scandals over tainted foods and toys from China. Whether or not re-importation will be introduced in the United States is a hard question to answer. The introduction of Medicare Part D has abated the pressure on political action to address international price differences for drugs, particularly with Canada. However, we learn from history that without resolution of the underlying issue, the issue will continue to surface.

Estimating the impact of parallel trade is a fairly complicated task, much more complicated than assessing the impact of price referencing. Parallel trade has two types of impact on the business:

1.   Impact on price, as companies may reduce price in higher-priced markets to limit the flow of parallel trade product. Avoiding parallel trade by setting a lower price at launch is likely to be more effective than attempts to stem the flow after registration of parallel imported product has been granted and actual trade is occurring.

2.   Actual impact of parallel trade on local sales, as well as regional and global profit. Loss in profitability is related to the loss in actual price charged between the destination and source countries, which is the margin that is gained by the arbitraging parallel trade company.

The impact of both effects of parallel trade is hard to separate as they are in a clear trade-off with respect to each other. Let's examine each of the effects separately in detail first.

Impact of parallel trade on price

To illustrate the impact of parallel trade on price, let's analyze an example. Figure 12.6 shows a hypothetical example of a trade-off between local market potential and the impact of parallel trade.

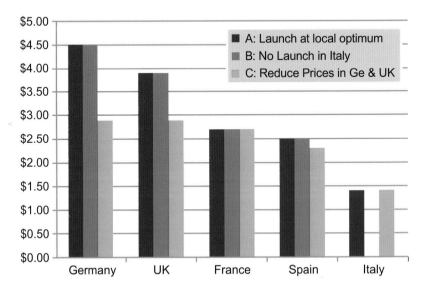

Figure 12.6   Example of EU-5 pricing strategy options

The figure illustrates three of many options to handle the impact of parallel trade.

a)   Launch in each market at the local optimum price. We can take advantage of the sales potential in every market at local willingness-to-pay or the highest feasible price under government control. Parallel trade is very likely to impact the market in the UK, where parallel trade is very common, and potentially Germany.

b)   Withholding launch in Italy, thus cutting off potential for low-cost supply to the higher-price markets in the EU. In reality this option can be the result of a stalled negotiation on price in Italy, as the company may decide to turn down any price below the anticipated or realized Spanish level.

c)   Launching at lower than optimal prices in Germany and the UK, whereby reducing the incentive for parallel trade. To avoid parallel trade in the EU, a price difference will generally have to be reduced to a 5–15 percent level, depending on sales level, countries involved, unit price level and ease of shipment.

We can identify the most attractive option to pursue through a close analysis of the options. Table 12.4 shows a typical analysis of the impact of the options as described above on the business in the EU-5 markets.

Table 12.4   Evaluation of options related to parallel trade avoidance

	Peak Sales Potential	Optimal Price	Price to Avoid Trade	Sales for Option A	Sales at Option B	Sales for Option C w/o Upside	Sales for Option C with Upside
Germany	250	4.5	2.9	188	250	161	193
UK	170	3.9	2.9	128	170	126	139
France	240	2.7	2.7	240	240	240	240
Spain	160	2.5	2.5	160	160	160	160
Italy	180	1.4	1.4	215	0	180	180
Total	1000			930	820	868	912

Total peak sales revenue for the EU-5 markets is estimated at $1 billion. This total sales potential is only theoretically achievable and not a choice in this situation. The realistic choices are options A, B and C. The impact of the three options has been estimated in an approximate way to illustrate the trade-offs.

- *Option A*

  Rough assumptions for parallel trade lead to reductions in sales for Germany and the UK. Incremental sales occur in Italy, although at a lower revenue per unit, reflecting a lower Italian price. Total peak sales under option A is $930 million, a $70 million loss in comparison with our theoretical benchmark.

- *Option B*

  Withholding an Italian launch has a large impact on total EU-5 revenues. Given the size of the Italian market in this example, it may not be surprising that this option is not very attractive at a total peak sales revenue of $820 million.

- *Option C*

  Reducing price in Germany and the UK will reduce the incentive for parallel trade, but will as a consequence reduce revenues in these countries. To accurately evaluate this option, we need to know the impact of price on product uptake in the UK and Germany (price-elasticity of demand data). Without any additional drug uptake, total revenue under option C is $868 million. Under arbitrary and merely illustrative assumptions, some additional upside is assumed in this example to increase sales to $912 million.

The example and illustrative estimates of resulting sales revenues in Table 12.4 show some of the key factors that drive decision making. In this case, the Italian market is too large to omit. Assumed parallel trade levels are fairly modest, in this example at 25 percent of sales, given the large price differential. The ability and willingness to control supply to Italian wholesalers will further influence decision making.

In Table 12.5, the impact is shown of a much smaller Italian (or other) market on the results of the analysis. In this case, the rational course of action is to not launch our drug in Italy, as its negative impact on other markets is larger than the benefit of launch.

Table 12.5   Slightly modified parallel trade case with smaller Italian market

	Peak Sales Potential	Optimal Price	Price to Avoid Trade	Sales for Option A	Sales at Option B	Sales for Option C w/o Upside	Sales for Option C with Upside
Germany	300	4.5	2.9	225	300	193	232
UK	250	3.9	2.9	188	250	186	204
France	220	2.7	2.7	220	220	220	220
Spain	160	2.5	2.5	160	160	160	160
Italy	70	1.4	1.4	116	0	70	70
Total	1000			908	930	829	886

The example is just illustrating the trade-offs and complexities of decision making related to price differences. To further complicate the situation, price referencing needs to be taken into consideration. Most EU markets use some form of price referencing in addition to the parallel trade mechanism to influence drug pricing. The above examples have been focused on the EU, where parallel trade is common practice. Assessing the impact on potential parallel trade or re-importation for the US is more complicated, as it requires some speculation with respect to future developments. Evaluation of a potential impact of US reimportation is a low-probability, high-impact issue with a high level of complexity.

PHARMACO-POLITICAL CONSIDERATIONS

Global price differences continue to be sensitive in pharmaceutical and political circles. Does it make sense to allow a much lower price for a new lung cancer drug in developing countries? How far should a company be willing to go with respect to offering HIV/AIDS drugs at cost or close to cost for compassionate use in lower- and middle-income countries?

Global policies with respect to global drug pricing have as much to do with management vision as they have with a quantitative assessment of impact on global profitability. Currently, the only markets with significant double digit sales growth are emerging growth markets such as China and India. Many companies will consider it worthwhile to invest in these markets and engage in some global pricing risks, even when the short-term returns are modest.

GLOBAL STRATEGY OPTIONS

Debating global pricing strategy options sometimes has the character of debating religion. Everybody has strong beliefs, but it is hard to get evidence that one is right. There is no one right answer, but it is important to come to a consistent viewpoint on the basis of beliefs and an analytical assessment of the situation. In developing a global strategy, we should not lose sight of the opportunities in individual markets. Issues in small countries are often as complicated as they are in larger countries, however we cannot afford to have an issue in Norway drive the strategy in the United States or France.

Figure 12.7 shows the relative share of global pharmaceutical sales by country. The distribution is likely to be somewhat different for individual therapy areas, but in general this view is sufficiently accurate. The figure helps to immediately put some things in perspective. The US and Japan are clearly dominating the global scene with a joint 62 percent of the global market. Europe and its individual country fragments form the remainder of the global scene. From a global perspective, Canada is almost irrelevant. Certainly it is not a worthwhile market to justify considerable concessions in the United States. In making global strategy decisions, we need to closely consider the share of global business, as well as the ability of any market to influence other countries and payer systems. A global pricing strategy usually entails a global competitive strategy with respect to a competitive benchmark, as well as a set of global and regional floor prices. Finding the right balance between maintaining global consistency and allowing local businesses to thrive is always hard. Frequently this is a trade-off between a short-term business objective and a long-term vision on the industry environment. For this reason, global pricing decisions need to be endorsed at the highest level in the pharmaceutical company.

As an example, let's consider decision making with respect to the price of a high-cost biologic for cancer or, say, psoriasis treatment in China. Due to affordability issues, we would want to set a lower price in China, as long

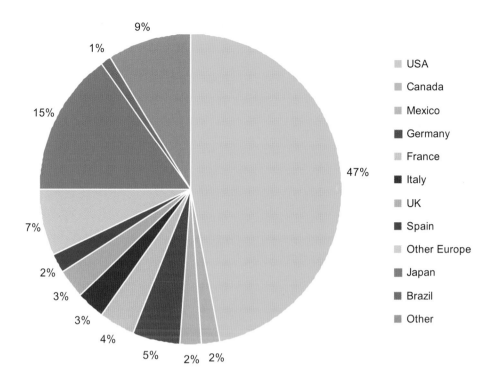

9%

1%

15%

7%

2%

3%

3%

4%

5%   2%   2%

47%

- USA
- Canada
- Mexico
- Germany
- France
- Italy
- UK
- Spain
- Other Europe
- Japan
- Brazil
- Other

Figure 12.7   Typical global sales distribution for prescription drugs

as cost of goods will allow us to still have a reasonable margin. However the mere fact that a price is lower in China, may suggest to a US Managed Care or European government payers that they are over charged. Global price differences for drugs and lack of public understanding and appreciation with respect to the complexities of the industry's cost structure cause a lot of challenges for pharmaceutical companies. In the past, this has frequently caused pharmaceutical companies to be very hesitant to make patented drugs available at lower prices in developing countries, as a negligible amount of profits for a China business may jeopardize the much larger business potential in the United States and Europe. In addition to global pricing concerns, we should consider that there is a broad range of affordability across each country. A better strategy than an across the board price cut may be to engage in income-based patient assistance programs. These programs place some administrative burden on physicians and the drug company, but they help avoid the risks of large list price discrepancies, while enabling patient access at more affordable prices. A more detailed discussion of these programs can be found in Chapter 18.

In the early 2000s the drug industry was struggling to deal with issues related to global pricing for HIV/AIDS drugs. AIDS-related health crises in middle- and low-income countries ignited governments in activating provisions of the global Agreement on Trade Related Aspects of Intellectual Property Rights (TRIPS) to enact compulsory licensing for emergency use of anti-retroviral drugs. Drug companies had been hesitant to supply HIV/AIDS drugs at lower prices because of past issues related to global price differences. For example in 1994, the US government chastised US industry for supplying pediatric vaccines at lower prices to developing countries on the basis of argued lack of full access in the US.

In recent years, compulsory licensing has once again come to the forefront of global industry concerns as India has systematically both rejected drug patents and at the same time instituted compulsory licensing activities for oncology drugs in favor of its own developed generics industry. Unfortunately, the global political environment has so far not seen any urgency in addressing this issue, thus creating a risk that other developing countries will follow. The act of balancing between providing access to lower income countries and avoiding a domino impact on higher-priced countries continues to be a hefty challenge that involves both commercial and ethical issues within a politically divided world. The strategic answer is unlikely to be the same for every company, but for any new oncology drug, pharmaceutical companies should think long and hard before they decide to enter the Indian market. Novartis's Gleevec (imatinib), often referred to as a miracle drug that has transformed many patient lives, has mainly benefited the local generics industry, despite the fact that Novartis has operated an unprecedented and generous patient access program across the world; they operated this program even in India, where generics captured 90 percent of the market.

In this Chapter …

We have looked at bringing everything together in an optimal global market access and pricing strategy. We looked in detail at price referencing and parallel trade and considered some specific examples to determine an optimal strategy.

13

Public Policy and Ethical Considerations

Profit versus Right to Healthcare

The drug industry is at an all time low with respect to its public reputation. As a result, an industry that should be hailed for bringing great improvements in patient well-being has stunningly slipped in image to or below the ranks of tobacco and gun manufacturers. The combination of perceived high prices and compounding drug safety issues have drawn more attention than the positive patient impact of the large number of curative and palliative treatments that the industry has brought. Rapidly increasing drug prices, initial industry resistance to Medicare reform, increasing awareness of global price differences and an initially inadequate reaction to the HIV/AIDS pandemic have harmed the industry and taken away its ability to garner support for a favorable industry policy in the United States. Whereas in the 1990s and in the early Bush administration era the Democrats were uneasy with the drug industry, during the 2008 elections, both Republican and Democrat tickets showed less patience with the drug industry and are, for example, supporting drug importation legislation. During the Obama legislation the drug industry's reputation may not have further deteriorated, but it certainly has not improved either. Meanwhile, in Germany further evidence of problems can be found in the introduction of the Arzneimittelmarkt-Neuordnungsgesetz (AMNOG) price control legislation, which was clearly born over government frustration with the industry and attempts by the British government to introduce price controls rather than existing reimbursement controls.

Over the last few decades, many international governments have interfered in pricing and/or reimbursement for prescription drugs and continue to do so despite the practical complications that it is causing. As the main payer for drugs, governments have frequently mandated price cuts, where their budgets did not adequately allow for increasing healthcare needs and available new technologies. Even in the United States, the country where free competition is holy and price control of any kind is generally "off limits" in political discussions, price controls for drugs have been suggested and seriously considered. Why do we have this discussion in a system that has traditionally relied on free market mechanisms to create equilibrium between consumer willingness-to-pay and investor willingness-to-fund?

Governments of many countries have intervened in drug pricing in various ways, the most extreme of which is direct control of price. As a result, setting and gaining approval for price and reimbursement of pharmaceuticals is a difficult process in each individual country. To add to the complexity, pricing and reimbursement decisions are frequently influenced by prices in other countries. Particularly in Europe and Canada, referencing of product prices to other countries is a widespread custom. Hence an unfortunate pricing decision or unsuccessful price negotiation in one country can have a huge impact on the global return on investment for a product. How have companies dealt with this and how do citizens in price controlled markets fare under this? Does the European model of government control work?

PATIENT ACCESS

As cost of healthcare is rapidly increasing around the world, patient affordability and access restrictions are increasingly influencing physician prescribing. Delays in availability and utilization restrictions of new drugs in pricing and reimbursement controlled markets, as well as de-listing of "life style" drugs, increasing co-payments and co-insurance rates have increased patient "responsibility" for drug cost. Lack of drug coverage for the elderly under the original Medicare benefit has made this group particularly vulnerable to drug cost increases and sensitive to price differences between the US and other countries, such as Canada. The Medicare Modernization Act (MMA) has improved drug coverage for Medicare eligible patients, particularly at the lower income levels, but left a significant cost burden on patients through the "doughnut hole" patient contribution and drugs that are not covered, at least until full implementation of President Obama's 2010 health care reform bill that is gradually reducing the patient cost by each year. Obama's Affordable Care Act (Obamacare) has focused on addressing lack of healthcare coverage for a large group of uninsured, however many uninsured have not signed up to the program and significant deductibles and co-payments remain, as willingness to pay the premium and subsidy funding is limited.

HEALTHCARE AND POVERTY

Access to healthcare is considered a fundamental human right by organizations such as the World Health Organization (WHO). Access to "essential drugs" has particularly been a hot topic over the last 20 years, as the HIV/AIDS pandemic has devastated lives globally, but particularly in developing countries, where access to healthcare, including drugs has been sporadic at best. Since then, healthcare concerns have shifted to oncology and diabetes, but the issues have been largely the same and yet unresolved. This is perhaps so because the focus of the healthcare access issue has largely been concentrated on drug pricing and patents, rather than a broader solution towards developing country healthcare needs to arrest the pandemic and provide care to patients. Global drug pricing decisions are made in an environment where social drug access interests and global free trade ideals are in violent conflict. Can a solution be found that is technically feasible and politically acceptable?

FUNDING OF NEW TECHNOLOGIES

Recent technology breakthroughs have started to result in a steadily increasing flow of innovative new drugs and treatments. Gene therapy and personalized medicine are expected to substantially improve health outcomes for diseases such as cancer, but are causing additional budgetary challenges for private and public health plans. Payers increasingly feel the need and justification to ration these high-cost treatments on the basis of formal labeling, evidence-based guidelines and health economic criteria. However the practical implementation of these controls face stiff practical, legal and political hurdles, as the collective experiences in the various global healthcare systems teach us.

HEALTH ECONOMICS

Making healthcare funding decisions can be very difficult for payers. Coverage denials on the basis of health economic criteria are generally hard to justify as they invariably result in discussions on the value of a life and a host of related ethical and legal considerations. Healthcare systems around the world have come up with vastly different answers to these challenges. Canada and Australia have introduced relatively tight health economic requirements, which are directly linked to national or provincial formulary decision making. The much debated NICE system in England and Wales is providing non-binding guidance with a very similar impact on technology utilization. Most other markets are flirting with health economics as a tool to support politically sensitive rationing decisions, however further evolution is likely to be very different from market to market.

In today's environment of soundbites and limited attention span it is hard to explain the complexity of the drug pricing environment. However, since mankind continues to have great needs for new and innovative drug therapies, it is important to provide incentives for drug development and provide relatively unrestricted patient access.

Compulsory Licensing

In the late 1990s Brazilian, South African and some other governments interfered in order to address the HIV/AIDS crisis in their countries by authorizing compulsory licensing to enable funding of broad access to necessary HIV/AIDS drugs. This happened in the midst of a complicated and emotionally charged political situation concerning the right to affordable healthcare. The basis for issuing compulsory licenses for patented pharmaceuticals is found in Article 31 of the Agreement on Trade-Related Aspects of Intellectual Property (TRIPS), which allows a government to, in essence, overrule the patents rights of a manufacturer by allowing for the production of a version of the patented drug in exchange for a reasonable license fee to the patent holder. What constitutes a reasonable fee is left up to the discretion of the government. Article 31 states that compulsory licensing is authorized "in situations of emergency or other cases of extreme urgency." Much debate has taken place on the right of governments to import generic versions of patented drugs from commercial Indian generics manufacturers until the Doha Declaration on the TRIPS Agreement and Public Health, adopted by the WTO Ministerial Conference in November 2001.

Governments have used the authority granted under TRIPS and the Doha Declaration to negotiate supply of HIV/AIDS drugs at lower prices or the cost of manufacture. Pharmaceutical companies have long resisted allowing for price differences between countries, as it leaves them vulnerable to some of the same governments who are demanding lowest available prices for drugs to preserve their national drug spending. To illustrate the point, the Clinton administration strongly chastized US pharmaceutical companies for supplying essential children's vaccines to developing countries at lower prices than the prevailing prices in the US and other developed countries, arguing that not all US children have access to the same drug. This incident was not only an implicit admission to a poor US healthcare policy, but also demonstrates that in any country national politics and economic interests tend to trump global solidarity.

In recent years, the Indian government has broadly instituted compulsory licensing in order to be able to provide authorization for the local generics industry to manufacture generic copies of the most innovative oncology drugs. At the same time, the Indian government has uniquely rejected patents for other oncology drugs.

Differential or Equity Pricing

RIGHT TO ACCESS

Should access to healthcare be available to all, independent of nationality, race, income and other demographics? It seems hard to say no to what seems to be a reasonable claim, but who will pay? What if countries simply don't have the money or choose to spend it differently, say on something drastically different, such as weapons? Any discussion on this topic is bound to be emotional and complicated due to a difficult mix of social, economic and political issues that underlie individual attitudes.

Should essential drugs be made available at low or near cost to suffering African and Asian populations? How about clean water, doctors, nurses and healthcare infrastructure? How about transplant surgery, the latest biotechnology drugs and the evolving personalized medicine advances? These questions raise the sheer impossibility of equal access, but can also just be an easy excuse to deny compassionate aid to needy populations anywhere. The drug industry has learned over the last decade that it cannot afford to ignore demands for subsidized supply of drugs, such as HIV/AIDS drugs to developing countries, despite reasonable objections and concerns over inadequate infrastructure and risk of resistance development due to improper use. Calls from WHO and UN have only slowly resulted in increased funding to meet healthcare needs due to the AIDS pandemic, frustrating aid organizations to provide meaningful assistance. Unfortunately, without this funding, the supply of low-cost drugs alone will not call a halt to the HIV/AIDS pandemic in developing countries. The World Health Organization has maintained a list of "essential medicines." Figure 13.1 states the WHO definition of essential medicines.

"Essential medicines are those that satisfy the priority health care needs
of the population.

They are selected with due regard to public health relevance, evidence
on efficacy and safety, and comparative cost-effectiveness.

Essential medicines are intended to be available within the context of
functioning health systems at all times in adequate amounts, in the
appropriate dosage forms, with assured quality and adequate
information, and at a price the individual and the community can afford.

The implementation of the concept of essential medicines is intended to
be flexible and adaptable to many different situations; exactly which
medicines are regarded as essential remains a national responsibility."

Ref: http://www.who.int/medicines/

Figure 13.1   WHO definition of essential medicines
Source: http://www.who.int/medicines/

Most of the drugs on the essential medicines list are multi-source products
and are available at relatively low cost. HIV/AIDS antiretrovirals were placed
in the list as no multi-source products were available. Even as patents of AZT
and other antiretrovirals drugs expired, a broad array is likely to remain on
the Essential Medicines list as the use of drug cocktails is essential for clinical
results. Unfortunately, developing countries are struggling with a large number
of diseases, such as malaria and tuberculosis, for which there is only limited
progress in new drug treatments. Given the cost of fundamental research
and development of potential drug candidates, typical developing country
medical conditions have suffered from a lack of financing for independent
researchers and limited financial incentive for commercial drug companies.
Recent collaborations between pharmaceutical companies and local research
institutions have perhaps set a new trend to address these needs.

HIV/AIDS drugs have perhaps only formed a starting point of raising a
fundamental conflict between the societal need for affordable healthcare on
the one hand and free trade principles on the other. Theoretically, it would
be possible to create a separate market for drugs for developing markets, for
which drugs companies would charge no or a very limited premium over the
marginal cost of manufacturing. An example of such a world is illustrated in
Figure 13.2.

Figure 13.2   Compassionate pricing simplicity: the new divide

Theoretically, this creation of two worlds would allow for the low-cost supply of drugs to the area, mainly consisting of low-income countries. In the developed world, companies could continue to charge market prices, which would allow for funding of new research and a reasonable profit for the drug company and its shareholders. This principle of "equity," "differential" or "compassionate pricing" has been strongly promoted by developing countries, the WHO and aid organizations as the solution to the developing world's healthcare crisis. Supported by a number of generics manufacturers, governments, including the South African and Brazilian governments, have pushed for compassionate drug prices at or near manufacturing cost levels. WHO and WTO have organized a collaborative effort to realize such a solution for essential drugs (WHO, 2001). However, there are some fundamental flaws in the two-world principle:

1.   Income and affordability is not an all or nothing situation. For example Brazil and South Africa, the most vocal advocates for compulsory licensing, are middle-income countries with a much higher income level than most developing countries. Where then to draw the line? How should this change over time as new economies grow?

2.   Implementation of a two-world market for drugs would require significant controls to avoid product flow from one world to

another either through tight distribution channels or Berlin wall-style separations.

3.   Governments would have to demonstrate a discipline to not use compassionately-priced drugs in international price referencing schemes and informal negotiations. The former may be achievable, but the latter is much harder to achieve. The European Union has actually issued statements to the effect that it would not reference drug prices that are granted as a result of compassionate pricing practices.

4.   Governments in developed countries may assign national healthcare needs a higher priority than developing market needs. In the United States, access and affordability of drugs has become a hot issue and it is not clear that politicians and the population would support more extensive subsidy arrangements in the light of the already perceived high drug subsidies paid to foreign nations. This may be illustrated by the crisis that US vaccine manufacturers were faced with, when chastized by Hillary Clinton et al. over lower vaccine prices to developing countries.

5.   Countries such as India and China have significant populations that are below the poverty level, but also have some fairly affluent populations.

It may be obvious from the above that a simple two-world subsidy arrangement, created by compassionate pricing, is practically unworkable. However, given the humanistic need and emotional pressure on the issue, it is hard to reject the proposition where other solutions seem problematic as well.

Given the practical complications of a global political solution, we need to continue to strive for collaborative programs between pharmaceutical industry, aid organizations, WHO, governments and university researchers to:

1.   Organize an integrated effort to fund and deliver healthcare and necessary drugs to areas of need. Distribution of compassionately priced medical devices and drugs should have adequate guards

against black market diversion. HIV/AIDS drugs are prime candidates to be included in such programs.

2.   Fund and organize development of new drugs to address key healthcare needs for developing markets that are currently not served due to affordability constraints. Malaria, tuberculosis and river blindness are some of the diseases that may fit this model.

Large pharmaceutical companies have significantly stepped up efforts to implement programs as suggested above. Funding will continue to be the critical factor in these collaborative efforts, as supply of drugs at cost still pose an insurmountable budget hurdle, not even considering the funding needs for healthcare infrastructure, without which supply of drugs are of relatively limited patient value and raise concerns of drug resistance and a further cascading of the HIV/AIDS pandemic. However, pointing out the key limitations in infrastructure has been a difficult issue for pharmaceutical companies, as it can easily be portrayed as an excuse to not make an effort to provide affordable drug solutions.

Global Trade versus Social Policy

Since World War II, the world has seen a lot of battles based on the differences in philosophy between a predominantly capitalistic-oriented society and one that is based on socialism or communism. Separations between Russia and Eastern Europe versus the United States and Western Europe have been a result of the large power struggle and the cold war between the two superpowers.

Since the fall of the Soviet Empire and the opening up of the iron curtain between East and West, the underlying political conflict has largely disappeared, but some underlying conflict between the driving philosophies in the two areas remain.

Most economists believe that free trade is an important vehicle towards achieving economic success. The European Union has strongly, even dogmatically, enforced its free trade principle between its member states which – particularly after the introduction of the common currency, the Euro – has resulted in price normalization between states. Essential to free trade are open borders, mutual recognition of product quality standards and elimination of tariffs and other additional charges.

Free trade discourages companies from differentiating in price between markets. Price differences that exceed a certain threshold will result in significant product flow from the lower-priced market to the higher priced market when trade is unrestricted. Therefore, in a perfect free trade world, prices are likely to be relatively uniform.

As demonstrated earlier in this chapter, compassionate and social considerations argue for adoption of differential or equity pricing principles in pricing essential goods. For a product like a truck, this may not lead to a great difference in pricing structure, as the manufacturing cost may not allow for a large discount, even when profits are eliminated. As has been explained in Chapter 1, the drug industry's cost structure is very different, such that individual drug companies may be enticed to sell certain drugs at a relatively low price, which may be unprofitable for the overall global business, but which will deliver a positive profit contribution when not allocating a global overhead for R&D and other central expenses. In absence of free trade, subsidizing lower-income countries this way can be a viable strategy, provided that the higher-priced markets accept this politically. This is where the practical problem lies. As illustrated in Figure 13.3, pharmaceutical pricing is a contant balancing between the two conflicting worlds of social considerations and free trade.

In 1994, US drug companies were heavily criticized for supplying vaccines to developing countries at prices that were significantly lower than the US prices. This criticism came from the US government under the initiative of Hillary Clinton, who was then spearheading healthcare reform attempts. International solidarity does not always weigh heavy when local economic or political arguments come into play. In all fairness, there are other examples as well. As mentioned earlier in this chapter, in 2001, discussions were held on differential pricing for HIV/AIDS and other essential drugs, organized by WHO and WTO and attended by representatives from industry, governments, NGOs, patient organizations and experts (WHO, 2001). As an expert pricing attendee to this meeting, I expressed my concern to European Union representatives over potential reference pricing by developed markets to the much lower "equity priced" drugs to developing countries. Approximately one year after the meeting, the European Union had adopted legislation, barring future importation of "differentially priced" drugs (defined as discounted by 85 percent or more) into the EU.

In the case of EU legislation to bar imports of "differentially priced" drugs, the gesture was probably largely symbolic. Collaboration of this kind will

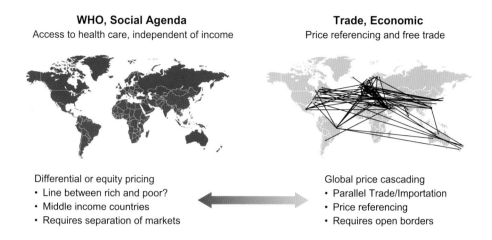

WHO, Social Agenda
Access to health care, independent of income

Trade, Economic
Price referencing and free trade

Differential or equity pricing
• Line between rich and poor?
• Middle income countries
• Requires separation of markets

Global price cascading
• Parallel Trade/Importation
• Price referencing
• Requires open borders

Figure 13.3   The conflicting worlds of social fairness and trade

however be a critical condition to reach consensus on a solution for the need for lower-priced drugs in a political economic environment that encourages and sometimes even demands free trade.

Over the last 10 years, companies have slowly evolved towards accepting larger price differences between high-income countries and middle/lower-income countries. This trend has been driven by stagnating growth in the US and Europe and increasing growth and affordability in particularly middle-income countries. At the same time, companies have found ways to better balance the need to maintain some consistency in global list prices, while allowing access to the less affluent through patient assistance programs and controlled net pricing programs. Some of these programs are also described as examples of Managed Entry Agreements in Chapter 18.

In this Chapter ...

We have discussed public policy and ethical considerations of global drug pricing. Given the public policy issues that the drug industry has been wrestling with, this is proven to be a highly important topic in drug pricing. The social right to healthcare, need to fund future innovation and free trade principles set the stage for some difficult public policy challenges for drug companies that try to introduce a globally consistent market access and pricing policy for their drugs.

14

Oncology and Orphan Drugs

Oncology and orphan drugs are both often mentioned in the context of high drug prices and related concerns. Both categories of drugs (and some overlap between the two) concern high unmet needs for targeted patient populations, but are under continuous public scrutiny due to their high cost to healthcare systems and some individual patients. For this reason, we will discuss both in this chapter.

Oncology is Different ... (?)

How different are oncology and other specialty drugs from typical "small molecules" with respect to pricing and market access considerations? How are payers treating these drugs differently?

US-based oncology companies and business units are particularly insistent that oncology is different. Although this is to some extent true, it is often used in a claim to "leave them alone" from commercial interference in decision making. This is certainly misplaced, as not taking payer management into consideration can lead to serious commercialization challenges in the US and even more so outside the US. In addition, payers worldwide are gradually becoming more comfortable in addressing their concerns over the impact of high-cost oncology drugs on their limited drug budgets, certainly where clinical benefits have only been demonstrated in comparison with a treatment with placebo.

PAYERS AND ONCOLOGY

There is a relatively wide discrepancy in payer management practices with respect to oncology, perhaps more so than in any other therapy area. At one end of the spectrum, NICE in England and Wales has rejected many oncology treatments that other markets have endorsed over lack of demonstrated cost-effectiveness. The emphasis is on "demonstrated." It is particularly hard to demonstrate cost-effectiveness for a treatment for which the critical outcomes measure is overall survival, unless the survival improvements are relatively short and hence unimpressive. It takes longer trials and patient follow-up to demonstrate longer survival benefits. Ironically, drugs with the largest potential Overall Survival (OS) benefits are unlikely to be able to demonstrate this at launch. Consequently, they may decide to delay launch at the risk of letting potential competing drugs launch first. On the other hand, payers in the US have been generally hesitant to take very restrictive coverage decisions for FDA or compendia supported applications of drugs.

One persistently contentious issue in relation to cancer drugs concerns the burden of evidence with respect to survival benefits of patients. Any payer will prioritize OS over Progression-Free Survival (PFS), but the trade-off is not an easy one. As argued above, OS data sometimes take a long time to gather. In earlier treatment phases, where survival is usually the treatment goal, it may even be close to impossible to measure a meaningful OS, as the patient will likely experience cross-overs with multiple other treatments post-trial regimen failure. Consequently, a clean picture of OS is hard to obtain in these cases. PFS is typically deemed a good preliminary substitute when the magnitude is at least somewhat impressive (at least 4–6 months) and if the PFS improvement comes with clear patient quality of life benefits. Germany's IQWiG, a stickler for clinical end points, has endorsed the combination of PFS with patient quality of life improvements as an acceptable "benefit" in their formal benefits assessment.

Oncology drug pricing and the large number of NICE rejections have been a strong point of contention in England. It has led to special end-of-life approval criteria for diseases with less than 3,000 patients and ultimately the institution of a Cancer Drug Fund to fund cancer treatments that are deemed necessary and were not approved and NHS funded following NICE rejections. In order to "fix" the apparent issues with NICE evaluations for anti-cancer drugs, and perhaps some similar issues in some other therapy areas, a Value-Based Assessment (initially Value-Based Pricing) was introduced. A key component of the Value-Based Assessment is the weighing of cost-effectiveness with societal factors to allow for a higher cost-effectiveness cut-off point in diseases with a high societal urgency, oncology presumably being one of them. At the time of writing of the second edition of this book, the introduction of the Value-Based Assessment was still a highly contested issue. Australia, another health economics-driven market, has accepted a higher cost-effectiveness cut-off point for oncology.

A complicating factor in demonstrating value and cost-effectiveness in oncology is that it is often deemed unethical to experiment with new drug treatments in earlier lines of therapy, where the largest benefits are likely to be demonstrated. Most development programs first demonstrate (often palliative) improvements in the later stages of the disease, only to advance to earlier disease stage trials at a later date. At launch this creates a tendency to force prices below their ultimate value. Increasing price later to reflect that value is only theoretically possible. The UK has introduced a formal mechanism to re-price a drug on that basis; however it has never led to an actual increase.

In Germany, an evaluation of AMNOG rulings shows that oncology is treated more generously in terms of positive benefits rating than for example diabetes (Bouslouk, 2014). This is perhaps further illustrated by IQWiG's acceptance of PFS data as discussed above. One may wonder whether innovation has been stronger in oncology or whether the G-BA has been more hesitant in making tough rulings in oncology, but experience shows that most oncology agents get a "benefit" assigned and are able to negotiate prices that are in line with other European markets.

In France, recent changes require a "Medico-Economic" (health economic) data submission for drugs with revenue in excess of €20 million in the second year of sales and for drugs for which the drug company claims an ASMR of I, II or III. Although not specific to oncology, this is likely to affect this drug category significantly. A review of Transparency Committee rulings suggests that an Overall Survival benefit is necessary to achieve an ASMR of I, II or III unless no suitable treatment is available. Head-to-Head trials versus an appropriate comparator are always required in France, unless strong reasons for not doing so are available and accepted.

The United States market has generally been tolerant with respect to coverage of oncology drugs. Healthcare plans usually cover expensive drugs on the basis of label, but also typically allow unapproved uses when supported with clinical data and endorsed in compendia, such as the National Comprehensive Cancer Network (NCCN) compendium. Many states also mandate coverage of approved anti-cancer agents. As in other drug categories, plans can and do use formulary tier placement and prior authorizations to influence utilization.

ONCOLOGY PRICING

Pricing of anti-cancer drugs and other specialty drugs has come under intense public scrutiny. An annual cost of drug treatment in excess of $100,000 is not unusual, making it a high-cost item for health insurance companies and raising concern over patient co-payments, which amount to 20 percent under Medicare Part B and usually more under Medicare Part D or Healthcare Exchanges. A group of hematologists published an article in Blood (Blood, 2013), in which the authors criticize the drug industry over the high prices of CML drugs. The high cost of these drugs is an obvious concern in light of patient affordability at today's high co-insurance rates, particularly since many of these patients have now achieved survival rates that nearly approach the non-CML population. The article also criticizes US price increases for CML drugs. This is a complicated and contentious topic, particularly when considering that the US dollar devaluation against the Swiss Franc (Novartis's home country currency) explains 80 percent of the price changes. This is not to argue that affordability is not an important issue.

In the current environment, providers are critically looking at the added cost of drug improvements. As evidence of this trend, we should examine Memorial Sloan Kettering Cancer Center's decision to reject Zaltrap for colorectal cancer on its formulary (*New York Times*, 2012). In November 2012, three physicians from Sloan Kettering announced that the hospital had decided not to use Zaltrap as, at about $11,000 a month, it was twice as expensive but no more effective than a similar medicine, Avastin from Genentech. Cost burden on Medicare patients, who pay 20 percent of all cost, was said to have played an important role in the decision. Physicians explained that both drugs improved median survival by 1.4 months. Shortly after, Sanofi decided to offer a 50 percent discount on Zaltrap, stating that it had erroneously based its pricing decision on a comparison of label dosing between the two drugs rather than real-life dosing. A small majority of Avastin patients use only half the label dose in real life. Some have argued that the Zaltrap example is evidence of change in the US oncology environment. Others argue that this was simply a rather fundamental mistake by Sanofi to offer a drug with no apparent demonstrated improvement at double the price. Most payers globally have no concerns over rejecting more expensive drugs when no improvement is demonstrated, but have difficulty linking a monetary value to a demonstrated (even small) improvement for a devastating disease such as cancer. The German system is also clearly illustrating this philosophy, as the real hurdle for price negotiations under AMNOG is the recognition that there is a "benefit." Even a classification of "minor benefit" under AMNOG qualifies a drug company to go to the negotiation table with the joint sick fund "Spitzenverband" organization, whereas without an assigned benefit the drug is automatically forced to be priced at the cost of the existing treatment standard, without any negotiation.

There are several reasons why drug companies should keep a close eye on payer management of oncology drugs. Below are just a few:

- Drug budgets are increasingly tight, particularly under the long recession and Euro-crisis that has plagued economies, resulting in increasing payer management of drug pricing and reimbursement, not just in oncology, but in all disease areas.

- Oncology is getting more crowded and is expected to become even more so in the future as development pipelines have a heavy emphasis on oncology agents.

- Bio-similars are likely to increase the need for differentiation for new drug entries with strong evidence of benefit across the approved indication.

- In the United States, many health insurance agencies have introduced high co-insurance rates for expensive drugs, thus leaving a high patient "responsibility" and resulting price sensitivity. That, in combination with high oncologist awareness of the cost burden, can drive utilization to options with lower patient cost, particularly where the differences are perceived to be small or undocumented.

The need to demonstrate benefits over the existing treatment standard may be evident from the above. This may require some tougher development decisions in drug companies. However, the unmet need in oncology is still huge, with many cancer types still suffering from poor survival rates and patient quality of life. It is unfortunate that oncologists have chosen to criticize drug companies rather than praise the truly remarkable benefits of life-saving drugs in CML. We can only wish to see more of these innovations come to the vast number of patients in need.

BENEFITS AND LAUNCH TIMING

In Chapter 10 we discussed the BEST PRICE framework to identify what is driving success with payers in pricing and market access negotiations. The identification of benefits that payers care about was an important part of the discussion. In Figure 10.4 we illustrated this approach with a diabetes example. In order to demonstrate the particular challenges in oncology, we will explore a typical situation in this disease area.

Figure 14.1 shows a simplified example of a benefits analysis for a new solid tumor drug. The example is kept general for blinding purposes. In the clinical benefits category, OS is typically rated highest, followed by PFS and tumor response rates. Payers tend to place less value on response rate improvements, unless it is demonstrated to result in OS advantages. Impressive PFS improvements are often accepted as an indicator of likely OS benefits, and can be accepted pending further OS data collection when PFS is accompanied by clear patient QOL benefits. QOL benefits themselves are often downplayed by payers, unless they are tangible and specific. In the economic benefits category, payers with broad medical budget responsibilities are obviously interested in any medical cost offsets from the treatment, including reduced hospitalization, long-term care or complications from chemotherapy side effects. Work productivity is not typically considered a strong benefit to payers, as this falls

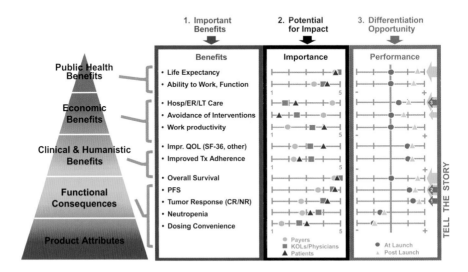

Figure 14.1   Benefits analysis for a typical oncology drug

outside their financial perspective. Health economics-driven systems (with the exception of Sweden) don't consider broader societal economics outside the national healthcare budget in their decision making. Public health benefits such as a notable increase in life expectancy for a disease, obviously not easily obtained, are extremely powerful claims that rise to the attention of politicians, media and the broader public.

In the performance section of Figure 14.1, a hypothesized differentiation versus standard of care is illustrated for both the launch and post-launch timeframe. As is typical in oncology, at launch we only expect to have tumor response and PFS data available. More compelling OS claims and more extensive data to show cost savings in reduced need for hospital care can only be obtained at a later timeframe beyond launch. The post-launch benefits analysis shows what most drug companies refer to as the aspirational value proposition. In reality a better name would be "Stuff that I don't have."

Decision making with respect to evidence availability at launch is a tough topic. Extending Phase III trials to include robust OS data limits the effective patent life and can offer a window of opportunity for competing drugs to launch first. It also increases clinical program cost and risk of clinical failure. Ironically, the most promising improvements face the highest hurdles in this decision. It obviously takes much more than 5 years to demonstrate a 5-year OS improvement. It takes much less time to demonstrate a much less meaningful 3-month OS improvement for the same condition. In some cases, risk sharing deals can offer a solution to this problem.

RISK SHARING

A large proportion of risk sharing deals involve oncology. Particularly in the UK and Italy, many deals involve this disease area for different reasons. In the UK, NICE evaluations tend to exclude oncology products from the market unless price adjustments are made, as other markets assign a higher value for most anti-cancer treatments. In Italy, the government has routinely used risk sharing deals to avoid paying for patients who do not respond as measured through a partial or complete tumor response rate. Australia for Yervoy did do exactly that to allow access for a potential (but unproven) improvement in survival for multiple melanoma, which is a particularly large healthcare challenge in Australia.

Risk sharing deals are discussed in more detail in Chapter 18.

EMERGING MARKETS

Oncology drugs play an important role in emerging market strategies for two reasons. First, given affordability concerns, many drugs can only be marketed in emerging markets through cash payment. Universal health insurance funds are insufficient in most markets to cover the latest-generation oncology drugs. However some countries, like Brazil, have moved to mandate significant coverage of these drugs for its private insurance industry. In most cases, drug companies can only meet willingness-to-pay and affordability through customized patient access programs, which both encourage compliance and ensure controlled distribution of discounted drugs. Some provinces in China have accepted deals where government, drug company and patient each pay a part of the cost, so that the drug has come within reach of those in need. Many different customized market access and funding solutions have been introduced in emerging markets.

Second, compulsory licensing is a particular threat for oncology drugs. Over the last few years, the Indian government has systematically issued compulsory licenses for oncology innovations. In addition, the government has denied drug patents for oncology drugs. Unfortunately, the global political arena has been unable and/or unwilling to address this threat to innovation in such an important disease area. Sharing of confidential data through a regulatory filing in India is probably unwise at this moment, as the strong local generics industry may be the only party to benefit. It is important to keep a close eye on compulsory licensing and intellectual property right developments in the developing world and carefully weigh the risks involved in doing business in these countries.

Orphan Drugs

The focus of this book is on the payer environment and its impact on drug pricing and market access in global markets. Orphan drugs are frequently discussed in this context, although most formal regulations with respect to orphan drugs involve FDA, EMA or other regulatory requirements for marketing authorization rather than review criteria for payers.

ORPHAN DRUG DESIGNATION

In the United States, orphan designation (or sometimes "orphan status") can be obtained for drugs or biological products under the Orphan Drug Act (ODA). For a drug to qualify for orphan designation both the drug and the disease or condition must meet certain criteria specified in the ODA and FDA's implementing regulations at 21 CFR Part 316. Generally a drug can qualify if it is for the treatment of a disorder with fewer than 200,000 patients in the United States. Besides various development incentives, tax credits and waiving of the prescription drug user fee, the drug benefits from seven years of market exclusivity.

The European Commission specified that Orphan medicinal products are intended for the diagnosis, prevention or treatment of life-threatening or very serious conditions that affect not more than 1 in 2,000 or a maximum of 250,000 persons in the European Union. The EU Regulation on orphan medicinal products (Regulation (EC) No 141/2000) establishes a centralized procedure for the designation of orphan medicinal products and puts in place incentives for the research, marketing and development of orphan medicinal products. The EU's definition of an orphan condition is broader than that of the USA, in that it also covers some tropical diseases that are primarily found in developing nations. Orphan drug status granted by the European Commission gives marketing exclusivity in the EU for 10 years after approval. Applications for orphan designation in the EU are examined by the Committee on Orphan Medicinal Products (COMP) of the European Medicines Agency (EMA). Applications for market authorization for designated orphan medicines are assessed by the Committee for Medicinal Products for Human Use (CHMP).

In addition to the United States and the European Union a large number of other markets including Japan (Orphan drug designation Japan) and Australia (Orphan drug designation Australia) have introduced similar incentives to encourage the development of drugs that treat orphan diseases.

An implication of the orphan drug designation is that marketing authorization agencies tend to be less strict in statistical evidence requirements for drug improvement claims. Given the small patient populations it would be practically impossible to enroll sufficient patients in a well-powered clinical trial to demonstrate statistically significant improvement in the appropriate end points. Trial recruitment may become lengthy or even impossible.

PAYERS AND ORPHAN DRUGS

Most payer systems don't formally distinguish orphan drugs from other drugs in pricing, coverage and reimbursement decision making. Of the large payer systems, only Germany has a formal exception of the need to demonstrate a "benefit" under AMNOG as long as annual retail (non-institutional) sales remain below €50 million. These drugs are still subject to price negotiations, but are exempted from an important hurdle and risk of reference pricing. For these drugs, G-BA makes a high-level benefits assessment for negotiation guidance. Once a drug passes the €50 million limit, a benefits dossier is due within three months and G-BA will make a benefit assessment after an IQWiG recommendation (see Chapter 22).

In reality, the orphan drug status will provide for some benefits in payer negotiations. Given the small patient population, payers tend to be less concerned about overall budget impact. Also, they are thoroughly aware of the challenges of demonstrating robust evidence of a claimed benefit for an orphan drug. They will generally accept lack of such evidence, provided that a strong underlying rationale is present. They may also insist on re-evaluation of the dossier after more patient experience is gathered, for example through a formal patient registry.

Ultra-orphan drugs are used for very rare debilitating diseases. There is no formal ultra-orphan drug status and only the UK has defined it as a drug for a condition that involves fewer than 1 in 50,000 people. Pricing for ultra-orphan drugs is under a lot of debate. With prices in excess of $100,000 per year, some exceeding half a million dollars, ethical issues arise in light of both costs to the healthcare system and the individual patient (due to for example US co-insurance rates). Willingness-to-pay for orphan drugs and ultra-orphan drugs originates from a realization that there are no other treatment options available for often devastating conditions in combination with the fact that it is hard to fund the research that is required to meet regulatory data requirements for these innovations. The value and willingness-to-pay becomes a point of contention when the patient improvement is marginal, as is illustrated in a payer research example in Chapter 15 (Figure 15.5 and associated text). Hefty debates have taken place in the Netherlands over reimbursement of new drugs for Pompe disease and Fabry disease, as in 2012 the College Van Zorgverzekeringen (CVZ), the Dutch advisory body for reimbursement decision making, recommended discontinuing reimbursement of these drugs over the relatively limited impact of the drugs at very high cost (€400,000 to

€700,000 per year for Pompe disease). Ultimately, the government decided to continue reimbursement for prescribing in two specialized hospitals (in conjunction with an undisclosed price reduction).

In the United States, smaller regional health plans can be heavily affected by just a few patients with an orphan disease. These plans tend to decide on coverage on an individual patient basis, as cases arise. Given the high cost of treatment, verification of diagnosis and disease management support can be very important in cost management.

High cost of treatment and unmet needs in both oncology and orphan drug categories create complex ethical issues in both pricing and coverage decision making. As the cost of healthcare continues to outpace the consumer price index (CPI), governments and private insurance companies are increasingly faced with a need to make tough decisions. In light of those decisions, drug companies need to clearly identify their added benefits and evidence in support of those benefits. Those that don't can look forward to more pricing and coverage rejection than we have seen in the past.

In this Chapter …

We discussed the complex areas of oncology and orphan drugs. Although subject to the same formal payer approval requirements, both categories typically benefit from more latitude in decision making. Payer willingness to intervene has gradually increased under cost and economic pressures. This trajectory is expected to continue.

15

Payer and Pricing Research

Research and Payer Understanding

One way of better understanding payer decision making with respect to a new drug and its optimum price, is the use of market research with payers, payer influencers and prescribers, hereafter referred to as "payer and pricing research." Payer and pricing research has many similarities with general market research with physicians and patients, but there are also a couple if important differences that are critical to understand.

One of the most critical aspects of payer and pricing research is the need to avoid bias. When physicians give answers on prescribing questions for a new drug, they generally have no interest or intent to mislead the interviewer; after all, why should they? When a question relates to price the situation tends to be different, as decision makers, whether direct consumers or prescribing physicians for drugs, tend to strongly prefer lower prices. Consciously or subconsciously respondents of pricing research tend to overstate the importance of price in their decision making. The degree of bias is very dependent on the research methodology. Quantitative methodologies, such as a discrete choice method are designed to minimize the potential for bias. When well executed (not a trivial assumption), this method can be assumed to be reasonably reliable and without bias. Other methodologies, such as the Van Westendorp method, can provide good insights on client perceptions, but can easily cause bias. Methodologies and means to avoid or reduce bias are further discussed in this chapter.

Before diving in to the design of an interview program, one should ask "Who pays for this?", "Who are the decision makers?" and "What is the decision-making process?" Whether a hospital drug in the US, a retail pharmacy drug in Spain, or either of these in China, we need to create a very different set of questions and evaluations. A hospital drug may be covered through the hospital budget and reimbursed by the patient's health insurance carrier through a capitated treatment fee based on the condition for hospitalization. If the cost of the drug exceeds the overall daily reimbursement, we obviously would like to expand reimbursement to the hospital, or we may have some serious market access issues. Similarly, how does an outpatient treatment fit into the reimbursement rules in, for example, France or the UK? Without this knowledge, any pricing study is useless.

Before initiating payer and pricing research it is important to identify what the primary goals are. Particularly in support of early drug development decision making, it may not be so important to get an accurate estimate of price. It may be important in this stage to support key choices between development options instead. As a consequence, a well-designed qualitative research program with a mix of payers and prescribers may best serve this purpose.

In support of launch of a new drug, payer and pricing research tends to be more involving and require a mix of methodologies. It may, for example, be important to explore general willingness-to-pay and price impact on formulary decision making through in-depth qualitative discussions before testing final price within a pre-defined range through a discrete choice program.

Whatever research methodology is used, it is very important to build the research program to obtain a solid understanding of customer thinking, which is carefully linked to past behaviors and degrees of freedom that they have within the healthcare system and market access and pricing approval and control mechanisms.

A number of years ago, when I was responsible for global pricing and reimbursement in a drug company, we were working with a vendor on a pricing study for a new drug in the neuroscience field. We held individual interviews in a focus group setting with pharmacy and medical directors of a mix of US payers. I was not able to personally attend the first few interviews and as I arrived at the research site, I found the team concerned about the responses obtained from the interviewees. "They are not going to reimburse unless if we price it at generic levels," was the frustrated response from the team at my inquiry of the initial findings. One of the particularly discouraging interviews was still in progress and I asked to include some additional questions in the interview, related to past decision making on some ad hoc case studies for recent new drug approvals within the interviewee's healthcare plan. As the discussions evolved, it turned out that this particular pharmacy director had very little control over drug placement on formulary, as the plan has an open access policy. Today there are very few of these plans available, but that is not the point in this example. It was probably a combination of a focus group setting and insufficient exploratory discussion in the initial interview stage that had allowed responses dictated by frustration rather than reality to go undetected.

One example from my consulting experience may further illustrate how important it is to choose methodologies that provide both answers and thorough understanding of customer motives. In this case I was asked to provide a proposal for payer and pricing research to support development and go/no-go decisions for a new drug for treatment of an auto-immune disease. During conversations with the client it became apparent that an extensive and expensive quantitative research program had already been completed. A problem arose when a senior executive, having discussions with two Managed Care contacts, found opinions that were at direct odds with the research findings. What to believe: two unstructured discussions or the extensive quantitative research program? Apart from the fact that it is emotionally difficult not to believe the results of a half-million dollar or so research program, it was hard in this case to identify the issue. Obviously the product manager (guided by a market research vendor with little experience in payer research) had failed to build sufficient understanding of payer preferences and decision making, for example through in-depth qualitative interviews. Without this understanding, it is very difficult to properly design a quantitative research program and the probability of mistakes is very high. Also, it creates significant challenges when anybody is challenging the results and conclusions on the basis of a general customer understanding. Quantitative research results only really make sense to somebody who understands the underlying customer preferences and behaviors. Even if the quantitative results of this example were correct, which they were not, they were not fully understood, which resulted in an issue. Quantitative research programs can be very useful, when well designed with thorough understanding of the key customer decision parameters and influencing elements (mostly obtained through well designed in-depth qualitative discussions with key customer segments).

Hopefully the above has illustrated the need to carefully choose an appropriate methodology (or methodologies) to best suit the situation and objective of the research program. Careful design of the actual interview guides and stimuli used to test hypotheses are obviously equally crucial for good results. A combination of common sense, understanding of the payer environment and experience in executing these programs are of vital importance to ensuring that you can actually believe the results of the research. That is something to keep in mind to avoid having to explain to senior management why that half-million dollar project gave results that nobody understood or trusted.

Carefully choose research methodology and research instruments and/or work with a qualified vendor who has the experience to guide you through the process and who you can trust to execute the program well.

Before deciding on a research program and its methodology, it is advisable to critically evaluate the situation and build some hypotheses. What do you think that the answers to the research will be? How uncertain are you about each of these? How important is it at the current stage of development and decision making to validate the hypotheses and get the answers? In some cases, for example a new disease area, it may be hard to even formulate hypotheses. In this case it may make sense to start with an exploratory research program, which can inform a more robust subsequent program.

The next sections provide more background and insights on the most commonly used payer and pricing research methodologies. It is not the intention to give a complete overview of all possible methodologies, but rather to describe key elements and to contrast between them in order to better understand how and when they can best be used.

Qualitative Payer and Pricing Research

A qualitative payer and pricing research program should provide good insights into critical elements related to payer and prescribing decision making that can be expected to have an impact on the drug's development program and/or its price setting. The key word is "insights." In essence, we need to understand the customers' thinking with respect to treatment options and unmet needs in the therapy area under consideration, the value that the new treatment brings, and the willingness to prescribe and fund the new treatment in the light of the labeling and the provided clinical and outcomes evidence.

Payers generally make their pricing and reimbursement decisions within the structure of the payer system. This enables them to justify sometimes difficult decisions and guarantees consistency of decision making. Payer and pricing research should therefore be aimed at understanding how each of the healthcare systems will view a new drug, its particular characteristics and the therapy area treatment standards and unmet needs.

Evaluating past behaviors through the discussion of case studies is a generally good way to complement stated payer opinions and intent. It helps to limit the impact of potential bias in research responses. It is frequently helpful to combine discussions on product situations with similar past examples as case study validations to responses. Using case studies particularly helps in ensuring that the interviewee is linked to his or her day-to-day actual world rather than what he or she would like it to be. In, for example, considering a diabetes treatment in France, it is useful to consider how the previous diabetes drugs were reviewed. How were Victoza and Januvia or Onglyza reviewed? What were their comparators and what ASMR score did they achieve? What comments were made in the review summary and what restrictions have been placed on reimbursement? What price was granted and how does it compare to the comparator and other countries? All these questions can yield answers with important indications on how a new compound may perform during pricing and reimbursement reviews.

Payers cannot be experts in each of the therapeutic areas that they make coverage decisions for. It is important to have a good understanding on how they rely on formal or informal advising committees or individual advisors in reaching their final decisions. In reality, it is important to have a good understanding of both the perceptions of payers of a disease area and its treatments, and the advice and messages that they will likely receive from key opinion leaders in the field. The responses from payers can indicate what can be expected in terms of pricing and reimbursement approval. In some cases it is particularly useful in indicating the hurdles that can be expected and the gap that payer perceptions may show in comparison with KOLs.

A good qualitative research program examines all key assumptions that are underlying the business case and are essential for commercial success of the new drug in development. We can easily identify the main components by reviewing the PODiUM and BEST PRICE frameworks that are discussed in Chapters 9 and 10 and by carefully considering and analyzing knowledge gaps with respect to elements that are key to the specific situation and opportunity. Most of the elements of the PODiUM evaluation are not unique to a market access and pricing assessment. A close collaboration in a cross-functional team is important in order to avoid duplication of efforts and inconsistency in assumptions and chosen strategies. Analyses for most elements may have already been done prior to the market access and pricing assessment; however, they frequently need further validation and detail to ensure a good baseline for the planned research.

The "money flow" element of the PODiUM evaluation is most unique to the MA&P assessment. Examining the financial perspectives of prescribers and MA&P decision makers is extremely important for a complete view of the situation, particularly for medical benefits and pharmaceutical benefits that are frequently initiated and/or used in a hospital setting. Let's consider an example of a medical benefit such as a pediatric vaccine that is administered in a pediatrician's office. Reimbursement rates for the vaccine and its administration are taken into consideration for choice of vaccine in addition to any clinical arguments that there may be for a particular choice. Before the Medicare Modernization Act of 2003, Medicare only reimbursed drugs that were administered to US patients in the doctor's office. As a result, Medicare patients with rheumatoid arthritis would be fully eligible for reimbursement of Remicade, but would not qualify for reimbursement of Enbrel or Humira, since these could be self-administered by the patient. Private insurance companies on the other hand were struggling to handle the increasingly costly therapy area with some alternatives (such as Enbrel and Humira) usually handled as a pharmacy benefit, and other drugs (Remicade and Orencia) handled as a medical benefit, which is more difficult to be managed in some plans and does not provide opportunities for contracting. Concern has also frequently been expressed by those managing plans over physician incentives to prescribe Remicade after investment in on-site infusion suites and with an ongoing upward creep in Remicade dosing. Reduction of Medicare Part B reimbursement rates from AWP-based reimbursement to ASP + 6 percent (see Chapter 19) have reduced physician incentives to prescribe more expensive medical benefits. This has particularly been a point of contention among oncologists, who saw part of their compensation stream disappear. The key point to consider in the context of conducting pricing research is that we need to be aware of the impact of funding flow on decision making, particularly since many interviewees are likely to understate its importance during research.

Price and willingness-to-pay are dependent on the perceived value of the product offered. Therefore it is crucial to give the respondent a realistic and complete picture of the benefits of the drug and some realistic expectations on the impact that these benefits will have on patient well-being and economics of disease management. For particularly complicated disease areas that has implications with respect to the stimuli used. A target product profile (TPP) may not sufficiently bring benefits of a drug to life, put it in the right context of the disease challenges and may not adequately address the specific evidence provided. These elements are all important in providing a respondent with a full picture that is not understating nor overstating the value provided. It is also important that we particularly address the benefits that payers care most about in drafting our drug profile for testing. To ensure that we do this appropriately, we can use the Benefits Analysis from the BEST PRICE framework described in Chapter 10, together with our TEMPLE framework (Chapter 11) to identify our high-level payer value story.

Figure 15.1 is an illustration of a benefits analysis example that identifies what are the most important points of differentiation versus the standard of care that are at least a medium priority, but preferably a high priority for payers. A good cross-functional debate is important to bring out the most promising benefit claims, as we need to link medical unmet needs, evidence of benefits and humanistic and economic consequences of treatment success versus failure. In some cases we need to do this for different indications under consideration or even patient sub-populations within an indication. The right side of Figure 15.1 shows the TEMPLE framework that we can use to help us define the high-level payer value story. Particularly in earlier development phases, it is not necessary to get into detailed messages in support of the pillars. Highlighting the most important value claims and their impact should suffice. Geographic focus of the research will have an impact on the importance of payers across the benefits. Particularly for economic benefits, the emphasis across these benefits will be different between NICE in the UK, G-BA in Germany, a typical Medicare Part D plan in the US or Oregon State Medicaid.

What information of the above analysis is used next to a TPP in the payer and pricing research is a matter of experience and some testing. In any case, it is important to ensure that any medical claims are consistent with what KOLs would advocate or at least not shoot down at time of launch. It's all about creating a test setting that is mimicking reality as much as practically possible.

Most components of a qualitative research program are conducted through structured in-depth discussions. The actual pricing component of a research study needs to be carefully structured to avoid response bias. We all like to get a good deal. As a consequence we tend to lower our stated willingness-to-pay when we suspect that the interviewer is trying to decide on price through the research. There are several methodologies that are used in pricing research.

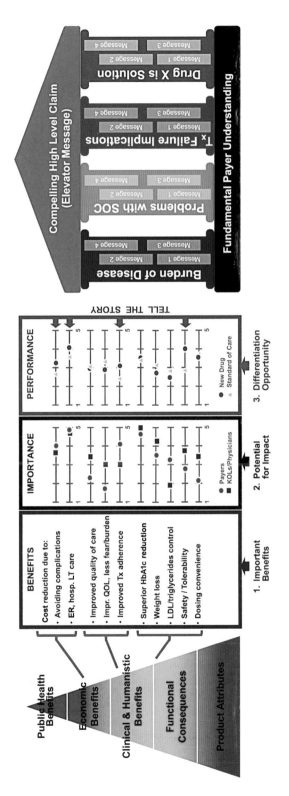

Figure 15.1   Payer research stimuli development

Each methodology has its own advantages and disadvantages and some have more potential for bias than others. We will discuss the most common methodologies in the remainder of this chapter.

Van Westendorp

A frequently used research methodology for pharmaceuticals is the "Van Westendorp" methodology. The method is essentially evaluating a perception of reasonable pricing. It is successfully used in many other industries as well (Van Westendorp, 1976).

Essentially, an interviewee is simply asked three or four questions related to a new product, as shown in Figure 15.2.

1. At what price do you feel that the product is reasonably priced?

2. At what price do you feel that the product is priced too low and you would question the value of the product? (Usually not used in pharmaceutical research.)

3. At what price do you feel that the product is expensive, but you would still use it?

4. At what price do you feel that the product is too expensive and you would not use it?

Figure 15.2   Van Westendorp approach

A concern with a methodology, such as the Van Westendorp approach, is that it is very likely to result in some bias from the respondent. Is it very clear what the purpose of the research is, and some respondents will be tempted to "game" the research to influence the company to set an attractive price. This further illustrates the point that for an accurate price determination, more robust quantitative methods, such as a discrete choice or monadic design must be considered.

There are ways of minimizing bias, by ensuring that the respondent has to justify his or her response and/or for example by preceding the research with a case study example, where the respondent has to justify past decisions in a similar situation. This tends to make respondents more rational and less prone to bias. A key issue in evaluating the research results and obtaining meaningful data is whether the respondent has strong awareness of price levels for various product options in the research category. If the interviewee has very low awareness, the responses are likely to be less accurate, but also show that the respondent is less price-sensitive. This is probably less true for professional purchase decision makers, such as Managed Care pharmacy directors or government-pricing decision makers, as they will likely do detailed homework before an actual decision is made.

The analysis of results from the Van Westendorp methodology is illustrated in Figure 15.3. According to the formal description of the method, each of the intersections of the curves has a specific meaning, as defined in Table 15.1 and indicated in Figure 15.3.

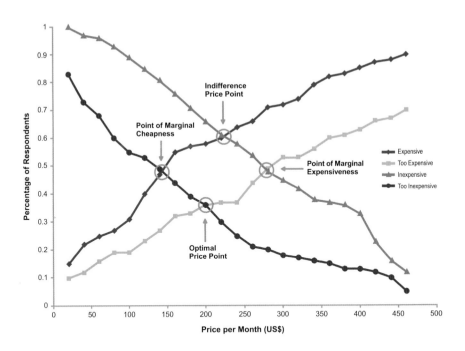

Figure 15.3   Graphic representation of Van Westendorp research results

According to Van Westendorp, the IPP reflects the median price that is actually paid for a market leader, if a similar product is already on the market. The optimal price point will lie between the Point of Marginal Cheapness and Point of Marginal Expensiveness. This seems like a reasonable assumption for products that already have a similar version on the market.

Table 15.1   Van Westendorp's key intersections

Abbr.	Price Point	Description
IPP	Indifference Price Point	The point at which an equal number of respondents believe the test product is *expensive* as believe it is *inexpensive*
PME	Point of Marginal Expensiveness	The point at which an equal number of respondents believe the test product is *too expensive* as believe it is *inexpensive*
PMC	Point of Marginal Cheapness	The point at which an equal number of respondents believe the test product is *expensive* as believe it is *too inexpensive*
OPP	Optimal Price Point	The point at which an equal number of respondents believe the test product is *too expensive* as believe it is *too inexpensive*

For application in pharmaceutical pricing, the Van Westendorp method has its own place in examining perceptions of price. The method is useful in cases where there is no clear reference or multiple potential references for the price of a new drug or treatment. An example could be a radically new treatment for a disease without existing treatment options or a breakthrough improvement over an existing treatment. The "too inexpensive" question does generally not work very well with pharmaceutical payers and is usually omitted. The largest power of the Van Westendorp method in its application for prescription drugs lies in the opportunity to identify the underlying perceptual reference that is the basis for the "expensive" and "too expensive" responses.

For very innovative pharmaceuticals, for which no clear price reference is available, I would recommend a "Modified Van Westendorp" question sequence without any aid on price levels for suggested references. The respondent should be asked for a justification after every step though. Figure 15.4 shows a way in which this can be done.

1. At what price do you feel that the product is reasonably priced? Why did you choose this price level? What has been your reference in your choice and why?

2. At what price do you feel that the product is expensive, but you would still use it? Why did you choose this price level? What has been your reference in your choice and why?

3. At what price do you feel that the product is too expensive and you would not use it or put restrictions on its utilization? Why did you choose this price level? What has been your reference in your choice and why? What restrictions would you consider imposing on its use?

Figure 15.4   Modified Van Westendorp approach

The above method can be further strengthened by showing a list of prices for comparative drugs or treatments after question 3. This way the interviewee can adjust his or her answer after seeing actual price data or further justify the choice. The discussion and the nature of the dialog can help the experienced interviewer to validate accuracy of the responses.

Figure 15.5 shows and example of an orphan drug with a wide range of prices reflecting the high reference of other orphan drugs on the market, but also indicating that the value proposition is not sufficiently compellingly defined and is challenged by payers. Many respondents in this case gave a very low response, reflecting the low price levels of existing but insufficient current treatments. Only few payers were willing to believe in its claimed breakthrough value.

Now consider the example in Figure 15.6. As mentioned earlier, "too inexpensive curves" are often meaningless in drug pricing. Payers don't have a concept of too inexpensive that would turn them off. They love generics and have generally no quality concerns with generics and their low price. As a matter of fact, even the "inexpensive" responses are generally very sensitive to bias. Figure 15.6 has a "too expensive" curve that has some interesting characteristics.

In prices around about $220 per month the curve is relatively steep, as is usually the case around a perceptual or competitive benchmark. Then at about

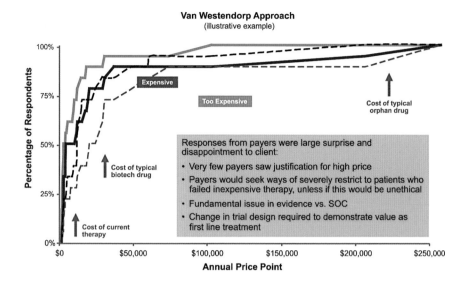

Figure 15.5   Van Westendorp results for an Orphan drug with a sub-optimal value proposition

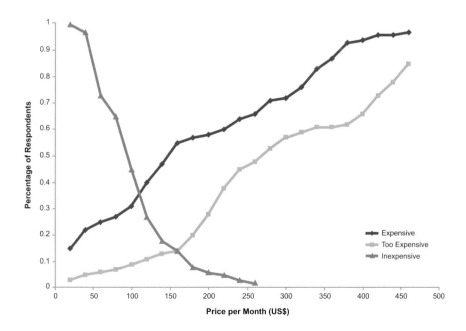

Figure 15.6   Van Westendorp results for a typical drug situation

$450 another relatively steep increase occurs. When using the Modified Van Westendorp line of discussion, the interview provides justifications for the responses, which usually clearly coincide with one or more break points in the pricing curve. These price points are often direct or indirect competitors, but frequently other perceptual barriers, such as a perceived limit on daily or monthly drug cost or the treatment cost in another therapy area that has some commonality.

Van Westendorp's pricing theory tells us that the optimum price is below $160, probably near the IPP at about $110 per month. A good quantitative study would probably indicate that the optimal price point could indeed be $160, or close to $400 as both of these points are just below prices where rapid drop-off in acceptance takes place. It may be clear from the above that the Van Westendorp method is helpful in finding perceptual price points, but not necessarily reliable in setting an exact launch price. Other methodologies, such as the discrete choice methodology are much better suited for this as they provide true price–volume relationship rather than just an "opinion" on what is reasonable or expensive.

Monadic Testing

The purest method of quantitatively measuring the optimal price point is the monadic test method. With this method, each interviewee is only asked to make one purchasing decision for one price point. For meaningful results, a relatively high sample size is required, which makes this approach a costly one. To properly conduct the research, each interviewee should be asked to indicate a product choice from among a number of options, including our product of interest. The product descriptions include price as one of the parameters. Across respondents the price is randomly varied to allow analysis of price impact across a price range of interest. Because every respondent only sees one price point or co-payment level together with other parameters, we can avoid bias, provided that the rest of the study is set up correctly. Some other important aspects to consider:

- Respondent willingness-to-pay is only of interest where he/she has indicated to be interested in the option offered by us. Willingness-to-pay will be low and is not of interest to us where the respondent has indicated not to wish to use our option in the first place! This is a common mistake that can lead to serious underpricing.

- Whether or not a respondent is aware of prices of existing treatment options can impact the results somewhat. In this context, we need to decide whether to show prices of other choice options. Showing prices can overemphasize price; not showing them may not be realistic either. We can decide to use both approaches, but in a few cases where I have seen both used, the results were only marginally different.

Monadic testing can be a good choice in cases where the cost per interviewee, including interviewer cost and respondent recruitment and honoraria, is modest. Internet surveys with consumers are an example of such a potential situation. Cost of internet research is largely driven by fixed programming cost and analysis. Physician and payer interviews tend to be expensive under this method due to the relatively high cost of recruitment and honoraria. Another situation where the method tends to be feasible from a cost perspective is patient willingness-to-pay research in emerging markets, where the lower cost of interviewers can outweigh the local cost of more complex discrete choice methodologies.

Cutting corners in the choice of pricing research methodology is always very tempting, as intuitively the approaches such as the Gabor–Granger seem like a reasonable compromise to cut cost. The example in the following section shows that one should be extremely careful in choice of methodology and accepting compromises that may undermine the validity of the research results.

Gabor–Granger

An approach that is inappropriately loved for its simplicity is the Gabor–Granger methodology, which was first introduced by A. Gabor and C.W.J. Granger in 1961 (Gabor, 1961). The interviewee is shown a profile of a product and is asked whether they would buy the product at a certain price level. This is repeated for various price points in random order.

The Gabor–Granger method is dangerously attractive as a methodology, because it provides a seemingly complete set of responses for every price point with a false hope of accuracy based on randomization of the questions. The reality is that the respondents will be highly aware of the fact that the interviewer wants to establish price after the first question, thus causing a high risk of bias. Also, the method usually does not offer alternative choices, thus not realistically modeling the purchasing process.

To illustrate the importance of using a more robust methodology, such as the monadic approach, consider the comparison in Figure 15.7 between the two research methodologies, applied in the same research for a price optimization challenge in a non-reimbursed prescription drug situation. The Gabor–Granger methodology indicates the lowest tested price point as statistically significantly better than all the other price points; it may even make sense to choose a price lower, as lower price points were not tested. The more reliable monadic test shows a different result and a higher optimal price. Poor pricing research methodologies tend to usually lead to an underestimate of willingness-to-pay, as is the case in this example. Pricing studies only seldom involve multiple research methodologies. If the Gabor–Granger was chosen as the sole methodology in this study, the researchers would probably have believed the research results, which would have resulted in a serious pricing mistake.

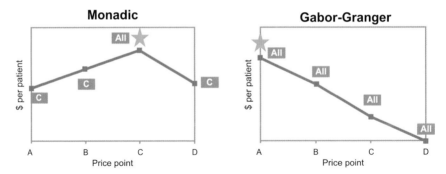

Patient price sensitivity testing with two methodologies
Black boxes indicate statistical significance of differences with other price points
Both study methods show different revenue maximizing price points, each with statistical significance

Figure 15.7   Pitfalls of the Gabor–Granger research methodology
Source: Multi-national price elasticity study for a non-reimbursed drug (blinded)

To further illustrate the problems associated with Gabor–Granger, let me give an example of a pricing project that I did many years ago when I was in the industry, working with one of the pricing research vendors. As we were arguing research methodologies, I expressed a concern over using a proposed Gabor–Granger methodology. As we had a substantial sample, I asked for a sub-analysis of data for respondents that started with a higher price point and going down versus the ones that started with a lower price point and going up. The results were clearly different and showed the bias that is inherent to the methodology.

Conjoint Analysis

Conjoint studies are extensively used to establish customer preferences in support of various marketing and forecasting objectives. In this established use these studies provide great customer insight. Market researchers are frequently tempted to include one or two pricing questions, or to do an entire pricing study with this methodology. Adding a few pricing questions to a marketing conjoint study can add value, but can be misleading when over-interpreted. An accurate price determination requires a thorough assessment with more than a few questions.

A conjoint pricing study can give reasonable results, but is generally not recommended as it has no advantages and a number of disadvantages in comparison with the discrete choice method, which is discussed in the next section. In conjoint studies, interviewees are asked to rate their level of interest for a number of profiles, representing variations of a number of product attributes. Through statistical analysis the choices are translated into insights with respect to the impact of each variable on decision making. The number of interviewees required is statistically determined by the number of attributes tested and the number of choices for each attribute.

A flaw of using the conjoint method in pricing studies is that it does not reflect the prescribing decision. Having a preference for elements of a profile is in reality meaningless unless a physician makes a positive prescribing decision for a particular patient. When a product is a second preference for every patient, you are likely to sell nothing. The discrete choice methodology mimics this prescribing process better, certainly in cases where a limited number of appropriate options are available. In very crowded markets, with many similar alternatives, it may make sense to use a conjoint methodology as physicians may not even be able to clearly articulate their preferences between the available options. Since sample sizes and related cost of executing a discrete choice is similar to cost of a conjoint program, there is usually not a good reason to not choose a discrete choice method. Discrete choice is discussed in the next section.

Discrete Choice

The discrete choice methodology is probably the most frequently used quantitative pricing research methodology, as it provides reasonably accurate pricing data at a cost which is much lower than that of the monadic testing method. In this method, the interviewee is shown a number of situations on cards (or a web screen) and is asked, for each situation, to make a prescribing decision; a choice between various specific options. Ideally, the situations shown represent a variation of various key drug attributes, including price or reimbursement status, whatever is appropriate in the healthcare system under consideration. In markets, such as the United States, we need to first evaluate the impact of price on reimbursement status with payers, and then assess the impact of reimbursement status, and other drug characteristics, on physician prescribing. Let's focus on the physician research part for the following example.

Suppose that we want to investigate the impact of US Managed Care formulary status on specialist prescribing of a new anti-depressant. For the purpose of this research methodology discussion, it does not matter what the drug profile is, but obviously when we execute this program, it is very important to have a well validated set of stimuli. Poorly developed stimuli will lead to poor quality research. Let's assume that we have done extensive payer research, mapping out how Managed Care makes its decisions depending on the price we set and contracting offers that we make. We have also done qualitative research with specialists, which has given us good insights on the factors that influence specialist prescribing behavior, as influenced by Managed Care decision making on tier placement (second, third tier) and other potential restrictions, such as step edits.

The discrete choice research will have to contain various parameters, describing patient type (for example first depression diagnosis, failure of first SSRI, treatment resistant), other patient characteristics (gender, age), the drug's label and key claims (efficacy, side effects), as well as patient reimbursement (co-payment) and related restrictions (step-edit or not). Each interviewee is exposed to a number of profiles such as: newly diagnosed female patient, 55 years of age. Then the physician is offered various existing treatments and a new treatment option. The new treatment option includes a description on approved indication, efficacy, safety claims. For all drug choices an insurance coverage status is stated as well. This exercise is repeated for a number of different patient situations with the same interviewee. Across a sample of interviewees, various dimensions in the profile can be tested, without every interviewee seeing all possible permutations of parameters. The relationship between prescribing and the underlying parameters is established through a regression analysis.

Depending on the situation, it may make sense to validate physician behaviors through analysis of their actual behaviors in a number of representative analog situations in the same or other therapy areas. In some cases, it may also make sense to further examine patient reactions to co-payment.

Linked Decision Making

In conducting pricing research we have to realize the complexity of the decision-making process for prescription drugs. We have discussed this aspect in Chapter 1. Physician prescribing is influenced by payer restrictions, as well as patient preferences and concerns. There are of course many other influencers, such as medical societies and their guidelines, individual KOLs as they advise formulary decisions and publish studies in peer reviewed journals, as well as the pharmacist who in some cases may get questions or cost complaints from the patient. In addition, each country has its own complexities of national, regional and local rules and regulations. For example in a German region, there may be a quota in place for the maximum share of patients treated with a certain expensive drug in a category with multiple options. In the US, Accountable Care Organizations provide incentives for provider groups and their physicians to identify cost savings. Figure 15.8 illustrates how that could influence our Dinner for Three dynamic. Our payer research should take these factors into consideration to our best ability.

Besides evaluating the influence of surrounding stakeholders on payers, physicians and patients, we need to decide how we incorporate interactions between these three parties in our pricing analyses.

Figure 15.9 shows an illustrative example of an interlinked decision model for a typical US prescription drug situation. The prescribing physician makes a prescribing decision on the basis of patient condition and other characteristics, informed by label and other medical and drug information against the background of his/her training and experience. That decision is influenced by payers through coverage decision making, involving potential prior authorizations, step edits and co-pay tier placement. Patients can influence the decisions through either pro-active requests for a certain brand

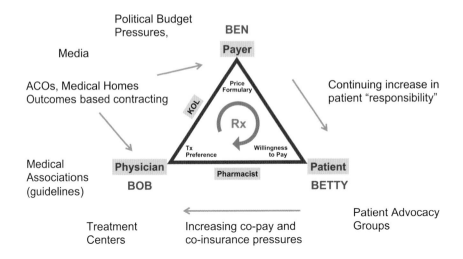

Figure 15.8   Dinner for Three with its influencers

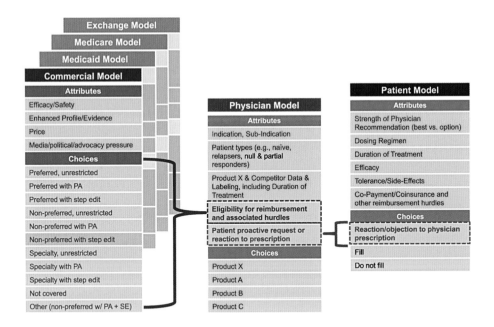

Figure 15.9   Interlinked US pricing model

or through an objection at the pharmacy when they are exposed to a high co-payment (where not offset with a coupon). It is very important to evaluate the dynamics of interaction between physicians, payer and patients and take these into consideration in the design of the interlinked model. After deciding on the model structure and the links, we can populate each of the components with a quantitative research program. With that data we will now have a price-revenue relationship that can help us to evaluate an optimal price.

In reality, the US market has many payer segments and sub-segments that behave somewhat differently. For example, Medicare Part D plans have significant restrictions and patient co-payments, particularly for specialty drugs. Employer sponsored plans tend to offer more extensive coverage, but there are various degrees of management within the segment. We need to make sure that we appropriately analyze each of the payer segments that are important for our situation and prepare an appropriate segmentation that is representing the specific drug situation. Incorporation of patient behavior, such as acceptance of co-pays, impact of coupons, can either be done through market research or through patient level data analysis for a number of good analogues. Which one is more appropriate depends on whether appropriate analogues can be identified, whether good data is available and how much the prescribing decision of a treating physician is influenced by patient requests and co-pay objections.

As a consequence of the fragmented nature of the US market, we are likely to find large differences in willingness-to-pay and optimal price. Medicare Part D and Exchange plan patients are likely to be more sensitive to co-pays, as co-pays are higher and average income levels are likely to be lower. Also, coupons cannot be used for Medicare patients. We can maneuver pricing across these segments with list price and discounting strategies. By maintaining a higher list price and contracting with selected customers in exchange for formulary concessions, we can optimize our business. These analyses can often be analytically complex as contracting and formulary decisions need to be assessed on their impact on a local level in consideration of spill-over effects between geographies. We do need to carefully consider MCO willingness and timing post launch for contracting.

In ex-US healthcare systems the interlinked model for pricing analysis usually looks simpler. In a country such as France, the national pricing and reimbursement authorities will be the main players on the payer side for drugs that are dispensed in the retail pharmacy. Most patients have no co-payment, thus eliminating the need to look at detailed patient willingness-to-pay considerations. In countries such as Italy, Spain and Sweden we need to consider the role of regional payers and sometimes hospitals next to the national payer. This situation is illustrated in Figure 15.10 as the left blue rectangle, where the model only involves the behavior of national and regional/local payers. In Spain, the impact of co-payments can be substantial as well, as these have been increased to 40-60% for non-retirees for non-chronic treatments. Therefore in Spain we need to consider a more comprehensive model, which includes national/regional payers, physicians and patients.

Cash pay markets or non-reimbursed situations in reimbursed markets require focus on the physician-patient interactions without consideration of the payer. This is substantially different from the OTC market situation as the physician is still the essential decision maker, albeit strongly influenced by his/her perception of patient affordability or willingness-to-pay, as well as the patient's actual response to the prescription and its cost. In Figure 15.10 the red rectangle is representing the non-reimbursed pricing model, where physicians and patients interact and their joint behaviors drive optimal price.

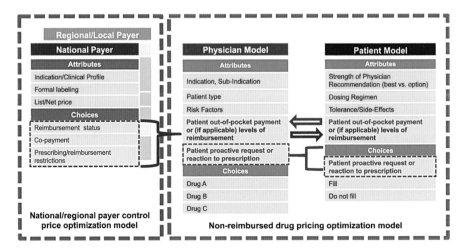

Figure 15.10   Interlinked pricing model variations

"Don't Try This at Home"

Pricing research is complicated and is very different from general market research. Avoiding bias is a key consideration in the design of a pricing research program. This is related to the fact that interviewees tend to consciously or subconsciously want to "game" research when they perceive it to be to establish optimal price and willingness-to-pay. Everybody likes a good deal.

A number of times I have been consulted by pharmaceutical company employees who had completed sometimes expensive quantitative research programs with market research companies that upon examination did not have deep pricing research experience. Sometimes these programs were not preceded by qualitative research resulting in incorrect choice options. Other times a faulty methodology resulted in an underestimated willingness-to-pay.

Any research program that is not coupled with a thorough understanding of the motivations and reasoning behind decisions is bound to be unreliable and will potentially lead to very costly commercial mistakes. Working with an experienced vendor is critical in assuring reliable results. For this reason I gave this closing section of this chapter on pricing and payer research the title "don't try this at home."

In this Chapter ...

The importance of payer and pricing research is discussed. The role of in-depth qualitative discussions is described, as well as a number of quantitative research techniques. The importance of avoiding bias has a large impact on methodology choice and executing research. Poor choice of methodology and poor formulation of research questions can easily lead to a dramatic underestimation of willingness-to-pay and suboptimal price setting. Pricing mistakes generally have a huge impact on profitability and return on investment.

PART D
Market Access and Pricing Strategy Implementation

16

Corporate Market Access and Pricing Function

The global market access and pricing function is organized very differently across pharmaceutical companies. There is not a single right solution, particularly since the function needs to be integrated with the rest of the organization in the most effective way. In this chapter we will discuss some of the options and their pros and cons. We will also consider what is or should be part of market access and pricing (MA&P). Further, we will discuss work processes and essential tools to enable the function's role, both during the drug development stages and implementation of an agreed-upon strategy.

Pricing and Corporate Decision Making

Drug pricing is a function that needs to be closely managed globally. Pricing decisions have a large impact on a company's performance. Small differences in price can have a substantial effect on profits, since they flow straight to the bottom line. Pricing mistakes in one country can easily impact pricing in other markets.

A global pricing strategy involves trade-offs between markets. As discussed in Chapter 12, we may be forced to launch at a higher than optimal price in one market, to avoid price decline in another. In some cases we may have to decide not to launch a product in a country. Launch sequencing is frequently necessary to optimize long-term value. Coordinating pricing decisions is an important task for a global market access and pricing organization. Beside financial reasons, there are public relations reasons to be very cautious with pricing decisions. Unfortunately, the drug industry has managed to get a reputation that seems worse than that of the gun and tobacco industries. For an industry that cures debilitating diseases rather than design and sell products that kill, this is a truly poor performance from a PR perspective. The HIV/ AIDS crisis has ignited a lot of criticism over drug industry pricing practices. Whether this is fair or not, even today, the issue continues, as evidenced by the Blood article by US hematologists, which heavily criticizes US drug pricing and price increases for CML drugs, and public and payer price objections to Gilead's price for Sovaldi (sofosvubir), a new and highly effective Hepatitis C drug. Given this situation, pricing decisions need to be carefully weighed and consistently applied. Particularly for devastating diseases, such as HIV/AIDS and cancer, the company needs to carefully consider the impact of its pricing on patient access to treatment in all countries.

Pricing and Marketing

Philip Kotler's four Ps of marketing – place, product, promotion and price – clearly anchor pricing as one of the key elements of a pricing strategy (Kotler, 2007). Whether you include a fifth P for "people" or not, pricing is an essential element of the marketing mix and, as such, needs to be closely integrated with the marketing strategy.

Drug positioning, a core strategic marketing activity, needs to consider the most important value that a new drug can deliver for its customers. Increasingly, payers are influencing or even controlling the positioning that physicians are allowed to respond to in their prescribing. When a pharmaceutical company is promoting a use for its drug which is not reimbursed (even if within label), physicians will be confused and will ultimately balk. They may stop prescribing the drug in the first place, as it creates a difficult situation with patients. The payer value story needs to be very consistent with drug labeling and the marketing campaign. To achieve this, MA&P teams need to closely collaborate with the marketing team.

Notwithstanding the importance of a strong link to the marketing organization, MA&P teams need to be closely linked to many other groups as well, including clinical, strategic planning, regulatory, market research and public affairs. This will be further discussed in later sections of this chapter.

Market Access and Pricing Functions

"Market access" has been the new trendy phenomenon for the last few years. Another coined phrase has been "value proposition". Emphasis on both elements is to address the need to focus pharmaceutical development and commercialization efforts on payers, in addition to the classical focus on physicians and patients. Emphasis on both is extremely important to ensure progress in this area, but it is also important to be clear what the terms mean. If not, we see that each function translates the term in the way it wants to see it, very much like the airplane design example in Chapter 1.

Let's go back to the definition of market access, as explained earlier in the book:

> Market access is the discipline that addresses any financially based consideration or hurdle to drug prescribing and use, whether imposed by public or private third-party payers, or experienced as a consequence of patient affordability.

Key functions that are essential to the market access and pricing definition as described above are pricing and reimbursement (P&R), health economics and outcomes research (HEOR) and public policy (PP). The pricing group has traditionally been the keeper of pricing strategies, as well as coordinating efforts and insights to achieve pricing and reimbursement approvals with payers. The HEOR team offers key insights and analyses related to patient outcomes data and health economics modeling and data. The analyses are particularly important for health economics-driven markets. The public policy department particularly plays a key role in the later go-to-market stages, as pricing issues can raise sensitive policy issues, particularly in HIV/AIDS and cancer. MA&P departments need to closely collaborate with marketing and medical groups, but are usually kept as separate organizations.

MA&P activities span geographically from global to local. Most companies have global and local MA&P departments in place; some have regional groups as well. Organizational structures tend to be different on a global, regional and local level. This will be discussed further in a later section of this chapter. MA&P activities start early in development and continue until the end of the drug's effective life cycle, usually after patent expiration. Over the course of time the nature of the activities and the teams involved may change. In this context, it is

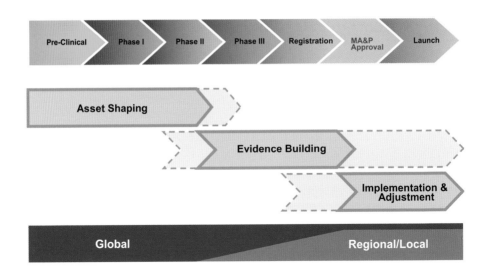

Figure 16.1   MA&P activity phases over a drug's life cycle

important to consider the three phases that we discussed in Chapter 7, which are shown in Figure 16.1.

Activities during the asset shaping stage are usually coordinated by the global group, as close collaboration with the research and development disciplines is essential. Involvement of regional and/or local functions is usually very limited at this stage. During the evidence building stage, perhaps about two years before launch, regional and local groups get increasingly involved as they need to get ready to ultimately take responsibility for implementation of the MA&P strategy. During the implementation stage the role of the global group is usually limited to coordination of global pricing strategies and the initiation of any strategy adjustments when necessary.

MA&P and the Drug Development Process

The MA&P department needs to be closely involved in the drug development and commercialization process to ensure that the payer perspective is considered in key decisions. Absent specific focus to make this happen, organizations will continue to act as they have done for many decades. Clinical and regulatory departments have collaborated for many years and have a very good mutual understanding of each other's needs. Adding the payer perspective to the regulatory one is greatly adding to the complexity of the number of individuals and perspectives involved. Without a conscious process to structure input and trade-offs between development options, change is likely to only progress slowly at best.

A structured approach will help towards analyzing all requirements for key decision points, such as a Phase III go/no-go decision. This is discussed in detail in Chapter 10 (under Assess Evidence Needs). Introducing a structured analysis of key options will initially lead to added work load, as teams are uncomfortable with perspectives from other functions. It is extremely important to overcome this initial hurdle, as it addresses the exact purpose of the exercise: bridging different experiences and perspectives into one key decision. Over time the process will be much easier, as teams get a better understanding of the trade-offs. It is like learning how to ride a bike: initial falls and bruises, but after you learn it is hard to imagine why it didn't come naturally. How easy it is to effectively get the functions to work together and reach consensus, may also depend on the structure of the MA&P group. HEOR teams have traditionally resided in R&D, whereas pricing teams are always in the commercial division. Building a team that crosses the commercial/R&D divide can be an organizational challenge, but will also help expedite the process of integrating MA&P considerations into the company's decision making.

Go-to-Market Efforts

Implementation of MA&P strategy, included in what today is frequently referred to as the "go-to-market" efforts is coordinated by the local MA&P teams, supported by the regional and/or global MA&P team. It is very important to have a strong local team in each country, with a solid understanding of the payer system, payer preferences and the role of key influencers. Established relationships in the market can be extremely helpful in ensuring a thorough understanding of the requirements for success for a new compound.

Characteristic of the go-to-market MA&P efforts is the involvement of a large number of disciplines. Beside the core groups of pricing and health economics, public affairs and medical groups play an important role in formulating and communicating key messages to key stakeholders in the medical/political community. All these efforts need to be coordinated in close collaboration with regulatory and marketing teams.

Pre-marketing activities with respect to MA&P activities are very important, as has been explained and argued in previous chapters in this book. The medical team should have a good understanding of the role of local regional and global medical societies on local treatment guidelines and prescribing habits. Particularly as reimbursement guidelines are increasingly aligned with medical treatment guidelines, influencing the medical community's views on good treatment practices is becoming more and more important.

Global Management of Price

Managing prices for a prescription drug is no doubt a role that needs to be fulfilled on a global level in the drug company. Local pricing decisions frequently have an impact on other countries on a global scale. A German price can impact the price in Japan. The French price influences the price in Canada. This is just a small selection of all global price links between countries, formal and informal. It is important for a drug company to establish a global pricing policy with guidelines for pricing relative to a competitive benchmark, as well as specified global and regional floors. Exceptions to the policy should be subject to central approval by executive management.

Figure 16.2 shows two examples of price floors set to address different situations. On the left side, for an innovative compound, the company decided to set one global price floor at $107 per unit. The right side of the figure shows multiple regional floors to address the large variability in achievable prices in each market. Given the amount of interaction and referencing ongoing between EU markets, it usually makes sense to define a European floor. This price floor should be set in Euros to minimize the impact of currency exchange fluctuations. Since the introduction of the Euro, exchange rate fluctuations have been less problematic as they created stability in comparison with the pre-Euro period. However, even today, the UK, Sweden and Denmark are still not part of the Euro-zone. In addition, recession-related steep price cuts in Greece, Spain, Ireland and Portugal in 2010 highlight the continuing challenge to maintain a consistent European pricing policy. Typically, Asian prices have a broad range as there is a broad range of population affordability and a mix of negotiated reimbursement systems and primarily cash out-of-pocket pay. South Korea and Taiwan tend to have relatively low prices as a result of their HTA-driven negotiations. China and India have a need for much lower than existing prices to enable reach of the broader less affluent and rural populations. Given the perceived future importance of China and India, many companies are finding

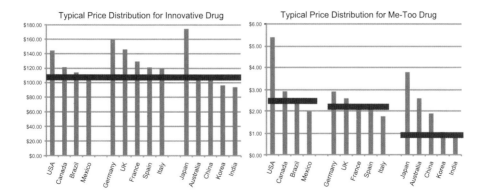

Figure 16.2   Global and regional floor examples

ways to allow for a lower launch price in these markets, thus taking on a higher risk of price cascading.

Market Access and Pricing Organization

There is no single solution to how to organize a MA&P organization. The group needs to be able to fit and function within the larger organization's design and processes. A customized approach to achieve this is certainly warranted when structuring this group. However in any situation, there are a number of sequential decisions to be made with respect to the general structure:

1. What is the *charter* of the group?

2. What is the high level organizational *process* that this group's activities fit into?

3. How does the group fit within the *larger corporate structure*?

4. Which *functions* need to be functionally aligned within the MA&P group?

5. How should the group be structured and aligned *geographically*?

6. Which *roles and responsibilities* should be handled globally and which regionally or locally?

In structuring a MA&P group, we need to start at a high level with the group's charter and the larger organizational process. Structure needs to follow strategy for a successful solution. It goes beyond the scope of this book to discuss how a MA&P organization would fit within each organization and its processes. However we will discuss some general considerations for the group's structure.

MA&P GROUP STRUCTURE

As was discussed earlier in this chapter, key disciplines for a MA&P organization are pricing and reimbursement (P&R) and health economics and outcomes research (HEOR). These groups need to collaborate with each other closely, and with other commercial and development disciplines. A complicating factor is that P&R is usually located in the commercial organization and HEOR in R&D.

Figure 16.3 shows an option of gathering a MA&P team in a classical functional organization with separate commercial and R&D divisions. The core global MA&P team is comprised of the global P&R and HEOR teams. These teams should have close links to regional and local P&R, HEOR and policy teams. Reporting structure is probably the most complicated part of creating

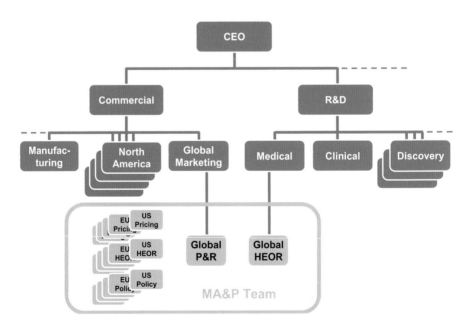

Figure 16.3   MA&P team option in functional global structure

the MA&P organization in this structure. First, will the MA&P organization report to the commercial or R&D organization? Both options exist today. When considering the nature of MA&P responsibilities – ensuring that payer needs are addressed in development and commercialization strategies – a strong case can be made that the MA&P organization should have a commercial focus and report to the commercial leader.

In structuring the MA&P organization itself, the following considerations should impact decision making:

- Structure of internal customer groups with the highest level of interactions, such as marketing, clinical, regulatory, regions, affiliates;

- Capabilities and experience requirements for individual leaders within the group.

Pricing and health outcomes disciplines, although very much involved with the same issues, tend to require different academic backgrounds. Pricing, traditionally a financial function, usually relies heavily on a marketing and business background. HEOR is usually best served with a public health and medical or pharmacy background. An integrated team that handles pricing and health outcomes requires a mix of these capabilities and experiences.

Figure 16.4 shows an example of how a MA&P team could be structured. Pricing and health outcomes specialists are organized by therapy area.

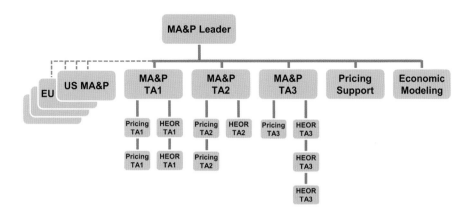

Figure 16.4   Example of a MA&P team structure

Additional functional pricing support and specialized outcomes support, for example in health economics modeling, complement the team. Some organizations have moved to create business units, where commercial and research groups are under one leadership by therapy area. The advantage is that under this structure it is relatively easy to add designated MA&P support.

Figure 16.5 shows an example of MA&P support under a business unit structure. The market access team is well set up to collaborate with other commercial and research disciplines that are united within the business unit. The challenge under this structure is to keep functional expertise in the pricing and health outcomes functional areas.

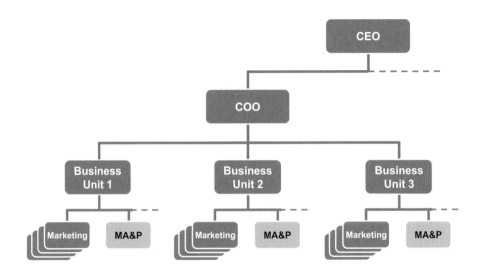

Figure 16.5   MA&P teams in a business unit structure

The previously mentioned examples are merely intended to provide some illustrative examples of the available options and trade-offs. In reality, each company is different and the organization is best served with finding a customized solution that best fits the organization's specific needs and the talent that it has on board.

GLOBAL VERSUS REGIONAL AND LOCAL GROUP STRUCTURE

In the typical group structure examples above, we have been mainly focused on the organization on a global level and its linkages to the regional and local teams. For both global and regional/local teams, the interaction between MA&P and marketing and medical is important in order to drive agreement on an integrated strategy. However on a global level, the activities are heavily focused towards working with the R&D and early marketing teams to ensure that a drug's value proposition is aligned with payer requirements. For regional and local teams, the efforts are focused on implementation. As a result, particularly local teams need to heavily interact with medical and government affairs disciplines. This difference can result in a need to choose a different organizational structure on a local level. Ensuring good collaboration and clear points of contact between the global, regional and local teams is of course very important, no matter what structure is chosen.

Role of Information Systems

Analyzing and tracking pricing and market access information is an important aspect of the MA&P function. Examples of information that is useful to collect in support of MA&P work are:

- Ex-factory and public prices for the company's own and competing drugs in therapy areas of interest;

- Reimbursement status of key drugs in therapy areas of focus;

- HTA assessment results and considerations for key compounds;

- Public statements about pricing strategies and events by competitors and press.

Maintaining a database of global prices is important to monitor competitive changes and support strategic pricing analyses. Changes in exchange rate can have a large impact on global price differences over time.

MA&P databases can either be stand-alone systems or well integrated modules of the corporate financial system. Each option has its own advantages. Stand-alone systems are much more flexible with respect to analyses and reporting, but are more work intensive, as financial data need to be imported. Creating a useful database within or connected to the financial systems is often cumbersome and expensive and imposes severe restrictions on customization, but does allow for an immediate link to real financials, such as sales, average in-market actual price, which allow for tracking of reported prices and price policies with real behavior.

In this Chapter ...

We have addressed organizational aspects of global market access and pricing in bio-pharmaceutical companies, including the roles and responsibilities and interactions with other parts of the commercial and research organization. We discussed a number of organizational structures, but noted that the right structure may be very different from company to company. We briefly looked at pricing information systems.

17

Market Access and Pricing Negotiations

How do we negotiate for a price in a price controlled market? How do we negotiate favorable market access at a price that we decided to set in a free pricing market? In many countries we may not actually sit across from a payer and engage in face-to-face negotiations. In some cases we may actually feel that we are just in a price taker situation as the process does not allow for more than very limited formal interactions and the payer rules seem very strict and directive. In other cases we may only be able to benefit from limited formal interactions. However, if we take a step back, take a longer-term perspective and consider the payer customer perspective (including their concerns), we may have more room than we think, as there are more opportunities to communicate than seemingly offered in the formal submission process.

In this Chapter we will discuss how we can optimize our chances of success in negotiating Market Access and Pricing results at national, regional or local payer levels. Frameworks, such as the relatively simple "Getting to Yes" (Fisher and Ury, 2011) can be very useful, but will need some substantial adjustments to fit to the prescription drug situation.

Prescription Drugs versus Other Products

As argued above, the prescription drug sales situation is very different from other negotiation settings. This is also apparent when we consider the "Dinner for Three" analogy that was discussed in Chapter 1. We usually negotiate with the payer, while physicians and patients may have a much more direct interest in each specific situation where the drug solution is needed. In addition, the payer needs to make a general coverage policy decision, where for some individual patients the need may be particularly compelling.

Considering the "Dinner for Three" analogy, we must ensure that the physician and patient perspectives are on the payer's mind during negotiations. Most payer decision-making bodies conduct a thorough medical review as part of the process, but we want to make sure that all elements are well understood and appreciated, particularly since we are often excluded from any discussions that take place during this part of the process. Also, the medical professionals that are frequently part of this process (or even career professionals in the Department of Health) may be more critical than their colleagues that are actively managing these patients in the clinic every day. In any case, it is very important that we identify areas where payers may have a different view from patients and treating physicians, and find ways to convince the payers of the importance of those aspects, particularly when they are central to our drug's value proposition. For this reason, preparations for prescription drug negotiations start long before the actual approval, as we need to make sure that the foundation for our ultimate value story is laid before we come with our drug solution. Pre-launch promotion for a new drug is not legal, so we want to make sure we don't advocate specific claims that we expect or hope to have. However, it is certainly appropriate to study and publish results of studies that evaluate the impact of shortcomings of existing treatment options, so that it is part of the evidence domain at time of launch. This is very important, since physicians tend to de-emphasize treatment shortcoming when there is no patient solution. We need to be careful that this behavior does not limit the realization of treatment shortcoming when we finally do have the solution at hand.

Negotiation Settings

So far we have discussed negotiations in fairly general terms. Let's now examine the typical settings that we may be negotiating in. Some settings may be largely characterized by dossiers and formal correspondence. Others will allow for frequent informal interaction. These differences are important considerations that have a large impact on how we execute our strategy.

NATIONAL GOVERNMENT PAYER

Government payers, such as Transparency Commission members and Economic Committee members in France, G-BA members in Germany or equivalent officials from other national pricing and/or reimbursement decision-making bodies tend to be very restrictive in their willingness to communicate with drug companies outside a formal consultation or other official setting. Usually during a national pricing or reimbursement process there are only a few opportunities for formal dialog and none for informal dialog. Members of a review committee that have had personal contact with the company, such as through advisory boards (if even allowed), usually have to excuse themselves from the decision-making process. It is understandable that payers are concerned with any potential perception of favoritism or even bribing, but it does make communication of a new drug's value proposition more challenging.

National payers are usually bound by formal approval rules and processes and are often more concerned with the drug budget than with overall medical cost, but this can differ from case to case.

REGIONAL GOVERNMENT PAYER

Regional government payers, such as the ones found in Italy and Spain, or for county councils in Sweden may act equally formal as their national counterparts, but they tend to be more closely concerned with the overall medical budget and can be more willing to structure meaningful and pragmatic deals.

PRIVATE PAYER

Private payers, such as Managed Care plans in the United States or equivalents in Canada, Brazil, China or others, can have a wide range of rules with respect to their decision making and the ability to approach these decision makers. Most organizations tend to be more flexible than government payers and will allow for company presentations and dialog with the pharmacy and medical directors.

HOSPITAL PAYER

Hospital decision making for prescriptions drugs is usually made by a drug formulary committee, comprised of pharmacists and clinicians. How approachable individual committee members are differs from setting to setting. Next to the drug formulary, for inpatient treatments, such as oncology or CHF, the hospital may utilize treatment protocols that are essential to consider in gaining utilization of a drug.

PROVIDER GROUPS

Provider groups, such as physician group practices can act as a payer in situations where they purchase and stock injectable and infusion drugs. Reimbursement can take place on the basis of an established formula (for example ASP + 6 percent for US Medicare) or as a capitated fee for a treatment. Particularly larger practices may be able to negotiate favorable net pricing deals.

For every payer, drug companies obviously need to be well aware of the limitations on communications of sales representatives and medical staff, which will be somewhat different from country to country and setting to setting.

Payer Perspective

Before we engage in negotiations, we need to be well aware of the specific situation that the payer is in, as well as what the objectives and priorities are for the payer. Payers are professionals who are tasked to ensure availability of new drug and medical solutions in appropriate trade-off with cost. Like everybody, they have specific motivations and concerns. Knowing what these are can be of great benefit in negotiations. Some typical questions that we need to ask ourselves:

- What is the perspective of this payer; is he/she only in charge of the drug budget, overall medical budget or an even broader societal perspective?

- What are the primary goals of the organization that I am negotiating with? Is it for example a commercial hospital with a primary profit objective or is it a not-for-profit community hospital that has other non-financial objectives? Is it a regional payer in Spain with heavy financial challenges or is it a more financially secure region?

- Does the disease area under consideration have a specific meaning for this payer? Is our disease area for example a national priority? How high does it appear on the budget? Are there any specific metrics in this space that play a key role in the decisions for this payer, such as quality metrics, fixed reimbursement rates (DRGs) or other?

- What is the time horizon that this payer is operating in? Does he/she take a long-term perspective or, given budget problems, are finances evaluated year by year?

- What decisions have been made in the past year or few years in this therapy area? How have these decisions been justified? What lessons can we learn from this that may apply to our situation?

- Does anybody in the sphere of influence have a particular affinity to the disease area, for example through direct personal exposure or other?

The more we know about the payer and his/her organization, the better off we are in our preparations.

Understanding the Payer's Point of View

A critical success factor for any negotiation is to understand how the other party will view the situation and how it fits with their priorities and preferences. When we are truly able place ourselves in the shoes of the payer, we are best situated to emphasize the appropriate arguments and reach a mutually acceptable solution. Our interests are hardly ever in complete opposition to one another. Finding common ground may offer a window for solutions. For example, the payer may

- want to lower budget impact where we may be more concerned about international implications of a lower price;

- be particularly concerned over this year's budget while we may be looking more over a three-year horizon;

- need to have the assurance not to look foolish when long-term outcomes data are less impressive than the preliminary data that the drug was approved on;

- be more concerned over creating an example of an exception than really caring about the budget impact of the individual case.

I will illustrate the latter point with some personal experience. Many years ago, I was responsible for a pharmaceutical business in the Netherlands as a new reference pricing system was introduced. The new system caused a lot of anxiety among the pharmaceutical industry and left my business with a loss of reimbursement for the drug that comprised nearly 40 percent of my business. The basis for the reimbursement loss was an unfortunate use of the WHO Daily Defined Dose data (WHO DDD) that was not really applicable to the use of the drug in the Netherlands, but was an integral part of the reimbursement limit calculations. Over a period of more than a year we engaged in two lawsuits against the government, an advocacy campaign to rally specialists and a number of in-person meetings with the key decision maker at the Department of Health. After six meetings the decision was changed in our favor.

What was the key to the favorable outcome in this situation? The lawsuit? Lobbying with specialists? Partly, but certainly not entirely. The key was thoroughly understanding the concerns of the Department of Health, which enabled us to jointly find a resolution. Lawsuits and lobbying with specialists helped create some urgency, but it was mainly the personal interactions with the decision maker that created a willingness to arrive at a mutually acceptable solution. From the Dutch government perspective it was critical to avoid exceptions that could undermine the system's integrity.

Interestingly, three months after getting a resolution of the case above, I received a formal reimbursement rejection from the Department of Health for a different new drug on a totally different basis. By then I was intimately familiar with the new Dutch reimbursement regulations and realized that this decision was not in line with the law. Rather than starting a lengthy and public appeals process, I placed one call to the senior legal person in the Department of Health, whom I knew from the previous issue. He was more than happy to quickly fix a painful mistake. All it took was a 15-minute call to the right person.

Both examples above allowed for a solution because of an intimate understanding of both the formal rules and the preferences and concerns of the payer and his organization.

Examining our Value Proposition

Now that we have a good view on the perspective and preferences of the payer (organization) and the formal MA&P rules, we need to examine our drug's value story and carefully customize it to best suit our negotiation. In Chapter 10 we discussed how we can use a Benefits Analysis approach to identify what are the key value messages to payers, physicians and patients. In Chapter 10 we showed a rather simple illustrative example for diabetes; in Chapter 14 we showed an oncological example. In both cases, we just considered payers as one homogeneous group. As we are more closely considering our negotiation angles with individual payers, we can decide to engage in some payer segmentation and prepare slightly different versions of our value story for each segment. Here are a few examples:

- US Employer-sponsored plans with various levels of control or specific cost management techniques for the disease area at hand; employer-sponsored versus Medicare Part D plans or Exchanges;

- Health economics-driven payer systems (such as the UK or Sweden) versus Therapeutic referencing systems, such as Germany or Japan. In both UK and Sweden, cost-effectiveness is a critical factor in the payer decision-making process; in Germany and Japan it plays a minor or no role;

- Private versus public payers in Brazil, Canada and many other markets.

When preparing for negotiations in a particular market or providing a briefing on the negotiation strategy for a certain payer segment, we can make a more customized assessment of particularly important benefits for a payer. We can also see how the payer perspective may be different from that of KOLs/physicians and patients. This will help us to identify which elements of our value dossier are important to emphasize in our pre-negotiation communications as well as during the actual negotiations. Here are a few illustrative examples:

ADHERENCE EXAMPLE

Let's consider an example of a new drug that is expected to provide long-term outcome improvements through the drug's relatively favorable tolerability profile and associated improved patient treatment adherence. First, payers are generally very skeptical of any compliance and adherence improvement claims. They have been disappointed in the past and have usually not seen these claims materialize in real life. By law, sustained release formulations cannot get a price premium over the original product forms in Canada for this reason. Most other payers will be equally sensitive and will only embrace adherence improvements enthusiastically if there is no additional associated cost. Second, even when the payer is honoring adherence claims, will he/she be ready to act on it? A number of years ago I was meeting with a pharmacy director from one of the larger US Managed Care organizations. I was trying to find out how he would respond to an adherence improvement that we were working on substantiating in the pharmaceutical company that I was working in. I had expected some push-back, but was surprised by the intensity of the resistance as he said "I don't really believe in these adherence improvements." As I was somewhat puzzled, I moved the discussion to a different example in the cardio-vascular space, where I felt he would have to agree that drug treatment adherence is critical. Then he finally said, "Well, most of my patients in this space would be in our Medicare Part D plans." Obviously, in the Pharmacy-Benefit-only Medicare Part D space, increased adherence would just imply increased drug cost; the only healthcare silo that he was responsible for in these patients. I hope that the example illustrates that we need to be alert for specific payer perspectives, as they play a key role in payer behavior. In many cases payers will not volunteer the information, but a good understanding of the specific payer system or segment should bring this out clearly.

BUDGET EXAMPLE

This case took place a couple of years ago in the UK. We were investigating an opportunity for a client, which involved a drug innovation that would require a small additional cost at acquisition, but would pay back and generate attractive savings in year 2. In payer discussions with Primary Care Trusts (PCTs; this was just prior to the change in the UK from PCTs to Clinical Commissioning Groups (CCGs)), they fully accepted the product concept and did not contest the cost savings that this innovation would bring, yet a majority of them were not willing to make a positive formulary decision. Why? At that time PCTs were in very bad financial shape and were simply unwilling to spend extra money one year for larger savings the next year.

Hopefully the above examples illustrate the impact that a payer's situation and role can have on the appreciation for our value proposition. We need to take this into careful consideration as we structure our approach in the negotiations. Working on customizing the value proposition in a cross-functional group is a very important part of a successful preparation for negotiations, as it offers a great opportunity to ensure that we have translated medical improvements into benefits that are of importance for the particular payer or payer segment that we are considering.

Payer Objections

We already discussed objection handling as part of our Payer Value Story in Chapter 11. However, we have to make sure that we look at the specific payer or payer segment to further customize our response; in some cases we may decide to pro-actively address a potential concern in the value story. In other cases we may consciously choose to handle the objection as it comes.

Objection handling is part of every negotiation, whether face-to-face or through a paper process. As long as we are well prepared, objections should not bother us too much. It is natural that if we try to "sell" our proposition there may be some push-back or need for clarification of certain aspects. Particularly in the European culture, pushing back and arguing is a natural part of the buy-in process. You might even say that if there is absolutely no push-back, we probably underpriced the product. We need to make sure that we carefully anticipate objections on the basis of a consideration of the specific payer situation and his/her perspective. Equally important, we need to structure the responses so that they are pertinent and meaningful to the payer. Example: If a payer is concerned about budget impact, then a response on medical cost offsets is only useful if the payer has a broader medical budget responsibility. If not, then we need to focus on the value that is underlying that cost saving rather than the cost saving itself.

Price

Price can obviously become a point of discussion in negotiations, either directly as price, or indirectly as budget impact or cost-effectiveness. In some cases it is raised in relation to the proposed patient population for reimbursement approval. Before we respond to a price objection, we need to carefully consider whether the timing is right and whether the objection is really a price objection.

Let's take a lesson from the "well-respected" profession of the second-hand car dealer. Let's assume we are visiting a dealership as we are shopping around for a used car. We are looking at a number of cars and the dealer has been eyeing us for a while until we seem to show an interest in a particular car, let's say a BMW which looks good and does not have too much mileage. There is no price sticker on the car and as we are gradually warming up to the thought of driving this BMW, the sales person is approaching us. I ask him: "How much is this car?" What will he respond? We may get one of a thousand responses, but if he is a professional car salesman, price will not be the response. Why? Because he has learned not to talk about price until the product is sold. We will hear about the great BMW quality, perfect shape of the car, the brand new tires, the low mileage, how good we will look in it, the GPS system and the great warranty program, but not price! We need to realize that often when we hear a price objection from a customer, price may not be the problem, but it is just an easy way out for the prospective purchaser. Every good sales person who gets a price objection first tries to guide the conversation back to value of the product. We should only consider closing the deal after the client has demonstrated that they understand the value proposition. Closing deals may be different between prescription drugs and cars, but the principles of salesmanship are not that different: sell first, and then close the deal.

The manner in which we "close the deal" is obviously dependent on the payer and related selling situation. Selling to a national payer is essentially trying to convince them to either 1) allow for a reasonable price (price controlled markets) or 2) approve broad reimbursement at the drug company determined price. In US managed care, price can involve a discount. In some international markets, negotiations may involve post-launch data to be supplied, a risk sharing deal with a discount, but in many cases the government will decide on the company concession by basically setting a lower price in a take-it-or-leave-it fashion. Whether we accept that "deal," depends on our insights with respect to the importance of making a deal to the payer. We tend to think that we have no negotiating power, but failure to close a deal can be a problem for a payer as well. The better we understand the attractiveness of a deal to the payer, the more empowered we are to negotiate an optimal outcome.

TIME PRESSURE

Our urgency in gaining MA&P approval can have a large impact on the result achieved. Payers are in no rush to add a new expensive compound to their drug lists. European governments have played the time card for many years to preserve their budgets, until the EU intervened with regulations on timing for pricing and reimbursement decision making. Payers may choose to delay a decision if they know that a second market entrant in the same drug class is on the horizon or if patent expiration of a reference compound is near. Particularly when our data are not fully up to the payer standards, we may give payers an easy excuse for an initial rejection.

BATNA

In "Getting to Yes" (Fisher and Ury, 2011) the Best Alternative To a Negotiated Agreement (BATNA) is introduced to help you evaluate how important a deal is. How far should we be willing to go if a deal seems infeasible? What concession would still make this a better deal than "no deal"? Assume we are negotiating a price with the national payer in Spain. From the perspective of the local Managing Director of our company, almost any price would be beneficial, as it would add to his/her bottom line. Of course, below a certain price point, the local profitability would become an issue, but the global organization will already have concerns at much smaller price concessions. For this reason, there is a lot of upside to incorporating the global or regional considerations as part of our negotiation strategy. Local teams are sometimes hesitant to do this as they see an associated risk of not making a deal, while in reality it will enhance the probability.

Let's consider a fictitious example for a national drug pricing negotiation in Italy with AIFA. Let's say we are introducing a new class of oral diabetes drugs and are finding that the AIFA representatives insist on a discount of 5 percent versus the existing gliptins (let's say Januvia), where we claimed to deserve at least a 10 percent premium (we asked for 15 percent premium). For this example, let's assume that the only justification that AIFA gives for the discount is that it only offers marginal improvements versus Januvia, which are not supported with long-term evidence. From a local perspective we are tempted to try to make a deal at parity, or even, if need be at the 5 percent discount. Not making a deal is clearly hurting the local Italian business. Even the delay of another negotiation round, with an uncertain outcome, may put the financials at risk for this year and next. From a European perspective, the Italian price tends to be towards the lower end of the spectrum. Therefore a 5 percent discount versus our comparator Januvia may create significant risks for price referencing and parallel trade within Europe and consecutive impact on pricing in Japan and Canada. When we model this out, similar to what we did in the parallel trade example in Chapter 12 (Tables 12.1 and 12.2), we may find out that we are better off not launching in Italy at all, rather than accepting the 5 percent discount. We would ideally leverage this to negotiate a higher price in Italy, or otherwise aim for a confidential deal, bringing net price down while maintaining a higher list price. A payer, who realizes that the global or

European team will never accept the offered 5 percent discount versus Januvia, is more likely to accept a higher price, because the BATNA for the global team is different. Global willingness to step away from a deal enables us to close a better deal.

Structuring Compromise

In situations where there is willingness to discuss mutually acceptable solutions, we should carefully go about analyzing the reactions and concerns from the negotiating payer. As mentioned earlier in this chapter, not all interests are 180 degrees opposed from each other. Managed Entry Agreements and Risk Sharing agreements (discussed in Chapter 18) can be good examples of such a solution. Without an open discussion with the payer, structuring compromise can be hard or impossible. In some systems, a compromise may only be realistic for the most innovative drugs, as they represent an important enough issue to the payer.

In this Chapter ...

We discussed how negotiations are different in the prescription drug space from most other business areas. We emphasized the need to carefully analyze the perspective of the payer and try to thoroughly understand his/her motivations and concerns. Finally, we critically reviewed timing and need to make price concessions and identified ways to structure a compromise.

18

Risk Sharing and Managed Entry Agreements[*]

Risk Sharing is a popular term in the pharmaceutical industry. Other terms heard are Outcomes-based Contracting, Innovative Contracting and the UK term Patient Access Scheme. More recently, the term Managed Entry Agreement has become commonplace.

With increasing frequency in Europe and Australia, and to a lesser extent in the US and other geographies, biopharma companies and payers are entering into agreements to provide some form of risk sharing or price protection as new drugs are adopted into formularies. The earlier ones among these include: Pfizer's Sutent (sunitinib malate) and Onyx/Bayer's Nexevar (sorafenib) anti-cancer drugs; Novartis's Aclasta (zoledronic acid), and Sanofi-Aventis/Procter & Gamble's Actonel (risedronate sodium), both osteoporosis drugs. Manufacturers have agreed to various deals in Italy, Germany and the US to provide drugs for free if no improvement is seen after initial treatment, or to reimburse health plans if for example bone fractures occur despite the osteoporosis therapy. Particularly in Italy and the UK, many deals have been closed that follow the same pattern. Particularly in oncology there are a large number of deals across countries.

There is a lot of misunderstanding and controversy about risk sharing in the pharmaceutical industry. Some love it, others hate it, but most of us are just confused about the topic. What is the risk and who is sharing? Will we miss out if we don't start closing these deals immediately? In this chapter, we will give you a structured four-step approach to help your decision making on whether you need to act, and for which opportunities.

---

[*] Sections of this chapter were previously published in the January/February 2010 issue of Pharmaceutical Commerce (www.PharmaceuticalCommerce.com). This chapter has been updated for the second edition.

What is Risk Sharing?

The fundamental idea of risk sharing is simple: in return for a pharmaceutical company's guarantee of efficacy, a payer will add a new product to its formulary that it would not have added otherwise. The concept is similar to a "money back" guarantee for consumer products – they provide a perception of quality and confidence. However it does raise the question whether pharmaceutical companies should provide insurance to insurance companies? That sounds like something that one should be careful about.

For new drugs, risk sharing can make a lot of sense, as the manufacturer has better insights into the strength behind its claims with respect to yet unproven long-term health benefits. A deal can help overcome challenges in addressing payer hurdles in providing meaningful long-term outcomes data prior to launch. For drugs at a later stage of their life cycle, one needs to be careful not to pursue the pharmaceutical equivalent of attempting to sell refrigerators to Eskimos. At this stage, payers are likely to have much better data on outcomes than the drug company.

"Alternative Pricing Schemes" Would Have Been a Better Name

Most risk sharing deals share no risk at all, if one takes the definition of "share" taught in kindergarten. It would have been better to refer to this large group of risk sharing deals, outcomes-based contracting and performance-based agreements as "alternative pricing schemes."

Risk sharing deals originated in Europe and Australia, where they served to overcome individual nations' particular pricing and reimbursement approval hurdles. In the United Kingdom, for instance, risk sharing deals have helped reduce cost per patient within National Institute for Health and Care Excellence (NICE) guidelines. As such, these deals are really poorly disguised price cuts.

Risk sharing continues to fascinate the industry, even though relatively few deals actually bridge the risk inherent to a long-term outcome of a pharmaceutical product. Payers tend to love these deals as discount opportunities. Health outcomes specialists support the use of their data in structuring agreements. But drug pricing professionals are very skeptical. They know from experience that price concessions have a domino effect across markets, and once a payer in one country or region gets a risk-sharing discount, payers elsewhere will demand the same net price.

If the benefits are slender, why is the industry buzzing about these deals? Often, payers are directly or indirectly demanding these arrangements, particularly in Europe, where centralized mechanisms give payers power over market access. Enticed by demanding payers, pharmaceutical companies have engaged in arrangements that provide short-term local success, but can have major long-term bottom-line repercussions.

Types of Risk Sharing Deals

Many pharmaceutical executives are unclear what makes a good risk sharing deal, one that is mutually beneficial to all parties instead of tilted towards one or the other. There are different types of risk sharing deals, and it is in executives' best interest to understand exactly how these deals work – and how to make deals work for them.

We have identified seven basic types of risk sharing deals. Each is based on two determining factors: is the deal based on population or individual outcomes, and is the agreement triggered by biomarker, short-term clinical, long-term clinical or financial data? Figure 18.1 gives an overview of the deal types.

1. THE BIOMARKER-LINKED REIMBURSEMENT DEAL

In this type of arrangement, payers make reimbursement conditional on results from biomarker tests. Herceptin is a good example. The drug is particularly effective in HER2-positive patients. Payers have made reimbursement contingent on a positive biomarker test that screens for HER-2 positive patients.

Biomarkers inherently limit a drug's eligible patient population, but can significantly enhance the product's value through a demonstrated higher effectiveness – it can command a higher price and market share, provided that the biomarker is available and reimbursed at the time of launch.

Biomarkers have started to play a very useful role in selecting patients with a higher probability of successful treatment. In some cases biomarkers have been

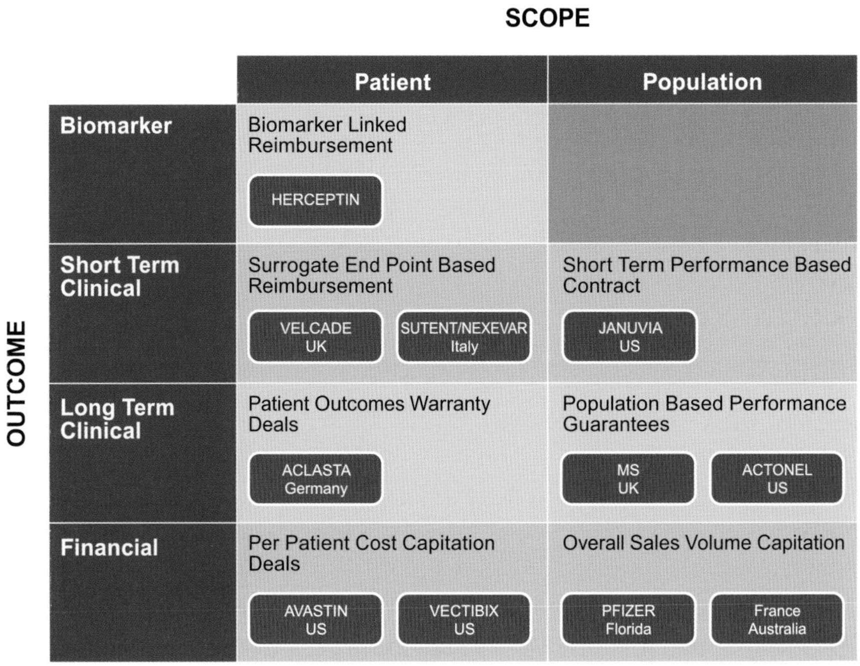

SCOPE

	Patient	Population
Biomarker	Biomarker Linked Reimbursement HERCEPTIN	
Short Term Clinical	Surrogate End Point Based Reimbursement VELCADE UK / SUTENT/NEXEVAR Italy	Short Term Performance Based Contract JANUVIA US
Long Term Clinical	Patient Outcomes Warranty Deals ACLASTA Germany	Population Based Performance Guarantees MS UK / ACTONEL US
Financial	Per Patient Cost Capitation Deals AVASTIN US / VECTIBIX US	Overall Sales Volume Capitation PFIZER Florida / France Australia

(OUTCOME — vertical axis label)

Figure 18.1   Risk sharing deal categories

considered and tested as part of the regulatory approval process and have been incorporated in the labeling. Payers can easily make reimbursement conditional on a positive biomarker test, provided that such a test is commercially available and reimbursed. Identifying a biomarker during pre-launch development can significantly enhance the value of a new drug through demonstrated higher efficacy rates. It will of course limit the treatment eligible population, but this should be more than offset by a higher value (and price potential), as well as a higher market share within the appropriate population. When a biomarker is introduced post-launch, it will add value in strengthening the value proposition for the patient segment that is positively affected. However from a commercial perspective it would have been much more attractive if it had been identified and developed earlier, so that it could have played a role in price setting.

From this is may be apparent that the identification and development of biomarkers is an important topic of discussion in drug development. It is further discussed in Chapter 7.

2. THE SURROGATE ENDPOINT-BASED REIMBURSEMENT DEAL

This is the most liked – and loathed – type of deal. Some argue that the surrogate end-point deal is sometimes necessary to bring a product to market; others say it is a problematic precedent-setting price discount. Today, it is part of everyday reality in Italy and the UK. These deals link reimbursement to meeting short-term surrogate endpoints, such as tumor response rates. However, clinical risk is not associated with surrogate outcomes, but rather with predictability of long-term outcomes that the deal does not address.

Sutent and Nexevar in Italy were introduced using this kind of deal and show some of the hazards of engaging in it. The Italian government reimbursement agency now frequently insists upon agreements that link reimbursement to demonstrated patient-specific efficacy; Sutent and Nexevar have been approved for partial reimbursement for the first three months of use. After three months, the government only pays for patients who respond under the agreed-upon response definitions.

The Velcade Case Study (on the following page) shows a frequently referenced UK-style surrogate endpoints-based reimbursement deal. Typical for the UK version of the surrogate end-point-based deal, rebating takes place for unresponsive patients per defined criteria on the surrogate end point.

Government insistence to not pay for non-responsive patients creates objections with many pharmaceutical pricing executives. It seems unfair to first reference a drug price to other countries and then to insist on paying only for a subset of treated patients. In reality, it has been no more than an artificial way to deal with differences in willingness-to-pay across countries, thus allowing a company to get more flexibility to deviate from a list pricing strategy in order to launch.

3. THE PATIENT OUTCOMES WARRANTY DEAL

Patient warranty deals are based on explicit guarantees regarding long-term patient outcomes. This type of agreement makes intuitive sense – it provides the payer an explicit guarantee that a product works as advertised.

An example of such a deal is the deal between Novartis and some German sickness funds, where Novartis refunds the cost of its bisphosphenate Aclasta for osteoporosis, for patients who suffer from a fracture despite taking the drug.

CASE STUDY: VELCADE – UK

The National Institute for Clinical Excellence (NICE) initially in 2006 declined to recommend Velcade for inclusion on PCT formularies. The new treatment was deemed not cost-effective as its cost was in excess of the £30,000 per QALY unofficial NICE threshold. Under a proclaimed "Risk-Sharing Scheme", it was agreed that the NICE ruling would be reversed under condition of Jansen-Cilag repaying drug treatment cost to NHS for patients with a less than 50 percent reduction in serum M-protein.

The arrangement between Jansen-Cilag and NICE helped overcome a hurdle to marketing Velcade, which could otherwise probably only be resolved through a straight price reduction of equal value to the NHS. The complexity associated with the deal and the added handling costs are unfortunate side-effects of bringing anti-cancer agents to the UK market, which has historically been a daunting task. Unfortunately for British cancer patients, passing on a UK launch continues to be a serious option for every new anti-cancer agent in development.

The warranty deal has several merits, but one stands out: the drug company is making a claim for which they have better information than the payer. From that perspective, it is truly a "risk sharing" partnership. A population-based deal (discussed later) may be more practical, as it may reduce administrative burden.

4. THE SHORT-TERM PERFORMANCE-BASED DEAL

This type of deal is rare. At launch, a pharmaceutical company usually knows a product's short-term clinical performance, diminishing the need for complicated risk-sharing deals.

However, an arrangement between Merck and Cigna for the diabetes drug Januvia is an interesting exception. This partnership involves guarantees on HbA1c as well as patient compliance, key aspects of achieving long-term health outcomes improvements.

The deal does not involve long-term health outcomes data guarantees, and as such does not bridge lack of data on long-term performance of the drug. However the deal seems to be a useful contract between the parties to

CASE STUDY: MERCK/CIGNA – USA

In a pricing approach that was radical for the United States, drug maker Merck forged a deal with insurance company Cigna to price diabetes medicines Januvia and Janumet based on how well patients control their blood sugar.

Merck gave Cigna bigger discounts on Januvia and Janumet in return for better placement on Cigna's formulary, meaning lower co-payments for Cigna's 7 million patients than for other branded drugs. Additional discounts were granted based on patients diligently taking the drug as prescribed. Not only did this deal give Cigna an incentive to carry through with patient compliance programs that urge people to take medicine at the right times and in proper doses, it also encouraged Cigna to support the utilization of Merck drugs in order to reap the benefits of the deal.

The deal was a win-win situation as more compliant patients meant fewer complications from the disease for Cigna and Merck benefited from selling higher volumes.

collaborate on optimizing compliance. The partnership component of this deal may be of great use in other situations. It would have been more appropriate if Merck had received a benefit from demonstrated HbA1c improvements rather than it resulting in a seemingly unfounded additional discount to Cigna.

In general, it does not make a lot of sense to bridge the clinical risk of a drug on the basis of short-term clinical measures. Short-term clinical performance is usually reasonably well known at launch, which suggests that there is little reason to create complicated deals to bridge that risk.

5. THE POPULATION-BASED PERFORMANCE GUARANTEE DEAL

In many ways, this is an ideal agreement, as it brings drug innovations to needy patients, thus benefiting health policy objectives and the pharmaceutical innovator. As its name suggests, reimbursement is based upon long-term outcomes of a patient population, rather than individual or short-term population outcomes.

The multiple sclerosis deal in the UK was one of the first true risk sharing deals. The situation was ideal for a population-based guarantee deal: the British

CASE STUDY: MULTIPLE SCLEROSIS – UK

In 2002, NICE evaluated four new multiple sclerosis drugs (Avonex, Betaferon, Copaxone and Rebif) and ruled them not to be a cost-effective use of NHS resources although they acknowledged apparent clinical benefits. As this ruling was seen as contentious, the NHS decided to engage in a risk-sharing agreement with the drug manufacturers and the risk-sharing scheme (RSS) was born.

For example, the NHS accepted Biogen Idec's proposed price for Avonex that costs around $18,000 a year in exchange for efficacy performance guarantees, which was monitored through a patient registry that was created for this purpose. Under the plan, multiple sclerosis patients are being followed for ten years to see the effect of the drugs in slowing the progression of the disease. In case that long-term targets could not be met, an ex-post discount was agreed. Between 2002 and today, over 9,000 people consented to be followed, the largest such study of MS therapies being undertaken anywhere in the world.

Implementation of the registry, which was an essential part of the agreement, has been more complicated than anticipated. Patient groups have been critical over the fact that after seven years, there is still no available data on two-year patient treatment results. Recent discussions have emphasized that analytical and political complexity of successfully implementing this kind of registry; this should certainly be a lesson for future deals.

government wanted to address high patient demand for MS treatments, despite a negative NICE ruling, while pharmaceutical companies were willing to guarantee long-term outcomes of new products. Both parties stood to gain and mutually bear risk. Unfortunately, the execution of the MS deal struggled from huge implementation issues and lack of coordination and collaboration between the many parties involved. On top of that, the initial data did not show impressive patient improvements over placebo after two years. Due to the unfortunate negative results and the enormous implementation struggles, appetite for real risk sharing deals has shifted to one for simple discounts instead.

The concept of the population-based performance guarantee deal type is actively explored on many fronts in the United States under the Coverage with Evidence Development (CED) classification. A number of device and drug reimbursement agreements with CMS follow the CED concept. Under these agreements, reimbursement coverage is provided by CMS, under condition that the patient is enrolled in a registry in which further evidence on the treatment's efficacy and safety is gathered over time.

The Sanofi-Aventis/Proctor & Gamble deal with Health Alliance in the United States for its Actonel osteoporosis treatment deal is a variation on the Novartis-German sickness funds deal guaranteeing outcomes. However in this deal, for patients taking Actonel and suffering fractures, Sanofi-Aventis will reimburse the medical cost for treating a fracture rather than just the cost of the drug treatment. It is unclear if an uncertainty of clinical outcomes forms the basis for this type of deal, rather than tactical life-cycle marketing objectives.

In 2012, the Australian government approved the inclusion of BMS's Yervoy for the treatment of metastatic melanoma in the Pharmaceutical Benefits Scheme (PBS). A risk sharing arrangement was an essential part of the approval (Yervoy Risk Sharing, 2012). The deal included restrictions on dose for first-line treatment, implementation of a real-world evidence verification of the claimed overall survival improvements, and a financial risk component. Particularly the overall survival guarantee portion of the deal is an important next step in addressing long-term outcomes data for a new and innovative drug that has substantial needs in the market.

CASE STUDY: AVASTIN – USA

Prior to the FDA approval of Avastin for use in breast cancer, there was a lot of public debate about the cost of this application of Avastin. Doctors and media targeted Genentech at the prospect of $100,000 per year on the drug, with some patients forgoing use of Avastin so as not to deplete family savings.

To avoid a PR challenge, Genentech launched the "Avastin Patient Assistance Program". The program provides an opportunity for eligible patients who are treated for an FDA-approved indication and who reach an annual dosage of 10,000 mg to receive Avastin free of charge from Genentech for the remainder of the 12-month period. The program is open to all patients receiving Avastin regardless of insurance coverage.

The initiative which essentially caps Avastin cost at $55,000 per calendar year seems to have been effective in addressing Genentech's challenges in the US.

6. THE PER-PATIENT COST CAPITATION DEAL

In general, the per-patient cost capitation deal ensures payers that cost will not exceed a certain limit. This is particularly important for payers concerned that a pharmaceutical product can support sustained use beyond what the payer may find reasonable. For example, in a deal with the Department of Health in the UK, Novartis agreed to pay for macular degeneration drug Lucentis when patients require more than 14 injections of the treatment, beyond which evidence suggests that it is not clinically useful.

Another example of this type of deal is the Avastin breast cancer deal in the United States (see Case Study on previous page). Following a lot of negative publicity Genentech effectively used a price cap to help alleviate cost concerns.

7. OVERALL SALES VOLUME CAPITATION

The final type of risk sharing agreement ties prices to sales. As part of a launch price negotiation in France, annual sales volumes must be agreed upon for several years. If the maximum volume is exceeded, the pharmaceutical company will pay penalties, be it in terms of rebates or price reductions. Similar deals are found in Australia, both for individual drugs and, across companies, for drug classes.

Sales-volume capitation deals are designed to address government budget concerns, but form a disincentive for innovation, as additional demand following better data can be punished severely.

Finding the Deal that Makes Sense

Pricing and health outcomes disciplines need to engage in close collaboration to ensure that the "right strategic deal" is pursued. There are some truly great opportunities for risk sharing deals. However, as with the "disease management" phenomenon in the 1990s, many healthcare companies are jumping on the risk sharing bandwagon because they do not want to feel left out, no matter the benefits in any given deal. It is up to each of us to identify these and not be distracted by neighbors who are attempting to sell refrigerators to Eskimos.

A simple measurement of a deal's viability is when both payer and pharmaceutical company see a benefit. The multiple sclerosis agreement in the UK is a role model example for a perfect fit of a risk sharing deal. The payer and pharmaceutical companies truly shared the risk, and, despite some implementation difficulties, patients gained access to the drugs and a difficult situation for the NHS was averted. Figure 18.2 is illustrating how various risk sharing deals can be seen to measure up with respect to the win-win aspect. Some deals represent a strong negotiation position from payers; others may be more truly a partnership. Most important is the idea of trying to find common ground as the best way to reach a meaningful deal.

True "risk sharing" agreements can be pursued for two reasons:

- A pharmaceutical company has in-depth information on a new product's characteristics at or prior to launch;

- Availability of key data to back up pharmaceutical company claims is dependent on the company's commitment to plan and execute these trials.

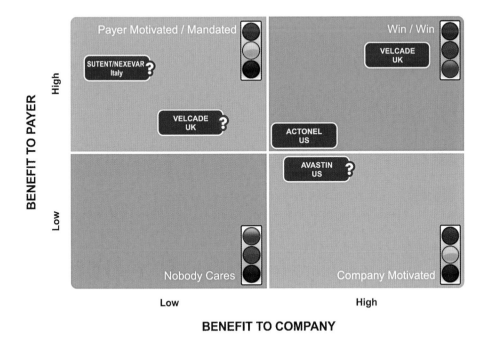

Figure 18.2   Looking for the win-win

Whether the deal is a true "risk sharing" deal or not, we should evaluate every opportunity for a risk sharing deal in a logical and structured fashion:

1. *Have a clear goal*

   What are we trying to achieve? When the objective of a deal is vague, we are not likely to come up with a meaningful deal that makes sense in the long run. Good deals *resolve issues* rather than create them.

2. *Look for the win-win*

   What is in it for the payer? If it is not a win-win deal, it is less likely to be successful or it may not be a good deal for one of the parties. Are we pursuing the right kind of deal?

3. *Consider longer-term impact*

   What is the long-term strategic impact on our business? Will we impact pricing in other countries? Are we just increasing the cost of doing business through admin and data collection cost?

4. *Make sure it is real*

   Can it be implemented? Even the much heralded MS deal in the UK was facing great implementation issues.

A deal that gets a positive report card after review on the above four criteria, is likely to be worthwhile pursuing.

Managed Entry Agreements

As mentioned earlier in this chapter, Managed Entry Agreements (MAEs) have been surfacing over the last few years. While originally risk sharing deals were focused on means to address concerns of payers related to clinical outcomes and financial risk, some more recent MAEs tend to be more pragmatically focused on addressing pricing-related issues in the negotiations through a more direct mechanism. In reality, Managed Entry Agreements are not different from most

Risk Sharing deals, but rather a more appropriate naming of what most risk sharing deals had actually evolved to.

To understand the movement towards MEAs we need to go back to the Multiple Sclerosis Risk Sharing deal in the UK and similar Outcomes-based Contracts in other countries. Through these deals, payers have started to realize that these deals come with a huge cost of program management with a very uncertain return on investment. As a result, patient access schemes in the UK initially required drug companies to pay for all costs of registry data gathering/ handling, then abolished data gathering altogether in favor of simple discount deals.

As payers have become more critical of risk sharing deals that involve a lot of data gathering, the pharmaceutical industry thinking has evolved to devise creative managed entry solutions that speed up access to innovative medicines while complying with local approval requirements. The new approach of MEAs is in essence just a more focused and less complex approach to overcoming payer objections. It was usually not about real risk sharing anyhow, but rather about structuring the right deal that can enable the local business without a disruption of global strategies.

Managed Entry Agreements in Emerging Markets

Managed Entry Agreements often refer to deals made with (usually government) payers as a way to address affordability and willingness-to-pay of lower- and middle-income countries in comparison with the United States and Europe. These MEAs can have a structure, ranging from simple discounts to more elaborate collaborations such as the "Vale Mais Saude" program created in Brazil by Novartis. This program is a comprehensive health management platform for chronic diseases, such as COPD, that aims to reduce hospital and medical visit resources by tracking patients and providing nutritional, wellness, sports, exercise and counseling services. Discounts are provided on a portfolio of brands.

Implementation Considerations

Even when a pharmaceutical company negotiates a deal that looks good on paper, it can easily fall apart over implementation issues such as data collection complexities and administrative burdens related to validation of claims related to the deal. To reduce longer-term cost and administrative burdens, it is important to have an exit strategy after a sufficient evaluation of the risk elements. Evaluating individual patient data for the rest of a drug's life cycle, just to calculate a rebate, is in nobody's interest.

Transparency of a deal can be a contentious issue. Payers can be concerned that a confidential deal will distort the market or form a substantial barrier to entry for new follow-on drugs. It may be difficult for a new player to negotiate price when they don't know what existing prices are. The German government has insisted that negotiated net prices under AMNOG are publicly known. The French government is very comfortable in keeping all deals confidential. As confidentiality is an important cornerstone of many risk sharing deals, it will continue to be a point of debate with payers.

Underlying all of these conditions is the answer to a fundamental question for pharmaceutical companies: is the deal adding any fundamental value to the company, or providing a competitive advantage? Pricing professionals need to convincingly answer "yes" before embarking upon a complicated and hard-to-implement deal. Certainly payers are less open to deals that involve a lot of administrative hassle.

The Future of Risk Sharing

It will be interesting to see how risk sharing and managed entry agreements will evolve. Outside the United States, existing practices on risk sharing are likely to continue, as government payers identified a way to demand prices outside international pricing bands that were previously guarded carefully. In other cases, drug companies have found ways to overcome limitations in relation to gaps in the evidence package.

In the United States, deals have so far been sporadic and with limited numbers of payers. They have the nature of experiments. However, there is a continuing flux behind the Coverage with Evidence Development (CED) concept, which fits within the population-based performance guarantee category. Accountable Care Organizations and other quality control mechanisms are likely to further impact support for innovative pricing initiatives. We can help establish a meaningful place for risk sharing deals by focusing on deals that "make sense."

If not, in a few years we will find them in a museum exhibit, right next to "disease management."

In this Chapter ...

We have closely examined "risk sharing" deals and "managed entry agreements" and identified seven kinds of deals that are generally included in the category. We identified likes and dislikes about each of them and considered a number of case study examples. We emphasized the importance of identifying a goal for a deal and the potential for a win-win opportunity with payers. We also highlighted the importance of considering implementation aspects.

PART E
Key Healthcare Systems

In this part, a number of key global healthcare systems are described in general terms. The purpose is to give an understanding of the key processes and driving factors and organizations that are involved in the various pricing and market access approval steps. To describe each system completely would go far beyond the scope of this book. Reports are available that serve that purpose.

Besides a technical description of each system, comments are included to highlight some of the real-life issues and the practical aspects around gaining approval. Many of these are the author's opinions, based on many years of experience in dealing with these healthcare systems.

It is important to realize that, although carefully structured and legislated, all these systems slowly evolve on the basis of the evolving medical science, political changes and experience gained through ongoing operations within the system. Changes in healthcare systems usually evolve slowly and in evolution rather than revolution. Many changes in one country are based on similar changes that have occurred previously in other countries, although usually in a somewhat adjusted local version. Interestingly, payers tend to frequently add new means of control without eliminating their old ones, thus creating increasingly complex systems.

In the second edition, many larger and smaller updates were made. Particularly the Chapters for the United States, France, Germany and the United Kingdom were significantly modified to incorporate substantial system changes. For the United States, the Affordable Care Act and many smaller changes and additions were made. For France, the introduction of Medico-Economic requirements in 2013 and for Germany AMNOG and many associated changes were introduced. Furthermore, all financial and health statistics were updated.

Key statistics for each country in the following chapters are obtained from *The Economist* (2013 [2]), World Bank (2013), Global Use of Medicines (IMS, November 2013) and Aspen (2013).

19

United States

Key Statistics

Population	318.8 m
GDP	$17,508 bn
GDP per capita	$54,920
Healthcare Budget (% GDP)	15.4 %
Health Budget per capita	$8,608
Drug Market Size	$328.2 bn
Drug Market Growth ('08–'12)	+3.0 %
Global Drug Market Ranking	1

Overview

Healthcare in the United States is mainly administered through private insurance or managed care organizations (MCOs) and government-run Medicare and Medicaid bodies. Besides employer sponsored health insurance offerings, MCOs also manage many government sponsored programs such as Health Exchanges, Medicare Part C/D and Managed Medicaid.

Rapidly rising cost of healthcare and broad access to affordable healthcare have been hot political topics over the last two decades. Substantial rises in healthcare cost have resulted in a rapidly rising share of uninsured in the United States to 15 percent of the population in 2013. In states like Texas, the uninsured share of the population was higher at about 25 percent. Furthermore, in order to contain insurance premiums, higher deductibles, co-pays and coverage restrictions have become more common place.

Upon implementation of President Barack Obama's Affordable Care Act, the distribution of insurance coverage has only slightly shifted. Figure 19.1 provides an estimate of the March 2014 breakdown of health insurance segments across the US population. At the time of writing of this second edition, enrollment in the healthcare exchanges reached 7 million patients or about 2 percent of the population (not all previously uninsured). In addition, previously uninsured adults have signed up for Medicaid and young adults under 26 have gained coverage as dependents on their parents' insurance plans. This may evolve further, but at least in 2014, despite these changes, the uninsured continue to form a significant group in the US healthcare environment.

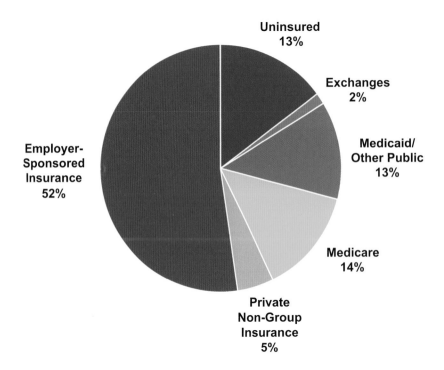

Figure 19.1   US population by payer segment

Pricing

Drug prices can be set without government restrictions in the US, although there are some post-launch limitations in pricing freedom for the government sector. Each company is free to determine the optimal price for its drugs in the private market, and adjust prices over time to address inflation or market-related considerations. However, pricing decisions and discounts and rebates granted to selected customers can have implications for reimbursement rates for Medicare, Medicaid and other government agencies.

List prices are calculated and/or published under various terms with slightly different definitions, as shown in Table 19.1. Many of the listed price levels are defined by government agencies to determine net reimbursement price. This will be discussed in subsequent sections of this chapter.

The use of the Average Wholesale Price (AWP) has been a very contentious issue and subject to a large number of federal, state and local lawsuits against drug manufacturers. The underlying problem has been that AWP has served as a basis for reimbursement calculations for Medicare and many other payers. AWP is typically set at about 20 percent to 25 percent above WAC by First DataBank. In reality, the AWP is not clearly related to the actual price paid, as discounts and rebates are generally applied. Today, ASP and AMP are more common price references for reimbursement calculations.

Table 19.1   US drug pricing definitions

Price Level	Definition
Average Manufacturer Price (AMP)	Benchmark used for Medicaid rebate calculations since 1990, defined as the average price paid to manufacturers for retail drugs
Average Sales Price (ASP)	Weighted average price of all non-federal sales to wholesalers, net of chargebacks, discounts, rebates and other benefits paid
Average Wholesale Price (AWP)	Most frequently used official list price for prescription drugs listed in sources such as the Red Book and First DataBank. AWP has been used extensively as a basis for reimbursement calculations by Medicare, Medicaid and Private Insurance. Use of AWP as a reimbursement reference has dramatically decreased over the last years, as ASP and AMP have been proven to be more sensible sources
Direct Price (DP)	See Wholesale Acquisition Cost (WAC)
Federal Upper Limit (FUL)	Federal price ceiling that applies to drugs with three or more generic versions
Maximum Allowable Cost (MAC)	Upper limit price that Medicare, Medicaid or a private insurance company will pay for a multi-source drug
Medicaid Best Price	Lowest price paid to a manufacturer for a brand-name drug, taking into account rebates, chargebacks, discounts and other pricing adjustments, excluding nominal prices
Wholesale Acquisition Cost (WAC)	Manufacturer list price for wholesalers, also known as Direct Price (DP)

Private Health Insurance

The US health insurance or managed care market represented a total value of $713 billion in direct premiums in 2012. The top 25 companies represent nearly two-thirds of the market. The largest company, United Healthcare holds an 11.7 percent market share (see Figure 19.2 for an overview of health insurance providers by size).

The large majority of US citizens have health insurance that is sponsored by their employer and administered by a private insurer or managed care organization (MCO). Employers are increasingly offering a menu of choices of coverage for the employee and his/her dependents, where the choices can involve multiple plans with for example different levels of freedom of choice with respect to the medical network, as well as levels of co-pay and deductibles and related premium differences.

MCOs are engaged in a balancing act, trying to keep their primary customers – employers and members – happy, while controlling cost of medical and pharmaceutical benefits. This has been a challenge, particularly since the cost of medical care has continued to rise rapidly. In trying to deal with cost

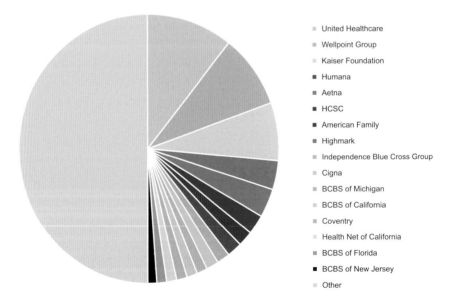

Figure 19.2   US health insurance market share by premiums
Source: NAIC, 2009

increases, early day MCOs tried many approaches to contain cost, including strict staff models, only allowing medical consultations with contracted staff physicians. At one time plans issued physician gag orders to stop physicians from informing patients of more appropriate treatment options that were not covered by the health plan. After staff models were rejected by many members, who strongly value the ability to choose their own physician, and physician gag orders were legally challenged, most MCOs evolved to a network model. These models offered one or more structures for their medical services, such as Health Maintenance Organizations (HMOs), Preferred Provider Organizations (PPOs) and some fee-for-service programs. With the emergence of PPOs, physician networks and contracted fees for healthcare services have become an important tool for managed care plans to negotiate lower physician fees as an important part of their financial model. For patients, PPOs offer a more flexible model and more provider choice than the rather restrictive HMO model. Fees for uninsured and for out-of-network services are much higher than what is actually paid by most health insurance companies for in-network services. As a consequence, uninsured patients generally pay much more for medical care by physicians and hospitals than insured patients do. This has added more pressure on the political parties to provide universal healthcare coverage to the population.

The March 23, 2010 Patient Protection and Affordable Care Act (ACA), frequently referred to as "Obamacare," has initiated substantial change in the US healthcare industry. The ACA law has the following components:

- Individual Mandate, requiring US citizens and legal residents to have qualifying healthcare coverage with a gradually increasing tax imposition for those not complying. The individual mandate, essential to avoid young healthy individuals to opt out of the program, has been heavily challenged by Republicans, but was upheld by the Supreme Court.

- Employers with 50 or more full time employees are required to cover healthcare insurance with tax impositions for those not complying. Implementation was initially per January 1, 2014, but was delayed over plan implementation problems.

- Medicaid expansion for all non-Medicare eligible individuals under age 65 with incomes up to 133 percent of the Federal Poverty Level (FPL). The Supreme Court ruled that this part of the program is optional for state participation; many states have opted out. Many participating states already had a higher coverage level than the mandated federal minimums.

- Creation of state-based Health Insurance Exchanges (Marketplace) for individual employees and small employers to purchase health insurance at competitive rates with low-income subsidies. Plans should offer four benefit categories (bronze, silver, gold and platinum) and a catastrophic option for individuals. Initial sign up was very slow, in part because of website problems, and more heavily weighted towards older individuals.

- Prohibition of limitations on pre-existing conditions and annual/lifetime coverage limitations. Establishment of a high-risk insurance pool for initial financing of patients with pre-existing conditions.

- Extended healthcare coverage of dependents up to the age of 26 and prohibition of rescissions of coverage.

- Various initiatives to improve quality and efficiency of health care, including Medicare payment links to quality performance in high-cost conditions (cardiac, surgical, pneumonia care), Accountable Care organizations (ACOs) and various bundled payment initiatives and pilots.

The above is only a general description of the elements of ACA. A more detailed summary is found in *Focus on Health Reform*. The impact of ACA on the pharmaceutical market and its payer segments is discussed in later sections of this chapter.

Pharmaceuticals

Prescription drug coverage is provided as part of comprehensive healthcare coverage for most MCOs. Private healthcare plans can provide drug coverage directly or through pharmacy benefits managers (PBMs), who handle formulary management and prescription processing on behalf of the health insurance company (or directly for the employer). Formulary negotiations between healthcare plans or PBMs and pharmaceutical companies are confidential and discount and rebate terms are generally not known to the public.

Since PBMs only handle drugs, their cost perspective tends to be limited to drug cost only, ignoring any broader medical cost consequences and savings that a comprehensive plan might consider valuable.

Most Managed Care companies manage pharmaceuticals as a medical benefit when administered by a physician or other medical staff and as a pharmaceutical benefit when dispensed through a retail pharmacy and self-administered by the patient. Whether a pharmacy benefit is handled by the plan or carved out and handled as a silo by a PBM can have important implications for the impact of certain evidence on formulary decision making. A PBM will generally not be sensitive to evidence that a new drug treatment is saving medical cost, since they will not be receiving any benefit from it. As an example, a new drug treatment that has the potential to reduce days of hospitalization or reduce other medical expenses will be looked upon favorably by any integrated health plan, because it will look at the patient benefit from a total cost perspective rather than a drug cost perspective only. PBMs have been under a lot of pressure for their limited focus on the pharmacy silo only; it will be interesting to see whether they will try to evolve to get more broadly engaged in medical management to address this criticism.

Most MCOs are careful to separate decisions on medical need for a drug from actual formulary placement. Their formal perspective tends to be that formulary inclusion is a medical decision, independent of cost, whereas its specific formulary tier placement is a financial decision. In reality this may only be true for the most innovative new drug entries.

Formulary management for pharmacy benefits is controlled by decision making by a pharmacy and therapeutics committee with membership of key disciplines of the organization, including pharmacy and medical directors. Drug formularies usually have multiple tiers with different patient co-pay levels. A three-tier formulary includes generics, preferred brands and non-preferred brands. Generics are incentivized with a very low co-pay of typically $10, even lower for chains such as Walmart. Plans increasingly use a specialty fourth tier and sometime a fifth tier for high-cost biologics. Specialty tiers frequently use a co-insurance (percentage co-pay), rather than a fixed co-pay to create more sensitivity to the high cost of biologics. A fifth tier is increasingly introduced as a non-preferred specialty tier with the fourth tier then serving as a preferred specialty tier. Typical four- and five-tier formulary designs are shown in Table 19.2.

Table 19.2   Four-tier and Five-tier formulary designs

Tier	Four-tier Description	Five-tier Description
1	Generic	Generic
2	Preferred Brand	Preferred Brand
3	Non-Preferred Brand	Non-Preferred Brand
4	Specialty	Preferred Specialty
5	—	Non-Preferred Specialty

Formulary designs have undergone dramatic change over the last 15 years, moving from rather simple formulary structures to multi-tier co-pay and co-insurance formularies. Figure 19.3 illustrates the development of employer-sponsored plan designs from 2000 to 2012. Since the early 2000s the three-tier plan design has been the dominantly used design. Since 2004, a fourth (and later fifth) tier has grown in prevalence, at least in part inspired by Medicare Part D practices. In 2013, about 23 percent of plans had introduced a fourth tier, a rapid increase from prior years.

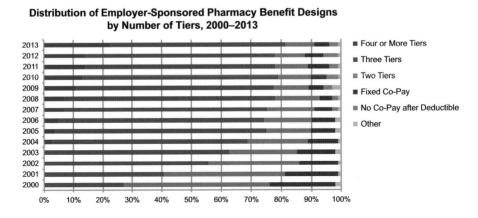

Figure 19.3   Private employer-sponsored plan evolution 2000–2013
Source: Kaiser/HRET Survey of Employer Sponsored Health Benefits 2013

Figures 19.4 and 19.5 illustrate the development of absolute and relative co-payment rates from 2000 to 2013. Gradually increasing co-pay levels, together with an increasing use of higher tier levels have resulted in an increased patient cost exposure. Co-insurance levels for fourth tiers are 32 percent on average

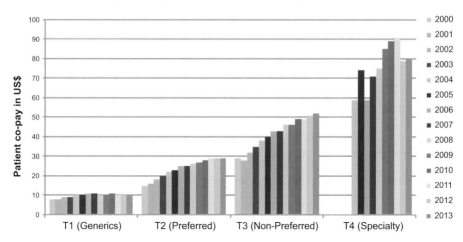

Figure 19.4   Private employer-sponsored plan co-pay development
Source: Kaiser Employer Health Benefits Survey 2013

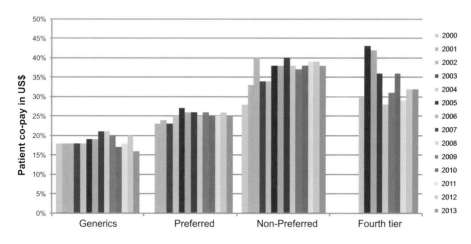

Figure 19.5   Private employer-sponsored plan co-insurance development
Source: Kaiser Employer Health Benefits Survey 2013

in 2013, which given the high cost of the specialty drugs in this category can amount to significant out-of-pocket payments for patients.

Management of biologics, particularly in oncology, has been and continues to be a difficult matter for healthcare plans. Co-insurance rates have further increased price sensitivity with patients. They have also raised considerable concerns over patient adherence to drug therapy. Figure 19.6 shows a case study in Multiple Sclerosis, indicating three- to six-fold increases in treatment discontinuations for co-payments reaching $250 (20 percent).

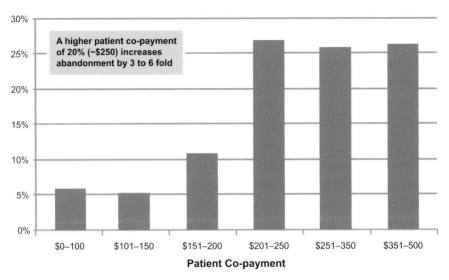

Figure 19.6   Impact of patient co-payment on prescription abandonment

Source: Association of Prescription Abandonment with CostShare for High-Cost Specialty Pharmacy Medications. Patrick P. Gleason et al. *Journal of Managed Care Pharmacy*. October 2009, Vol. 15, No. 8.

Medicare Part D and Exchange plans have substantial co-insurance rates and are hence of the highest concern with respect to patient willingness-to-pay and adherence to drug treatment. Many plans have an out-of-pocket maximum, above which only small patient co-payments are required. For these patients, cost sensitivity will naturally decline. See later sections of this chapter for more discussion.

PRIOR AUTHORIZATIONS

High-cost drugs are generally subject to increased scrutiny by healthcare plans through a prior authorization process, requiring the approval by the plan before a script can be filled at the pharmacy or can be used in an inpatient or office setting. There are several levels of intensity of information requirements, depending on the drug and therapy area. In many cases, prior authorizations (PA) are simply used to verify that the use is within drug labeling. This may include verification of diagnosis and proof of prior treatments used.

Given the cost of handling PAs it only makes sense for plans to use the mechanism for higher-cost drugs, particularly biologics, such as many anti-cancer drugs and TNF-inhibitors. Generally, plans may use it both to incentivize to try cheaper options first, as well as to ensure that high-cost drugs are used appropriately. In the case of anti-cancer drugs, plans will usually want to confirm that the indication is within labeling or endorsed in one or more of the recognized drug compendia. In many US states, coverage for approved anti-cancer drugs is mandatory, but plans can decide on formulary placement and management.

STEP EDITS

A tool that is frequently used by payers to enforce use of lesser expensive earlier lines of treatment, usually generics, is the step edit. Step edits, unlike prior authorizations (PAs), are not usually expensive to administer and can be effective in managing lower unit cost non-biologic drugs with a high budget impact. The lines between step edits and PAs can be blurred at times as some of the "easier" PAs that are electronically adjudicated at point of sale can practically act as a step edit.

CONTRACTING

What is the role of contracting? Under what circumstances does it make sense to contract and when not? This book will only address some of the high level concepts and practices on contracting with the main purpose of addressing how they impact a brand's market access and pricing strategy.

In a Managed Care contract, discounts are provided to the payer, usually in exchange for a more favorable formulary position. As an example, Januvia (Merck) and later gliptins such as Onglyza (AstraZeneca) have been competing in many healthcare plans for a second-tier formulary position in diabetes treatment. Similarly, manufacturers of Enbrel, Humira and subsequent anti-TNF market entries are trying to convince payers for a more favorable formulary position in rheumatoid arthritis treatment. For drugs without any close substitutes, there is generally no strong rationale to contract, unless it is to remove certain patient restrictions or when certain performance guarantees or long-term commitments are given by the payer.

Most US payers initially place new drugs on a third tier (fourth tier for specialty drugs) for six to nine months following launch. This gives payers the opportunity to evaluate physician experience, monitor initial demand and project future utilization and budget impact of the new drug. When anticipated demand is low, MCOs are likely to leave the drug on an unfavorable formulary position. When anticipated demand is high, MCOs are much more willing to discuss contracting to take advantage of discount-related savings at a higher utilization rate. Recently, more plans have moved to not cover or charge higher than typical Tier 3 co-payments for new launches until a formal review and formulary decision has taken place.

Contracting is usually attractive for MCOs when multiple drugs are available within the same drug class. Drugs in one class are often considered interchangeable for most patients, thus creating a likely large impact of co-pay differentiation on prescribing and market share. On the commercial side however, co-pay cards can largely offset the impact of an unfavorable co-pay tier. As a result of these co-pay cards, plans have increasingly resorted to step edits and PAs to force utilization of cheaper options first.

Depending on the nature of contracts in place, a high hurdle can be placed on subsequent entries. Consider, as an example, a drug class with two drugs, A and B. Drug A has a 70 percent share of sales within the plan on the basis of a contract, granting exclusive second-tier placement for a 10 percent discount. Assume that a competitor with a third Drug C of the same class wants to entice the plan to place Drug C on second tier. Since the plan would lose its 10 percent discount over 70 percent of drug class sales if it broke its contractual obligations with the manufacturer of Drug A, it would have to get a significant concession from the new player. For the MCO to just break even, the company would need to offer a 35 percent discount at an expected 20 percent market share or even a 70 percent discount at an expected 10 percent market share. In this simplified case, there is obviously a very high hurdle for a new entry. From the MCO perspective, giving exclusive preferred tier placement can provide a robust savings, but also limits opportunities to obtain later cost savings as others enter the market. MCOs are also hesitant to provide a preferred formulary position for new and relatively unproven drugs as they don't want to "push" physicians to prescribe lesser proven agents in lieu of confidential payments to the plan.

The drug companies' ability to contract with MCOs for a favorable formulary position is practically limited through its potential impact on Medicaid reimbursement through Medicaid "Best Price" provisions. See further discussion under Medicaid later in this chapter.

Medicare

Medicare provides coverage for elderly over 65, disabled under the age of 65 and patients with End-Stage Renal Disease (ESRD). Coverage is provided through four program parts:

- Part A: Inpatient medical and drug treatment;

- Part B: Outpatient treatment, including physician-administered drugs;

- Part C: Medicare Advantage plan, integrated medical and drug benefits, including self-administered drugs;

- Part D: Medicare coverage for self-administered prescription drugs.

Medicare Part A is offered free of charge. Other parts require a monthly fee. Medicare Parts C and D are structured under the 2003 Medicare Modernization Act and administered by competing private Managed Care plans under CMS specified coverage criteria and fees. Drug coverage for hospital inpatients under Medicare Part A is included in the diagnosis-related group (DRG)-based prospective payment made to the hospital.

MEDICARE PART B

Medicare Part B covers drugs that are administered in the physician's offices at a reimbursement rate of ASP + 6 percent. Physician administration fees are usually handled through a separate reimbursement code. Patients are mandated to pay a 20 percent co-payment for drugs and medical benefits, although many patients may not be exposed to this due to supplementary insurance coverage.

Due to formal ASP calculations and reporting mechanisms, there is a lag time between price increases and reimbursement adjustment. As a result, we need to be careful with larger price increases for medical benefits, as they may result in losses for particularly the least efficient purchasers, such as small group practices. For practices with a relatively large Medicare population this can pose an issue.

MEDICARE PART D

Medicare Part D has been instituted as part of the 2003 Medicare Modernization Act (MMA) to address a gap in insurance coverage for the elderly for retail prescription drugs.

Figure 19.7 shows the standard coverage design under the 2003 MMA with 2014 "Donut Hole" coverage gap numbers. Since 2011, Medicare Part D enrolees who have reached the donut hole get a 50 percent discount on brand drugs. Patient payments while in the donut hole will gradually decrease until 2020, when patients will pay 25 percent for both brands and generics, effectively eliminating the donut hole from their perspective. Table 19.3 shows the annual schedule of patient responsibility for brand and generic drugs.

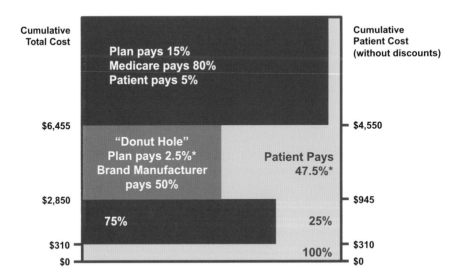

Figure 19.7   Standard Medicare Part D benefit design (2014 limits)

Table 19.3   Phase-out schedule of donut hole under Medicare Part D

Year	Brand-Name Drugs			Generic Drugs	
	Pharma. Mfgr. Discount	Plan Responsibility	Patient Responsibility	Plan Responsibility	Patient Responsibility
2014	50 %	2.5 %	47.5 %	28 %	72 %
2015	50 %	5 %	45 %	35 %	65 %
2016	50 %	5 %	45 %	42 %	58 %
2017	50 %	10 %	40 %	49 %	51 %
2018	50 %	15 %	35 %	56 %	44 %
2019	50 %	20 %	30 %	63 %	37 %
2020	50 %	25 %	25 %	75 %	25 %

Healthcare plans are allowed to offer a different benefit design, as long as the actuarial value of the benefit is equal to that of the standard benefit. In reality, most plans offer a tiered benefit structure rather than the standard 25 percent co-insurance for drug cost below the donut hole limit. This allows plans to encourage the use of a full range of inexpensive generics at very low co-pays and 25 percent and higher co-insurance rates for expensive biologic drugs. More than 90 percent of Medicare Part D enrolees have a specialty tier in their formulary design, which is substantially more than for employer-sponsored private insurance, where (in 2013) 23 percent of employers indicate the use of the specialty tier (see Figure 19.3). Under Medicare rules, drugs with a monthly cost in excess of $600 can be included in a specialty tier. The median co-insurance rate for these drugs is 33 percent, which leaves a significant cost burden and cost-sensitivity with the patient. See Table 19.4 for median patient cost sharing data for 2013.

Table 19.4   Median 2013 cost sharing for Medicare Part D plans

Tier	Prescription Drug Plan	Medicare Advantage
Generic	$2	$5
Preferred Brand	$40	$45
Non-Preferred Brand	$85	$90
Specialty	26%	33%

Source: Kaiser Family Foundation, 2013

Patient cost-sensitivity for Medicare Part D drugs tends to be very high due to the high co-pays and co-pay differentiation between tiers. In addition, co-pay offset cards cannot be used legally for Medicare Part D due to anti-kickback statutes. Another consideration is that a sometimes large share of patients may be dual Medicare-Medicaid eligibles, who have a much lower patient contribution.

Medicaid

Medicaid and the (State) Children's Health Insurance Program (SCHIP or CHIP) provide healthcare coverage for eligible low-income families. Medicaid and CHIP are federally subsidized programs that are administered by the states. The core program is shown in Figure 19.8. States can add additional coverage beyond what is indicated in Figure 19.8.

Medicaid covers inpatient and outpatient medical and pharmacy drug benefits. Pharmacy benefits can be managed through a Medicaid Managed Care

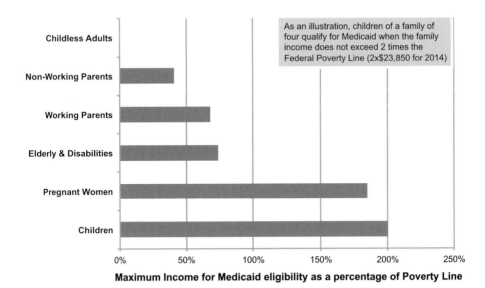

Figure 19.8   Income eligibility level for Medicaid/CHIP coverage

plan or managed through a state formulary with or without a Preferred Drug List (PDL) and state and federally mandated rebates. Medicaid beneficiaries, who are covered under Medicare Part D, that is "dual eligibles," have been covered under Medicare Part D since its introduction. Fifteen percent of the population and 28 percent of all children are covered by Medicaid.

Drugs supplied to Medicaid providers are subject to a mandated discount of 23.1 percent (was 15.1 percent until 2010) off the Average Manufacturer Price (AMP), or the difference between AMP and the best price offered to any private purchaser. Medicaid pricing can be increased annually up to the Consumer Price Index (CPI) rate. Any excess of price increases over CPI need to be offset with additional Medicaid discounts off AMP. Aggressive contracting in the private market can have implications for Medicaid pricing, as any lower price needs to be provided to the Medicaid population under the best price provision.

States have the ability to negotiate supplemental Medicaid discounts on top of the mandated federal rate in exchange for listing on a state's preferred drug list.

Many states have outsourced management of their Medicaid program to third party Managed Medicare organizations, who manage healthcare services and drugs as a managed care plan, albeit with much more limited coverage offered than the average employer-sponsored program.

Under Obamacare (ACA) changes, states have been offered the option to use temporary federal subsidies to extend Medicaid coverage for all non-Medicare eligible individuals under the age of 65 with incomes up to 133 percent of FPL. For a mix of political reasons and concerns over long-term budget implications, many states decided to forego the subsidies and not participate. Figure 19.9 provides an overview of the status of ACA Medicaid expansion in March 2014.

Hospital Drugs

Reimbursement of hospital administered drugs is dependent on the insurance segment and the point of care of the medical service provided. Drugs administered to inpatients are usually covered under fixed Disease Related Group (DRG) reimbursement rates, which are set and periodically updated

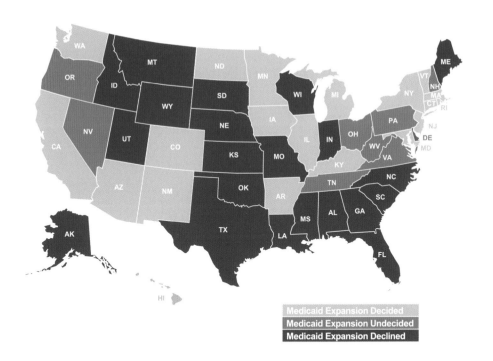

Figure 19.9   US state participation with ACA Medicaid expansion
Source: US Dept. of Health and Human Services – status per March 1, 2014

by CMS. Drug manufacturers can provide price concessions to hospitals in order to obtain a favorable position on a hospital formulary. Hospital price discounts have consequences for Medicaid best price provisions with the exception of hospitals that qualify for exemption under the 340B program.

Healthcare Marketplace (Exchanges)

A central part of the ACA of 2010 has been the institution of Healthcare Exchanges by January 2014, offering a competitive marketplace for individuals and small employers to buy health insurance. States were able to elect to build a fully State-based Marketplace, enter into a state–federal Partnership Marketplace, or default into a Federally-facilitated Marketplace. The latter Federally-facilitated Marketplace was established and operated by HHS in states where there was no willingness to establish a State-based or Partnership Marketplace. Figure 19.10 shows the nature of participation by state in the administration of the

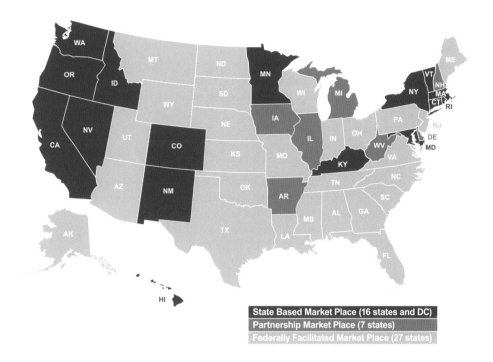

Figure 19.10   State health insurance Marketplace decisions
Source: Kaiser Family Foundation

Marketplace. Decision making was heavily driven by politics, with many Democratic states participating with a State-based marketplace and many Republican states opting out, thereby obtaining the Federally-facilitated option as mandated by ACA.

At the time of writing of this second edition, enrollment for the Exchanges had been very slow, with about 7 million patients enrolled by March 31, 2014. Initial operational struggles with the website, as well as a lack of perceived urgency for young healthy individuals led to low adoption and higher participation at higher age groups. Further evolution of enrollment across the Marketplace plan options (bronze, silver, gold and platinum) and related premium and coverage profiles will impact detailed strategies and tactics. However, with 63 percent enrolling in the Silver Plan and 18 percent in the Bronze Plan option through end of February 2014, deductible and co-payments will need to be very high, leading to very high sensitivity of patients to tier placement of covered drugs.

The introduction of the Marketplace plans, in addition to high co-pay Medicare Part D plans and gradually increasing co-pays and a fourth tier in employer sponsored health plans are gradually transforming the US pharmaceutical market into an even more fragmented and complex environment. Determining an optimal drug price in this setting requires increasingly complex analyses, as for any drug the payer mix between various payer types and their sub-segments need to be analyzed and modeled, while considering how co-pays may impact physicians prescribing and patient adherence to treatment. Figure 19.11 illustrates the high-level model of interactions that needs to be considered in this evaluation. More information about US price optimization methodologies is found in Chapter 15.

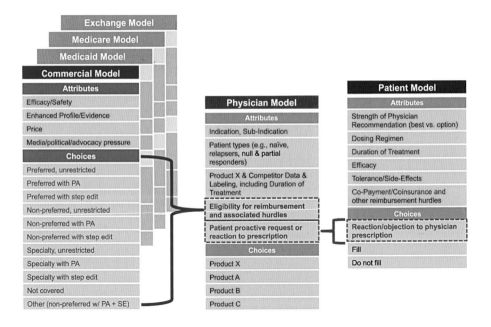

Figure 19.11   US Price optimization modeling across decision makers

Hospitals, Provider Organizations and Accountable Care Organizations

Hospitals and Provider Organizations are discussed together here as for each of them the organizational incentives and payment structures need to be closely considered as key drivers of their decision making. Accountable Care Organizations, instituted under ACA, can operate across hospitals and provider organizations.

Reimbursement of hospital-administered drugs is dependent on the insurance segment (Commercial, Medicare, Medicaid, Marketplace Exchanges) and the point of care of the medical service provided. Drugs administered to inpatients are usually covered under a fixed Disease Related Group (DRG) reimbursement rate, which are set and periodically updated by CMS. Drug manufacturers can provide price concessions to hospitals in order to obtain a favorable position on a hospital formulary. Hospital price discounts have consequences for Medicaid best price provisions with the exception of hospitals that qualify for exemption under the 340B program.

Hospitals with 340B status are able to obtain prescription drugs at steep discounts as their purchases qualify for federally mandated discounts and are exempt from Medicaid best-price calculations. Basis for the status is the relatively large share of low-income and uninsured individuals among the population that the 340B hospitals are serving. A contentious issue and likely basis for further regulation, is that in reality discounts are often applied to a broader population than the intended one, thus providing a windfall for hospitals and clinics as they can charge Medicare and private market rates for heavily discounted high-cost drugs and pocket the difference.

Physician groups and larger provider organizations can institute formularies and treatment guidelines not only driven by clinical considerations, but also by profitability reviews and contractual arrangements with insurance providers, including Accountable Care Organizations (ACOs). Particularly for medical benefit drugs, it is critical to thoroughly understand the organizational objectives, financial perspectives, health outcomes/quality metrics and utilization review systems of the prescribers and their direct decision-making environment. Under ACA, ACOs are eligible to share in efficiency savings that are achieved in the program, while maintaining specified health quality standards and improvements.

The United States environment continues to evolve rapidly and is likely to continue to do so as cost of healthcare continues to outgrow the economy and the ACA is unlikely to deliver the savings that justified its introduction in political circles. The future will tell.

Implications for List and Net Pricing Strategies

Due to the complexity of the US prescription drug market with its large number of payer segments (Employer sponsored plans, Medicare, Medicaid, other Government Agencies, Exchanges) and sub-segments, price setting can be complicated. First, what is the optimal price for each of the segments? Is price discrimination feasible between the segments? How do discounts in one segment impact other private and government segments? How does tier placement change prescribing and patient fulfilment? A methodology to evaluate list and net pricing strategies is discussed in Chapter 15.

20

Canada

Key Statistics

Population	34.9 m
GDP	$1,873 bn
GDP per capita	$52,620
Healthcare Budget (% GDP)	10.7%
Healthcare Budget per capita	$5,630
Drug Market Size	$22.0 bn
Drug Market Growth ('08-'12)	+3.1 %
Global Drug Market Ranking	9

Overview

Canadian healthcare is mainly handled through the publicly funded "Medicare." About 25 percent of healthcare spending is from private sources, either covered though private health insurance companies or through out-of-pocket funding. Pharmaceutical spending is funded through public programs (44 percent), private health insurance (36 percent) and patient out-of-pocket contributions (co-pays and deductibles; 20 percent) (Drug Expenditure in Canada, 2012).

Pharmaceuticals

Marketing authorization for new drugs is handled by the Federal Ministry of Health or "Health Canada" through the Health Products and Food Branch (HPFB). HPFB has two branches. The Therapeutics Products Directorate (TPD) handles pharmaceuticals and medical devices. The other branch is the Genetic Therapies Directorate (BGTD), which handles biological and radiopharmaceutical drugs, including blood and blood products, viral and bacterial vaccines, and genetic therapeutic products. After market authorization, multiple pricing and market access hurdles need to be passed before any drug can expect to attract substantial sales. Canada controls price at a national level and reimbursement at a provincial level, using almost the entire arsenal of pricing and market access control mechanisms that exist. About 40 percent of the population is covered through private healthcare plans, which tend to be much more liberal in their coverage policies, although drug prices are still subject to national control by the PMPRB, as described in the next section.

Pricing

Pricing of patented drugs is controlled in Canada by the Patented Medicines Price Review Board (PMPRB). Companies that are deemed to charge "excessive" prices can be ordered to reduce price and pay back any excessive revenues and potential penalties. The PMPRB was set up under the Patent Act of 1987, ending a period of compulsory licensing history in Canada, and under which the generic industry was given extensive opportunity to grow, while only having to pay minor fees to innovators. As a result of this situation, prices for all drugs were very low in Canada. In fear of large drug price increases, the PMPRB was charged to ensure that price premiums over comparable products are restricted to highly innovative pharmaceuticals. After initial launch price setting, prices can be increased annually by no more than the Canadian Consumer Price Index (CPI).

PMPRB uses a classification system to determine the means of price control. Since a revision in 2010, drugs are classified in one of four categories at PMPRB's discretion:

- Breakthrough;

- Substantial improvement;

- Moderate improvement;

- Slight or no improvement.

Each category has different rules related to the maximum price that can be charged by the manufacturer in order to be not deemed excessively priced. Each of them involves a combination of one or more of the following price tests.

MEDIAN INTERNATIONAL PRICE COMPARISON (MIPC) TEST

Under this test, the price shall not exceed the median price of France, Germany, Italy, Sweden, Switzerland, the United Kingdom and the United States.

THERAPEUTIC CLASS COMPARISON (TCC) TEST

The National Average Transaction Price and the Market-Specific Average Transaction Prices for each class of customer – hospital, pharmacy, wholesaler and province/territory – shall not exceed the price of comparator drug products.

HIGHEST INTERNATIONAL PRICE COMPARISON (HIPC) TEST

The price shall never exceed the highest of prices in the seven reference countries (stated under MIPC).

Figure 20.1 shows the price control measures in place for each of the four categories. The 2010 changes in PMPRB price rules offer some theoretical improvements over the previous version through an extra innovation class and opportunities of increasing net price to a previous level, for example after discontinuation of a deal in a market segment. However the set of rules and calculations have also become much more complicated in the process.

The ability to price at a premium is usually severely limited through a mix of MIPC and TCC-based limitations, depending on the classification. Historically, only few compounds obtain a favorable innovativeness rating, resulting in practical pricing freedom. As a result, drug companies sometimes decide not to launch new drugs in Canada, as a negative impact on US and other markets causes considerable concern.

Line extensions of existing drugs, which are classified as category 4, have to be priced in line with existing formulations. It is important to realize that new patented formulations, such as retard and other sustained release formulations are considered equivalent for purposes of price setting, independent of any perceived or demonstrated value.

Category	Description	Price Controls
1	Breakthrough	MIPC test
2	Substantial Improvement	Higher of: 1) Top of the TCC test* 2) MIPC test.
3	Moderate Improvement	Higher of: 1) Midpoint of: i) Top of the TCC test* and ii) MIPC test; and 2) Top of the TCC test*. If it is impossible to conduct a TCC test (i.e., unable to derive comparable dosage regimens or the prices of the drug products used for comparison purposes appear to be excessive), then use the MIPC test.
4	Slight or No Improvement (also applies to patented generic, line extensions and combination products)	1) Top of the TCC test*. 2) In the exceptional cases where HDAP does not identify any comparable drug products, use the lower of i) the bottom of the TCC test comprised of all superior drug products identified by HDAP and ii) the MIPC test. 3) If it is impossible to conduct a TCC test (i.e., unable to derive comparable dosage regimens or the prices of the drug products used for comparison purposes appear to be excessive), then use the MIPC test.

Figure 20.1   PMPRB drug classification system

Therapeutic reference pricing for branded drugs has been introduced to a limited extent in British Columbia but, at least so far, has not been further implemented in other parts of Canada.

Pan-Canadian Pricing Alliance

The pan-Canadian Pricing Alliance (PCPA), established in August 2010, is a joint provincial/territorial initiative to negotiate prices for brand name prescription drugs. Currently Ontario and Nova Scotia lead the initiative that is acting on behalf of provinces and territories except Quebec and Nunavut. Following Health Canada approval and CDR or pCODR review of the drug, the PCPA engages in pan-Canadian negotiations with the manufacturer. After an agreement is reached, individual provinces and territories make their own funding decision and can enter into a product listing agreement. Each product submission is assigned a lead province for the review process.

The PCPA has been a natural answer to the many Provincial Listing Agreements (PLAs) that have been closed as confidential agreements since the institution of the Common Drug Review. Confidential deals have been more acceptable to pharmaceutical companies than list price reductions for CDR. That same confidentiality has raised concerns, particularly with smaller provinces and territories, that they miss opportunities. Since there is little experience with PCPA, it will be interesting to monitor further evolution. Industry has many concerns over the impact of PCPA negotiations on the Canadian business environment, particularly if individual PLA agreements become harder to close or become part of broader class reviews.

Common Drug Review

Since 2003, new drugs are subject to the Common Drug Review (CDR) process if they are to qualify for provincial formulary consideration. All provinces (and territories) with the exception of Quebec follow the CDR recommendations. Quebec maintains its own independent system of drug evaluation (INESSS). The CDR reviews drugs through expert committees and is managed by the Canadian Agency for Drugs and Technologies in Health (CADTH, formerly CCOHTA). Comparative drug effectiveness and safety are evaluated, but of particular focus is the drug's cost-effectiveness. CDR recommendations can fall into the following categories:

- List;

- List with conditions;

- List in a similar manner;

- Do not list at the submitted price;

- Do not list.

Over the last 10 years 47 percent of drugs were not listed and 39 percent listed with conditions with only 3 percent listed as proposed and 2 percent not listed over price. These numbers substantiate the point that CDR listing is very difficult and often results in no or only partial approval for reimbursement in the labeled indication.

Since April 2014, the oncology version of the CDR, the pan-Canadian Oncology Drug Review (pCODR) is residing with the CADTH. Similar to CDR, pCODR reviews clinical and cost-effectiveness evidence and provides reimbursement recommendations to all provincial and territories except Quebec.

Provincial Formularies

Canada has 10 provinces (Alberta, British Columbia, Manitoba, New Brunswick, Newfoundland and Labrador, Nova Scotia, Ontario, Prince Edward Island, Quebec, and Saskatchewan) and three territories (Northwest Territories, Nunavut, and Yukon) that manage their healthcare budgets independently. In addition, the Non-Insured Health Benefits Program (NIHB) provides health benefits for eligible First Nations people and Inuit. Each province/territory maintains a formulary, access to which is highly dependent on the CDR/pCODR recommendations and negotiations with pharmaceutical companies. A common phenomenon among provinces is the negotiation of Product Listing Agreements (PLA) with pharmaceutical companies. These agreements allow for formulary listing under confidential terms, essentially similar to what is occurring in France, thus allowing companies to be less vulnerable to the international implications of price differences between Canada and particularly the United States. It also allows for price discrimination versus private plans. Provinces can, and often do, engage in these agreements even when there is a negative CDR or pCODR review. Quebec is the only Canadian province that does not base its coverage decisions on the CDR/pCODR. As discussed earlier in this chapter, the establishment of the pan-Canadian Pricing Alliance (PCPA) may bring a growing centralization of price and coverage negotiations, although it remains to be seen how the distinctly different styles of the provinces will fare under the alliance.

A number of provinces (BC, AB, SK and MB) have started to manage oncology spend through treatment protocol-driven formularies and central budget management.

Quebec is acting largely independent from other provinces and does not follow CDR and pCODR for coverage decision making. Decision making for provincial drug coverage, including a Province-wide hospital formulary is based on reviews and recommendations by the Institut National d'Excellence en Santé et en Services Sociaux (INESSS), the provincial health technology assessment agency.

Private Plans

As mentioned earlier in this chapter, private insurance plans fund 36 percent of Canadian healthcare versus 44 percent by public payers and 20 percent out-of-pocket expenses. Private plans are mainly employer-sponsored programs that offer healthcare coverage to employees and their dependents. Private plans have historically been much more liberal in their drug coverage policies than their public provincial counterparts. They cover most drugs except lifestyle drugs with co-insurance (percentage co-pays) that are not differentiated across drugs. Over the last few years, private plans have been maneuvering to exert more control over drug cost, but to date there is little evidence of individual agreements with pharmaceutical companies.

Health Economics

Health economics plays a key role in public pharmaceutical coverage decision making, both through the CDR/pCODR assessment, and the individual provinces, which look at both cost-effectiveness and budget impact evaluations.

Hospitals

As in most other countries, hospitals control their drug utilization through formularies and use their negotiating power, usually further strengthened through group purchasing organizations, to bring cost down. Price concessions to hospitals are usually confidential.

Outlook

CADTH has undertaken studies and held consultation sessions in late 2013 for a review policy for orphan drugs. At the time of writing of this second edition no decisions had been made.

A lot of attention is given to the Canada–EU Free Trade Agreement (CETA), which is expected to be ratified in 2015 or 2016. The agreement is expected to result in an effective lengthening of drug patent life by up to two years and provide drug companies with a right to appeal patent related rulings.

21

France

Key Statistics

Population	65.7 m
GDP	$2,721 bn
GDP per capita	$41,410
Healthcare Budget (% GDP)	12.0 %
Healthcare Budget per capita	$4,952
Drug Market Size	$36.7 bn
Drug Market Growth	+0.3 %
Global Drug Market Ranking	5

Overview

The French healthcare system, instituted in 1946, is designed to provide general population-wide health insurance coverage on the basis of three principles:

- Equal access, independent of place of residence and income;

- Quality of treatment;

- Solidarity, that is contribution to cost based on income.

The system is mainly funded through taxes and wage contributions and covers a large proportion of inpatient and outpatient healthcare costs, including drugs. Outpatient medical and drug cost that is not covered through the national program is mostly covered through complementary insurance programs (Mutuelles).

The French government has been attempting to tackle growing budget deficits and cost of healthcare for many years. Cost cutting and potential for far-reaching reform continues to exist across the system for all aspects of healthcare, including drugs at both inpatient and outpatient levels.

Patients must register with a referring doctor, usually a General Practitioner, who acts as a gatekeeper for specialist care. Patients have the option to go to specialists directly, but will be reimbursed at a lower rate if they do so.

Pharmaceuticals

The French healthcare system has one of the most tightly managed controls on pharmaceutical pricing and reimbursement. Prices for reimbursed products are negotiated prior to launch, which ultimately results in a contract with various volumes and other utilization controls and with potential future penalties on price or through rebates. Contracts are renegotiated every five years (this will likely change to two to three years). Prior to renewal of the contract, a thorough review of benefit and appropriate utilization is completed with potential resulting changes in the contract provisions.

Many of the controls in France, whether price-volume contracts, promotional taxes or recent potential limitations on physician visits for certain therapeutic classes (Charte de la visite médicale) are focused on control of drug utilization. Volume growth continues to be the number one cause of increases in drug cost.

The French government continues to struggle to maintain broad and quality access to healthcare with growing social security deficits, particularly under the current economic challenges. Besides budget challenges, the French environment has been plagued by the "Mediator Scandal." Mediator (fenfluramine derivative) was marketed by Servier and used extensively off-label as an appetite suppressant. Although Mediator's safety was questioned since 1998 and the drug was withdrawn from the Italian and Spanish markets since 2005, it took until November 2009 for the drug to be pulled from the French market. This resulted in investigations of AFSSAPS (now ANSM), some other public agencies and the pharmaceutical industry. As a result of the scandal, a number of reforms were made, resulting in:

- Limitations on off-label prescribing;

- Re-evaluation of several therapeutic classes leading to de-listing decisions for many drugs that are deemed obsolete;

- Requirements for disclosure of interests by experts and companies (further extended in 2014 to public disclosure of all physician payments on a publicly accessible website);

- Limitations on hospital promotion activities;

- Head-to-head clinical trials versus an appropriate comparator essentially mandatory unless a strong rationale can be provided for not performing this trial.

Since October 1, 2013 Medico-Economic data requirements are included in the review process for innovative and high-cost drugs. This will be discussed in more detail in later sections of this chapter.

Market Access

Market access for drugs is obtained through the following steps and key agencies:

Market authorization

> Granted by the Market Authorization Commission of the Agence Nationale de Sécurité du Médicament et des Produits de Santé (ANSM) – French Agency for the Medical Safety of Health Products (formerly Agence Française de Securité Sanitaire des Produits de Santé, AFSSAPS).

Actual medical benefit (Service Medicale Rendu; SMR) and improvement in actual medical benefit (Amélioration du Service Médical Rendu; ASMR)

> Assessed by the Transparency Commission (Commission de la Transparence) of the High Authority for Health (Haute Authorité de Santé, HAS).

Economic value

> Assessed by the Economic Evaluation and Public Health Commission (Commission Evaluation Economique et Santé Publique (CEESP)) since October 1, 2013

Price determination

> The Economic Committee for Healthcare Products (CEPS) sets reference prices and prices for reimbursable products on the basis of cost-efficacy assessments and price–volume negotiations. Analyses and recommendations from CT and CEESP serve as input into CEPS decisions. CEPS can also conduct its own assessment of medical benefits .

Reimbursement rate determination

> The National Union of Complementary Health Insurance Funds (Union National des Organismes d'Assurance Maladie Complémentaires, UNCAM).

In theory, France has free pricing for pharmaceuticals. However, prices for reimbursed drugs are controlled through the Economic Committee (CEPS). Very few drugs have been launched with commercial success without reimbursement. Third-generation oral contraceptives is one of the exceptions, as it is a class where women have been willing to pay for the latest generation branded drugs even though older generation drugs are available at full reimbursement.

Medical Benefit and Added Medical Benefit Assessment

The Transparency Commission is using two ratings to assess medical value. The Actual Medical Benefit (SMR) is a measure of the drug's utility, which is assessed on the basis of an evaluation of the nature and severity of the disease, drug efficacy/safety, place in therapy (line of therapy, prevention/curative/symptom control) and the existence and adequacy of existing treatment alternatives.

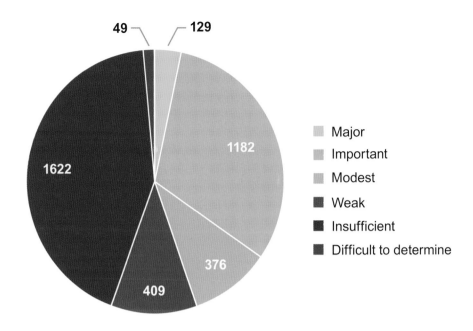

Figure 21.1   SMR ratings through March 2012

Source: http://www.theriaque.org, http://www.has-sante.fr/

The SMR rating is linked to a reimbursement rating, dependent on the severity of the disease; this is further explained in the reimbursement section of this chapter. Figure 21.1 shows an analysis of SMR ratings through 2012. The vast majority of drugs have been rated to have important or modest benefits, whereas very few have major benefits. Slightly over 15 percent of drugs were rejected on the basis of insufficient or difficult to determine benefit. In 2012, 72 percent of drugs received an "Important" rating, 9 percent "Moderate," 9 percent "Minimal" and 11 percent "Insufficient," relatively similar to the average prior to 2009.

Probably the most essential assessment by the Transparency Commission is the determination of the Level of Improvement in Actual Medical Benefit (ASMR). The Transparency Commission uses a scale from ASMR I to V to define the degree of improvement in benefit over the comparator drug (see Table 21.1 on following page).

Table 21.1   ASMR ratings of clinical benefit improvement

Rating	Improvement in Actual Medical Benefit
ASMR I	Major improvement (new therapeutic area, reduction in mortality)
ASMR II	Significant improvement in efficacy and/or reduction in side-effects
ASMR III	Modest improvement in efficacy and/or reduction in side-effects
ASMR IV	Minor improvement
ASMR V	No improvement

The ASMR rating that is granted is a very important measure for the price level that is obtained; however, it is also important to consider the selected comparator (or the best available therapeutic strategy) and the "appropriate" patient population for the new drug treatment.

Figure 21.2 illustrates that only a small percentage of products are granted a rating with major (ASMR I) or significant (ASMR II) improvement. Actually a total of 19 percent of cases have been assigned an ASMR of I, II or III since

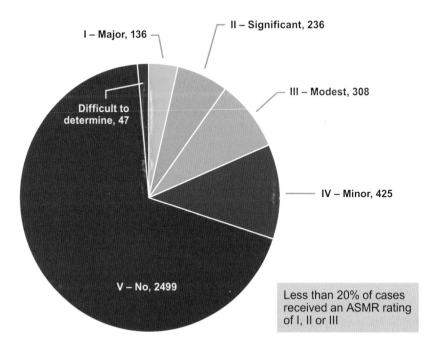

Figure 21.2   ASMR ratings through March 2012

Source: http://www.theriaque.org, http://www.has-sante.fr/

the institution of the ASMR rating system. From 2009 through 2012 88 percent of cases were assigned an ASMR of V or No Improvement. Prior to 2009 only 60 percent was assigned an ASMR of V. It has obviously become increasingly challenging to convince the CT of any clinical improvement.

For the declining share of drugs that received an ASMR of IV or better, individual ratings have become less favorable as well. Figure 21.3 shows that since 2007 the majority of ratings were ASMR IV. It is hard to determine whether the CT has become more tough, or if it has simply become more challenging to develop innovative drug solutions.

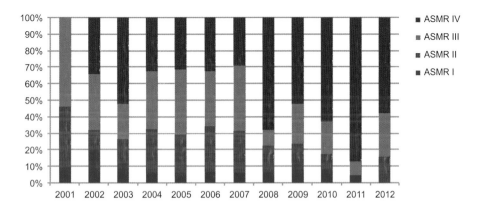

Figure 21.3   ASMR Improvement Ratings 2001–2012
Source: http://www.theriaque.org, http://www.has-sante.fr/

For drugs that are classified as providing either minor or no improvement, it is important to consider what the chosen comparator is. Usually, the comparator selection reflects standard of care for the patient population served or, when available, a close chemical comparator.

Medico-Economic Assessment

On the basis of the Social Security Financing Law of 2008, HAS was tasked with publishing recommendations and medico-economic opinions in order to pursue healthcare efficiency improvements. To this end, HAS instated its Economic Evaluation Commission (Commission Evaluation Economique et Santé Publique [CEESP]) on July 1, 2008. The role of medico-economic assessments was formalized in the "social security financing law plan for 2012" (Projet de loi de financement de la sécurité sociale pour 2012 - PLFSS 2012) in October 2012.

The institution of the CEESP followed concerns regarding the cost of expensive drug therapies without clinical superiority and very high cost of new therapies, including targeted therapies and orphan drugs (Harousseau, 2014). Medico-Economic reviews are required for all new drugs for which the drug company claims an ASMR rating of I, II or III, as well as drugs that are expected to have a significant impact on healthcare expenses. The latter has been defined as exceeding €20 million per year as of the second year on the market. Drug companies are obliged to submit a medico-economic dossier. CEESP will make Incremental Cost-Effectiveness Ratio (ICER) assessments in Euros per Quality Adjusted Life Years (QALY), but there are no pre-defined ICER thresholds.

Price Determination

The Economic Committee (CEPS) determines the price for a new drug on the basis of comparisons of treatment cost for the recommended indications mentioned by the Transparency Commission and the evaluations on clinical and economic value, expressed in the ASMR rating by the CT and Medico-Economic value opinion as reported by the CEESP. Prices are set at ex-factory level. Pharmacy retail and wholesale prices for reimbursable pharmaceuticals are regulated as well. Final pricing decision lies with the Department of Health.

There is a link between the ASMR rating achieved and the price premium gained over the comparator (see Table 21.2).

Table 21.2   ASMR rating impact on drug price

Rating	General Price Expectation
ASMR I, II, III	European Price (and subject to CEESP review since Oct 1, 2013)
ASMR IV	Price may be higher than comparators (usually 5–15%)
ASMR V	Reimbursement only if price lower than comparators

A company that would have the "courage" to launch a new beta-blocker in France would no doubt get the most widely used generic beta-blocker assigned as a comparator. This means that, unless a very high level of benefit improvement can be demonstrated (ASMR I, II or perhaps III), a generic level price will be assigned. On the other hand, a compound that is launched following a new class entrant, such as Galvus following Januvia, will still command an acceptable price, which may be a small premium or most likely about 5 to 15 percent below the first entrant, depending on the ASMR rating (IV or V) and the underlying clinical data differentiation. Input from discussions with French payers suggests that French payers increasingly feel that ASMR IV drugs do not require a price premium as a real additional benefit would result in garnering a rewarding large market share.

As a result of the *"accord cadre"* agreement between the Economic Committee and the Association of the Pharmaceutical Industry (Les Enterprises du Médicament, LEEM) highly innovative drugs with ASMR I, II or III are guaranteed a price which is not lower than the lowest observed in Germany, Spain, Italy and the United Kingdom for at least the first five years of reimbursement listing. These products are subject to the customary volume agreement on sales, which is linked to the indication for which the favorable ASMR rating is granted. For ASMR III drugs the level of sales should also not exceed €40 million in the third year of marketing to maintain the international price reference guarantee.

When high ASMR ratings (I, II or III) are achieved, the comparator is not as critical for price setting, but may still play a role in determining an appropriate clinical use, that is patient population for which a volume agreement will be drafted. For any patient that is well served with cheaper, perhaps even generic alternatives, the demonstrated value versus standard of care will be thoroughly challenged before reimbursement is granted. This will likely be clearer as the first results of the Medico-Economic reviews by CEESP will impact CEPS negotiations. At the time of writing of this second edition there was not yet clarity on its impact. As a background for price setting of high-cost drugs, we should consider a recommendation from the Ministry of Health to curb drug prices at €50,000 per patient per year..

Some oncology drugs, such as Glivec and Herceptin, received an ASMR I, reflecting the improvement in reducing mortality that was demonstrated. This has been an important enabler of introducing a consistent European price, thus avoiding downward price cascading through international price referencing and parallel trade.

France has had a reference price system since 2003, which is only used for reimbursement determination for generics.

Reimbursement Rate Determination

The SMR rating of medical benefit translates by law into a reimbursement rate, as shown in Table 21.3. The National Union of Complementary Health Insurance Funds (UNCAM) can authorize a change in rate of +/– 5 percent from the indicated rate.

Table 21.3   SMR rating and reimbursement

SMR Rating	Reimbursement Rate
Important	65%
Moderate	30%
Weak	15%
Insufficient	0%

As an exception, drug treatments for severe chronic diseases such as cancer are reimbursed at 100 percent when included on a special list by approval of the Minister of Health. Products where de-listing is impending, such as vein tonics, are listed at a reimbursement rate of 15 percent. After a positive review, a product is granted reimbursement for five years through placement on a positive list of reimbursable pharmaceuticals. Reimbursement is reviewed after five years or when a major change occurs in the profile, such as the approval of a new indication or the availability of significant clinical data. Most patients in France have additional insurance coverage through employer-sponsored "Mutuelles." As a result, patients are generally not confronted with co-payments.

Hospital Drugs

Hospitals can purchase and dispense drugs that are authorized by the Ministry of Health after evaluation of SMR and ASMR by the Transparency Commission. Hospitals are generally responsible for the procurement of drugs for inpatient use. The cost of these drugs is covered through an all-in T2A DRG-like daily reimbursement rate for all medical care.

Some high-cost drugs, not included in the T2A system, have a separate reimbursement after approval by the Ministry of Health. Drugs that are placed on this special hospital reimbursement list are subject to national volume restrictions and tight regional budget monitoring by regional health agencies (Agences Régionales Sanitaires; ARS).

Hospitals frequently participate in regional buying organizations to negotiate favorable prices with drug manufacturers.

22

Germany

Key Statistics

Population	81.9 m
GDP	$3,556 bn
GDP per capita	$43,420
Healthcare Budget (% GDP)	11.2 %
Healthcare Budget per capita	$4,875
Drug Market Size	$42.1 bn
Drug Market Growth	+3.8 %
Global Drug Market Ranking	4

Overview

Germany has a predominantly mandatory healthcare system that is run by competing sickness funds. Employees with an income below €4,350 per month (2013) are mandated to join one of the 134 sickness funds for their healthcare insurance. Insurance premiums are income dependent. Employees with incomes that are above €4,350 per month have the option to join one of the private health insurance plans. In reality only about 10 percent of employees are covered by private health insurance plans.

Healthcare-related decision making is delegated to a large number of self-governing multi-disciplinary committees under the ultimate control of the Federal Ministry of Health (Bundesministerium für Gesundheit, BMG).

Healthcare coverage is comprehensive and includes inpatient and out-patient treatment as well as drugs. Outpatient care is delivered through a network of independent private physicians and, increasingly through physician group practices.

State-level physician associations play a strong role in budgeting and cost containment, as they allocate funds by specialty across the region within their allocated regional budget and provide guidance on economic drug utilization.

Pharmaceuticals

Formal decision-making responsibility on coverage and related aspects of market access for pharmaceuticals is handled by the Federal Ministry of Health (BMG), the Federal Joint Committee (Gemeinsamer Bundesausschuss, G-BA). Many of the operational decisions are handled by a number of multi-functional committees of members of sickness funds, physicians groups, pharmacists and other key interested parties.

FEDERAL INSTITUTE FOR PHARMACEUTICALS AND MEDICAL DEVICES (BUNDESINSTITUT FUR ARZNEIMITTEL UND MEDIZINPRODUKTE, BFARM)

BfArM holds responsibility for licensing of new pharmaceuticals (with the exception of blood, blood products, sera and vaccines) and medical devices in Germany.

PAUL EHRLICH INSTITUTE (PAUL EHRLICH INSTITUT, PEI)

PEI holds responsibility for licensing of blood, blood products, sera and vaccines in Germany.

FEDERAL JOINT COMMITTEE (GEMEINSAMER BUNDESAUSSCHUSS, G-BA)

G-BA is the most important self-governing body, responsible for all German reimbursement decision making and guidelines, including reference pricing groups. G-BA has been evaluating added benefits for pharmaceuticals as part of the AMNOG (Arzneimittelmarkt-Neuordnungsgesetz) process for prescription drug price negotiations since January 2011.

G-BA has representatives from sickness funds, providers and patients. Patients do not have voting rights.

INSTITUTE FOR QUALITY AND EFFICIENCY (INSTITUT FUR QUALITAT UND WIRTSHAFTLICHKEIT IM GESUNDHEITSWESEN, IQWIG)

IQWiG conducts effectiveness and drug benefits analyses if mandated by the Federal Joint Committee. IQWiG's benefits analyses have become an integral part of the benefits assessment part under AMNOG. G-BA is however the final decision maker.

FEDERAL ASSOCIATION OF SICKNESS FUNDS (GKV – SPITZENVERBAND OR SPITZENVERBAND DER KRANKENKASSEN, GKV)

The GKV was formed in 2008 to combine six sickness fund organizations (AOK, BKK, IKK, Verband der Ersatzkassen, Deutsche Rentenversicherung Knappschaft–Bahn-See and Spitzenverband der Landwirtschaftlichen Sozialversicherung). GKV is responsible for the setting of reference prices. Since 2011, the GKV is also responsible for prescription drug price negotiations with drug companies under AMNOG.

Pricing

Until the introduction of AMNOG on January 1, 2011 pharmaceutical prices were not controlled in Germany with the exception of some price freezes and mandatory rebates. Pharmaceutical companies were free to set ex-factory prices at any level they desired. Only pharmacy and public prices are set by law on the basis of the ex-factory price. A long-standing mandatory 16 percent rebate on patented and non-reference priced drugs was reduced to 7 percent in March 2014, while a moratorium on price increases was extended until the end of 2017.

AMNOG

In November 2010, "AMNOG," the Arzneimittelmarkt-neuordnungsgesetz (Law for Reforming the Market for Pharmaceuticals) passed in the German parliament, effectively ending free pricing in Germany. AMNOG is a federal price control system based on the assessment of the benefit of newly authorized pharmaceuticals in comparison with existing treatment alternatives. The reform came into effect on January 1, 2011 for all newly licensed pharmaceu-ticals. Initially, high-volume drugs launched prior to January 1, 2011 were scheduled for review (Bestandsmarktbewertung), but as part of coalition ne-gotiations towards the end of 2013, further reviews of marketed drugs were cancelled.

The introduction of AMNOG was politically inspired and was hastily enacted and implemented. As many elements were not clearly defined, it cre-ated massive confusion and frustration, both with government officials who were chartered with implementation and with the industry, due to uncertainty with respect to Germany as a viable market for its drugs.

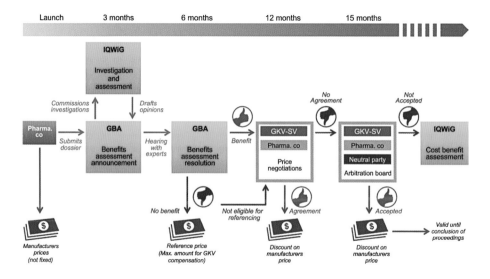

Figure 22.1   AMNOG Process

Source: http://www.bmg.bund.de. GBA: joint federal committee, IQWiG: Institute for quality and cost effectiveness in healthcare, GKV-SV; federal associations of sick funds

Figure 22.1 illustrates the AMNOG process starting at the time of drug launch. Within three months after launch, pharmaceutical companies are obliged to submit a scientific dossier demonstrating its therapeutic benefit compared to the treatment alternatives unless drug sales can be expected to be less than €1 million per year or the drug has orphan drug status. Orphan drugs don't require a filing until annual sales reach €50 million per year. The dossier needs to address very detailed requirements as defined in German Social Code,

Book Five (SGB V), section 35a. Since all available clinical trial data need to be reported, dossiers can amount to 30,000 pages or more.

Following dossier submission, G-BA normally commissions IQWiG to prepare an opinion on added benefit of the new drug versus one or more existing "comparators." For example in the case of Brilique (ticagrelor, AstraZeneca), IQWiG defined four patient sub-populations and selected different comparators and benefits ratings for each of them. There are six benefit levels that can be assigned:

1. Major added benefit over comparator;

2. Significant added benefit;

3. Slight added benefit;

4.   Unquantifiable added benefit;

5. No added benefit proven;

6. Less than comparator.

Figure 22.2 illustrates the relative ratings assigned by G-BA through Feb 20, 2014. Notably, not a single drug has achieved the "Major Benefit" status. The "unquantifiable added benefit" category has not been assigned since 2012. Instead, to reflect quality of the evidence, a new metric "Quality of additional benefit" has been introduced with the potential ratings:

•   Evidence of additional benefit;

•   Indication of additional benefit;

•   Hint of additional benefit.

The G-BA has deviated from IQWiG benefits opinions in a number of cases. A notable example is IQWiG's refusal to accept viral load as an acceptable surrogate end point for Hepatitis C drugs. IQWiG's opinion raised many eyebrows in the clinical community and was rejected by G-BA. Selections of treatment comparators and head-to-head trial requirements have been extremely strict and highly controversial in a number of cases. A much debated example is

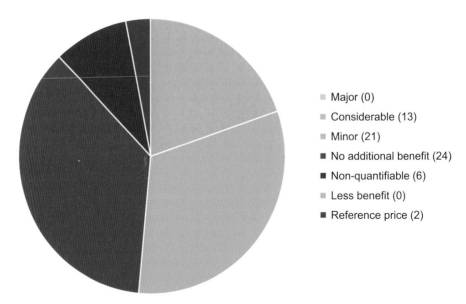

**Figure 22.2   Highest assigned benefit category by drug under AMNOG
through February 20, 2014**

Source: M. Bouslouk, 2014

the decision on Trajenta, a follow-on entry in the DPP4/gliptin market. Due
to the G-BA ruling, effectively declaring it no better than generically available
metformin and sulfonylurea, Trajenta would not be allowed to get a similar
price to the already marketed gliptins. The fact that the criticized clinical trials
were designed many years before the hastily enacted AMNOG law was not
considered. A better solution would have been to compare later entries in a
class to the first entries. The rather blunt therapeutic referencing mechanism
would have yielded Trajenta a fairer price than the more "flexible" AMNOG
assessment.

Orphan drugs automatically qualify to proceed to price negotiations, as
they are assumed to have a "benefit" under AMNOG as long as annual retail
(non-institutional) sales remain below €50 million.

Pharmaceuticals without added benefit are price referenced versus the
identified comparative benchmarks without negotiation, whereas innovative
pharmaceuticals with attested added value, even in only one sub-population,
are subject to price negotiations with the Federal Association of Sickness Funds
(GKV-SV) or "Spitzenverband." The negotiations between the Drug Company

and Spitzenverband are not regulated through any specific metrics, but are supposed to take the following elements into consideration:

- Clinical comparator;

- Additional benefit rating;

- Price benchmarks;

- Prices for the same drug in 15 EU reference countries (Austria, Belgium, Denmark, Finland, France, UK, Greece, Italy, Ireland, Netherlands, Portugal, Sweden, Slovakia, Spain, Czech Republic).

When the negotiations are not successful, an arbitrage phase is entered through a neutral arbitrage board. When either of the parties does not accept the arbitrage results, IQWiG is commissioned to start a cost benefits assessment.

Within the first year after marketing authorization (during the benefit assessment as well as the subsequent price negotiations) the pharmaceutical company is free to set the price. After one year pricing is controlled and per a recent ruling in 2014, rebates will be published. Negotiated prices are fixed for at least two years unless new evidence is submitted in a dossier by the manufacturer.

REBATES

Prior to the introduction of AMNOG, rebates were already an increasingly popular phenomenon in Germany. Particularly for generic drugs it has become customary for companies to reach agreements with sickness funds to obtain favorable treatment in exchange for confidential rebates. For branded drugs there is a lot of discussion on rebates, but in most cases it does not make sense to consider rebates, as the sickness funds tend to have little inclination to influence prescribing for one brand within a therapy area. A notable exception was the case of short-acting insulin analogs. G-BA ruled on the basis of an effectiveness assessment by IQWiG that insulin analogs should no longer be eligible for statutory reimbursement unless they are not more expensive than human insulins. They were classified as "me-toos." Faced with dramatic loss of sales, the insulin manufacturers engaged in (confidential) contracts with the sickness funds to offset the cost differences and maintain reimbursement. The insulin case can be seen as a pre-cursor for what AMNOG is now doing in a broadly institutionalized manner.

Reimbursement

Reimbursement of pharmaceuticals is controlled by the Federal Joint Committee and several other committees on behalf of the Federal Ministry of Health. Reimbursement decisions are officially not linked to price, but rather to the offered value. In reality, price and budget impact play a key role, particularly for drugs with similar therapeutic options in the same chemical class. Since the early 1990s the German authorities have gradually built a rather complex system of reimbursement and spending controls, which have effectively resulted in noticeable price elasticity in physician prescribing behavior.

Germany has not implemented a positive list, although such a list has been legally approved several times. Instead, the government uses a negative list for drug categories that are excluded from mandatory reimbursement by the sickness funds. Drug exclusions from reimbursement and usage restrictions are outlined in the physicians' mandatory Drug Prescribing Guidelines (Arzneimittel-Richtlinien, AMR). The following groups of drugs are generally not reimbursed:

- Drugs for "trivial" diseases, such as the common cold for insured patients over 18 years of age;

- "Inefficient" drugs, that are not deemed effective for the desired purpose or have not been established with certainty to be effective;

- "Analog" or me-too drugs; drugs which have been found to not show any benefits over cheaper equivalents;

- Drugs that are used outside their approved labeling;

- "Lifestyle" drugs, including erectile dysfunction drugs;

- OTC drugs except for selected drugs used in severe patient conditions and for children under the age of 12.

Sickness funds are formally not authorized to fund clinical research or the use of unlicensed drug indications. Rules and conditions for reimbursement of off-label drug use are still under review and further clarification.

Today, there are four complementary ways in which the German healthcare system controls reimbursement and drug utilization:

- Benefits assessment of pharmaceuticals through AMNOG;

- Price referencing;

- Target prescribing volumes or quotas;

- Prescription guidelines.

Essentially, the four reimbursement and utilization control elements are effectively controlling price for "similar products," holding physicians to a maximum annual drug expenditure per patient, and enforce specific prescribing limitations on selected drugs for which cheaper alternatives should be used as first line. Particularly, prescribing quotas (minimum percentages of scripts for generically available drug options in a class) have become more commonplace as a cost management tool. A more detailed description and discussion is found in the sections below.

German patients over the age of 18 years are subject to a co-payment for pharmaceuticals, which amounts to 10 percent of the drug price, with a minimum co-pay of €5 and a maximum of €10 per prescription. Annual co-pays are capped at 2 percent of gross annual income (1 percent for serious chronic conditions). Co-payments are waived for drugs that are priced 30 percent below the reference price or drugs that have a negotiated rebate contract.

Price Referencing

Germany and The Netherlands share the perhaps dubious honor of being the innovators in the introduction of what is internationally known as reference pricing. In Germany the term "price referencing" is used, since formally it is not used to set price, but rather to establish reimbursement limits. Since the introduction of this system in Germany and The Netherlands, it has been used in many other countries, mainly in Eastern Europe, but also in other countries such as Australia, Italy, Spain and British Columbia in Canada. In most countries, including Italy and Spain, reference pricing is limited to generics. However in Germany (and The Netherlands) it is used to also limit reimbursement for drugs within the same therapeutic class.

The WHO Anatomic Therapeutic Class (ATC) classification of drugs is used to identify groups or clusters of at least three similar therapeutic drugs, such as for example ACE-inhibitors or cholesterol-lowering agents. These groups contain both patented and unpatented drugs with, as a result, generally widely ranging prices. Sub-groups can be used to differentiate between various drug delivery forms, for example oral versus an injectable form. For each sub-group a calculation of the average cost per day is made to determine a "reimbursement limit" for the group. Calculations are first made for groups with the same chemical active ingredient, then across groups of drugs deemed therapeutically equivalent. For every drug that is priced above the reimbursement limit, the patient has to pay the difference as a co-payment. Reimbursement limits are calculated annually based on actual range of prices of generic options and number of generic options available. A more extensive discussion of reference pricing systems can be found in Chapter 4.

Not all therapeutic classes have been included in the German price referencing system. It has proven to be challenging to use the system for all therapeutic areas. Much debate has been ongoing on the criteria for what constitutes a class of therapeutically "similar" or "substitutable" drugs. Under the German system, in order to be excluded from a group (that is formed with ATC-4 level drug options, such as all statins), criteria have been defined in terms of demonstrated medical and therapeutic value. The burden of evidence in terms of randomized direct comparators is frequently costly and impractical to obtain prior to launch. Since 2004, the Federal Joint Committee can request the Institute for Quality and Efficiency to undertake a Health Technology Assessment (HTA) to support G-BA decision making.

A much-noted example was the grouping of cholesterol-lowering agents in the earlier days of implementation of the price referencing system. Lipitor was included in the group of cholesterol-lowering agents with many generics, as the Federal Joint Committee ruled that the demonstrated efficacy differences at the higher dose ranges were not deemed sufficient to exclude Lipitor from the reference group. At the lower reimbursement limit, Lipitor lost its leading market share practically overnight, showing the effectiveness of the reimbursement limits with respect to physician prescribing and patient sensitivities to co-payments.

Target Prescribing Volumes

The use of prescribing budgets and spending guidelines has been an evolving element of German healthcare reform since 1993. In various forms, German physicians have been held responsible for their prescribing behaviors under threat of sickness funds audits and personal financial penalties. As a result, physicians today are more cost conscious than most, if not all of their European counterparts.

Currently, sickness funds operate with prescribing target volumes by state. Regional physician associations are responsible for the allocation of the regional target volumes over specialties and eventually individual specialists and general practitioners, which reflect both differences in cost of drug treatment by area of specialty and the mix of retirees and non-retirees by practice.

Physician penalties for exceeding prescribing targets and their previous budget equivalents have been a source of much debate over the years. When exceeding their prescribing targets physicians are typically advised in writing to review their prescribing behavior. When the targets are exceeded repeatedly or by significant margins, physicians need to justify individual prescription decisions through an audit, and may be forced to compensate the sickness funds for excess spending. In reality the latter hardly ever occurs, as physicians have become very careful to not disproportionally use expensive drugs.

Besides overall prescription targets, sickness funds also monitor generic prescribing and for certain highly prescribed drug classes monitor a required minimum use of a leading (generic) substance and average daily cost of prescriptions (through a comparison with the daily defined dose, DDD).

Prescribing Guidelines and Controls

Standard treatment programs (disease management programs) are put in place for diabetes, breast cancer, coronary heart disease asthma and COPD. In addition, for some therapeutic areas, regional physician groups with drug budget responsibility increasingly set up prescribing guidelines and quotas, which mandate the use of generic treatment options as a first line of treatment. Quotas have been used to limit the use of one specific drug (usually a generically available molecule) within its class. For example when Risperdal (risperidone) was the first atypical to lose its patents, some regions in Germany put limits on the percentage of patients that could be treated with atypicals other than risperidone.

For expensive "special" pharmaceuticals co-signing ("Zweitmeinung") was in place from 2009 until the institution of AMNOG, when it was abolished.

Parallel Trade

Pharmaceuticals that are available on the shelf in Germany, but sourced from lower price markets in Europe, are subject to the same reimbursement conditions as their locally distributed equivalent. Wholesalers and pharmacists are frequently financially incentivized to dispense parallel traded drugs. Pharmacists are obliged by law to dispense parallel traded substitutes when their price is at least 15 percent or €15 below the German equivalent. Since European and German law allow for re-packaging of products sourced from other European markets, hurdles to substitution for parallel traded pharmaceuticals are very low.

AMNOG regulates that original products with a negotiated rebate should have priority over parallel trade drugs.

Health Economics

The role of health economics in pricing and market access decision making in Germany has been hotly contested since the introduction of the first German HTA agency in 2000. The original role of health economics was determined to be very similar to the role of the National Institute for Health and Care Excellence (NICE) in the UK. The British designed standards for "excellence" did not meet with some of the German laws and preferences and the mandate of the Institute of Quality and Efficiency (Institut fur Qualität und Wirtschaftlichkeit im Gesundheitswesen [IQWiG]) was redirected to be more focused on effectiveness evaluations in support of reimbursement decision making.

Health economic evaluations are not mandated for reimbursement evaluations, but can be undertaken by pharmaceutical manufacturers at their discretion. Since the introduction of AMNOG, the role of IQWiG has been re-defined; IQWiG now mainly focuses on supporting the G-BA with effectiveness and benefits analyses in support of G-BA decision making under AMNOG.

Hospitals

Pharmaceuticals for inpatient use are covered under the hospital budget and reimbursed by the sickness funds under a disease-related group (DRG) reimbursement rate system. Hospitals negotiate prices directly, frequently through buying groups, with pharmaceutical companies. These confidential agreements can be very meaningful in terms of hospital savings, particularly for generics and for drugs for which treatment is initiated in the hospital for continuation of further treatment in the retail setting. Sales to hospitals for inpatient use are not subject to AMNOG and do not count towards the small products and Orphan drugs revenue limitations for benefits reviews.

Future Developments

Germany continues to be under change and reform, although much has become more clear since the initial introduction of AMNOG; a period that was confusing for industry and government officials alike. At the time of writing of this second edition, public disclosure of rebates was just announced by the government, a decision which will severely harm the negotiating position of the Spitzenverband, as drug companies can ill afford to have favorable German prices cascade over the world.

Germany will continue to be a country that is worth monitoring carefully. Payers from other countries will certainly do the same.

23

Italy

Key Statistics

Population	60.9 m
GDP	$2,005 bn
GDP per capita	$32,920
Healthcare Budget (% GDP)	9.0 %
Healthcare Budget per capita	$3,436
Drug Market Size	$26.2 bn
Drug Market Growth	+2.9 %
Global Drug Market Ranking	7

Overview

The Italian National Health Service (Servizio Sanitario Nazionale, SSN) provides tax-funded comprehensive medical care to the entire population, essentially free of charge. Since 2001 healthcare is a shared responsibility between the central government and 21 regions. The central government is empowered to determine essential levels of care, which must be guaranteed to every citizen in the country. Regions are funded by the central government on an age-adjusted per capita basis. The regional authorities are responsible to provide medical care; they have the freedom to provide care beyond the essential levels of care, but they must finance this from their own resources. The regionalization process of healthcare is largely implemented, but is still evolving.

Most patients are covered under the national system; about 15 percent of the population is covered under private health insurance.

Local health units are responsible for the actual delivery of healthcare by private physicians and other healthcare providers. Public and private hospitals are generally reimbursed on the basis of diagnosis-related group (DRG) fees. Access to hospitals is free of charge to patients.

General physicians act as gatekeepers for specialist and other secondary and tertiary levels of care.

Drugs

The Italian Medicines Agency (Agencia Italiana del Farmaco (AIFA)) has responsibility for market authorization, pharmaco-vigilance, pricing and reimbursement for all pharmaceuticals for human use since July 2004. The creation of AIFA was part of an overhaul of the Italian healthcare system, aiming to control disproportionate growth of drug expenditures.

Pharmaceutical expenditures through retail pharmacies are capped in 2013 at 11.35 percent of public health expenditures. Hospital budget drug expenses are capped in 2013 at 3.5 percent of public health expenditures. Containing drug budgets has been a government challenge. In recent years, particularly hospital budgets continued to exceed the previous 2.4 percent cap.

AIFA is controlled by the Ministry of Health (Ministerio della Salute) and the Ministry of Economics (Ministero dell'Economia). AIFA has a very broad range of responsibilities touching all healthcare and industry-related aspects of the pharmaceutical industry:

- Guarantee access to healthcare and its safe and appropriate use;

- Promote rational use of pharmaceuticals and the dissemination of information on pharmaceuticals;

- Provide pharmaceutical expenditure governance in the framework of economic and financial viability and competitiveness of the pharmaceutical industry;

- Encourage and reward innovation and investments in research and development in Italy.

It is interesting and encouraging to see that AIFA is both responsible for managing its healthcare budget and ensuring the viability of a competitive pharmaceutical industry with appropriate R&D investments. However in reality that does not mean that price negotiations in Italy are an easy task.

Pricing and Reimbursement

The current price setting system, introduced in 2004, moved away from the formal use of average European prices in price calculations. The number of formal approval steps has been drastically reduced as well. As a result, AIFA reports that since its institution in 2004, the pricing and reimbursement approval process time was reduced from 300 days to about 90 days, although the actual average time for approval of new chemical entities was slightly higher at 131 days in 2006. In 2014 implementation was under way of temporary sale of drugs in the non-reimbursed C Class, pending negotiations, as well as a more rapid review process for orphan drugs, hospital drugs and medicines of great therapeutic and social relevance (Tafuri, 2014).

Within AIFA the Pricing, Reimbursement and Market Analysis department (Prezzi, Rimborso e Mercato, PRM) handles reimbursement evaluations and price setting for pharmaceuticals. AIFA relies on a number of technical-scientific consultative expert committees. The two most important ones for pricing and reimbursement evaluations and decision making are:

- Technical Scientific Committee (Commissione Tecnico Scientifica [CTS]) provides consultative opinions on market authorizations and provides reimbursement classifications. CTS has taken over from the previous National Medicine Evaluation Board (Commissione Unica del Farmaco [CUF]);

- Committee for Pricing and Reimbursement (Comitato Prezzi e Rimborsi [CPR]), which is charged with the actual price negotiations with the drug companies.

Pricing is determined on the basis of the evaluation and reimbursement decision by the Technical Scientific Committee (CTS). A rating of the innovativeness of the drug treatment in comparison with the standard of care and other existing treatment options, as well as an assessment of the appropriate patient population that should be considered for the new drug, plays a key role

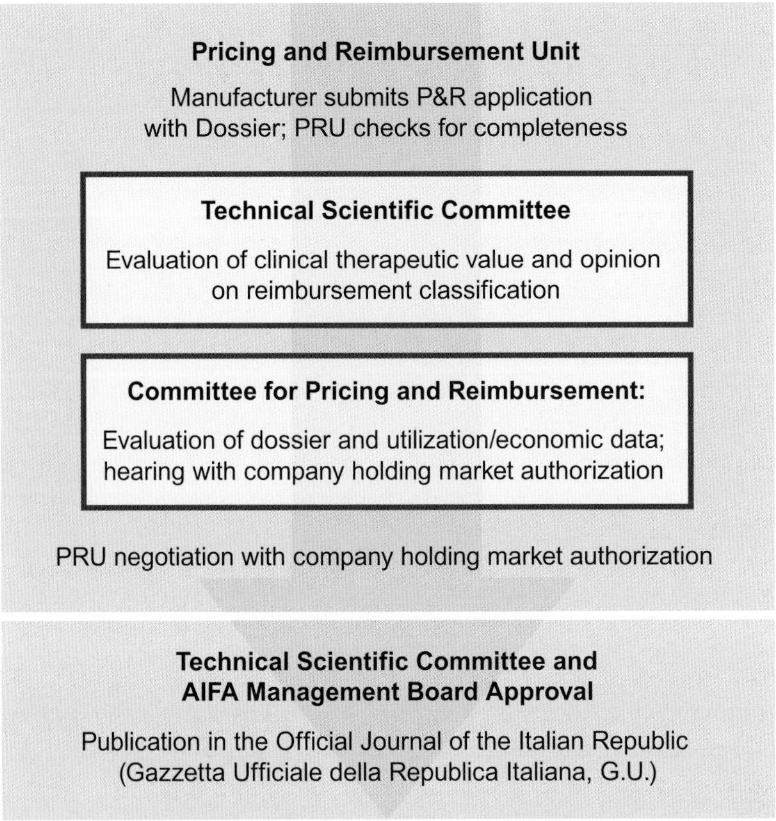

Pricing and Reimbursement Unit

Manufacturer submits P&R application
with Dossier; PRU checks for completeness

Technical Scientific Committee

Evaluation of clinical therapeutic value and opinion
on reimbursement classification

Committee for Pricing and Reimbursement:

Evaluation of dossier and utilization/economic data;
hearing with company holding market authorization

PRU negotiation with company holding market authorization

**Technical Scientific Committee and
AIFA Management Board Approval**

Publication in the Official Journal of the Italian Republic
(Gazzetta Ufficiale della Republica Italiana, G.U.)

Figure 23.1   AIFA pricing and reimbursement approval process

in the evaluations. Reimbursement and pricing decisions are closely linked. At the time of writing of this second edition, a new algorithm for determination of innovativeness was under public consultation and subsequent finalization.

When a drug is not reimbursed, it is placed in the non-reimbursed Class C and pricing and trade mark-ups are free of government controls.

The Interministerial Committee for Economic Planning (CIPE) has defined some criteria to determine prices of reimbursable pharmaceuticals:

- Product therapeutic characteristics (indications, posology and method of administration, duration of treatment or length of course of therapy, mechanism of action);

- Therapeutic value compared to existing drugs in the same therapeutic category; direct clinical comparisons;

- Pharmaco-vigilance data;

- Price of the drug in other EU Member States;

- Prices of similar products within the same pharmaco-therapeutic group;

- Internal three-year market forecasts and market value of all pharmaceuticals in the pharmaco-therapeutic group;

- Number of potential patients (annual basis; disease prevalence);

- Budget impact for the National Health Service (pharmaco-economic studies).

Prices are negotiated on an ex-factory level. Wholesale and pharmacy prices are determined in accordance with fixed mark-ups. Off-patented drugs are subject to price referencing.

Reimbursement

Decision making with respect to the Italian reimbursement scheme is handled by the Italian Medicines Agency (AIFA) under the advice of the Technical Scientific Committee. The National Pharmaceutical Formulary (Prontuario Farmaceutico Nazionale, PFN) is a positive list of all drugs approved for reimbursement. In addition, certain drugs listed as non-reimbursed, can be reimbursed for particular, usually chronic conditions, under supervision by specialized regional healthcare centers.

The National Pharmaceutical Formulary is updated every year, except when the 11.35 percent cost ceiling for pharmaceuticals is exceeded, in which case the list is updated every six months. Table 23.1 shows the reimbursement categories that the National Health Service uses to classify the reimbursement status of pharmaceuticals. A previously existing Class B for non-essential drugs, reimbursed at 50 percent was eliminated in 2001.

Table 23.1   Reimbursement categories

Reimbursement Category	Reimbursement Rate	Description
Class A	100%	Essential pharmaceuticals
Class A with Note	100%	Only reimbursed under specified conditions
Subgroup H	100%	Only reimbursed under specialist supervision in hospitals
Class C	0%	Not reimbursed
Class C (nn)	0%	Not reimbursed; not yet AIFA reviewed
Class C-bis	0%	OTC; not reimbursed

AIFA recently implemented law 189/2012 which includes two provisions:

- Creation of a new Class C (nn) category for drugs that can be sold without reimbursement prior to AIFA reimbursement review and decision making. Companies can apply for placement on this list immediately after receiving market authorization;

- Orphan drugs, selected other therapeutically important drugs (at the discretion of AIFA) and hospital-only drugs can be reviewed in parallel with the EMA market authorization process, thus expediting reimbursement.

Class H is a sub-group of Class A, which can only be used in hospitals under specialist supervision. All other Class A drugs are available in hospitals under equal reimbursement arrangements to the outpatient setting.

Regions

The introduction of 21 regions in 2001 has initiated a continuing trend towards budget delegation to the regions. Particularly under the recent austerity measures, the Italian healthcare regions have had to make tough coverage decisions. Regions organize tenders for multi-source products, but also manage market access conditions for brand drugs, depending on their review and interpretation of the value provided. Under the impending new innovation rating system (and algorithm), regions are obliged to provide market access for drugs that obtained a high innovativeness rating by AIFA on a national level.

The introduction of regional budget controls has been additive and has not eliminated the central price control system. This two-tier approval system is creating some tension between national authorities and regional budget holders in both Italy and Spain, where a similar trend has evolved. Particularly when considering an alternative pricing scheme or risk sharing deal (a real one and not just a response-rate-based price cut), national authorities are not set up to make the deal and regional decision makers don't have the practical ability. National authorities seem hesitant to let go of their pricing controls, yet until this happens, regions will be hampered in their ability to truly manage cost.

Hospitals

Hospitals maintain a formulary of drugs for use in its institutions and reimbursed by the Department of Health. Hospital formulary drug choices must be compliant with the Hospital Pharmaceutical Formulary (Prontuario Terapeutico Ospedaliero Aziendale, PTOA). Criteria for inclusion on the PTOA are clinical efficacy, risk/benefit evaluation, cost/efficacy evaluation, pharmaco-vigilance and patient compliance. Hospitals get a mandatory 50 percent discount off the approved public price. Many high-cost retail drugs are managed through the hospital budget in Italy.

Health Economics

Health economic evaluations in Italy have only limited impact on pricing and reimbursement decision making at a national level and are mainly included in dossiers at the initiative of pharmaceutical companies. Budget impact analyses and clinical and patient outcomes data have probably more impact than formal cost-effectiveness evaluations and models. Particularly on a regional and hospital level, budget impact analyses are more important.

Risk Sharing

Italy has been very active in adopting "risk sharing" deals for particularly oncology drugs. In one of the earlier deals, Bayer provides a discount of 50 percent on Nexevar for the initial two months of treatment. After a tumor response is established, and only for those patients, reimbursement is granted at 100 percent. Although termed a risk sharing deal, this is in effect a price reduction that was apparently required to sway AIFA to grant reimbursement approval. Many similar deals have since been adopted for oncology drugs. A study by Russo (2010) showed that oncology drugs with risk sharing deals had a much faster regional formulary adoption than their counterparts without a risk sharing agreement. For a detailed discussion of risk sharing deals see Chapter 18.

Many drugs have been enrolled in drug data registries over the last five or so years. Drug registries have been a powerful means for the Italian health authorities to track post-launch clinical performance of new drugs.

Future

The Italian healthcare system has always been characterized by continual change, although many of the underlying philosophies of cost management remain the same. The new innovation algorithm upon an initial view looks very complicated and academic. The future will tell whether it will be finally introduced in a more practical format.

24

Spain

Key Statistics

Population	46.2 m
GDP	$1,312 bn
GDP per capita	$28,410
Healthcare Budget (% GDP)	10.7 %
Healthcare Budget per capita	$3,027
Drug Market Size	$19.9 bn
Drug Market Growth	+1.7 %
Global Drug Market Ranking	10

Overview

The Spanish National Health Service (Sistema Nacional de Salud, SNS) provides universal healthcare coverage to essentially the whole Spanish population. Healthcare is funded through general tax funds. Since 2002 healthcare is provided to patients through 17 regions, which act within national guidelines, but have become increasingly independent over the last five years. About 9 million people have supplemental private insurance for additional services, such as dental or to circumvent long SNS waiting lists. General practitioners act as a gatekeeper for secondary healthcare services.

The economic recession and Euro-crisis has hit Spain particularly hard and has resulted in some drastic austerity measures in the healthcare sector.

Pharmaceuticals

The AEMPS is the authority in Spain which is responsible for the grant of national marketing authorizations and mutual recognition procedures over medicinal products. Within AEMPS, the review of applications is handled by the Evaluation Committee for the Therapeutic Utility of Human Drugs (Comité de Evaluacion de los Medicamentos de Uso Humano, CODEM).

Pricing and Reimbursement

Pharmaceutical prices for reimbursed prescription drugs are controlled through the Comisión Interministerial de Precios de los Medicamentos (CIPM), which is a sub-department of the Ministry of Health and Consumer Affairs. The commission also has representatives from the Ministry of Finance and the Ministry of Industry.

Prices for new chemical entities are determined on the basis of manufacturing and R&D costs, budget impact and international price comparisons, particularly with France and Italy. Since the introduction of the Medicines Act in 2006, AEMPS and CIPM have a mandate to manage reimbursement lists to promote "rational use of medicines," making inclusion on the reimbursement list more specifically contingent on the demonstration of some form of innovation. The 17 regions can nominate external experts that evaluate the utility of new drugs. The Spanish government has mandated a number of across-the-board price cuts over the years to address budget issues.

The Spanish Ministry of Health instituted substantial patient co-pay increases in July 2012 to address the tough budgetary situation of the government. Table 24.1 shows an overview of co-pay rates and caps by income and age group. Co-payments for non-retirees can be substantial as there is no capitation. Some additional comments:

- Retirees with minimum wage and some other population groups (unemployed without income, etc.) will not have co-pays;

- Since October 2013, more than 50 hospital-distributed drugs for home use have a 10 percent co-pay up to €4.20 per drug;

- More than 425 drugs have been moved to the negative list (FiercePharma, 2012); these drugs have no reimbursement.

Table 24.1   Patient co-payments as of July 1, 2012

Income	Prescription Drug Co-Payment	
	Retired	Other
Under € 18,000 per year	10% up to € 8.26 per month	40% (no cap)
From € 18,000 to € 100,000 per year	10% up to € 18.59 per month	50% (no cap)
Over € 100,000 per year	60% up to € 62 per month	60% (no cap)

Co-pays for some chronic drugs are 10% and capped for all income levels. Some high-cost drugs are controlled through the "visados previos de inspeccion," a prior authorization system, which reviews that the drug is used for its authorized use prior to approval. Today, this review is done by regional inspection services.

Wholesale and pharmacy mark-ups are fixed by law.

Reference Pricing

For off-patented products that have been on the market for more than ten years, reference-based pricing was introduced. Reference price groups include all pharmaceuticals with the same active substance and route of administration (ATC-5 classes). The reference reimbursement rate is calculated as an average daily dose (ATC DDD) for the three lowest products in the category. Pharmacists are obliged to substitute when a price exceeds the reference price for the drug; patient co-payment of the price difference is not an accepted option.

Regions

Spain's 17 healthcare regions have full budget responsibility since 2003. Regions use prescribing controls and incentives to increase cost awareness and influence physician prescribing habits. Depending on their individual focus, regions are experimenting with different monitoring and control tools, such as prescribing by active ingredient, electronic prescription monitoring, use of drugs in high medical needs areas and so on.

Health Economics

The influence of health economic data on pricing and reimbursement decisions is limited in Spain. Many companies submit budget impact analyses, but health economic submissions are not mandated and its place in the approval is not specified in the new Pharmaceutical Law.

Parallel Trade

Spain has been a country of focus in the long-lasting battle on parallel trade in the European Union. At the time of accession to the European Union in 1986, Spain and Portugal were excluded from parallel trade until 1995. Since that time, companies have been trying to combat parallel trade from Spain, as its low prices caused significant issues within Europe. In the course of this battle it has served as a legal experimentation ground for parallel trade. A number of court rulings have in essence enabled a practice of price discrimination between drugs intended for the price controlled local Spanish market and the export market. Drugs companies since then have charged higher prices for drugs that, given purchasing patterns, can reasonably be assumed to be exported, given a normal growth of internal market use. In addition, some companies have set up local distribution, thereby circumventing local exporting wholesalers.

25

UK

Key Statistics

Population	62.2m
GDP	$2,255bn
GDP per capita	$36,250
Healthcare Budget (% GDP)	10.0 %
Healthcare Budget per capita	$3,609
Drug Market Size	$23.9bn
Drug Market Growth	+3.4 %
Global Drug Market Ranking	8

Overview

The National Health Service (NHS) in the UK is responsible for providing all aspects of healthcare to its citizens, including control of pricing and supply of pharmaceuticals. Since its inception in 1948 the NHS has been charged to provide universal healthcare to all UK citizens. Each of the countries, England, Scotland, Wales and Northern Ireland have NHS organizations that manage healthcare and health policies. NHS organizations in Scotland, Wales and Northern Ireland are managed by their devolved governments. NHS England has decentralized the majority of health services, including emergency care, elective hospital care, maternity services, and community and mental health services through the institution of 211 Clinical Commissioning Groups (CCGs), GP-led organizations that handle local medical and pharmaceutical funding decisions within NHS guidelines and budget. CCGs replaced Primary Care Trusts (PCTs) in April 2013 as part of a large NHS England reorganization that was intended to bring medical and pharmaceutical policy decision making closer to practicing physicians (Commissioning, 2013). NHS England remains responsible for direct commissioning of services outside the remit of clinical commissioning groups, namely primary care, public health, offender health, military and veteran health and specialised services. NHS England's 27 area teams (ATs) are created to maintain a single operating model for primary care and eliminate duplication of effort in the management of the four primary care contractor groups (medical, dental, eye health and pharmacy).

Drugs

Market authorization is granted through the European Medicines Agency (EMA) or through the Medicines and Healthcare product Regulatory Agency (MHRA) who hold the formal drug registration authority in the UK. After obtaining regulatory approval, each of the NHS organizations can grant full reimbursement of drugs to its citizens. NHS England and NHS Wales use clinical and cost-effectiveness guidance from the National Institute for Health and Care Excellence (NICE) on reimbursement coverage through decision making on a local level. Similarly, in Scotland, the Scottish Medicines Consortium (SMC) issues advice on all new licensed medicines to NHS Health boards and Area Drug and Therapeutics Committees (ADTCs), who then make recommendations on which medicines should be used in their area. The "voluntary" Pharmaceutical Price Regulation Scheme (PPRS), controls profits (and hence pricing) of UK branded pharmaceutical companies. Each of the above will be discussed in more detail in the rest of this chapter.

Pricing

Prices of branded prescription drugs in the UK are indirectly controlled through the voluntary PPRS between the Department of Health (DH) and the Association of the British Pharmaceutical Industry (ABPI). Under PPRS, participating manufacturers agree to repay excess return on capital to the NHS under an agreed method of calculation. For any company that does not "voluntarily" sign up to the scheme, the DH can impose profit and price controls through section 33 of the Health Act 1999. These manufacturers have also received a 15 percent price cut effective January 1, 2014. PPRS was renewed in late 2013 to take effect on January 1, 2014; details are discussed later in this chapter.

New chemical entities (NCEs) have free pricing as long as the company remains within the PPRS profit guidelines. Price changes later in the product's lifecycle can generally only be achieved through "price modulation," where a price increase needs to be offset by a price decrease for another product, thus maintaining budget neutrality to the NHS. Except through price modulation, price increases have generally only been granted for individual and unique cases of small companies. Extension of the PPRS agreement has gone hand in hand with price cuts for branded pharmaceuticals in 2005, 2008/2009 and price freezes and rebates in 2014.

The PPRS determines the prices at which reimbursement to the pharmacist occurs for branded prescription pharmaceuticals. Manufacturers' prices are set at a 12.5 percent distribution margin below the NHS price. Generic prices are controlled through the Drug Tariff, which is the reimbursement rate, adjusted monthly to account for in-market discounts granted by manufacturers. As a result, upon patent expiration, drug reimbursement rates tend to fall rapidly, particularly for highly prescribed drugs that attract multiple generic entries. The NHS reported £1 million a day in savings on Lipitor (atorvastatin) once generics were available (*PharmaTimes*, 2013).

The new PPRS agreement of 2014 included drug expenditure growth caps. Drug companies will make rebate payments based on actual growth rates that exceed the agreed-upon caps. Plans for Value-Based Pricing (VBP) have been adjusted to a "Value-Based Assessment" (VBA), where NICE's value and cost-effectiveness assessment will be linked to reimbursement decision making rather than price. More information and discussion of Value-Based Pricing and Value-Based Assessment is found later in this chapter and in Chapter 5.

Reimbursement

Formulary listing decisions are made by each of the local trusts and commissioning groups within the NHS organizations under guidance of NICE and SMC. Drugs are reimbursed at 100 percent of the NHS price.

Patient Co-payments

Patients pay a fixed co-pay per script of £8.05 (April 2014) in England for each prescription item with various age- and condition-related exemptions. There are no co-payments in Scotland, Wales and Northern Ireland.

Health Economics

For England and Wales, the National Institute for Health and Care Excellence (NICE) is responsible for making clinical effectiveness and cost-effectiveness evaluations for drugs and medical procedures. Much debated is the measure of cost-effectiveness which is considered the cut-off point for positive NICE recommendations. NICE expresses cost-effectiveness in terms of cost per QALY (Quality Adjusted Life Years). Although clearly not the only measure, a cost per QALY of £20,000 and below tends to be considered cost-effective. Pharmaceuticals with a cost per QALY in excess of £30,000 tend to be considered not cost-effective. Since the inception of NICE in 1999, its recommendations have been challenged frequently, as can be expected, but generally its recommendations have been used by the NHS and local Clinical Commissioning Groups (CCGs) and previously the Primary Care Trusts (PCTs). One of the most noted cases has been the NICE ruling for four multiple sclerosis (MS) drugs that were found not to be cost-effective by NICE standards. Full reimbursement was nevertheless granted to MS patients under a risk sharing agreement, which is further described in the risk sharing section later in this chapter and in Chapter 18. See further discussion under "Risk Sharing Deals" below. Another case that has been contentious has been the NICE evaluation and subsequent restrictions in the use of drugs for the treatment of Alzheimer's Disease (AD). Patient groups have unsuccessfully challenged the decision to not fund use of these drugs in mild AD patients, where they are deemed to have relatively little impact on the patient's condition and hence lack cost-effectiveness. This decision was only reversed a few months before Aricept patent expiration.

Under a lot of pressure from the public, NHS England re-assessed their approach with respect to late-stage cancer patients. A lot of criticism has been voiced that the NHS is providing very little in terms of palliative care for late-stage cancer patients, where other healthcare systems are more liberal. Indeed, even the very strict Australian authorities tend to use a higher cut-off point for cost-effectiveness decision making for oncology drugs. The outcome has been that for smaller disease areas a broader assessment of patient benefits can be used for "end of life" situations, resulting in a positive NICE recommendation despite a cost per QALY that is above the £30,000 unofficial cost-effectiveness limit. As a result, agents for renal cell carcinoma have been positively endorsed for reimbursement. As far as the rationale for only including smaller disease areas is concerned one might wonder how that seems fair from the perspective of a patient suffering from a more common cancer. In addition to end-of-life coverage criteria, the Cancer Drug Fund (CDF) was established, which provided budget and a funding approval mechanism for cancer drugs that were granted a negative advice by NICE. See further discussion under "Value-Based Assessment."

Clinical Commissioning Groups

In England, CCGs commission the majority of health services, including emergency care, elective hospital care, maternity services, and community and mental health services (*Functions of Clinical Commissioning Group*, 2013). They are responsible for around 60 percent of the total NHS budget. CCGs are led by general physicians. Each of the 211 CCGs maintains their own drug formulary, which is informed by local priorities and decision making in consideration of various advising bodies, including NICE. A point of contention continues to be the fact that NHS England and Wales are supposed to provide funding for pharmaceuticals that have been given a positive NICE recommendation. CCGs frequently do not, or do only to a limited extent, include these drugs on their formulary, complaining that no additional funding is provided. The CDF has resolved the issue for cancer drugs, but not for other therapy areas.

Many CCGs are struggling to balance their budget and, as a result, tend to be very cautious in adopting new higher-cost drug therapies, even though NICE-recommended therapies are supposed to be covered.

Risk Sharing Deals and Patient Access Schemes

Risk sharing is probably the most popular discussion item among pharmaceutical market access and pricing specialists. For most of today's deals that seem to be captured in this category, the name "risk sharing" seems a misnomer, since there is not much "sharing" but rather a price adjustment in the form of a discount to fit within the cost-effectiveness requirements. Today, the arrangements are called "Patient Access Schemes" in the UK.

As mentioned earlier in this chapter, a first and perhaps only real risk sharing deal in the UK occurred in 2002, when NICE made a negative recommendation for four new multiple sclerosis drugs. In order to address an apparently sensitive issue to the government of potentially having to discontinue funding of ongoing patient reimbursement for the four MS drugs, the NHS engaged in discussions with the four companies that held the marketing license for the four MS agents, which resulted in probably the first actual, and perhaps one of the few real, risk sharing deals. As part of this arrangement, full reimbursement has been granted for all eligible MS patients where, in exchange, the four companies funded a 10-year patient registry, that was to validate the health claims for the four compounds, which were based on a long-term extrapolation of two-year data. The agreement also included potential financial consequences of measured underperformance of the drugs per the registry in relation to the claimed cost per QALY by the manufacturers. In reality, the implementation of the registry proved to be very complicated and the first interim data from the registry did not show favorable improvements in clinical outcomes for the new drugs in comparison with placebo. As a result the deal was discontinued and enthusiasm for Patient Access Schemes (PASs) with a data collection component cooled down significantly in the NHS. Current expectations are also that the pharmaceutical company bears any cost of program implementation.

PASs are usually initiated by pharmaceutical companies that try to resolve cost-effectiveness issues. These include positive endorsements of Velcade by NICE, as J&J committed to pay drug cost for non-responding patients, and capping of reimbursement for Lucentis after 14 cycles, where Novartis has committed to supply drug for free beyond the 14 cycles. Since then many more PASs have been implemented. Under initial VBP plans PASs were to be abolished, however this was reversed with the announcement of the 2014 PPRS agreement.

Risk sharing deals are discussed in a broader context in Chapter 18.

Value-Based Assessment

Value-Based Pricing (VBP) was announced as the replacement of PPRS as a means of controlling price in the UK. The methodology was meant to introduce price control rather than the previous reimbursement control, by linking an NHS price setting algorithm to a cost-effectiveness evaluation by NICE. Cost-effectiveness determinations would be adjusted by various factors, including innovation and societal needs. After a few years of discussion and much critique, plans for Value-Based Pricing were modified to a Value-Based Assessment approach. At time of writing of this second edition, finalization was still pending as part of the 2014 PPRS agreement, but in essence the following essential elements are clear:

- Cost per QALY-based cost-effectiveness evaluations by NICE will be adjusted with a societal impact factor to determine reimbursement eligibility;

- Price continues to be set by the manufacturer;

- The Cancer Drug Fund has been extended through 2016;

- Patient Access Schemes will continue to be used to enable reimbursement approval for drugs that don't meet reimbursement standards because of cost.

Value-Based Pricing is further discussed in Chapter 5.

Early Access to Medicines Scheme

Starting April 2014, drugs for serious diseases can qualify for reimbursement under the new Early Access to Medicines Scheme (EAMS). Under the programs, drugs for severely ill patients with life-threatening and serious debilitating conditions that earn the new designation of "Promising Innovative Medicine" (PIM) can qualify for approval. Likely candidates for the PIM designation are orphan drugs and selected off-label uses of existing drugs. Criteria for PIM designation had not been clarified yet at the time that this second edition was written. Since EAMS is a "devolved matter," it is up to the relevant authorities in Scotland, Wales and Northern Ireland whether they follow England in the scheme.

Unfortunately, there is no funding for EAMS. Qualifying drugs can only be distributed free of charge by the manufacturer until EU marketing authorization is granted.

EAMS decision making takes place in three stages:

1.   Promising Innovative Medicine designation

Drugs for life-threatening or seriously debilitating conditions can obtain a PIM designation several years before approval. PIM designation is granted at a special scientific meeting of the MHRA. PIM status does not guarantee EAMS designation.

2.   Early Access Scientific Opinion

MHRA reviews available efficacy and safety information from Phase II and/or Phase III data and issues a benefit-risk opinion. If the opinion is positive prescribers are informed and the company is authorized to make the drug available free of charge.

3.   Licensing and rapid commissioning

After obtaining marketing authorization from EMA, the drug goes through the standard NICE appraisal on the basis of evidence collected during the scheme and will be commissioned by NHS England like other drugs.

Future Developments

At time of writing of this book, implementation of Value-Based Assessment was still under discussion and EAMS was just starting implementation.

26

Japan

Key Statistics

Population	127.6m
GDP	$4,975 bn
GDP per capita	$38,990
Healthcare Budget (% GDP)	10.2 %
Healthcare Budget per capita	$3,958
Drug Market Size	$111.3 bn
Drug Market Growth	+3.0 %
Global Drug Market Ranking	2

Overview

The Japanese healthcare system has offered universal healthcare to its citizens since 1961 through three mandatory insurance programs: the National Health Insurance (NHI), the Employees' Health Insurance and the Government-Managed Health Insurance. The Employees' Health Insurance is a group of more than 1,800 mid- and large-size company associated health insurance programs. For smaller firms, the government provides a collective health insurance, which is called Government-Managed Health Insurance. Those who are not covered by the Employees' Health Insurance are required to participate in the region-based National Health Insurance, for which the municipalities (more than 3,000) act as the independent insurers.

A network of largely private hospitals and clinics is reimbursed on a fee-for-service basis, although a DRG-based system is gradually being implemented over time. Patients pay a co-insurance rate, ranging from 10 to 30 percent, depending on the insurance program and whether the patient is the employee or a dependent.

Drugs

New drug applications are reviewed by the Pharmaceutical and Medical Devices Agency (PMDA), an agency within the Japanese Ministry of Health, Labor, and Welfare (Korosho). Korosho also determines coverage policy and pricing for healthcare products that are purchased by hospitals and pharmacies.

Pricing for New Drugs

National Health Insurance Prices are established by the Central Social Insurance Medical Council (Chuikyo) a separate body within the Korosho. Every other year, the Korosho selects 20 members for the Chuikyo from academia and various interest groups, including the Japan Medical Association (physicians), the Japan Pharmaceutical Association (pharmacists), and Rengo, the Japan Trade Union Confederation (employees).

Japanese prices for drugs are controlled by the Korosho in accordance with a very structured system, consisting of internal reference pricing and an adjustment based on international prices.

COMPARATIVE METHOD

Most drugs are approved on price under the comparative pricing method. In this method, pricing is determined on the basis of a selected comparator and an improvement related premium over the price of that comparator. Selection of the comparator is based on a sequential analysis of indication, mode of action and the chemical structure of the new agent in comparison with existing drugs.

It is very important to evaluate the impact of development decisions on drug price very early in drug development. Decisions on, for example, choice of indication can have a dramatic effect on price, as it is the first factor that determines the choice of comparator.

After selection of the drug comparator, the relative usefulness and innovativeness of the new agent are assessed to determine an appropriate price premium over the comparator drug. Table 26.1 gives an overview of various categories (1 through 6) with different price premiums and related requirements. Historically it has been difficult to qualify for the highest level of price premium as the requirements for qualification are very tough.

Table 26.1   Pharmaceutical price premium requirements (JPMA, 2014)

1	Premium for innovativeness (rate: 70–120%) Applied to new drug products in the NHI price lists meeting all of the following requirements:	
	1)	The newly entered drug has a clinically useful new mechanism of action.
	2)	The newly entered drug has been shown objectively to have greater efficacy and safety than existing (comparator) drugs in the same class.
	3)	The newly entered drug has been shown objectively to improve treatment of the indicated disease or trauma.
2	Premium for usefulness I (35–60%) Applied to new drug products in the NHI price lists that meet two of the three requirements listed above:	
3	Premium for usefulness II (5–30%) Applied to new drug products in the NHI price lists that meet one of the following requirements (excluding products to which the innovativeness premium or usefulness premium (I) is applied):	
	1)	The newly entered drug has a clinically useful new mechanism of action.
	2)	The newly entered drug has been shown objectively to be more effective and safe than existing (comparator) drugs in the same class.
	3)	The newly entered drug has been shown objectively to offer, as a result of formulation improvement, greater therapeutic usefulness than other drugs in the same class.
	4)	The newly entered drug has been shown objectively to improve treatment of the indicated disease or trauma.
4	Premium for pediatric use (5–20%) Applied to new drug products in the NHI price lists meeting all of the following requirements:	
	1)	The newly entered drug is explicitly shown in the Indications section or Dosage and Administration section to be indicated for children (including infants, suckling infants, newborns, and low-birthweight infants).
	2)	The premiums for pediatric use must not have been given to comparator drugs available in the NHI price lists.
5	Premium for marketability I (10–20%) Applied to new drug products in the NHI price lists meeting all of the following requirements:	
	1)	Orphan drugs pursuant to the provisions of Article 77-2 of the Pharmaceutical Affairs Law in the NHI price lists for which the orphan indications for the disease or trauma are the main indications of the drugs concerned.
	2)	The premium for marketability (I) must not have been given to comparator drugs available in the NHI price lists.
6	Premium for marketability (II) (5%) Applied to new drug products in the NHI price lists meeting all of the following requirements (excluding products to which marketability premium (I) is applied):	
	1)	New drugs in the NHI price lists for which the main indications correspond to separately specified indication categories with a small market scale among drug indication classifications specified in the Standard Commodity Classification of Japan.
	2)	The premium for marketability (I) or (II) must not have been given to comparator drugs available in the NHI price lists.

"Drugs with less novelty" are drugs which are deemed too similar to an existing drug to warrant any premium. These drugs are priced on parity to the comparator drug (normally on a daily cost basis) and do not qualify for an increase in price under Foreign Price Adjustment rules (see later in this chapter).

COST-PLUS METHOD

Selected drugs, for which an appropriate comparator cannot be assigned, can qualify for cost-plus-based pricing. The method is based on an analysis of manufacturing and other costs related to the new drug. Despite the perception that many have in association with the name, the cost-plus method provides for good opportunities for a reasonable price in comparison with other healthcare systems. Cost-plus priced drugs are still subject to foreign price adjustment rules.

FOREIGN PRICE ADJUSTMENT

Prices that are calculated on the basis of the comparator or cost-plus method are subject to a Foreign Price Adjustment (FPA). Under FPA the price is compared to the average price of the United States, France, Germany and the UK and corrected up or down depending on the outcome of the comparison. In reality, under the FPA calculation formula, drugs with a poor internal price comparator and premium, can boost up its price to roughly 50 percent of the difference between the Japanese and average foreign price point. The other side of the coin is that if the local Japanese price determination leads to a much higher price than the foreign average, a price reduction can take place. The following calculations are used:

AFP = Average Foreign Price for US, France, Germany, UK

ICP = Internally Calculated Price (comparator method or cost-plus)

If $ICP \geq 1.5 \times AFP$: $[1/3 \times ICP/AFP + 1] \times AFP$

If $ICP \leq 0.75 \times AFP$: $[1/3 \times ICP/AFP + 0.5] \times AFP$

There are some additional limitations on the applicability of FPA calculations:

- Foreign prices that are more than five times higher than the lowest foreign price are excluded from calculations;

- When the highest price is more than two times the average of the other prices, two times the average price is assumed for that country price in cases where at least three foreign prices are available.

In addition, price increases under FPA cannot be applied when:

- Only one foreign price is available for FPA;

- Different forms (for example strengths) of the drug lead to higher and lower foreign prices;

- The drug is priced under the "similar efficacy comparison-based price setting" (drugs with less novelty).

The Japanese FPA rule is a largely underestimated opportunity to impact price in Japan. Carefully planning prices and related sequencing for launch between the US, France, Germany and the UK can have a dramatic impact on the profitability of the Japanese opportunity for a new drug.

The FPA was originally introduced to address an apparent weakness in the Japanese pricing system to reward for significant drug innovation. Even under the most favorable innovativeness premium of 120 percent, it is hard to reach an acceptable price level for an innovative drug unless the comparator is an already high-priced drug.

Pricing Adjustments for Listed Drugs

Differences in purchase price of drugs by medical institutions and the NHI reimbursement price can form a source of income for these organizations, particularly when pharmaceutical companies provide discount incentives to encourage use of their drug. Chuikyo has been trying to handle this issue since the 1980s through various price adjustment formulas that have evolved over the years.

Every two years, excess margins are corrected through a forced price reduction to reflect the actual net price offered to physicians. These corrections are referred to as R-zone price adjustments. A calculation of adjusted NHI price goes as follows:

WAWP = Weighted Average Wholesale Price to

Hospitals/Pharmacies before tax

NHI Price = WAWP + [1 + Consumption Tax Rate] + Adjustment

The current Adjustment rate is 2 percent.

Further price reductions can take place due to changes in indication, changes in dosage or administration and when drug sales are significantly exceeding original sales revenue expectations.

GENERICS

When a first generic is entering the market its price is set at 70 percent of the originator brand price. Oral generics are set at 60 percent after more than 10 generically equivalent drugs are available. New generic market entries are set at the lowest available price level. When more than 20 generic drugs are available new entries are priced at 90 percent of the lowest price.

Outlook

Korosho has announced plans to further decrease prices of generics from 70 percent to 50 percent of the original brand price. In addition, prices for long-listed drugs have been identified for price cuts. Long-listed drugs are off-patent drugs for which generic substitution rates are below 60 percent based on volume. Both initiatives should be seen in the context of the stated Korosho intent to increase generic substitution rates to at least 60 percent of the off-patent drug market, more than double the rate achieved by 2013.

27

Australia

Key Statistics

Population	$22.7 m
GDP	$1,384 bn
GDP per capita	$60,970
Healthcare Budget (% GDP)	9.7 %
Healthcare Budget per capita	$5,939
Drug Market Size	$14.0 bn
Drug Market Growth	+4.9 %
Global Drug Market Ranking	12

Overview

Australia's Medicare provides comprehensive healthcare coverage for all residents. Medicare provides reimbursement on the basis of an established Medicare Benefits Schedule (MBS) fee and provides 100 percent coverage for inpatient care and outpatient general practitioner consultations. Specialist fees are covered at 85 percent of the MBS fee. Almost half of Australian residents take advantage of private healthcare insurance options to avoid long public hospital waiting lists, improved accommodations and ancillary treatment services.

The Medicare system is funded through general taxation and a 1.5 percent Medicare levy on income. High-income individuals who don't take private health insurance are levied an additional 1 percent on income.

Drugs

Australia's Pharmaceutical Benefits Scheme (PBS) controls prices of drugs that are reimbursed under its scheme. Patients pay a maximum co-pay of A$36.90. Concessional patients, which are unemployed, elderly and a group of sickness payment beneficiaries, pay a lower co-payment of A$6.00. Safety net provisions from the PBS provide for lower concession level co-pays for general patients for which payments exceed A$1,421.20 per calendar year. Concession patients pay no co-pay when calendar year payments exceed the Concession Safety Net of A$360.00. All co-pays and Safety Net numbers are for 2014. Patients pay additional co-payments when a drug company sets its price above the approved PBS price level.

Reimbursement Approval

Listing on the PBS is subject to review by the Pharmaceutical Benefits Advisory Committee (PBAC) and final approval by the federal minister of the Department of Health. The PBAC can recommend one of three levels of approval for reimbursement:

- "Unrestricted";

- "Restricted Benefit" in accordance with specifically defined conditions, specified in the Schedule of Pharmaceutical Benefits;

- "Authority Required" from Medicare Australia prior to prescribing by "phone approval" or in writing.

PBS listing decisions are made on the basis of a broad set of criteria, including clinical need, effectiveness, side-effects and cost-effectiveness. Unless significant effectiveness or safety evidence is submitted, the price evaluation is likely to be based on a cost-minimization approach. Under cost-minimization the net impact to the drug budget must be zero or cost-saving.

Therapeutic Referencing

Therapeutic referencing is an essential part of the Australian reimbursement system. The PBS classifies drugs in therapeutic classes and determines a single reimbursement rate for all drugs in the class when they are deemed essentially equivalent. To obtain a higher reimbursement than the one established for a class, approval needs to be obtained through PBAC.

In 2007 the Australian government introduced a change in the therapeutic referencing system under the "PBS Reform" package (Commonwealth of Australia, 2010). The most important change due to PBS Reform has been the establishment of separate formularies for single-source (branded) and multi-source drugs. This allowed the government to pursue higher cost savings from generics through forced price reductions at patent expiration in therapeutic reference classes without a direct impact on prices of patented drugs and related incentives for drug innovation. The drug formularies are:

- F1: single brand drugs;

- F2: drugs with two or more PBS listed brands.

Until January 2011, the F2 formulary was broken down in an F2A and F2T part, depending on level of discounting prior to 2006 to provide for a smooth transition on price revision requirements for generics. Reference pricing does not take place between F1 and F2 formularies.

Health Economics

The subcommittee of the PBAC reviews pharmaco-economic submissions that manufacturers need to prepare to qualify for reimbursement. On the basis of the nature of a drug's innovativeness PBAC will determine whether the company needs to show incremental cost-effectiveness or cost-minimization in comparison with an appropriate reference drug. Generally, new drugs with a request for a premium over its therapeutic reference or otherwise are expected to increase patient treatment cost, need to justify the higher drug cost through a demonstration of cost-effectiveness.

Australia has been one of the first countries to implement strict cost-effectiveness requirements as part of its pricing and reimbursement approval process. Showing cost-effectiveness is a critical success factor in gaining price approval for innovative high-cost drugs.

Therapeutic Group Premium

For some therapeutic sub-groups the PBS has defined a Therapeutic Group Premium (TGP). Individual drugs in those drug groups are considered similar in efficacy and safety. The TGP is the price difference between the premium brand prescribed and the benchmark (base) price for the drugs in this class. For drugs prescribed in this group, the patient needs to pay for the TGP in addition to the normal co-payment. A prescriber can obtain an exemption from the TGP, mainly on grounds of adverse events and drug interactions.

Risk Sharing

The Australian PBAC has entered in many pricing agreements with the pharmaceutical industry. Most of the agreements involve a sales volume cap with a rebate mechanism, either for the drug or for the entire drug class. Various other deal types have been used to address specific PBAC concerns for a drug listing.

A particularly interesting deal has been negotiated in 2012 between BMS and PBAC for Yervoy, a drug indicated for metastatic melanoma. As with many anti-cancer drugs, Yervoy only had Progression-Free Survival (PFS) data available, which did not meet the PBAC preference for more meaningful Overall Survival (OS) data. Since melanoma is a highly prevalent disease in Australia, PBAC has been motivated to bridge the data gap. A risk sharing agreement was reached where OS data was to be gathered through a patient registry. Upon availability of the OS data, BMS is required to pay a rebate when the data fall short of the claims made during price negotiations (PBAC, 2012).

28

Brazil

Key Statistics

Population	198.7 m
GDP	$2,158 bn
GDP per capita	$10,860
Healthcare Budget (% GDP)	10.3 %
Healthcare Budget per capita	$1,121
Drug Market Size	$28.5 bn
Drug Market Growth	+14.6 %
Global Drug Market Ranking	6

Overview

The Brazilian healthcare system is controlled by the Ministry of Health that holds responsibility for public health policy and oversight of the public and private health provider network, including broad powers of control of healthcare and the drug industry. The latter is evidenced by its authority to grant compulsory licenses for the manufacture of patented products as it has done for HIV/AIDS drugs.

The market is developing as a two-tier market with fairly basic universal healthcare coverage through the Sistema Único de Saúde (SUS) and a growing supplementary private insurance market, organized under the Agência Nacional de Saúde Suplementar (ANS).

SUS

The Brazilian government established universal healthcare for the population in 1990 following the recognition of the right to healthcare in the Federal Constitution of 1988. Sistema Único de Saúde (SUS) was established to federally coordinate healthcare that is delivered and funded at federal, state and local level. The Brazilian government has prioritized access to public healthcare, but coverage remains relatively poor due to limited financial resources. Poor funding of SUS has created a lot of frustration among the population. Individual patients routinely needed to file lawsuits to gain reimbursement. Another large issue is the availability of physicians in the rural areas. In 2013 the Rousseff administration launched "Mais Medicos" (More Doctors), a crash program to recruit thousands of foreign doctors to work in Brazil's poor and remote areas.

PRIVATE HEALTH INSURANCE

Private insurance, which is funded by employers and households, covers about 30 percent of the population, but makes about 55 percent of the total expenditures. There is a large overlap in facilities used by SUS and private insurance companies, which creates many complexities. Since the insurance is supplementary, patients can use public services, but get additional access to procedures and drugs that are not covered under SUS.

United Health Group acquired a 90 percent stake in the largest Brazilian health insurer and hospital operator Amil in late 2012 in a move to invest in the rapidly increasing healthcare needs of the Brazilian middle class.

Starting January 2014, private health plans have been mandated to cover 36 oral anti-cancer treatments for home care. The list of drugs will be reviewed every two years by a "technical group" within Agência Nacional de Saúde Suplementar (ANS), the umbrella organization for private health insurance companies in Brazil.

Pharmaceuticals

The Brazilian Sanitary Surveillance Service (Agência Nacional deVigilância Sanitária – ANVISA) is an organization that autonomously operates within the Department of Health to oversee drug licensing, patent review, manufacturing licensing and healthcare cost control. ANVISA regulates medical equipment, cosmetics and hospital services and oversees reference pricing for similar and generic drugs.

Pricing

Price control is handled by the Drug Market Regulation Chamber (Câmara de Regulação do Mercado de Medicamentos - CMED), an inter-ministerial body with membership of the Ministries of Health, Treasury, Justice, Development and the Civil House. Drug companies need to obtain CMED approval for prices for new drugs and line extensions. Drug price approvals are classified in six categories with different approval requirements. This is shown in Table 28.1.

Table 28.1   Price approval requirements for six drug categories

	Description	Price Requirements
1	New molecular entities with additional benefits relative to current treatment options	Lowest price of nine comparator countries: Australia, Canada, Spain, the US, France, Greece, Italy, New Zealand, Portugal, and country of origin
2	New molecular entities with *no* additional benefits relative to current treatment options	Price cannot exceed cost of previously available treatments in the country
3	New formulations of existing products – same manufacturer	Price cannot exceed the average of currently available versions
4	New formulations of existing products – different manufacturer	Price cannot exceed the average of currently available versions
5	New combinations of existing products	Price cannot exceed the cost of previous treatments available in the country
6	Generic drugs	Prices must be at least 35 percent lower than the reference drug

Reimbursement

The Brazilian government is constitutionally obliged to provide drugs free of charge to its population. In reality, the government only reimburses a limited number of drugs. The National Essential Drugs (RENAME) program, inspired by the WHO Essential Drug List, supplies drugs for chronic diseases, such as diabetes, hypertension and mental health. The "Public Drugstore" program supplies most essential drugs for these conditions at low cost to the broader population under federal sponsoring. Most private insurance companies also don't cover drugs, leaving most of the drugs funded by patients without any reimbursement. Hospital drugs, such as chemotherapy for cancer patients can be covered on the basis of an established reimbursement rate based on the specific diagnosis.

CONITEC

In December 2011, the Comisión Nacional para la Incorporación de Tecnologías en el SUS (CONITEC) officially replaced the Comissão de Incorporação de Tecnologias (CITEC). CONITEC was tasked to assist SUS on coverage decision making through health technology assessment. Specific emphasis was placed on faster analysis (within 270 days), greater transparency and improved drug access (using expanded healthcare financing from 2013 to 2016). CONITEC requires:

- Scientific evidence comparing efficacy and safety versus existing SUS-funded drugs;

- Cost-effectiveness analyses versus existing alternatives;

- Budget impact estimates.

Whereas CONITEC is focused on providing reimbursement guidance for the public SUS sector, we may see some impact on the private health insurance industry that is facing many coverage demands and limited funding as well.

Compulsory Licensing

Brazil has taken a strong stance on HIV/AIDS drug pricing and has used its rights to engage in compulsory licensing under Article 31 of the Agreement on Trade-Related Aspects of Intellectual Property (TRIPS). In May 2007, the Brazilian government issued a compulsory license for Merck's Efavirenz as it claimed to need lower-cost antiretroviral drugs to execute its broad HIV/AIDS treatment program. Since then, the government has used the threat of compulsory licensing to negotiate better terms for these drugs.

Productive Development Partnerships

The Brazilian government has pursued establishing public/private partnership agreements for the manufacture of biotechnology drugs and other health technologies. The "Productive Development Partnerships" (PDPs) are intended to boost local manufacturing of high-technology products through technology transfer. Greater independence from multinational drug company decisions on discontinuations of manufacturing is stated as an important reason.

Outlook

Rapid growth of the private health insurance section and public pressure to improve universal healthcare coverage in Brazil make for an interesting situation, which is not atypical given the growth stage of the country. It will be important to monitor how the two-tier healthcare system will further evolve under various local political agendas as current policy proposals both include expanded public financing and tighter regulation of the private insurance sector.

29

China

Key Statistics

Population	1,350.1 m
GDP	$10,450 bn
GDP per capita	$7,740
Healthcare Budget (% GDP)	3.6 %
Healthcare Budget per capita	$278
Drug Market Size	$81.7 bn
Drug Market Growth	+22.3 %
Global Drug Market Ranking	3

Overview

The Chinese healthcare system has evolved and is likely to continue to evolve rapidly over the years to come. Prior to the 2009 health care reform, only a relatively small proportion of healthcare cost was covered by insurance, particularly in rural areas. Today, even in rural areas, the majority of patients have at least some health insurance coverage

The National Health and Family Planning Commission (NHFPC) has actively promoted health insurance coverage in rural areas through its New Rural Cooperative Medical System (NRCMS) since the old commune-based cooperative medical scheme collapsed. The new scheme offers voluntary insurance for the population that is not covered under other existing employer-based plans and is funded by participant contributions and national and local government subsidies. Since its institution in 2003 the NRCMS has been introduced in most of China's rural counties with about 95 percent participation of the eligible population (Source: NHFPC). The insurance system is mainly focused on inpatient treatment and limited or no outpatient treatment. Co-payments are usually high (can be 50 percent of cost).

The Basic Medical Insurance (BMI) offers health insurance programs for urban employees and urban residents. Under the employee program, employers in urban areas have to offer health insurance to their employees. The program is funded by employer and employee contributions and government subsidies. As dependents are usually not covered, they can get coverage under the resident program, which usually has a different coverage and (higher) co-pays. Healthcare coverage and co-pays differ from program to program and province to province.

Drugs

Drug coverage is limited under BHI and even more so under NRCMS, as both plans are focusing on basic coverage at limited insurance cost. Branded drugs are increasingly covered, but it can take a number of years before listing is accomplished. High-cost biologics are generally not covered. Drug distribution is complex and involves multiple layers of national and regional distributors and hospitals.

The BHI formulary is maintained by the MLSS. The formulary is officially renewed every two years, but in reality much less frequently. The MLSS maintains a national A-List formulary and a provincial B-List formulary. National Category A drugs have to be included in regional formularies; for Category B drugs the provincial authorities have the freedom to substitute or eliminate up to 15 percent of the listed drugs.

The National Development and Reform Commission (NDRC) is responsible for setting of ceiling prices for all BHI formulary drugs, including Category A and Category B in China. Provinces and local governments can use tenders to obtain prices below the national NDRC ceiling price. Drug coverage under the BHI can still involve a substantial patient co-payment (10–50 percent depending on geography).

For most innovative pharmaceuticals, the Chinese market is essentially still a cash market. However, this could change over the years to come as the government is working to fulfill its commitment to establish "universal healthcare with safe, effective, convenient and low-cost healthcare services" by 2020. Today, patient affordability and cost-related compliance play a major role in the physician's prescribing decision. In markets where some branded options are insured, the physician needs to work with the patient to trade-off between partially reimbursed (co-pay) options and more expensive non-reimbursed drugs.

In late 2009, the Chinese government announced the institution of the National Essential Drug System in order to bring down drug cost. To achieve this, the Ministry of Health (now NHFPC) introduced a Chinese version of the WHO Essential Drug List. Retail prices of drugs on this new National Essential Drug List (NEDL) are controlled through reference prices set by the central government and provincial decision making on actual authorized prices. Competitiveness is further encouraged through the use of public tenders in each region. These controls and the mandatory elimination of hospital mark-ups on NEDL prices are intended to make essential drugs more affordable for the population. The NEDL list has been updated in 2013.

Outlook

The Chinese healthcare system seems to be at a crossroads with respect to further potential development options. In more affluent provinces and cities, employers push for more comprehensive plans that cover a broader range of medical procedures and a "richer" drug formulary with a larger selection of patented drugs. In many respects, these areas are very comparable to typical Western economies with significant purchasing power, making them attractive customers for medical and drug industries.

Next to growth in the private insurance model, there is a strong on-going push for universal healthcare coverage for the large Chinese population. Great progress has been made since healthcare reform in 2009, but affordability will continue to pose limitations on the Chinese government's ability to address medical needs in largely underserved areas.

30

India

Key Statistics

Population	1,236.7 m
GDP	$2,102 bn
GDP per capita	$1,700
Healthcare Budget (% GDP)	3.5%
Healthcare Budget per capita	$59
Drug Market Size	$14.0 bn
Drug Market Growth	15.1 %
Global Drug Market Ranking	13

Overview

The vast majority of the Indian population is unable to access quality healthcare due to cost as less than 15 percent of the population has health insurance coverage. Central and state government employees are insured through the Central Government Health Scheme (CGHS) and Employee State Insurance Scheme (ESIS). Army, railway and oil companies have relative good coverage of medical and drug expenses, but comprise only a very small proportion of the Indian population. The government of India has encouraged the institution of private health insurance through its Insurance Regulatory Development Authority Bill (IRDA) which regulates and protects the rights of insurance holders.

Drugs

The Indian Ministry of Chemicals and Fertilizers' Department of Pharmaceuticals controls retail prices for drugs that are considered "essential drugs." Administration of the "Drug Price Control Orders" is handled by the National Pharmaceutical Pricing Authority (NPPA) that was established shortly after the Drug Price Control Order of 1995 was issued to control prices for 74 controlled substances.

The Department of Pharmaceuticals announced the Drug Price Control Order 2013 (*Gazette of India*, 2013), extending price control to 384 (multi-source) drugs that are listed on the New List of Essential Medicines (NLEM) of 2011, including many anti-cancer, anti-infective and HIV/AIDS drugs. Intent of the measure was stated to be to bring more affordable drugs to rural communities. The order sets a limit on retail prices that is determined as an average of all available forms with a market share over 1 percent for each NLEM chemical substance.

Wholesale and retail margins for drugs are fixed through an agreement between the Organization of Pharmaceutical Producers of India (OPPI) and the All India Organization of Chemists and Druggists (AIOCD). Wholesale and retail margins are 10 percent and 20 percent respectively, which after taxes leads to a retail price of approximately 65 percent over the ex-factory drug price (OPPI, 2008).

Patient Access Programs

As in other emerging markets, the pharmaceutical industry has engaged in various ways to address affordability challenges for branded drugs across the Indian population. These programs continue to be essential as companies try to balance low patient affordability and challenges related to price differences between countries (product diversion, price referencing, pharmaco-political issues). Most programs involve patient registration by an independent agency, who handles drug refills with discounted rates or free goods. Novartis has had a very liberal program for Glivec, distributing free drug to patients, despite continuous patent challenges and strong generic presence in the market.

Roche has initiated a multi-branding strategy in India for Herceptin, Mabthera and Pegasys. Under this program they market lower-cost brand versions through a partner in smaller cities to reach areas with lower affordability and sometimes compete with generic copies. It can also serve as a strategy to reduce the risk of compulsory licensing. The Roche program is just an example as many other programs are in place in India.

Compulsory Licensing

Industry expectations have been that the Patents (Amendment) Bill of 2005 would ensure that India recognizes drug patents despite its history and large interests in its generics industry. In passing the Patents Bill, India was supposed to become in compliance with the Trade Related Aspects of Intellectual Property Rights (TRIPS) agreement. It was expected to be a major change in Indian pharmaceutical policy which motivated many multi-national companies to introduce new innovative drugs.

Unfortunately, the Indian government has chosen to systematically ignore patent rights for particularly oncology agents by issuing compulsory licensing permits to local generic companies. Compelling population needs can motivate governments to enact a provision under TRIPS to engage in compulsory licensing under health emergencies; however the Indian government seems to go very far in its interpretations as it has systematically issued compulsory licenses for a broad range of oncology drugs. Under these circumstances, companies need to think very carefully before they decide to file for registration in India for any innovative drug, particularly oncology drugs.

Outlook

As India's economy is growing rapidly, the expectation is that private insurance coverage will continue to grow. However, for all practical purposes, India will continue to be a cash market for the foreseeable future.

As in many other emerging markets, handling of affordability gaps between the small affluent and large poor population leads to healthcare policy challenges and pressure to institute price controls.

As far as the drug industry is concerned, uncertainty over India as an attractive investment opportunity has only become greater. Five years ago, the Indian government was stating intent to support a strong local R&D industry.

Today we know that only local companies are likely to benefit from reward of innovation in the form of a five-year reprieve from price control. Most of the locally gathered technology is likely to stem from technology gained through compulsory licenses. US and European government support to address this issue seems only lukewarm, perhaps due to the poor public reputation of the industry.

For all practical purposes, India will continue to be a cash market for the foreseeable future.

31

South Korea

Key Statistics

Population	5.0 m
GDP	$129 bn
GDP per capita	$25,710
Healthcare Budget (% GDP)	6.3 %
Healthcare Budget per capita	$1,616
Drug Market Size	$11.3 bn
Drug Market Growth	6.3 %
Global Drug Market Ranking	14

Overview

The South Korean healthcare system has two components: The National Health Insurance (NHI) and Medical Aid (MA). NHI is a social insurance system that covers all citizens. MA provides healthcare to lower-income groups, which are 3.6 percent of the population (Eun Young Bae, 2013). Universal healthcare coverage was achieved in 1989. The health insurance program falls under the responsibility of the Ministry of Health and Welfare. The National Health Insurance Corporation (NHIC) serves as the insurer. Implementation of reviews and fee schedules is handled by the Health Insurance Review and Assessment Service (HIRA).

Drugs

Market authorization for prescriptions drugs is granted by the Korean Food and Drug Administration (KFDA) after review of efficacy and safety. Government reimbursement decision making involves the review by HIRA and negotiations with the NHIC. After successful negotiations, the Ministry of Health and Welfare formally approves the reimbursement at the agreed price, notifies the manufacturer and places the drug on the positive list.

The South Korean positive list was established in 2006 when for innovative drugs the cost-effectiveness-based price evaluation was initiated to replace the old international average pricing calculations for A-7 countries (US, UK, France, Switzerland, Italy, Japan, Germany). The institution of the positive list was part of a rationalization plan under which many drugs were de-listed over a period of five years (2007–2012).

Patients generally pay a co-payment of 20 percent on inpatient drugs and 30 percent on outpatient drugs. Co-pays are lower for elderly and for the treatment of cancer (5 percent) and rare diseases (10 percent). There are annual caps on patient co-pay contributions.

HIRA: COST-EFFECTIVENESS

The Health Insurance Review Agency (HIRA) is chartered to evaluate clinical usefulness and cost-effectiveness of any new drug on the basis of a dossier submitted by the pharmaceutical company. Drugs without a recognized clinical usefulness need to demonstrate cost savings as a condition for approval (cost minimization). Where a benefit is demonstrated, a cost-effectiveness evaluation is done, determining the Incremental Cost-Effectiveness Ratio (ICER) as a basis for price determination. There is no formal ICER cut-off criteria established; disease severity is one of the drivers of ICER acceptability. The Drug Benefit Coverage Assessment Committee (DBCAC) prepares the analyses for a formal recommendation by HIRA. The DBCAC has 21 members and includes representatives from the Korean FDA, consumers, medical experts and HIRA. DBCAC recommendations include positive list inclusion/exclusion and restrictions by indication.

NHIC: PRICE NEGOTIATIONS

Following the reimbursement advice from HIRA, the pharmaceutical company can start price negotiations with NHIC. Cost-effectiveness criteria usually are a starting point rather than an indication of acceptable price, as the NHIC usually tries to extract additional concessions. Because of this, and the fact that South Korean prices tend to be very low in comparison with European and most other Asian markets, companies frequently choose to not accept the NHIC price demands. Recent introduction of risk sharing deals may provide some solutions; see a brief discussion later in this chapter. In case of unsuccessful negotiations with the NHIC for an "essential drug," the Benefits Coordination Committee (BCC) mediates and can set a compulsory price. Essential drugs are drugs which meet all of the following criteria:

- There are no alternative treatments;

- The indication is for life-threatening diseases;

- Used for rare diseases;

- Recognized by the committee as clinically necessary.

Cancer drugs imatinib (Glivec), dasatinib (Sprycel) and anti-HIV drug enfuviritide (Fuzeon) were assessed by BCC after negotiation failure.

After successful negotiations, the Health Insurance Policy Review Committee endorses the price for final approval and publication by the Ministry of Health and Welfare.

PRICE VOLUME AGREEMENTS AND RISK SHARING

Since 2009, drug pricing approvals are subject to a Price Volume Agreement (PVA). Under the agreement, prices are cut by 10 percent when the agreed-upon sales volume is exceeded by 30 percent or more. At the time of writing of this second edition, there were calls to increase the PVA price cut to 20 percent.

Following the English Patient Access Scheme model, the South Korean government has started to engage in risk sharing deals with pharmaceutical companies. Under these deals, companies provide confidential rebates in exchange for reimbursement coverage. In March 2014, three of these deals were made; many are likely to follow.

GENERICS

Cost management of generic drugs has received a lot of government attention in South Korea. Since January 2012, cost containment policies resulted in an increase of mandated post-generic entry price cut from 20 percent to 30 percent for originator drugs. Initial generics are priced at 59.5 percent of the original drug price. Original brand and all generics must drop price to 53.55 percent of the original price after a one-year grace period. European-style reference pricing systems continue to be under consideration in South Korea.

References

Adams, Ben. Lipitor generics help NHS save £1m per day. *PharmaTimes* (May 15, 2013). http://www.pharmatimes.com/Article/13-05-15/Lipitor_generics_help_NHS_save_%C2%A31m_per_day.aspx.

AMCP, 2009. AMCP Guide to Pharmaceutical Payment Methods, 2009 Update (Version 2.0). *Journal of Managed Care Pharmacy*. Supplement August 2009. Volume 15, No. 6-a.

Aspen, 2013. Regional Leader Investor Presentation. *Aspen*, November. http://www.aspenpharma.com/SiteResources/documents/2013%20Investor%20Information/Regional%20Leader%20Investor%20Presentation%202013.pdf.

Blachier, C. and Kanavos, P. *Pharmaceutical Pricing and Reimbursement – France*. http://ec.europa.eu/enterprise/phabiocom/docs/tse/france.pdf.

Blood, 2013. The Price of Drugs for Chronic Myeloid Leukemia (CML); A Reflection of the Unsustainable Prices of Cancer Drugs: From the Perspective of a Large Group of CML Experts. Hagop Kantarjian et al. *Blood*, April.

Bouslouk, M., 2014. *G-BA: Latest Results of early benefit assessments and price negotiations*. Pharma Pricing & Market Access Outlook Europe Conference, London, February 25.

CEPS. Website. http://www.sante.gouv.fr/ceps/.

Commissioning, 2013. NHS England. http://www.england.nhs.uk/ourwork/commissioning/.

Commonwealth of Australia, 2010. The Impact of PBS Reform. Report to Parliament on the National Health Amendment (Pharmaceutical Benefits Scheme) Act 2007. *Commonwealth of Australia*, January.

CommSec, 2013. *FinFacts:* iPad Index: Argentina the most expensive; Malaysia the cheapest. http://www.finfacts.ie/irishfinancenews/article_1026585.shtml.

Correa, M. Carlos, 2002. Implications of the DOHA Declaration on the TRIPS Agreement and Public Health. *Health Economics and Drugs, EDM Series No. 12*, June.

DiMasi, J.A., 2007. "The Cost of Biopharmaceutical R&D: Is Biotech Different?" *Managerial and Decision Economics*, 28: 469–79.

Drug Expenditure in Canada, 2012. Canadian Institute for Health Information, 1985–2012. https://secure.cihi.ca/free_products/Drug_Expenditure_2013_EN.pdf.

Economist, The, 2009 (1). Big Mac Index, *The Economist*, February 4.

Economist, The, 2013 (2). *The Economist: The World in 2014.*

Eun Young Bae, 2013. *Value based contracting for medicine: the experiences of South Korea*. Gyeongsang National University, November 5. http://www.nhis.gov.gh/files/Value%20based%20contracting%20for%20medicine_revised.ppt.

Farkas, C. and Henske, P., 2006. "Reference Pricing For Drugs." *Forbes*, June 14. http://www.forbes.com/2006/04/13/pharma-reference-pricing-cx_cf_0414pharma.html.

FiercePharma, 2012. *The drug reign in Spain is leading to lots of pain*. Eric Palmer. FiercePharma, August 31. http://www.fiercepharma.com/story/drug-reign-spain-leading-lots-pain/2012-08-31.

Focus on Health Reform, Summary of the Affordable Care Act. http://kff.org/health-reform/fact-sheet/summary-of-new-health-reform-law/.

Forbes, 2012. The Truly Staggering Cost of Inventing New Drugs. *Forbes*. http://www.forbes.com/sites/matthewherper/2012/02/10/the-truly-staggering-cost-of-inventing-new-drugs/.

Forbes, 2013. India's Solution To Drug Costs: Ignore Patents And Control Prices – Except For Home Grown Drugs. John LaMattina. *Forbes*, April 8. http://www.forbes.com/sites/johnlamattina/2013/04/08/indias-solution-to-drug-costs-ignore-patents-and-control-prices-except-for-home-grown-drugs/print/.

Functions of clinical commissioning group, 2013. NHS Commissioning Board; Commissioning Development Directorate, March. http://www.england.nhs.uk/wp-content/uploads/2013/03/a-functions-ccgs.pdf.

Gabor, A., 1961. "On the price consciousness of consumers." *Applied Statistics*, 10: 170–88.

Gazzetta Ufficiale. http://www.gazzettaufficiale.it/.

Gazette of India, 2013. Ministry of Chemicals and Fertilizers. Drugs Price Control Order 2013. http://pharmaceuticals.gov.in/dpco2013gaz.pdf.

Global Use of Medicines: Outlook through 2017. IMS Institute for Healthcare Informatics, November 2013.

Graham, John R., 2002. "The Fantasy of Reference Pricing and the Promise of Choice in BC's Pharmacare." *Public Policy Sources*; The Fraser Institute.

Harousseau, J.L., 2014. *Update on the new HTA*. Pharma Pricing and Market Access Outlook Europe Conference, London, February 25.

HAS Website. http://www.anaes.fr/anaes/anaesparametrage.nsf/HomePage?ReadForm.

IMS, 2009. *IMS World Pharmaceutical Market Summary*, November.

Jommi, C. "Pharmaceutical Pricing and Reimbursement – Italy Profile." *Università Bocconi Milano.* http://ec.europa.eu/enterprise/phabiocom/docs/tse/italy.pdf.

JPMA, 2014. Pharmaceutical Administration and Regulations in Japan 2014. *Japan Pharmaceutical Manufacturers Association.* March. http://www.jpma.or.jp/english/.

Kaiser Family Foundation, 2013. *Medicare Part D Key Trends 2006–2013.* http://kff.org/medicare/issue-brief/medicare-part-d-prescription-drug-plans-the-marketplace-in-2013-and-key-trends-2006-2013/.

Kotler, P., 2007. *Principles of Marketing*, 12th edition, Prentice Hall.

LEEM. Website. www.leem.org/htm/accueil/accueil.asp.

NAIC, 2009. *National Association of Insurance Commissioners.* http://www.naic.org.

National Comprehensive Cancer Network (NCCN) compendium. http://www.nccn.org/professionals/drug_compendium/content/contents.asp.

New York Times, 2012. Sanofi Halves Price of Cancer Drug Zaltrap After Sloan-Kettering Rejection. Andrew Pollack. *New York Times*, November 8. http://www.nytimes.com/2012/11/09/business/sanofi-halves-price-of-drug-after-sloan-kettering-balks-at-paying-it.html?_r=0.

NICHSR, 2009. Glossary of Frequently Encountered Terms in Health Economics. United States National Library of Medicine (NLM). National *Information Center on Health Services Research and Health Care Technology (NICHSR).* Health Economics Information Resources: A Self-Study Course. October 5. http://www.nlm.nih.gov/nichsr/edu/healthecon/glossary.html.

OPPI, 2008. Indian Drug Market Profile. *Organisation of Pharmaceutical Producers of India.* http://www.indiaoppi.com/India%20OTC%20Profile%202008.pdf.

Orphan Drug Act. http://www.fda.gov/regulatoryinformation/legislation/federalfooddrugandcosmeticactfdcact/significantamendmentstothefdcact/orphandrugact/default.htm.

Orphan drug designation Australia, Australian Dept. of Health website. http://www.tga.gov.au/industry/pm-orphan-drugs.htm.

Orphan drug designation Japan, Japanese Ministry of Health website. http://www.mhlw.go.jp/english/policy/health-medical/pharmaceuticals/orphan_drug.html.

Orphan Medicinal Products, EU Commission website. http://ec.europa.eu/health/human-use/orphan-medicines/index_en.htm.

PBAC, 2012. November 2012 PBAC Outcomes – Positive Recommendations. http://www.pbs.gov.au/info/industry/listing/elements/pbac-meetings/pbac-outcomes/2012-11/positive-recommendations.

Pharmo, 2004. *Pharmo Report: Farmacotherapie tegen elke prijs?* Pharmo Instituut, Netherlands.

PhRMA, 2009. *Pharmaceutical Profile 2009*. http://www.phrma.org/files/attachments/PhRMA%202009%20Profile%20FINAL.pdf.

PPRI, 2007. Pharmaceutical Pricing and Reimbursement Information: Italy, October.

Pronk, M.H., Bonsel, G.J. and Van Der Kuy, A., 2002. "De budgetbeheersende functie van het Geneesmiddelenvergoedingssysteem." *Nederlands Tijdschrift Geneeskunde*, September 14, 146(37): 1729–33.

Russo, P., 2010. "Time to market and patient access to new oncology products in Italy: a multistep pathway from European context to regional health care providers." *Annals of Oncology*, 21: 2081–87.

Schöffski, O., 2002. *Diffusion of Medicines in Europe*. Friedrich-Alexander Universität Erlangen-Nürnberg, Lehrstuhl für Gesundheitsmanagement.

Tafuri, Giovanni, 2014. Italy: *Update on the Reform Agenda*. Pharma Pricing and Market Access Outlook Europe 2014 Conference, London, February 25.

Thomas, M., 2005. "The Change of Cost: Reference-based Pricing and the Statins." *The Canadian Journal of Cardiology*, 15(5): 535–8.

Van Westendorp, P., 1976. NSS-Price Sensitivity Meter (PSM): A New Approach to Study Consumer Perception of Prices. *Proceedings of the 29th ESOMAR Congress*, Amsterdam, 139–67.

Wagstaff, A., 2009. *Reforming China's Rural Health System*. The World Bank. Washington DC.

WHO, 2001. Report on the workshop on differential pricing and financing of essential drugs. World Health Organization and World Trade Organization secretariats. Høsbjør, Norway, April 8–11.

WHO EURO, 1999. *Definitions from EURO European Centre for Health Policy*, ECHP, Brussels. http://www.who.int/disasters/repo/13849_files/n/definitions_EURO_ECHP.pdf.

World Bank, 2013. World population statistics. http://data.worldbank.org/indicator/SP.POP.TOTL.

Yervoy Risk Sharing, 2012. *PBS Public Summary Document: Ipilimumab*, November. http://www.pbs.gov.au/info/industry/listing/elements/pbac-meetings/psd/2012-11/ipilimumab.

Index

If you have found this book useful you may be interested in other titles from Gower

Transforming Big Pharma
Assessing the Strategic Alternatives
John Ansell
Hardback: 978-1-4094-4827-3
e-book PDF: 978-1-4094-4828-0
e-book ePUB: 978-1-4724-0364-3

Applying Lean Six Sigma in the Pharmaceutical Industry
Bikash Chatterjee
Hardback: 978-0-566-09204-6
e-book PDF: 978-1-4724-2521-8
e-book ePUB: 978-1-4724-2522-5

Pharmaceutical Process Design and Management
Kate McCormick and D. Wylie McVay Jr
Hardback: 978-1-4094-2711-7
e-book PDF: 978-1-4094-2712-4
e-book ePUB: 978-1-4094-5622-3

Licensing, Selling and Finance in the Pharmaceutical and Healthcare Industries
The Commercialization of Intellectual Property
Martin Austin
Hardback: 978-1-4094-5079-5
e-book PDF: 978-1-4094-5080-1
e-book ePUB: 978-1-4094-8483-7